The Six-Day War

A RETROSPECTIVE

EDITED BY

Richard B. Parker

University Press of Florida
*Gainesville/Tallahassee/Tampa/Boca Raton
Pensacola/Orlando/Miami/Jacksonville*

01 00 99 98 97 96   6 5 4 3 2 1

Library of Congress Cataloging-in-Publication Data
The six-day war: a retrospective / edited by Richard B. Parker.
    p. cm.
  Includes bibliographical references and index.
  ISBN 0-8130-1383-6 (cloth: alk. paper)
    1. Israel-Arab War, 1967—Diplomatic history—Congresses.
I. Parker, Richard Bordeaux, 1923–
DS127.2.S58 1996 95-43804
956.04'6—dc20   CIP

The University Press of Florida is the scholarly publishing agency for the State
University System of Florida, comprised of Florida A & M University, Florida
Atlantic University, Florida International University, Florida State University,
University of Central Florida, University of Florida, University of North
Florida, University of South Florida, and University of West Florida.

University Press of Florida
15 Northwest 15th Street
Gainesville, FL 32611

To all those who lost their lives in this foolish war

Contents

List of Maps and Illustrations   viii

Foreword by Harold H. Saunders   xi

Preface   xv

Chronology   xvii

Introduction, L. Carl Brown and Richard B. Parker   1

1. Origins of the Crisis, *L. Carl Brown*   13

2. The United Nations Response, *I. William Zartman*   74

3. The Israeli Response, *Bernard Reich*   119

4. The Other Arab Responses, *C. Ernest Dawn*   153

5. The View from Washington, *Donald C. Bergus*   189

6. Conspiracy Theories, *Richard B. Parker*   237

7. Conclusions, *Richard B. Parker*   289

Appendix. List of Panelists and Observers   321

Selected Bibliography   325

Index   331

)

Maps and Illustrations

Map 1. The Syrian-Israeli border in 1967, 26

Map 2. United Nations Emergency Force deployment, May 1967, 84

Syrian president Nuredin Atassi, Damascus, December 1966, 10

Panel 1 (*left to right*): William Zartman, Shimon Shamir, L. Carl Brown, and Salah Bassiouny, 23

President Gamal Abd al-Nasser and Field Marshal Abd al-Hakim 'Amr in the Sinai, May 1967, 43

Georgiy Kornienko, Soviet Foreign Ministry, 1967, 52

UN Deputy Undersecretary General Sir Brian Urquhart, 81

F. T. Liu, UN Truce Supervision Organization, Jerusalem, 1967, 96

Israeli Prime Minister Levi Eshkol, Sea of Galilee, April 1967, 98

Arthur Goldberg, U.S. permanent representative to the UN, with deputy William Buffum, 1967, 105

Gideon Rafael, Israeli permanent representative to the UN, 1967, 106

Ephraim Evron, minister counselor of the Israeli Embassy, Washington, 1967, 128

Israeli Foreign Minister Abba Eban calling on President Lyndon Johnson, May 1967, 134

General Meir Amit, Mossad director, in the Sinai, June 1967, 136

King Hussein of Jordan and President Nasser, Cairo, May 1967, 171

Tahsin Basheer, member of Egypt's UN delegation, 1967, 182

Donald Bergus, chief of U.S. Interests Section of the Spanish Embassy, Cairo, 1967, 193

Undersecretary of State Eugene Rostow and President Lyndon Johnson, June 1967,   198

Pro-Israeli demonstrators at the White House, June 1967,   215

Ambassador Lucius Battle and UAR Foreign Minister Mahmoud Riad, Cairo, 1966,   248

Richard Helms, director, CIA, 1967,   258

President Lyndon Johnson and Soviet Premier Aleksei Kosygin, Glassboro, New Jersey, June 1967,   296

Foreword

How often have countries and groups triggered violent conflict unintention-
ally? How often have we assumed an orderly policy-making process in the
heat of crisis when decision making was actually an unknowable mix of
people, ideas, and actions with unintended consequences? Can we ever
understand these complex interactions well enough to "do better next time"?
These are but three of the questions this book addresses.

This book is unique. It probably will not be possible to assemble again
even this many individuals who were in policy-making positions during the
1967 Arab-Israeli War. The dialogue among them is invaluable, even though
any discussion on a subject of this kind must necessarily leave some questions
unanswered. In complex human interactions, some questions have no defini-
tive answers.

The conference from which this book emerged was uniquely and unusually
well organized. The project manager, who was also the conference moderator, worked with others before the conference to cull from experience and
existing literature the unanswered questions surrounding the larger one of
whether the 1967 war could have been avoided. He circulated them to all
participants in advance and invited their revisions. Participants were asked
to make oral presentations—not to write academic papers—in order to
preserve the freshness of human perspective which is key to understanding
policy making. He invited as many key participants as could come and
allowed for their full participation in the discussion. He equipped each panel
chair with questions to answer. Most unusually, he charged each panel
chairman with bringing some kind of synthesis to the presentations and
discussion by writing—after the discussion—a synthesis of the perspectives
to be used as an introduction to the print version of the presentations
and discussion.

Thus, what would otherwise be a confusing record of oral presentations
and discussions is given overall structure in advance so that readers can go
through the interaction among participants with a sense of what they are

looking for in that interaction. This may be a new design for a book of this kind; if so, it bears emulation. It transforms the confusion of a solid conference record into a well worked out conclusion—tentative though it may be—from the various perspectives aired. It makes a coherent volume out of material that by its nature—perspectives from different vantage points—cannot by itself be coherent.

Even though I was serving in the White House and was dealing with this situation in 1967, the discussion of key questions brought to the surface a number of points of view that made me think about angles I had not previously examined as I should have. The book thereby contributes a more fully rounded picture of the war than does any single author's volume, no matter how good.

The human interaction in the course of the conference that is apparent in the presentations and in the discussion brings the subject alive in the same multifaceted way that the real-life crisis was lived. If the book does nothing—and it does much more—it gives the reader a sense of the incompleteness of knowledge with which senior policymakers must operate in dealing with most major international problems. No textbook on international relations could contribute the same impressions that this book creates. A textbook feels compelled to bring order to the policy-making process. It is anything but, and only a book of this kind, produced by people and an editor who were involved, could convey that sense of partial knowledge, sharply conflicting perspectives, irrational actions, divided governments, and failure of even the closest friends to understand each other.

These are only some of the ways in which this book stands out from all others on this subject. Although it focuses on one major international event, the interactions surrounding that event are relevant to countless others.

This book will be required reading for all students of Middle East history in this period. It will match recent books on the Cuban missile crisis—some produced after similar dialogues among participants—as case studies in crisis management and policy making. It will interest students of international relations as a case study in how governments really interact. Although it is not in the same genre, it has the same interest value as *The Guns of August*.

Harold H. Saunders

HAROLD H. SAUNDERS was a member of the National Security Council staff in the White House during the period of the Six-Day War. Later, he flew on the Kissinger shuttles in 1973–75 and was assistant secretary of state for Near Eastern and South Asian Affairs when he helped draft the Camp David Accords in 1978 and the Egyptian-Israeli peace treaty in 1979. He is director of International Affairs at the Kettering Foundation.

Preface

This book is about a conference held on the twenty-fifth anniversary of the June 1967 war between Israel and its Arab neighbors. Inspired by, but not modeled on, a set of similar conferences held to discuss the Cuban missile crisis of 1962, the purpose was to assemble a group of knowledgeable survivors from the various states involved to discuss the origins of the crisis and the perceptions and misperceptions that lay behind it. Although of primary interest to Middle East specialists and historians, the informed general reader will also learn from it much about the disorder of diplomacy.

The discussions among Americans, former Soviet officials, and Cubans about the 1962 missile crisis have revealed that it was even more dangerous than anyone had realized at the time. The world came close to a nuclear exchange with untold consequences. The 1967 crisis, although it at one point threatened to provoke a U.S.-Soviet military confrontation, did not raise the specter of nuclear exchange as vividly as the Cuban missiles had. On the other hand, the war was a major turning point in the Middle East, and we are still dealing with its consequences.

The root causes of the 1967 war lay in the unresolved issues arising from the creation of the state of Israel in 1948. That a war was coming sooner or later if those issues were not resolved was accepted wisdom among people in the area. The question was not whether but when. Certainly war was not expected in 1967, and why it happened when it did is still a matter of debate.

After three days of discussion involving a number of key individuals, it was clear that a good deal of work must be done before the debate over origins will be settled, but we have a clearer idea of the questions that must be answered. Readers will find much that is new here.

The conference was attended by representatives of the former Soviet Union, Syria, Jordan, Israel, Egypt, the United States and the United Nations. Sponsored by the Middle East Institute, Johns Hopkins University, and the Center for the Study of Foreign Affairs of the Department of State's Foreign Service Institute, it was held at the institute's facility in Rosslyn, Virginia,

June 3–5, 1992. The organizer and chairman of the conference was retired ambassador Richard B. Parker, who was political counselor of the American embassy in Cairo at the time of the war.

This volume would not have been possible without the help of a good many people. Thanks go to Dr. Timothy Childs, who gave the seed money without which nothing else would have happened. Completion of the project depended on the financial support of the United States Institute of Peace, the Foreign Service Institute, the Samuel Bronfman Foundation, Merle Thorpe, and Joan Bingham.

Another vote of thanks goes to Ambassador Dennis Kux, director of the Center for the Study of Foreign Affairs, his deputy, George Sherman, and their staff, who had the vision to see the importance of the project and whose administrative support was vital to its success. Not only did they make the conference possible, but they also managed to provide us with a verbatim transcript of the proceedings, at the cost of much personal labor. Particular gratitude goes to Mary Lou Bothwell, who took charge of all administrative arrangements and supervised preparation of the transcript.

Finally, special thanks go to Cathi Grosso of the Middle East Institute, who managed the finances, and to Sarah Bright, also of the institute, whose role in the painstaking preparation of the manuscript was indispensable.

Chronology

Feb. 23, 1966. Leftist military coup in Damascus.

Nov. 13, 1966. Israeli attack on Samu', Jordan.

April 7, 1967. Air battle over Syria. Six Syrian MIGs shot down.

May 12. Alleged statement by Chief of Staff Yitzhak Rabin that Israel will occupy Damascus and overthrow regime if Syrians do not stop cross-border activities.

May 13. Syrian Foreign Ministry issues statement claiming Israel has aggressive intentions toward Syria. Soviets warn Egyptians that Israel is concentrating ten to twelve brigades on the Syrian border preparatory to an attack scheduled for May 17. The Syrians had passed a similar warning to the Egyptians earlier in the month. Egypt's Supreme Executive Council meets in Cairo and decides to respond by mobilizing and sending troops into Sinai.

May 14. Syrian UN representative George Tomeh calls on UN Undersecretary Ralph Bunche with instructions to express his government's serious concern about Israeli intentions. Egyptian troops begin moving into Sinai. General Muhammad Fawzi, Egyptian chief of staff, flies to Syria to survey situation and coordinate with Syrians.

May 15. Syrian delegate to the Israel-Syria Mixed Armistice Commission (ISMAC) expresses great concern to its chairman about the alleged Israeli buildup in the Tiberias area. Chairman says he has seen no sign of it. General Odd Bull of the UN Truce Supervision Organization (UNTSO) reports that there is no sign of Israeli military buildup but notes that Israelis don't really need to have one in order to attack. General Fawzi returns to Cairo and reports to the armed forces commander, Marshal Abd al-Hakim 'Amr, that there are no signs of Israeli troop concentrations and the Syrians themselves are not mobilized.

May 16. Egyptians request UN Emergency Force (UNEF) commander, General Indar Jit Rikhye, to effect withdrawal of his forces from observation posts along the border. Rikhye refers the request to the UN. UN Secretary-General U Thant requests clarification from Egyptian representative, Muhammad al-Kony. Al-Kony queries Cairo, which instructs him to tell U Thant that Egypt will rebuff any attempt to get it to withdraw request. U Thant informs al-Kony that partial withdrawal is unacceptable and if the Egyptians instead mean full withdrawal, they should address their request to U Thant himself.

May 17. U Thant informs al-Kony in writing that there are no recent indications of troop movements or concentrations that should give cause for concern.

May 18. Egypt requests complete withdrawal of UNEF.

May 19. Egyptian High Command issues orders for occupation of Sharm al-Shaykh, which controls access to the Gulf of Aqaba via the Strait of Tiran.

May 21. UNEF withdraws from Sharm al-Shaykh. Egyptian troops move in to occupy it.

Night of May 21–22. Supreme Executive Council in Cairo agrees Strait of Tiran should be closed to Israeli shipping.

May 22. Egyptian President Gamal Abd al-Nasser informs officers at Bir Gifgafa airfield in Sinai that a decision has been made to close Strait of Tiran.

May 23. Radio Cairo announces early in the morning that Strait of Tiran has been closed to Israeli ships and ships carrying strategic cargo to Israel. U Thant meets with Nasser and other members of Egyptian government in Cairo. U Thant tells Nasser he was surprised by the announcement regarding Tiran, which was made while he was en route to Cairo, and that he thought it made war inevitable.

May 24. Egyptian Minister of War Shams Badran leaves for Moscow. Radio Cairo announces Egypt has mined the Gulf of Aqaba (this report is never confirmed). Egyptian Foreign Minister Mahmoud Riad warns that entry of an Israeli ship into the gulf would be considered an act of aggression.

May 25. Badran meets in Moscow with Prime Minister Kosygin, Foreign Minister Gromyko, Deputy Foreign Minister Semenov, and Defense Minister Grechko. Kosygin tells him that everything Cairo has done to date is correct but that the situation is very dangerous. Now that the Egyptians have made their point, they should try to defuse the crisis in order to consolidate their gains.

May 26. Israeli Foreign Minister Abba Eban meets with President Johnson in an effort to find out the extent of support the United States will give to Israel on reopening the Strait of Tiran by force. Johnson reaffirms support for Israel but refuses to say the United States will do whatever is necessary to reopen the strait. He tells Eban that Israel "will not be alone unless it decides to go alone." His meaning is not clear.

May 27. Soviet ambassadors in Cairo and Tel Aviv deliver Soviet plea for restraint to Nasser and Israeli Prime Minister Eshkol in the early hours of the morning. The Israeli cabinet meets and divides evenly on the question of whether to go to war.

May 28. Badran delegation leaves Moscow. At the bottom of the steps to the aircraft Marshal Grechko tells Badran to stand firm, as the Soviets are behind Egypt.

May 29. Nasser tells the National Assembly Badran has brought a message of support from Moscow.

May 30. King Hussein of Jordan flies to Cairo and signs a mutual defense agreement with Nasser. The agreement, modeled on the Egyptian-Syrian treaty, binds the parties to use all means at their disposal to repel an attack on either one. Meir Amit, Mossad chief, travels to Washington to seek further clarification of U.S. position. He sees officials at CIA and Department of Defense before returning to Israel on June 3.

May 31. Marshal 'Amr tells Foreign Minister Riad he looks worried and tells him not to be, that he could reach Beersheba with one-third of his forces.

June 1. Nasser receives former U.S. Treasury Secretary Robert Anderson and agrees to send his second vice-president, Zakariya Muhieddin, to Washington to discuss ways to defuse the situation. There is a cabinet reshuffle in Israel. Moshe Dayan is given the defense portfolio, which had been Eshkol's. Right-wing Menachem Begin and Joseph Saphir are brought in from outer darkness and given cabinet rank without portfolios. This is promptly dubbed a war cabinet.

June 2. Nasser warns his senior officers that the Israelis will strike in a few days. His warning goes largely unheeded.

June 3 Eshkol's kitchen cabinet, after hearing Amit's report from Washington, decides to recommend war to the full cabinet the following day.

June 4. Israeli cabinet votes to go to war.

June 5. Israelis strike.

Introduction

The six-day war between Israel and its Arab neighbors in June 1967 burst upon an unsuspecting world as suddenly as a summer storm. In retrospect it should not have been all that surprising. None of Israel's neighbors was prepared to negotiate peace with it or even to accept its existence indirectly. Indeed, none of the Arab states, whether sharing a border with Israel or not, was yet ready openly to acknowledge that the 1947 UN General Assembly decision to partition Palestine into an Arab and a Jewish state, followed by the 1948–49 Arab-Israeli war, had brought into existence a state and a new regional reality that must be the focus of subsequent diplomatic actions.

The violently negative response to Tunisian President Habib Bourguiba's 1965 proposal that the Arabs should at long last face up to reality and accept the partition decision clearly demonstrated that the Arab world was not yet ready to adopt a realistic appraisal of the power balances. Away from the public eye, Arab-Israeli contacts, while intermittent, had never been lacking. The many negotiations between the Jordanian Hashemite dynasty and Israeli leaders (beginning even before the creation of Israel) and the Anglo-American–sponsored efforts to orchestrate a settlement between President Gamal Abd al-Nasser of Egypt and Prime Minister David Ben-Gurion of Israel demonstrate that serious Arab-Israeli diplomatic probings, both direct and indirect, had long existed. But all such endeavors had to be secret because the touchstone of Arab ideological purity remained support for the Palestinian cause and a refusal to accept the Zionist entity. No more damaging charge could be brought against a rival Arab government than to accuse it of failing to meet this test.

Nor had Israeli actions contributed to an atmosphere of accommodation. Quite the contrary, the Israeli policy of retaliation in force against Arab infiltration across the border, coupled with a tough and often provocative posture in various negotiations in the Mixed Armistice Commissions set up in 1949 to deal with border problems, hardly induced Arab governments or Arab public opinion to consider moving toward settlement.

Even the kindliest interpretation of Israel's regional strategy during roughly the first two decades of independence must leave considerable scope for the argument that Israel had adopted the classic dicta of hard-liners, past and present: "The only thing our enemies understand is force" and "The enemy of my enemy is my friend." The Israeli collusion with Britain and France in attacking Egypt as a stark finale to the 1956 Suez crisis further established what had long been an Arab perception: Israel was an instrument of continued Western imperialist domination of the Middle East.

Accordingly, the attitudes of the people and the leadership caught up in the Arab-Israeli confrontation provided ready tinder for a rapid move at any time from a state of no-war/no-peace to armed combat. Moreover, the actions of any one state (or of even a single person) might provide the necessary spark. This was ominous enough in itself, but exacerbating the situation was the cold war involvement in regional politics. From the beginning of the cold war, the superpowers had used the Middle East, at least that portion of it that John Foster Dulles was later to label "the northern tier," for their skirmishing.

With the death of Stalin in 1953, followed soon by Khrushchev's rise to power, Soviet activism in the Middle East moved southward in step with a more subtle Soviet policy toward the formerly colonized world. Those Third World leaders whom Stalin had distrusted as bourgeois nationalists were transmogrified by Khrushchev into revolutionary proto-communists. The turning point in the Middle East was the marriage of convenience between Nasserist Arabism and the Soviet bloc, the banns having been proclaimed with the 1955 Soviet-Egyptian arms deal. The marriage was never all that smooth, and it only aggravated the diplomatic instability. Nasser wanted the Soviets to neutralize Western power, but he warily monitored possible Soviet support for local communists or, even more disturbing to him, for radical regimes or movements that might escape Egyptian leadership in the Arab world.

In the meantime, the United States had gained a preemptive position as champion of Western interests in the region following decolonization and the fallout from the abortive 1956 Anglo-French attack on Egypt. The U.S. government's definition of American interests before 1967 was, first, denial of the region to the Soviets and, second, access to its oil on "reasonable terms." After 1967, the security of Israel was added to this list, even though reconciling it with the other two interests was often difficult, if not impossible, at least on the tactical level.

The Soviet Union sought regional advantage at the expense of the United States, but always without risking too much. To neither superpower was the Middle East as crucial as Central Europe. This setup was, in the best tradition of the earlier "Eastern Question" diplomacy, a pattern of super-power struggle by proxy. The one unstated superpower rule was that outright warfare was to be confined to the Middle East. Aside from that, no holds were barred. Arms deals, propaganda blitzes, covert action, warfare confined to the Middle East, and even detente constituted the spectrum of policies implemented by the rival superpowers.

This was a much more complex diplomatic game than the image of superpower patrons and regional clients would imply. It was also much more unstable. Whereas cold war diplomacy provided regional states some insurance against complete destruction at the hands of regional enemies—neither superpower being willing to accept such a defeat for its client(s)—the need to attend simultaneously to regional and superpower alignments increased the likelihood of initiatives being taken that might be unexpected or even irrational. Even so, what cries out for explanation now, a quarter-century later, is that a scant three weeks before June 5 no one—statesman, scholar, or soldier, Eastern or Western, Israeli or Arab—had predicted a general Arab-Israeli war in June or even in 1967. Even the Egyptian leadership appeared not to have anticipated an actual fight; the timing, it was believed, was not right. Had not Nasser himself often heaped scorn upon the radical Arab leadership for seeking a showdown with Israel before necessary preparations were in place? Nasser's publicly stated position well into 1967 was that the Arab forces were by no means yet ready to take on Israel. After all, the best one-third of Egypt's forces were tied down in Yemen, where since 1962 they had been supporting the republican forces in their struggle against the ousted royalists. Moreover, the civil war in Yemen had brought in its wake an inter-Arab struggle pitting Egypt against Saudi Arabia, with each seeking to line up Arab and foreign support.

Malcolm Kerr in his classic *The Arab Cold War* (Oxford University Press, 1978) deftly depicted the prevailing climate: "It was not hard to imagine, early in May 1967, that the mounting tension in the Arab world would lead to some sort of violent outbreak. The conflict to which all signs seemed to point, however, was between Arab revolutionaries and conservatives. The old quarrel with Israel seemed irrelevant" (p. 126)

What, then, about the superpowers? The United States, after a once promising but ultimately abortive effort to patch up relations with Nasser during the Kennedy administration, then sought to bring the Yemen civil war to a close in a way that would protect Saudi Arabia (and Western access to Arabian peninsula oil) without aggravating the polarization within the Arab world, which would give the West additional headaches. Most troublesome of all, the United States was increasingly mired down in Vietnam. The last thing the Johnson administration wanted was yet another international hot spot that might call for American action.

There remains the question of whether either Israel or the Soviet Union had sufficient motivation to play with fire and provoke a crisis that might lead all the way to war.

The Soviet Union over the previous twelve years had shown that it was not averse to taking limited Middle Eastern initiatives that might serve to strengthen Arab revolutionaries (the natural candidates for Soviet patronage) at the expense of the Arab conservatives (more nearly in the Western camp). The Soviets adopted an essentially pro-Arab, anti-Israel public posture that fit with the overall Soviet self-image as the world leader of liberation movements against Western capitalist forces and their Third World lackeys.

At the same time, the Soviet Union also had reason for prudence. It was still absorbing the dramatic events of October 1964—the ouster of Khrushchev and the advent of Brezhnev and Kosygin, plus the nuclear detonation that made China, the increasingly anti-Soviet giant, into the Communist world's second nuclear power. Soviet eyes, like those of the United States, were surely more concentrated on East and Southeast Asia than on the Middle East. Although the American post facto image of Vietnam is of a quagmire that the United States could and should have avoided, the Soviets in the mid-1960s saw their powerful rival upping the military ante in Vietnam in a way that might oblige an equivalent Soviet response. A still somewhat shaky post-Khrushchev regime, pressured by both its huge Chinese neighbor and its superpower rival and taunted by Third World radicals for not being revolutionary enough, might well opt for a diversionary action in the Middle East. It would seem more plausible, however, to assume that the Soviets scarcely sought a major crisis and, even less, a confrontation with the United States in the Middle East.

For Israel, the first months of 1967 were not promising. The GNP growth rate, double-digit in many recent years, was projected to decline to a mere 1 percent, and unemployment was above 10 percent. Israeli leaders saw no prospects for improved relations with any of the Arab states or, for that matter, with the Soviet Union.

Enough to put the Israeli leadership and body politic in a surly mood? Yes, and these underlying problems must have played their part in the battle of words and deeds between Israel and its neighbors that preceded the crisis itself. Yet to suggest an Israel disinclined to tolerate even inadvertent offense from any of its neighbors is one thing. To suggest an Israel with a long-range plan to provoke and sustain a crisis culminating in the preemptive Israeli military strike that actually occurred is quite another. The evidence to date from Israeli sources supports the view that Israelis no more expected the series of crisis-producing actions Nasser took beginning on May 13, 1967, than did anyone else, not excluding—it seems clear—even Egyptians and other Arabs. That the Israelis might have had a long-range plan (or plot), crucially dependent on specific, sequenced steps by the principal adversary that no one believed possible, simply does not pass the test of logic or common sense. Nevertheless, elaborate theories that the war was a result of a U.S.-Israeli (or Soviet or Syrian) plot began circulating as soon as the Egyptian defeat occurred.

Nor was 1967 a replay of 1956 for Israel. There were no great powers encouraging Israelis to take forceful action, although there are serious allegations that Lyndon Johnson gave them a green light to attack when they did. France, Israel's old comrade in arms and arms supply, under President Charles de Gaulle, was showing strong signs of playing the Arab card. The British were almost totally out of the picture. It is true that in President Johnson the Israelis seemed to have a friend, and the Arabs quite the contrary, but we must not read back into time before June 1967 the pattern of massive military and financial support that later characterized the American-Israeli relationship. In any case, however pro-Israel President Johnson might have been, his Vietnam venture left him disinclined to urge anyone to raise more trouble in yet another world area.

Thus, the broad contours of the situation prevailing just before the crisis can be reduced to the following interrelated factors:

- The potential for Arab-Israeli enmity to explode into another round of warfare was omnipresent, but
- The most ominous signs of regional stress in early 1967 were between the several Arab states.
- Most of the regional and international actors neither expected nor sought an Arab-Israeli confrontation at that time. Most of those involved had strong motivation to avoid (or at least postpone) any such test of strength. Even those whose motivation was possibly more ambivalent had little reason to expect the rapid runup to a full-blown crisis leading to war.
- Finally, the ultimate irony of the June War is that the person most responsible for taking initiatives that created the crisis leading to war in June 1967 was the regional actor with perhaps the strongest motivation to postpone indefinitely any confrontation with Israel: Gamal Abd al-Nasser. A compelling cast of statesmen from many different countries figures in any serious study of the

origins of the war, but none is more prominent and ultimately more enigmatic than Nasser. He stands out as the preeminent protagonist around whom the crisis leading to war unfolded. Nasser, in his *Philosophy of the Revolution* (Public Affairs Press, 1955), wrote of "a role in search of a hero" (p. 87). In 1967 the role that found its hero was not what Nasser had sought or others had expected.

The Scenario

Although some details are still disputed, the following is a summary of major events leading up to the June War.

On May 13, 1967, Soviet officials warned the Egyptians that Israel was concentrating forces on the Syrian border preparatory to a large-scale attack on May 17. According to Egyptian accounts, the warning was explicit as to the numbers of troops and their location. The numbers vary from ten to eighteen brigades, depending on one's informant. (There were in fact no such troop concentrations on the ground at the time.)

The timing of the Soviet warning was unfortunate. There was already considerable tension along the Israel-Syrian border. The Israelis were making efforts to incorporate into Israel the demilitarized zones left over from the 1948 war, and Palestinian paramilitary groups operating out of Syria were conducting sabotage operations in Israel. The tension had escalated into an air battle over Damascus on April 7 during which the Israelis shot down six Syrian planes. Egypt's refusal on that occasion to come to Syria's aid under their November 1966 mutual defense agreement had occasioned much sarcastic comment in the conservative Arab media.

Egypt had come in for equally bitter attacks for failing to respond when Israel attacked the Jordanian village of Samu' on November 13, 1966. Samu' was the largest Israeli military operation since the 1956 Suez campaign, and it inflicted a stinging defeat on the Jordanian army. This incident is generally agreed to be the beginning of the escalation in tensions that led to the war, but such an outcome was not apparent at the time. In responding to the public outcry, Jordan attacked Egypt for sheltering behind the UN Emergency Force (UNEF), which had been patrolling the Israeli-Egyptian border since the Israeli withdrawal from Sinai in 1957. Although Cairo brushed off these complaints at the time, it is evident that they rankled more than the Egyptians were willing to admit.

On May 13 the tension went up a further notch over reports that on May 12 the Israeli chief of staff, Yitzhak Rabin, had threatened to occupy

Damascus and overthrow the regime there if the Syrians did not stop the paramilitary incursions into Israel. That Rabin made such a statement is still an article of faith with many Israelis as well as Arabs, but the allegation apparently was the result of a United Press International reporter's distortion of a briefing by the Israeli chief of military intelligence, General Aharon Yariv. Various statements by other leading Israelis, however, had given the clear impression that it was only a matter of time before Israel struck at Syria unless the latter did something to stop the cross-border infiltration. In attempting to clarify Israeli attitudes, Yariv had confirmed apprehensions that Israel would resort to military measures. The question was not whether but when and on what scale.

Nasser and his vice-president and military commander, Marshal Abd al-Hakim 'Amr, evidently concluded after receiving the Soviet report that they could not afford not to respond with some military action to deter Israel from attacking. (According to some former Egyptian officials, they had not responded to a similar report from the Syrians a few days earlier because they had not believed it.) The question that remains unresolved is whether Nasser and 'Amr were, as they claimed, merely reacting to events or had in fact been waiting for a pretext to confront Israel. Hard as it is to see how they could have felt they were ready for such a confrontation, their actions do not make much sense if they thought otherwise.

The first Egyptian step was to order full mobilization on May 14 and to start sending troops into the Sinai immediately. According to Nasser, his military commanders thought that to be effective their troops must have freedom of action, which would require UNEF to withdraw from its observation posts along the border. Accordingly, on May 16 the Egyptian chief of staff requested the UNEF commander, Indar Jit Rikhye, an Indian general, to effect such a withdrawal. He referred the request to UN Secretary-General U Thant, who was responsible for UNEF. U Thant balked at what seemed to be a request for partial withdrawal and replied that it would have to be all or nothing—complete withdrawal or none. The Egyptians then requested total withdrawal on May 18. U Thant acceded to this request immediately, and Rikhye received orders early on May 19 to begin an orderly withdrawal. Most of UNEF was still on the ground when war came on June 5, but the contingent at Sharm al-Shaykh, which controlled the Strait of Tiran, the entrance to the Gulf of Aqaba, had been withdrawn and that position occupied by Egyptian paratroops on May 21.

On May 22 Nasser told a group of air force officers at a base in Sinai that as of May 23 the Gulf of Aqaba would be closed to Israeli shipping and strategic cargoes bound for Israel. His statement was broadcast over Cairo radio in the early hours of May 23. During the day the Egyptians affirmed that oil was considered strategic cargo.

The Israelis had enjoyed freedom of passage through the Strait of Tiran ever since their occupation of Sinai in 1956. They had stated publicly and unequivocally as far back as 1957 that any interference with that passage would be casus belli. (See Foreign Minister Golda Meir's statement of March 1, 1957, setting forth Israel's understanding of the conditions under which it was withdrawing its troops from Sinai.) Israel's position was well known in Egypt.

Frantic diplomatic maneuvering to find some way of avoiding the looming confrontation ensued. The United States, which had been committed in writing since 1957 to support freedom of navigation in the Gulf of Aqaba, favored a British proposal for creation of a multinational force that would keep the Strait of Tiran open. This stance appears to have been based on a conviction in Washington that the Egyptians would not oppose such a force militarily. (That conviction was contested by the American Embassy in Cairo.) In the event, for lack of enough other states willing to join in, such an effort was unworkable, and the proposal never approached implementation.

At the same time, the administration in Washington had been urging restraint on the Israelis and the Egyptians to buy time for a peaceful resolution of the crisis. As of late May the American government thought it had an Israeli commitment not to attack for a period of roughly two weeks, while Nasser had given a commitment not to begin hostilities. The Israelis, however, decided to ignore their commitment, and they struck with overwhelming force on June 5. By June 8 Egypt's forces could no longer resist, and a cease-fire was accepted on June 9. Meanwhile, the Israelis had responded to Jordanian firing across the border and seizure of a UN enclave at Jerusalem by smashing the Jordanian army and occupying all the territory between the old armistice line and the Jordan River, the so-called West Bank. They then turned their attention to Syria and occupied the Golan Heights after fierce fighting.

Motives, Perceptions, and Reactions

Even though the sequence of events is fairly well established, there are many questions about motivation, intentions, and perceptions of the parties involved. Why did they do what they did?

The Soviets

There has been much speculation but no irrefutable evidence as to why the Soviets gave the warning to the Egyptians in the way that they did. In fact, Soviet sources even question whether the warning was given by them as described by the Egyptians. Neither the Soviet nor the Egyptian archives on this period have been published, and we have only reminiscences to go on. Our puzzlement is increased by the fact that various qualified military observers testified at the time that the alleged Israeli troop concentrations did not exist, and it is difficult to see how a state with the Soviet Union's presumed intelligence capabilities would think they did. Did the Soviets know the report was false, or were they victims of an intelligence fabrication or a disinformation effort by somebody? Did they expect a limited reaction from the Egyptians? Were they seeking to have Egypt bolster Syria? Were they seeking to complicate life for the Americans and divert them from Vietnam? Were they pursuing a grand scheme to unite the Arab world? Did they hope to discipline Nasser and make him more dependent on them by luring him into a trap? All of these possibilities have been advanced seriously as explanations at one time or another, and many writers here assumed that the Soviets knew the report was false and passed it deliberately, with a specific end in view.

Egypt

Why did the Egyptians choose to react as they did, particularly after they had heard from their own military early on that there were no troop concentrations? They had plenty of time either to pull back or not to push for a confrontation. Why did they not stop the escalation? The memoirs of senior Egyptian military officers indicate that they knew they were no match for the Israelis. How could Nasser and 'Amr have believed otherwise, particularly given Nasser's public and private statements that Egypt was not ready for such a fight and given the presence of a third of his army in Yemen? What made them go over the brink as they did?

Syria

Little is known about the Syrian decision process at this point. A plausible argument can be made that the Syrian leadership, which repeatedly proclaimed its support for a "people's war of liberation," was seeking to drag Egypt into a confrontation with Israel and that Syria was the source of the false report of Israeli troop concentrations. What was Syria's true role in this affair? We are in almost complete ignorance in that respect.

Syrian president Nuredin Atassi tells a rally in Damascus on December 7, 1966, that his government will send arms to the Jordanians to help them overthrow their government because it did not react more strongly to the November 13 Israeli raid on Samuʻ. The man on Atassi's right is Syrian strongman Gen. Salah Jadid. By permission of AP/Wide World Photos.

Israel

According to one Israeli historian, the Israeli cabinet met on May 7 and decided that if Syria did not heed Israeli warnings about the border incursions, Israel would launch a limited retaliation raid. Is that true? What exactly did General Yariv say in his briefing for the press and military attachés on May 12? Was Meir Amit, the director of Mossad, told during his visit to Washington on June 1–2 that the Americans would bless an Israeli attack on Egypt? If so, who in the U.S. government told him that? In any event, did the Israelis think they had a green light from President Johnson to do what they did? Were the Israelis waiting for a pretext to strike at Nasser, as some writers allege?

The United States

Why was Washington so slow to respond to the crisis? (It took a week following the Egyptian request of May 16 for UNEF to be withdrawn before the first high-level message was sent to Cairo, and it had been overtaken by events before it was sent.) Why did the United States not honor its reiterations during the crisis of its support of the Tripartite Declaration of 1950, which committed it to oppose all forceful changes of territory in the region? Toward the end of May, Lyndon Johnson apparently resigned himself to the fact that the Israelis were going to strike, although he continued to urge them not to do so. To the Israelis it was important to avoid a repeat of the Eisenhower administration's reaction to their 1956 attack on Egypt, and Johnson's attitude was critical to their decision to strike. What persuaded Johnson to relax his opposition and to go along with the attack in 1967?

Jordan

Why did the Jordanians opt to join the fighting on June 5? Did King Hussein have any realistic alternative? How much control did the Jordanians have over their armed forces, given the appointment of the Egyptian general Abd al-Mun'im Riad as the nominal commander as a result of King Hussein's May 30 visit to Cairo? Is it true, as claimed by Egyptian pundit Mohamed Heikal, that King Hussein had warned the Egyptians on May 1 that the Syrians were trying to ignite the situation along the Syrian front in order to compel the Egyptians to come to their rescue? If so, what was the basis for Hussein's belief?

The United Nations

Was there a communications problem between the Egyptians and the UN? Specifically, is it true, as some have claimed, that the Egyptians never intended for UNEF to vacate Sharm al-Shaykh and had not originally intended to close the Strait of Tiran? Could the UN have accommodated a request for redeployment rather than withdrawal of UNEF? Why did U Thant not try to stall on the Egyptian request for withdrawal? Why did no one call for an emergency meeting of the General Assembly or ask for a meeting of the Security Council to discuss the Egyptian request? Why did U Thant or a senior member of his staff not go to Cairo as soon as the crisis began?

The Conference

In an effort to explore these questions with knowledgeable survivors and students of the crisis from those countries principally involved, the Middle East Institute, together with the Center for the Study of Foreign Affairs at the Department of State's Foreign Service Institute and the Conflict Management Program of the Johns Hopkins School of Advanced International Studies, sponsored a conference on June 3–5, 1992, to mark the twenty-fifth anniversary of the war. It was held at the Foreign Service Institute in Rosslyn, Virginia.

The conference was organized into seven panels that discussed in turn the origins of the crisis, the UN response, the Israeli response, Arab responses, the U.S. role, conspiracy theories, and a summing up. Attendance was by invitation only, and some professional involvement in the problem was a primary qualification. A chronology of the crisis precedes this Introduction, and brief identifications of the panelists appear in the Appendix.

As the reader will discover, the conference answered some questions but not others. Much work remains to be done before we can be certain of the Soviet, Egyptian, and Syrian roles in particular, but there are also unanswered questions about the American and Israeli roles. The findings are discussed in chapter 7, "Conclusions."

The first six chapters are organized by panels. An introductory essay by each panel chairman is followed by an edited verbatim transcript of the presentations and discussion on each topic. The transcripts have been reduced to the maximum possible extent consistent with clarity.

CHAPTER I

✒ Origins of the Crisis

L. Carl Brown

"'Where shall I begin, please your Majesty?' he asked. 'Begin at the beginning,' the King said gravely, 'and go on till you come to the end: then stop.'"

This unhelpful regal advice from *Alice's Adventures in Wonderland* illuminates the daunting problem facing this first session. The beginnings of events, great and small, are not all that discernible.

Is there a precise moment, a point of no return, a Caesar crossing the Rubicon, to be found in events leading to the June 1967 war? Or is there instead a more general context that predisposed the move toward war, somewhat like the classic explanation by Thucydides of what caused the Peloponnesian War: "What made war inevitable was the growth of Athenian power and the fear which this caused in Sparta."

Surely the answer concerning the June War, as is usual for wars, is that the origins must be found in both the general context governing the attitudes and actions of the parties, plus one or several proximate causes.

For the most part, this first panel has concentrated on the proximate causes of the June War. Not that the participants ignored the deeper historical roots of an Arab-Israeli confrontation that had previously provoked two wars (1948–49 and the 1956 Suez War) and produced no peace treaties. Rather, the participants, knowing this historical background all too well, have tended to concentrate on asking what immediate events triggered the June War. Even so, a careful reading of the transcript reveals interesting, and often contradictory, assumptions advanced by the different participants concerning the general context.

Attention to the proximate causes of the conflict dictated the choice of subjects—the Israeli "threat," the Soviet warning, and the Egyptian response—because most studies of how the June War began highlight one or more of the following factors as setting off the crisis:

- The Israeli threat to take punitive action against Syria, which, so the argument goes, the government of Israel must have known would necessarily provoke an Egyptian response.
- The Soviet intelligence report (clearly false) passed to the Egyptians of the mobilization of a large number of Israeli troops near Israel's northern border in seeming preparation for a major attack on Syria.
- The reaction of Egypt's Nasser, first demanding the withdrawal of UNEF forces and then announcing a blockade of the Strait of Tiran.

The Israeli "Threat"

In seeking to reconstruct the Israeli position in 1967, Shimon Shamir makes four points.

- Israeli actions fitted into that country's basic strategy of retaliation against Arab attacks, large or small, in accord with the general Israeli antipathy to a static defense. Consistent with the retaliation strategy was a pattern of issuing warnings that would serve either to deter or, failing that, to legitimate later action. This is what Israeli public opinion had been conditioned to expect, and any government not so acting would risk losing domestic support by appearing weak or indecisive.
- Shamir sees two Israeli schools of thought regarding how to deal with the radical regime in Syria. One group believed caution was indicated since overly assertive Israeli action against Syria might well bring about some form of Soviet intervention. A corollary was the idea that perhaps prudent diplomacy might even induce the Soviet Union to rein in its Syrian client. Others, however, especially the Israeli Defense Forces (IDF), felt that a tough military response to any Syrian act against Israel was better policy.
- Did Israel present an extraordinary threat to Syria? In reviewing the available evidence, including the May 12 United Press International dispatch, Shamir concludes that the threatening Israeli statements were within the framework of conventional warnings consistent with the well-established Israeli policy: warn to deter and then, should deterrence fail, retaliate. Shamir does accept, however, that Nasser could easily have interpreted the Israeli statements, especially as construed, inadvertently, by the Western media and, probably deliberately, by

Soviet and Syrian media, as part of an Israeli plan to topple the government in Damascus.

- As for lessons to be learned, Shamir suggests that if criticism of Israel is appropriate, the point would be that Israel "did not realize the delicacy of deterrence and warning. . . . Warnings of this kind are context dependent." The irony, he adds, is that the Eshkol government, "the most moderate Israeli government in years," probably felt compelled to keep issuing warnings over an extended period so as to counter domestic discontent.

The Soviet Warning

In addressing the question of why the Soviets gave the Egyptian government the false warning of Israeli troop mobilization near the Syrian border, Vitaly Naumkin outlines three possible alternative motives.

- The Soviets wanted a war.
- They hoped to avoid large-scale hostilities by securing a balance of military capabilities in the area, which would be accomplished if Egypt lined up in support of Syria.
- The Soviets' intelligence report was part of a "routine maneuver" intended only to prepare their regional clients for a possible war.

In setting out possible inducements for the Soviets to provoke an Israeli-Arab war, Naumkin presents what he describes as three unrealistic options, one weak option, and a single motive that might be plausible.

The unrealistic options are that the Soviets believed the Arabs would win such a war; that they sought an Arab defeat that would make the Arab states, with nowhere else to turn, even more reliant on the Soviet Union; or that they wanted a confrontation with the United States.

Naumkin's weak option is that the Soviets sought a scenario in which Israel would suffer heavy losses; this, in turn, would bring about American intervention and produce "another Vietnam" situation for the United States.

The more plausible motive was that the Soviets hoped to bring about an Israeli setback sufficient to strengthen Arab leftist regimes, and thus Soviet influence in the Middle East, and perhaps even to set up conditions for a regional settlement of the sort that would favor Soviet interests.

Were the Soviets, then, willing to risk an Arab-Israeli war? The answer would seemingly depend on the Soviet appraisal of Arab military capacity against Israel. Naumkin suggests that the Soviet appraisal in Damascus at the time was that the Arabs could avoid defeat only if Egypt, Jordan, and Syria formed a united command.

Yet Naumkin also maintains that during the May 25 meetings in Moscow with Egyptian Minister of War Badran, Prime Minister Kosygin warned against Egypt's initiating hostilities but stated that the Kremlin was confident of Egyptian victory if war came, the Arab military potential being much greater than that of Israel. There were as well Marshal Grechko's overly encouraging words to Shams Badran. Set against these bullish appraisals of Egyptian and Arab military potential are the many sources indicating that the Soviets were counseling caution from mid-May on. All this adds up to a confused picture of both Soviet thinking and action.

Naumkin suggests a resolution of this confusion by discounting, again, a Soviet urge to pick a fight with the United States. He discounts as well the notion that the Soviets had a firm strategy of offering their Arab clients sufficient support eventually to prevail. Instead, he believes that a strong anti-Israeli and anti-Semitic tendency in much of the party leadership was decisive in shaping the Soviet course. Certain high Soviet officials (such as Mikhail Suslov, the ideology secretary of the Communist Party), Naumkin concludes, may have wanted Israel to attack and be labeled the aggressor. It is not that the Soviets expected an Israeli defeat, but neither did they anticipate the devastating Arab defeat that occurred.

Naumkin's analysis, which must rely on speculation in the absence of adequate archival sources, seems to paint a picture of Soviet brinkmanship made even murkier by considerable intra-governmental rivalry. The image of a monolithic Soviet leadership all moving in lockstep along firmly fixed policy paths does not provide the answers needed, but the alternative that Naumkin suggests leaves questions unanswered as well. For example, Naumkin first cites the overly sanguine appraisal of Egypt's military prospect that Kosygin communicated to Shams Badran—which would certainly have encouraged Egyptian adventurism—but Naumkin's concluding remarks single out the same Kosygin as "a very restrained and responsible politician . . . [who] played a positive role."

The same confusion reigns concerning how and to whom in the Egyptian government the Soviets gave the intelligence report about alleged Israeli mobilization. Naumkin considers various possibilities: Soviet Ambassador Pojidaev gave the intelligence report to the Egyptian government, or a KGB official gave it to his Egyptian counterpart, or Soviet military advisers in Egypt passed it on. Or, yet another option, the intelligence report was not in fact officially given to the Egyptians.

Complicating the search for an answer is the lack of any reference in the Soviet Foreign Ministry archives to a May 13 meeting of Pojidaev with Egyptian Foreign Ministry officials. Even when all the archival material becomes available, a technical problem will continue to frustrate researchers: Soviet ambassadors were not allowed to refer in their cable traffic to the content of instructions sent from Moscow. They could only report that such and such a message had been delivered. Moreover, many Soviet diplomatic and policy decisions apparently were made without documentation, and determining origins and motivation at this remove may be difficult.

Yet the undisputed historical record, confirmed by several of the conference participants, is that an inaccurate Soviet intelligence report was passed to the Egyptians. It would satisfy the human desire for certitude to determine precisely how this was done, just as it is always relevant to determine as accurately as possible the modus operandi of the different bureaucracies involved. Still, Naumkin concludes that incertitude on this particular point does not appreciably affect the overall analysis of the Soviet role, a conclusion that seems warranted.

The Egyptian Response

In discussing Egyptian actions, Salah Bassiouny emphasizes what he sees as the incommensurability of the two regional protagonists, Egypt and Israel. Israel, he argues, was "well-prepared and with a deep understanding of the enemy and waiting for the right opportunity to provoke the war." Egypt, on the other hand, was completely tied up with domestic and inter-Arab issues. Israel had managed to develop a solid working relationship with its superpower patron, the United States. The Egyptian-Soviet link, by contrast, was more an arrangement for supply of matériel and military advisers, without any real identity of strategic outlook, perhaps even less of shared values, between the two.

Another major theme running through his account is the abysmal lack of coordination between Egypt's military and diplomatic establishments. Bassiouny reconstructs Egyptian perceptions and actions from the vantage point of a Foreign Ministry official at the time. It makes for a bleak picture of divided Egyptian leadership.

Concerning the elusive identity of the Soviet official who gave the faulty intelligence report to the Egyptian government, Bassiouny is categorical: On May 13 Soviet Ambassador Pojidaev requested an urgent meeting with the Egyptian foreign minister. The latter was not available, and the undersecretary of the ministry, Ahmad Hassan al-Feki, received Pojidaev. After hearing his report, which Pojidaev insisted was a Soviet intelligence finding, Feki sent an urgent message to the foreign minister and to the presidency. The Foreign Ministry also knew that the KGB liaison officer had delivered the same message to his Egyptian counterpart, but Bassiouny is not sure whether that took place before or after the Pojidaev-Feki meeting. A similar report was given to Anwar Sadat, president of Egypt's National Assembly, when he stopped over in Moscow on the way home from Pyongyang on the same day.

Bassiouny notes that "it was not customary for the Soviet ambassador to deliver such reports to the foreign minister, it had never happened before," and by this unprecedented move, plus the report to Sadat, the Soviets sought to leave no doubt that some "Egyptian action" was required.

Examples abound to show that the Egyptian Foreign Ministry was thereafter kept poorly informed. Chief of Staff Muhammad Fawzi left for Syria on May 14 to investigate and returned the following day to report that neither Egyptian nor Syrian intelligence could confirm any Israeli mobilization, but the Foreign Ministry was not informed of his report. Moreover, the Egyptian decisions to demand the withdrawal of UNEF from Sinai and to close the Strait of Tiran were taken without any request to the Foreign Ministry for a legal or political assessment. Only after the fact was the foreign minister made aware of the decisions.

Bassiouny was a member of the Egyptian delegation that visited Moscow on May 24–28. Again, the pattern of divided leadership prevails, seemingly on both sides. The Soviets, Bassiouny reports, were urging Egyptian de-escalation and assurance to the United States that Egypt had no intention of initiating hostilities. Not only that, but Bassiouny reports that the Soviets advised Egypt to "open the strait [of Tiran] for oil shipments to Israel." To underscore the importance of this Soviet advice, Deputy Foreign Minister Semenov took Ambassador Feki to his dacha on May 26 for a meeting that lasted until 4:00 A.M. At that long session the main theme stressed by Semenov "was an appeal to Egypt to avoid war." (This contrasts with the interpretation of the Moscow meetings given by Naumkin.)

Feki kept Cairo informed daily of these developments, but other reports of a quite different nature were being sent back to Abd al-Hakim 'Amr by the head of the delegation, Shams Badran, the minister of war. Badran even told Bassiouny as they were flying back to Cairo to change the conclusions of the report he was writing because of Marshal Grechko's last-minute message of support at the Moscow airport. [Grechko, the Soviet minister of defense, reportedly told Badran as the delegation was leaving that the Soviets would fill all the Egyptians' requests for arms, that the Soviet Union would enter the war on Egypt's side if the United States entered the war, and that "if something happens and you need us, just send us a signal."—*Ed.*]

Both Feki and Bassiouny deemed Grechko's parting words mere window dressing, but Feki remained pessimistic about being able to counter the Badran-'Amr plan to accept all risks, including war.

Bassiouny sees Egyptian mismanagement of the crisis as resulting "from the political system initiated by both [Nasser and 'Amr]." His interpretation accords with that of several Egyptian military and political leaders writing after the June War who describe a keen rivalry between Nasser and 'Amr, producing a situation in which Nasser was "hostage to the power of 'Amr and the army."

The Discussion

Karen Dawisha, commentator, concentrates on the Soviet role. Observers, she notes, have no trouble in accepting that the leadership in Egypt, Israel, and the United States differed over policy options, but there is a tendency to "assume unanimity on the Soviet side." Such was probably not the case, and she suggests that while an (unlikely) Arab victory would be the most favorable outcome for the Soviets, even an Arab defeat might advance Soviet goals by tying down the United States in a region where Soviet maneuverability was much better than in Southeast Asia. It would also silence Chinese criticism, torpedo detente, put an end to Romanian and Polish flirtation with Germany's Ostpolitik, and set the stage for a crackdown on domestic dissidents, including Soviet Jews.

The general discussion is mainly concerned with clarifying or contradicting (and thus at times confusing) details of the proximate causes of the June War as presented by the earlier speakers.

Meir Amit, drawing on his experience as head of Mossad, maintains that Soviet policy in this instance accorded with what he called the "Cuban model" of brinkmanship, escalating to a point at which a crisis risks getting out of hand, followed by a tactic of backing off and seeking to reap the benefits gained.

In the case of the June War, he notes that following the March 31 death of Marshal Malinovsky, Soviet hawks succeeded in replacing him with Grechko as head of the Ministry of Defense. The Brezhnev-Grechko alliance, he argues, was one of the main factors in provoking the June War.

Amit also observes that the late Moshe Sneh, leader of the Israeli Communist Party, had an intimate, unofficial meeting with Soviet Ambassador to Israel Chuvakin, who told him that the war would be over in twenty-four hours and in the end there would be no Israel. This point perhaps ties in with Amit's interpretation of Nasser's postwar resignation speech, in which the Egyptian leader explicitly stated that he had carefully calculated the balance of forces and decided that the Arabs could win.

As for when and how the Soviet warning was passed to Egypt, Georgiy Kornienko declares himself "absolutely positive" that "no instructions were given to Ambassador Pojidaev to pass any information on May 12 or 13 or around that date." He advances a different chronology, maintaining that only as late as May 20 did the Soviet ambassador, acting on instructions from the Soviet Foreign Ministry, refer, inter alia, to intelligence "which needed verification" about Israeli brigades near the Syrian border. The following day the Soviet ambassador, on instructions from Moscow, called on Nasser. The instructions made no mention of the alleged Israeli mobilization, and their main point was to urge Egyptian restraint.

Was Pojidaev perhaps acting on "back channel" instructions? Kornienko insists that it was impossible that a Soviet ambassador could act on instructions from the KGB or the Politburo, bypassing the Foreign Ministry. Victor Israelyan concurs but adds the intriguing comment that Brezhnev in December 1967 spoke to him of "changing" Soviet Middle East policy. Soon thereafter Pojidaev was replaced. Was this punishment for acting without instructions? Bassiouny, for his part, reaffirms that Pojidaev did indeed call on the Egyptian Foreign Ministry.

Tahsin Basheer accepts as beyond dispute that Nasser both demanded the withdrawal of UNEF and announced the blockade of the Strait of Tiran without having consulted the Soviets. Basheer, however, insists that the Soviets deserved criticism for the lack of warnings immediately thereafter, not to mention the ambiguity of Soviet advice even later that month. He also offers a different interpretation of the Nasser-'Amr rivalry, namely, that the two remained close right up to the outbreak of the June War and that the rivalry was between aides of the two leaders.

Ernest Dawn adds a significant chronological detail based on his close reading of the Arab press at the time. The government-controlled Syrian press sought to convert a domestic crisis into an alleged Zionist-imperialist plot as early as May 7, a view that was picked up by Tass and by the rest of the Arab press except for Egypt's. Not until May 15 did the major Cairo dailies start reporting "Zionist-imperialist" involvement in a threat to Syria.

Dawn notes as well that Israeli leaders could understandably have felt that the strategy of retaliation was effective. Shamir adds that this helps explain Israeli actions; only now, in a more extended time frame, can the limitations of Israel's retaliation strategy be perceived.

A careful reading of the transcript brings out several other questions and useful lines of inquiry that were presented.

- What was the impact on later events of the massive Israeli raid in November 1966 against Samu' in Jordan, in retaliation for attacks against Israel mounted from Syria?
- What was the import of Israeli Ambassador Gideon Rafael's trip to Moscow in the spring of 1967? His purpose was to express concern that a regional crisis might be emerging, but he received only a cold reply from the Soviets.
- What transpired during Soviet Foreign Minister Gromyko's visit to Cairo soon thereafter?
- Was Nasser's removal of UNEF forces justified under the circumstances? Should it have been seen by the Israelis as an acceptable limited response? Or was it an unacceptable change of the rules of the diplomatic game?
- Can a point of no return be agreed upon? If so, was it the removal of UNEF? Or the announced blockade? Or some earlier or later event?

This session did not produce general agreement either on points of fact or on interpretation, nor was such to be expected. Moreover, the design of this first session tilted the discussion toward the implication that a close look at Egypt, Israel, and the Soviet Union would serve to identify what caused the crisis leading to war. But this approach, probably sounder than any other that might have been chosen, leads to a concentration on events in May 1967 to the virtual exclusion of earlier events. It also diverts attention from inter-Arab rivalries. Stated more broadly, it produces a tendency (as both Bassiouny and Shamir suggested, the former in his opening remarks and Shamir in his closing summation) to concentrate on microhistory instead of on the broader context.

Even so, one major finding did emerge: Egypt, Israel, and the Soviet Union all demonstrated a large measure of intergovernmental differences and rivalries, with resulting ambiguities in policies adopted and actions taken.

Moreover, even though interpretations were presented that leaned toward charging conspiracy or at least duplicity on the part of others, the most plausible interpretation would seem to be that no long-range plans to entrap others existed and that, ironically, the three parties highlighted in this session were all more nearly responding to circumstances suddenly and surprisingly thrust upon them than acting from carefully crafted, long-term strategic plans.

The discussion also shed light on another important general finding, never disputed once raised but often ignored: Public opinion constrains political leadership regardless of where the political system lies on the scale from democracy to dictatorship. Clearly, public opinion, or public expectation, was a major factor shaping policy in both Egypt and Israel. A later session will reveal that such constraints were operating equally on other major players in this dangerous game, including Jordan, Syria, and the United States.

Finally, the many questions left unanswered, the stark disagreement on crucial details among participants who had been in a position to know, and the occasionally sharply differing, while plausible, general interpretations advanced by the several participants all together add up to yet another lesson to the historian. Reconstruction of past crises, while offering myriad advantages not available at the time of crisis to those making decisions at that time, must always be an uncertain, incomplete, and thus disputed enterprise.

It is thus no criticism to conclude that perhaps the conference did not even manage to "begin at the beginning," but on balance it was a useful beginning for both what was revealed and what was left in doubt.

Panel 1

Chairman: Dr. Leon Carl Brown, Princeton University
Speakers:
   Ambassador Shimon Shamir, U.S. Institute of Peace: "The Israeli 'Threat'"
   Vitaly Naumkin, Russian Center for Strategic Research and International
      Relations: "The Soviet Warning"
   Ambassador Salah Bassiouny, National Center for Middle East Studies,
      Cairo: "The Egyptian Response"
Comment: Dr. Karen Dawisha, University of Maryland

Richard Parker: The purpose of this conference is twofold. One is to set the record straight, to the extent we can. There is still controversy about who said what when and what it meant and who did what and whose motives were good and whose were not. Each of the states represented here, except Jordan, comes in for some allegation of being involved in a plot. The second purpose is to see what lessons are to be learned. Did this war have to happen? How could it have been prevented? What should we do next time we have a situation like this?

The conference is inspired in the first place by the conferences and meetings

Panel 1 (*left to right*): William Zartman, Shimon Shamir, L. Carl Brown, and Salah Bassiouny at the conference. Courtesy of Foreign Service Institute.

we have had with the Soviets and with the Cubans on the Cuban missile crisis, but it is not modeled on those talks, which took the form of a round table. We are rather more structured. We have a conventional American format of panels.

The purpose of the panels is to provide a framework for discussion. Our principal goal is to get a discussion started among the members of the panel, and between the panels and the people around the room, the observers. There are to be no papers.

Carl Brown: As a historian who many years ago had a very limited experience in the Foreign Service, I find this an opportunity to have a talking archive for the next three days. A thoughtful historian once stated, "The past, too, is a foreign country." We're talking about the past, about a war. It was a traumatic experience. Our intention now is to see what lessons we can gain from it. I therefore encourage all of us to approach this exercise with complete candor and without any feeling of a need to protect, to defend, to go out of the way to explain this or that administration's policy, this or that country's policy, or the like. I would be inclined to argue, as perhaps many of you would agree, that this war, like most wars viewed from a twenty-five-year perspective, was a tragedy for all parties, winners and losers alike. What we can learn from it now?

The Israeli Threat

Shimon Shamir: I will try to make four points in my presentation: to indicate some general elements of Israeli security doctrine before 1967 that are relevant to the issue of "the road to war"; to reconstruct the Israeli position vis-à-vis the specific Syrian challenge on the eve of the war; the main part of my presentation, to examine the allegations that an Israeli threat to Damascus caused the escalation to war; and to draw some lessons from that affair.

In the years preceding the 1967 crisis, from the end of the 1948 war, Israel was subjected to harassment by its neighbors: infiltration by armed civilians, raids by Palestinian guerrillas, and clashes with regular troops across the armistice lines. There were, of course, fluctuations in the intensity of this pressure on Israel's borders and hinterland, but it remained a constant element in Israel's life.

In the perception of Israelis at that time, this pressure constituted a real danger to the survival of their state. With today's hindsight, this may seem a somewhat exaggerated concern, but we are talking about Israel of the 1950s and most of the 1960s, an Israel not at all certain that time was not working in favor of its Arab adversaries or that their overwhelming numerical and territorial superiority might not one day decide the outcome of the conflict. In that period, a growing number of Arab states had been taken over by radical revolutionary juntas that made intensive efforts to unify the Arab ranks and forces, that invested vast resources in building up, with Soviet support, extensive war machines, and that frequently voiced pledges to eradicate Israel from the map. The Israelis felt that if this harassment were allowed to continue unanswered it would gradually erode their strategic credibility and viability. For them it was an existential problem, requiring a firm response.

Israel's answer to this challenge was the retaliation doctrine. Whenever Arab incursions reached a level that the Israelis deemed insufferable, a reprisal raid would be launched against a specific target across the border, usually by a unit of elite forces, with the aim of exacting from the other side a price that would be more painful than that suffered by the Israelis. The retaliation strategy was designed to convey a message to the perpetrators of the attacks against Israel or to the governments that tolerated or even encouraged them: If there was no peace on the Israel side, there would be no peace on the Arab side either.

In retrospect, this strategy can be summed up as a failure. The message did not get through. More often than not, retaliation generated escalation rather than pacification, as was quite evident after the Qalqilya raid, some time before the 1956 war. Yet the retaliation doctrine was not abandoned. It may be that many of the decision makers simply did not realize that reprisal was futile. It is also plausible that the mechanism that Kenneth Boulding identified as "the sacrifice trap," namely the inability to abandon a strategy whose implementation had required painful sacrifices, was also at work here, since many of those who fell in the daring operations were the flower of Israeli youth. And, of course, there were domestic pressures, for the public wanted its government to show a strong arm. Above all, the Israelis felt that no alternatives to this strategy existed. Sealing the borders by some sort of technological defensive systems was not seen as practical. Moreover, that tactic would have contradicted one of Israel's core tenets at the time: that Israel's quantitative and territorial disadvantage could be overcome only by a mobile offensive strategy, avoiding what one general called "the concentration camp strategy," namely seeking protection behind barbed wire. Retaliation was therefore Israel's only possible answer.

The element of this strategy that is perhaps the most relevant to our subject is that in almost all cases, reprisal operations were preceded by warnings from political or military leaders to the effect that Israel would respond to violence by violence at the time and place of its choosing. The reasons for such warnings were obvious. First, there was some hope that perhaps they might bear results and the situation would indeed calm down. Second, if unheeded, the warnings could legitimize the military action that would eventually be taken as a last resort. And third, they could serve as a signal to the Israeli public, which was sometimes in a state of agitation, that even if there was no immediate military reaction to the Arab hostilities, the government was not neglecting its responsibility for Israel's security and had made all the necessary contingency plans to respond in kind.

The main facts of the escalation along the Syrian border are too well known to need detailed elaboration. In January 1965, Fatah started guerrilla operations across the Israeli borders in the north. In 1966, the new Soviet-backed Ba'ath regime in Syria adopted a doctrine of Popular Liberation War (partly to compete with the Nasserite regime), leading to ideological endorsement of, and operational assistance to, the Fatah operations. There were numerous clashes in the disputed demilitarized zones, and the kibbutzim in that area—Bet Katzir, Ha'on, Gonen, and Kfar Szold—often came under Syrian fire. The Syrian project of diverting the Jordan's headwaters in order to preempt the Israeli National Water Carrier scheme [to divert Jordan waters to the coastal plain.—Ed.] was another source of tension and military clashes. The number of Fatah operations—mining, shelling, and

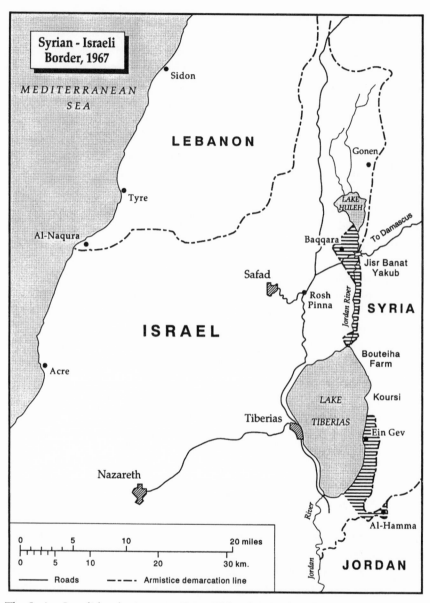

The Syrian-Israeli border in 1967. From Richard B. Parker, *The Politics of Miscalculation in the Middle East* (Bloomington: Indiana University Press, 1993).

sabotaging targets within Israeli territory—increased at a rapid pace. In the four weeks that preceded May 15, 1967, there were fourteen serious incidents along the border and within Israeli territory.

From the Israeli point of view, these developments constituted a qualitatively new level of threat, for several reasons. (1) It was the first appearance in the arena of an independent, organized Palestinian guerrilla movement devoted to a relentless campaign against Israel. (2) It was the first time that a major Arab regime had endorsed such a campaign, openly proclaiming escalation as its strategic aim. (3) The regime enjoyed extensive Soviet support. (4) There was the possibility of more Arab states rallying to this camp, a threat indicated by the conclusion of the Syrian-Egyptian defense pact of November 1966.

How did Israel respond to this challenge? Two schools of thought were discernible among the Israeli elite. One proposed prudence and silent work through diplomatic channels. (The government at that time was headed by Levi Eshkol, one of the most moderate prime ministers in Israel's history.) This school argued that the Soviet backing of Syria dictated extra caution. It was even believed that this patronage could be turned into an advantage by inducing the Soviets to use their influence to restrain the Syrians. Statesmen like Abba Eban referred to "the spirit of Tashkent"—an alleged Soviet disposition to seek peaceful accommodations—as grounds for hope that this diplomacy might succeed.

The other school of thought, emanating mainly from the defense establishment, was skeptical of the diplomatic option. It maintained that the diplomatic channels were either ineffective or had already failed. The Syrian regime was viewed as totally committed to the campaign against Israel and therefore to be deterred only by force. The air force action on April 7, which downed six Syrian MIGs, was a manifestation of this approach. The military school maintained that there was no escape from resorting, after proper warnings, to the retaliation strategy and that delaying the activation of this option would dangerously erode Israel's deterrence.

An important element in this line of thought was the distinction between the nature of hostilities emanating from Syria, on the one hand, and those coming from Jordan and Lebanon, on the other. Whereas the governments of Jordan and Lebanon were basically interested in keeping the peace and often regarded the irregulars operating against Israel as a menace to themselves as well, the attacks from Syria were directly supported by the government in Damascus. Accordingly, Israeli strategists consistently stressed the difference between the types of operations required in each case. With Jordan and Lebanon, the objective was to motivate their governments to seal their borders against incursions into Israel. With Syria, the aim was disciplining the Syrian government itself and compelling it to reverse its offensive policy. In other words the former had to be "empowered," whereas the latter had to be taught a lesson.

This internal Israeli debate created a confused and self-contradictory situation. While the upholders of the military option consistently projected a firm Israeli posture, the supporters of the diplomatic option stalled the habitual military reaction. It was thus inevitable that the Arabs and the Soviets, always predisposed to give greater credibility to Israel's military postures, were driven to the conclusion that if Israel remained militarily inactive, it could mean only one thing: that it was secretly preparing an exceptionally large operation. In reality, Israel was genuinely hesitant. A clear manifestation of its perplexity was the misguided raid on Samu', which was evidently triggered by the situation with Syria yet directed against a target in Jordan.

In this part of my presentation, I shall examine the allegations, voiced by Soviets and Arabs and believed by many others, that the crisis of May 1967, which led to the outbreak of the war, was caused by Israel's preparations to launch an imminent massive attack against Damascus. My attempt to answer the various questions concerning the Israeli "threat" will be arranged, for analytical purposes, under two headings: military operational preparations and verbal warnings.

Operational Preparation: Did Israel amass eleven, thirteen, or eighteen brigades along the Syrian border?

The Soviet-Arab reports on Israeli troop concentration along the border with Syria, which quoted different numbers of brigades in their various versions, are no longer believed by anybody. By now it is quite obvious that such a concentration did not exist. The allegation was refuted by General Muhammad Fawzi (the Egyptian chief of staff), who stated clearly in his memoirs that he had checked the situation on the ground and reported finding no changes along the Syrian-Israeli border. A similar denial was issued by UN Secretary-General U Thant, who relied on reports from the field sent by UNTSO (UN Truce Supervision Organization) observers. The refusal of Chuvakin, the Soviet ambassador to Israel, to accept the Israeli invitation to visit the area and see for himself is another indication to the same effect. Above all, the basic facts speak for themselves. The Israeli army at that time hardly had the number of brigades required for such a concentration. If there had been a massing of more than ten brigades in the north, Israel would also have had to put some brigades along the Jordanian and the Egyptian borders. This would have meant a general mobilization. Anybody who has witnessed such a mobilization in Israel knows what it means: The whole country is paralyzed, vehicles are inducted, businesses close down, roads are jammed with military traffic, and so on. Nothing like that took place.

Could there have been some deceptive troop movements that the Soviets and or Syrians construed as a genuine threat? It is unlikely. Attempting deterrence by means of deceptive maneuvers, without the backing of substantial military forces, would have been careless and contrary to Israeli doctrine and practices. Such movements could not be expected to achieve any of the Israeli objectives.

Were there some movements on the ground in preparation for a subsequent operation? Possibly a "signals exercise"? Israeli generals interviewed on this question denied any such activities. General Aharon Yariv recalled that plans for various types of reprisal operations had been submitted to the chief of staff, General Yitzhak Rabin, at that time but he had rejected them all. In this context, it is plausible that some reconnaissance activities took place, but they would not have amounted to any extraordinary changes in the ground forces. Besides, as Yariv recalled, the general staff was preoccupied at that time with the problems of the Independence Day (May 15) parade in Jerusalem and the risks of possible Jordanian interference.

Did the Israeli government take a decision on May 7 to launch an attack against Syria? In its weekly meeting on that date, the cabinet indeed discussed the deteriorating situation along the borders, but there is no evidence that a resolution on imminent attack was adopted. *Ma'ariv* reported on the following day that the inclination of the cabinet was first to exhaust all political methods. Political scientist Michael Brecher, who raised the possibility of such a resolution, nevertheless described it as conditional: It called for a retaliation operation if Syria did not heed the warnings and if all other measures failed.

Were there Israeli contingency plans that may have fallen into the hands of the Soviets or Syrians, triggering an alarmed reaction? Such contingency plans must have existed. Preparing a wide range of military options is the normal function of planning bodies in any general staff. However, it is highly implausible that the experienced Soviet intelligence, had it succeeded in laying hands on such plans, would have confused them with operational orders.

Many sources allege that on the eve of the crisis Israeli leaders announced that they would carry out a large-scale military operation with the intent of occupying Damascus and toppling the Syrian regime. Nasser, for example, said in his May 22 speech: "In recent days Israel has been making aggressive threats and boasting. On May 12 a very impertinent statement was made. Anyone reading this statement must believe that these people are so boastful and deceitful that one simply cannot remain silent. The statement said that Israeli commanders have announced they would carry out military operations in order to occupy Damascus and overthrow the Syrian government."

The statement referred to by Nasser is quoted, and accepted as authentic, by many writers on the origins of the 1967 war. They attribute it to Eshkol or to Rabin, citing May 12 as the date when it was made. In fact, no statements related to this subject were made on May 12 by either Eshkol or Rabin. Is it possible that such a statement was made on another date or by another Israeli spokesman? The issue certainly deserves to be systematically scrutinized.

Could the source have been Eshkol? The context of Nasser's criticism and his reference to "Israeli commanders" do not support the attribution of the statement to Eshkol. The prime minister did in fact make public statements on a possible action against Syria on other days. On May 11, in a speech at a Mapai Party meeting, he said that Israel took an extremely grave view of the recent attacks and, if there was no other way out, Israel might be forced to take "retaliatory measures no less drastic than those of April 7." On May 13 Eshkol told Israeli Radio that Israel had already shown that it was "able to respond at the place, the time and by the method of our choosing" and that "if they try to sow unrest on our borders, unrest will come to theirs." The tone of these statements was certainly grave, but the remarks did not in essence deviate from the conventional retaliation formulas used by Israelis in such situations. Eshkol's warnings said nothing about an imminent action, an attack exceeding a retaliatory operation, or an intention to occupy Damascus.

Could the disputed statement have been made by Rabin? He made several comments on the border situation (although none on May 12) in line with a well-established tradition that in the week preceding Independence Day, Israeli leaders, particularly the chiefs of the army, delivered speeches and gave interviews on the state of the country's security. Yet the messages Rabin delivered in his Independence Day interviews on May 13–14 did not go beyond pointing out the difference between retaliation against Syria and against Jordan-Lebanon. As noted previously, this was a repetition of a formula often used in the past (for example, in September 1966). The allegation that on May 11 Rabin declared on Israel Radio that "the moment is coming when we will march on Damascus"—a statement that for some reason was not repeated in the Israeli press—is highly questionable. I could find no corroboration in any available records, in broadcast monitors, or in anybody's recollection. The Israeli press might have been muted, but foreign correspondents certainly would have reported the story. Besides, it is highly unlikely that Rabin would use such a phrase.

A source of the "threat to Damascus" allegation might have been the not-for-attribution briefing to foreign correspondents given by the chief of intelligence, General Aharon Yariv, on May 12—as I pointed out in the chapter I wrote on the origins of the 1967 war for the *Middle East Record* (vol. 3, 1967 [Jerusalem 1971], pp. 183–204). The briefing officer was described in the press reports only as a "highly placed" or "qualified" source, but some writers, such as Eric Rouleau, concluded that the source was Rabin.

Yariv's briefing is the most strongly worded Israeli statement made at the time, but even his formulations fall short of the allegations. Here are excerpts from the *Middle East Record:*

[There is a need for an] answer that will convince the regime that the profit they had from what they call the "Popular War of Liberation" . . . will turn into a loss. The regime's popular base is very narrow. [Palestinian operations] are closely supervised by Syrian intelligence. . . . We must make it clear to the Syrians that they cannot continue this way, and I think that the only way to make it clear to the Syrians is by using force. . . . I could say we must use force in order to have the Egyptians convince the Syrians that it doesn't pay. . . . I think that the only sure and safe answer to the problem is a military operation of great size and strength. . . . But not everything that is sure is possible, and I think there are reasonable chances to find a solution to the problem by military action short of this kind of action. [Israel needs action that will warn the Syrians of the dangers of] a probable or possible or imminent all-out confrontation [with Israel, but to this end there exist alternatives between the extremes of a counterguerrilla war and] all-out invasion of Syria and conquest of Damascus.

I would say that as long as there is not an Israeli invasion into Syria extended in area and time, I think the Egyptians will not come in seriously . . . they will do so only if there is no other alternative. And to my eyes "no alternative" means that we are creating such a situation that it is impossible for the Egyptians not to act because the strain on their prestige will be unbearable.

Yariv made clear that he blamed the Damascus regime and favored the use of force. Yet he weighed, and discarded as unfeasible, several options: "a military operation of great size and strength"; the "extreme" of an "all-out invasion of Syria and conquest of Damascus"; "an Israeli invasion of

Syria, extended in area and time"; or any action that would create a situation in which the Egyptians would feel compelled to intervene. A careful reading of Yariv's statements shows that he spoke of an operation designed to *warn* the Syrians (and the Egyptians) of the dangers of an all-out confrontation, not an operation that would itself be the confrontation.

Other parts of Yariv's briefing were clearly polemical, directed against unnamed interlocutors—evidently the civilian politicians upholding the "spirit of Tashkent." Yariv argued that the Soviets would not restrain the Syrians.

Because of this, he said that he personally would have preferred a large operation but, given the impossibility, he had to choose a more limited option.

Could it [the allegations of a threatening statement by Israel] have emanated from the reporting on Yariv's briefing? Yariv's carefully worded, elaborate presentation was not easy to summarize, but correspondents managed to do so reasonably well [for example, AP's McClure and the *New York Times*'s Feron; see "Documents" section at the end of this chapter]. The report filed by the UPI correspondent was somewhat less sensitive to nuance, and it may have inadvertently created the impression of a direct threat to the capital of Syria. UPI reported faithfully that the Israeli warning was conditional ("if Syria continues its new campaign of sabotage in Israel"), and it makes clear that no all-out war was intended ("would fall short of all-out conflict"). However, by telescoping Yariv's characterization of the types of military operations considered and by strongly connecting the contemplated operation to the toppling of the government of Damascus, the report magnified the image of Israel's belligerent intentions.

A chronological examination of the sequence of events in the process of rising tension shows that this reporting of Yariv's briefings had a great impact in Moscow, at the UN, in Arab capitals, and in other political centers. An angry broadcast on Radio Damascus on May 13 at 1:15 P.M. gave the full text of the UPI dispatch, explicitly naming UPI as the source. Ambassadors of the Security Council's member-states were summoned to the Syrian Foreign Ministry and warned that Syria would not stand alone in the face of the threat. It may very well be that Nasser's perception, quoted here earlier, reflected his reading of the UPI dispatch. He could have reasoned that "a military action intended to topple the Damascus army regime" could definitely mean the occupation of Damascus. He must have known from the experience of his own regime in the 1956 Suez war (as we all should realize from the survival of Saddam Hussein after Desert Storm) that a Middle Eastern military regime cannot be toppled from the outside by any means short of capturing its capital. Accordingly, the UPI correspondent's addition "to topple the government of Damascus" is really crucial here.

To sum up: On the eve of May 15, the date of Egypt's movement into Sinai, Israel was engaged neither in military preparations for nor declaration of an imminent all-out attack on Syria—let alone a drive to occupy Damascus. The allegations to this effect were simply wrong.

According to Israeli security doctrine and practices, if the situation in the north had not improved, it is likely that a military operation would eventually have been launched. It could have been relatively more ambitious than previous operations against Syria, but would still have remained within the parameters of Israeli retaliation raids. The risks of Soviet reaction deterred Israel from undertaking a more extensive operation. It may be recalled in retrospect that even after the war broke out, Soviet deterrence was the cause of vacillation and delays among the Israelis before they brought themselves to launch the offensive on the Golan Heights. The risk of Egyptian involvement was another consideration that influenced the Israeli strategists (hence their puzzlement when the Egyptians became involved after all).

Surely, the Israelis did issue warnings, some of them quite strongly worded. Feron of the *New York Times* called them "stronger than those usually heard in responsible quarters." But all the warnings were made within the framework of the long-established retaliation pattern, with which people and governments in the Middle East were familiar. In mid-May, Israel was still in the "warning phase" of the strategic scenario, and at that stage admonitions were still conditional. For the Israeli government, the preferred outcome of its warnings would have been a Syrian consent to pacify its borders with Israel, a response that would have made military action unnecessary. A government that intends to launch an attack on a formidable fortress, as the Golan Heights were at that time, does not go about publicizing its intentions through all public channels—unless it still hopes that the attack can be averted.

In the event—unintentional as this may have been—the Israeli statements did evoke alarm and definitely contributed to the escalation of tension. This response was the result, in my opinion, of an unhappy combination of circumstances. A number of factors functioned as catalysts in this process: the coincidence of the Independence Day "season" of security-minded patriotic fervor; the intensive and insufficiently sensitive reporting in the media; and the poor quality of the assessment of Israel's political dynamics among its adversaries.

But the key for understanding the process is the internal debate between the two inclinations among Israel's decision makers, which jumbled two contradictory strategies. The deceleration of the "reprisal rhythm" in the course of that debate led, paradoxically, to escalation. This result was ironic because at the helm was the most moderate government Israel had produced in years, a government in which "doves" like Eshkol and Eban strove to exhaust all the possibilities of diplomatic channels. Yet the extended time between warnings and action only made the adversaries more suspicious and apprehensive: they were "waiting for the other shoe to drop." It was a textbook case of misconception in international relations, which perhaps lends support to the argument that a dovish position can sometimes lead to conflagrations that a hawkish position may prevent.

If there is a place for criticism of the Israelis on this account, it is perhaps that when they issued their warnings they did not adequately realize the delicacy of the deterrence mechanism. They delivered a message and it backfired. Obviously, deterrence is a delicate business. Alexander George, who wrote extensively on this question, explained how deterrence warnings depend on the existence of a logic on the other side that is similar to the logic of those who try to deter. Deterrence signals are not received at face value but are always "context dependent." When the context is "wrong," the import of the message can easily be altered.

When the Israeli government eventually discovered that its messages were unexpectedly generating alarming consequences, it made efforts to downgrade its warnings. The prime minister's office asked the press to tone down Eshkol's statements in their reports. The news of a recent incursion from Syria was suppressed. Even a poem included in the program of the Independence Day pageant was "re-edited" to excise verses that admonished "Aram," Israel's biblical enemy in the north. But all this came too late; the countdown had already started and Israel was no longer in control.

At any rate, the actions of the Soviets and their Arab clients can hardly be justified on the basis of the Israeli pronouncements. If they were genuinely alarmed by the Israelis' behavior, they had many ways to ascertain the situation along the borders and clarify Israel's intentions. (Of course, all this argumentation is unnecessary for those analysts who maintain that the Soviet-Arab move against Israel had been planned long before the May 11–14 Israeli warnings and would have been made anyway).

The 1967 conflict was a classical case of inadvertent war. None of the parties wanted an all-out war: The Israelis did not believe it could happen, the Egyptians were entirely unprepared, it contradicted the Soviets' global policy, and the Syrians could only lose by the confrontation. In this sense the Israeli strategy was much less counterproductive than that of the others.

Perhaps the final word has already been given by the organizers of this conference. In punctuating the title of my presentation in the program, they put the Israeli "threat" in quotation marks. This is indeed the essence of what I have tried to argue here.

The Soviet Warning

Vitaly Naumkin: To be concrete in talking about the Soviet warning, I will begin with various versions [of the Soviet motives in the crisis] that were put forth by different participants in this conference and by other authors, especially in the readings [provided to the conferees]. Because we still have no access to the Soviet archives, we must regard these possibilities as theoretical only.

The first version is that the Soviet Union was interested in this war being fought: It incited the Arab governments or provoked them, and the Soviet leadership of that time bears a great share of responsibility for the path that the war followed. The second version is that the Soviet Union was not interested in the war and didn't do anything to bring it about, but by developing the military capabilities of the Arab states the Soviets tried to secure a balance of forces in the region and to prevent the eruption of large-scale hostilities. The third version is that the Soviet Union didn't care about the future of the conflict at all but was preparing its Mideast partners for a possible war—just making a routine maneuver.

If we accept any of these versions, each of which has supporters and arguments in its favor, then we'll face other questions. The main question is, what goals had the Soviet leadership been pursuing by carrying out this or that course? This is especially important in case Moscow's policy was active, well planned, and directed toward certain results. Thus, if the USSR was interested in the war, then why? Why did Moscow need a new war? Combining some speculative assumptions with substantive positions of the authors and participants, we can draw up here five alternative goals.

- The Soviet Union believed in an Arab victory if the Arabs united their forces and pursued the goal of eliminating the Jewish state as an institution—not, of course, physically.
- The Soviet Union wanted Israel to be defeated, not because Moscow aimed at the liquidation of the state but because it was trying to create favorable conditions for the resolution of the Arab-Israeli conflict or to strengthen the Arab leftist regimes and its own position in the Arab world and the Middle East.
- The Soviet Union hoped that the Arabs would be defeated because, according to some authors, the Soviet Union envisioned all that in fact happened and hoped thereby to strengthen its influence in the Arab world.

- The Soviet Union, understanding that if Israel suffered heavy casualties the United States would come to the rescue, was trying to create a second Vietnam for the Americans. This view was expressed also in some documents [given to the conferees].
- The Soviet Union wanted an open confrontation with the United States and its original allies.

We can see that the first option is absolutely unrealistic. The last option, the confrontation with the United States, is as unrealistic as the desire of the Soviet Union to eliminate the Jewish state, and there are questions about each of the other options. We must know, first of all, how the Soviet government was evaluating the military capabilities of Israel and the Arab countries and what scenarios were envisaged by the Soviet leadership. From this point of view we can see that the third option, the defeat of the Arabs, is also unrealistic. The fourth option—I'll talk about it later—is also weak.

So I prefer the second option: The Soviet Union wanted Israel to be defeated, not aiming at liquidation of the state but at its own interests. In this case we must ask what Moscow had to undertake to implement its plan and whether it was wise to push its allies forward to bring about the war by providing this information [the warning about Israeli troop concentrations]. I think this also is not true, and if in fact the information was provided to Egypt, it would hardly have been a part of some plan of the Soviet leadership.

As for the Soviets' evaluation of the Arab military potential, I would like to refer to the remarks of the former Soviet ambassador to Syria, Anatoly Barkovsky. He informed me that they were thinking in his embassy that the Arabs would be able to launch a blow against Israel and avoid defeat only if Egypt, Syria, and Jordan had formed a united front under a united command, but not if Syria, for instance, entered the war by itself.

Victory, even if all the forces were united, was excluded because the United States would never let it happen. And the Soviet military experts in Syria thought that Israel militarily was much stronger than the Arabs. Such were their reports to Moscow. The Syrians were talking a lot about a possible attack by Israel. But, according to Ambassador Barkovsky, the Syrians didn't believe in such an attack, and in practical terms they were not ready for war. Barkovsky and the head of the military advisers in Syria learned about the June War only after it had begun. He also said that the Syrians were not pushing the Egyptians to start the war and were not undertaking any actions to that end.

Let's return to the matter of the Soviets passing false intelligence to Egypt about the concentrations of Israeli divisions. There are several versions of what actually happened. The first is that Ambassador Pojidaev [in Cairo] passed the information. The second is that an officer from the KGB was responsible. The third is that military advisers passed it, and the fourth is that the information wasn't passed at all. In the archives of the Ministry of Foreign Affairs of Russia, we couldn't find any mention of any meeting between Pojidaev and Ahmad Hassan al-Feki on May 13, 1967. This meeting probably never took place, but it does not mean that the information was not passed by someone else. I doubt, however, that in this case it would have decisively influenced the developments in the area.

So let's consider now the information that is at my disposal. On May 16, Ambassador Pojidaev was received by Egypt's foreign minister, Mahmoud Riad, and minister of war, Shams Badran. I cannot judge whether the information about troop concentrations was passed or not, for several reasons. First, the real archives concerning the 1960s are not open yet, so it is difficult to find the documented truth. Second, the mechanisms of documenting the information even about the 1960s will be difficult whenever the archives are opened. For instance, Soviet ambassadors were not allowed to disclose the content of incoming messages from Moscow. In their cables to Moscow they reported only that they had passed a message, without mentioning its essence. And so we know that Pojidaev was reporting in his cables that messages had been passed to the Egyptian leadership, but he did not mention their nature. We can [only theorize] that the message concerned the military-political situation in Israel and Israeli moves or concentration of Israeli troops near the Syrian border. One of the former senior diplomats in the Soviet Foreign Ministry at that time confirmed that the information might have been passed by Pojidaev, but the diplomat had seen in some cables words indicating that this information was operational intelligence data that needed checking. So it [the report of troop concentrations] was not confirmed as finalized, definite information.

Part of the problem is that some such foreign policy actions were documented not in the Foreign Ministry archives but in the archives of the Politburo of the Communist Party [currently the Presidential Archive], to which none of the researchers has had any access up until now. Furthermore, many political decisions of that time were undertaken orally, without any documentation. That was virtually the case, for instance, with the movement of Soviet troops into Afghanistan. We know that this state of affairs existed not only in Moscow but in other capitals as well. For example, according to my knowledge, after the June War the Johnson administration made the decision to give Israel the opportunity to [remain in position] until the Arab-

Israeli problem was resolved, and the decision was conveyed orally, as some of the participants can confirm.

Even without knowing the exact content of the conversation between Ambassador Pojidaev and Mahmoud Riad or Shams Badran, we can still make certain assessments on the basis of the information about Pojidaev's meeting with Nasser on May 22. According to a Soviet diplomat in Cairo, President Nasser, while receiving the Soviet ambassador, conveyed his gratitude to the Soviet leadership for supplying him with information on the military-political situation in Israel and the moves of the Israeli troops near the Syrian border. It was clear from Nasser's words that the Egyptians had previously received such information from the Syrians but would never have believed it had it not been supported by the Soviet intelligence. Nasser also thanked Moscow for its military support and asked it to speed up arms supplies provided under the bilateral agreement, in particular to equip SU-7E fighters used by the Egyptian air force with air-to-surface missiles. The Soviet side rejected Egyptian requests on the grounds that there was no agreement [to supply such equipment].

The next important meeting is the secret visit of Minister of Defense Shams Badran to Moscow between May 25 and 28. This secret visit has been described in all the books, of course. Badran and two other participants in the negotiations, Ahmed Hassan al-Feki and Ambassador Salah Bassiouny, one of the conference participants, confirmed that the Soviet leadership asked the Egyptians to be cautious, to be careful. According to information passed to me in a private talk by Ambassador Pavel Akopov, one of the participants in the negotiations, Badran had two meetings with Kosygin, on May 26 and 27. Badran told Kosygin that Nasser was absolutely sure that Israel would attack and that Egypt would have to fight. A special request was passed to the Soviet government to provide all necessary support to the Arabs. In this connection, Badran reportedly informed Kosygin about Nasser's idea of launching a preventive blow against Israel. In this case, the Egyptian minister stated, there would be every chance of achieving victory, but even if Israel attacked first, Egypt and the Arabs would never be defeated. During the first day of the talks, Kosygin gave Badran no answer. It is possible that the general situation and Nasser's plan, in particular, were discussed at the Politburo session on the same date.

The next day Kosygin passed to Badran the opinion of the Soviet leadership: The Soviet government could not agree with the Egyptian plan for a preventive strike, because if Egypt attacked Israel it would be considered an aggressor by everyone, and Moscow would have to take the same stand. At the same time, Kosygin said that the Kremlin was sure of Egyptian victory if war was inevitable, as the military potential of the Arabs was much greater than that of the Israelis. First Deputy Foreign Minister Vladimir Semenov, the head of the Middle East Department, Alexei Schiborin, and Pavel Akopov were also participants in these talks.

It is difficult to know whether the Egyptians consulted the Soviets while taking the decision about redeployment of their forces in the Sinai [two weeks before the Badran visit to Moscow]. But even if the Soviet political leadership was not consulted, the intelligence [about Israeli troop buildup], if it was passed by the Soviets, might have encouraged Nasser to redeploy forces.

One version of what happened, in my opinion, deserves special attention: that the false intelligence was forged by the Israelis themselves, who were trying to provoke the Arabs to undertake steps that would give Tel Aviv a pretext to launch a war. Such a version is supported by a lot of former Soviet diplomats and military people. Taking into consideration this option, I think the Soviet representatives talking with Egyptians before the war were constantly urging them to be cautious. Of course, the Egyptian leadership was pushed forward by the well-known words of Marshal Grechko, and also lesser-known words of the Soviet leaders, that the Egyptian army was the best and strongest army in the region. Some participants in these talks told me that Brezhnev was saying such things to Nasser.

Let's suppose that some of the Soviet leaders were in fact pushing the Egyptians toward war. Where were the roots of this strategy? There might be some proofs of this position if in fact it was held. Suppose it originated from some geopolitical concept based on orientation toward the Arab world with the intent to extend unlimited support to Arab efforts to solve their problems with Israel through military means. But the Kremlin didn't possess such a geopolitical vision, as manifested by the absence of a clear-cut Middle East policy. There were real forces that were oriented toward the Arab world, but maybe they were only a limited group of military commanders who were not actually affecting the decision-making process. It was difficult for them to influence the leadership. Grechko had been promoted to the post of minister of defense just before the war. He was not a member of the Politburo and he was not a real politician. Of course, the top military were looking for favorable conditions, and they were seeking the approval of the political leadership of the country, and that was a factor. But I think that even the military did not wish to involve the Soviet Union in any kind of war or to provoke any war in the Middle East. I tend to exclude also the possibilities that there was a desire to confront United States or to defeat Israel. The confrontation hadn't acquired such rigid forms, Israeli-American cooperation was not so clearly defined as in the seventies, and the military response wouldn't have been adequate to the threat. Nor can we speak about any kind of group interest or lobby. The level of centralization in political life in the Soviet Union excluded such options.

I think that the decisive role, if the Soviet warning did really take place, was played by a quite different factor. There was a strong anti-Israeli tendency in a big part of the party leadership. Some key figures in the Soviet leadership saw Israel and Zionism as major sources of ideological danger. Personalities like Mikhail Suslov, who was supervising foreign policy, would have successfully played a role in pushing forward the decision for passing the information, because without the decision of the Politburo none of the ambassadors would have been allowed to pass it. Those people could have had in mind weakening Israel's position by making Israel attack first and to be considered an aggressor in the future.

I consider absolutely wrong the interpretation according to which the Soviet leadership had in mind the probable defeat of Egypt. The blockade of the Strait of Tiran was unexpected by Moscow. During the visit to Moscow, Badran couldn't get any opinion from Kosygin about that action. Even after that, in the talks between Pojidaev and the Egyptian leadership, there were lots of words said about the necessity to be careful and not to be provoked by Israel.

Kosygin generally expressed himself as a restrained and responsible politician, and he played a positive role in my opinion during those days. But in the cables of Pojidaev to Moscow, we could detect some euphoria, and we can judge that maybe Pojidaev would have been in favor of some decisive actions. Maybe he was oriented to somebody in Moscow who was wishing to take these decisive actions.

In concluding, one can assume that the Soviet stance toward the Middle East conflict on the verge of the June War reflected and assumed all the features of Soviet foreign policy at that time. Its inconsistency was determined by a combination of ideological approach and pragmatism: On one hand there is talk of a strike force spreading its influence abroad, trying to expel its rivals from the region, while there is caution and unwillingness to take risks and an absence of vision and planning on the other. Moscow didn't plan a war in the Middle East that would have resulted in the defeat of Israel, and surely it didn't want the Arabs to be defeated. More than that, while there might have been some circles in the Soviet party apparatus who were eager to pass such information to the Egyptian leadership and to divergent groups, the rise of tension in the region and the prospect of being dragged into conflict with the United States caused concern to the Soviet leadership and at the same time guerrilla actions against Israel, carried out from Syrian territory, were regarded by the Soviets as an exercise of the legitimate right to fight Israeli expansion.

The Egyptian Response

Salah Bassiouny: I think these two speakers have made my job difficult. Let me say that the June War was the normal outcome of eleven years of tension since the war in '56. The Arab-Israeli conflict at that time was far from an overture to a settlement. Developments and events since the Suez war were conducive to anything but peace: The Arab world in '57 was spellbound by the confrontation with the United States over the Eisenhower doctrine, and there were the uprisings in '58 in Lebanon and Jordan, the Iraqi revolution, and the Egyptian-Syrian union, when Gamal Abd al-Nasser was the uncontested hero and leader. The Egyptian-Syrian union broke up in 1961, followed by socialist-oriented policies in Egypt and Egyptian intervention in Yemen. Yemen was a sort of Vietnam to Egypt, although the outcome in Yemen was different. During the next ten years [after 1956], politics, economy, and warfare were directed not toward Israel but toward the stability and power of the political system in Egypt and to the prevailing inter-Arab feuds that peaked during that era. Israel was fought by slogans and by some incursions of Palestinian guerrillas from Syria. It was also at that time that Israel, which had learned the lessons of '56, prepared itself for the right time for its coming war. Not only did it change its basic strategic alliance from Europe to the United States, but it also prepared its war machinery in a formidable way and went ahead with its nuclear program. Here we have two adversaries, one with all its effort diverted to side matters inside Egypt and the Arab world, the other well prepared, with a deep understanding of the enemy, and waiting for the right opportunity to provoke the war.

So the scene was prepared to secure the required objectives. During the three months preceding the June War, the assessments of the Egyptian Foreign Ministry were consistent in warning of an increased threat of war by Israel on the Syrian and Jordanian fronts. The Department of Research in the ministry, which receives the assessments of Egyptian general intelligence, was stressing in its reports consecutive warnings on that situation. Those warnings were based on (a) Israel's stable relationship as an ally of the United States; (b) Israel's procuring of sophisticated arms from the United States; (c) Israel's military operations against Jordan and Syria, which went beyond the scope of a limited retaliation; (d) Israel's assessment of Egypt's power to participate in the war; (e) the presence of UNEF on the borders;

and (f) the escalation of tension between Egypt and the United States, which could push Israel to undertake a military action against Syria to embarrass the Egyptian leadership in the Arab world.

At that time Egypt did not consider itself part of the military confrontation. In fact, the probability of the withdrawal of UNEF was not under consideration. The issue was how, through political means, to deter Israel from attacking Syria. Also, in the assessment of the Egyptian Foreign Ministry, Israel ten years after the Suez war had realized the maximum of its military capability and urgently needed to use it with a military balance in its favor. The analysis of Israeli policies and statements led to this end. Based on these assessments, the foreign minister, his assistants, and our ambassadors abroad referred to Israeli intentions during meetings in Cairo and abroad.

On May 13, the Soviet ambassador to Cairo, Ambassador Pojidaev, asked for an urgent meeting with the foreign minister, who was not then available. The meeting was arranged by Ambassador Muhammad Shoukri, chief of the cabinet of the Foreign Ministry, who asked Ambassador Feki, the undersecretary of the ministry, to receive the Soviet ambassador. The meeting took place in the office of Ambassador Shoukri. During that meeting Ambassador Pojidaev presented the report on Israeli troop concentrations on the Syrian border. Of course Ambassador Feki then sent an alarming report to the foreign minister and to the presidency, based on the Soviet ambassador's repeating during that meeting that this was Soviet intelligence, that it should be seriously considered in the light of Syrian fears and the reported Israeli massing of ten to twenty brigades on the Syrian border. Neither the Foreign Ministry nor Ambassador Feki referred later on to the question of withdrawal of UNEF. We know that the liaison officer of the KGB delivered the same report to the director of Egyptian intelligence, Salah Nasr, the same day. I do not know whether it was delivered before or after the meeting in the Ministry of Foreign Affairs. However, there is a question which should be asked here. It was not customary for the Soviet ambassador to deliver such reports to the foreign minister; it never happened before, so why did the Soviets choose to act in this way? Was it to confirm or reconfirm the seriousness of the situation and to leave no doubt that an Egyptian action is required? Probably that was their intention.

We know that this report was checked by the chief of staff, General Fawzi, and Egyptian military intelligence officials during their trip to Syria. General Fawzi came back the second day with a report that neither Syrians nor Egyptian military intelligence could confirm such massive concentrations of troops. The report of Fawzi was put aside, and either Arab pressure on

President Gamal Abd al-Nasser and Field Marshal Abd al-Hakim 'Amr at an airbase in Sinai on May 22, 1967, announcing the Egyptian decision to close the Strait of Tiran to Israeli shipping and strategic cargo bound for Israel. *Al-Gumhuriyya*, May 23, 1967.

Nasser or Abd al-Hakim 'Amr's staunch stand played their part in the decision on the withdrawal of UNEF from Egypt. The Foreign Ministry was not informed of the report of General Fawzi or of the sudden and ill-timed request for the withdrawal of UNEF. I believe that Mahmoud Riad, the foreign minister at that time, was present during the decision-making process and did not oppose this decision. In fact, he failed to ask for any legal or political assessment from his cabinet or the United Nations Department or the legal adviser's office of the Ministry of Foreign Affairs. As I explained earlier, no prior studies had been requested and apparently the foreign minister was not in a position to oppose or postpone this decision.

We were only informed in the ministry when we learned of the first reaction of U Thant from our ambassador in New York. It was then that we reminded the foreign minister of the implications, particularly of U.S. commitment of February '57 to Israel [regarding freedom of navigation in the Gulf of Aqaba]. From that day on, the developments and decision making were a mystery to most of the ministry's officers. Cables were seen by only a few in the minister's cabinet and Ambassador Feki. Three days later, after the decision to close the Strait of Tiran, I left with the Egyptian delegation to Moscow, which was headed by Shams Badran, minister of war.

During four days of talks, the main issue raised by the Soviet leadership was a request to de-escalate, and this could be done only by reassuring the Americans that Egypt had no intention of starting a war and by agreeing to open the strait for oil shipments to Israel. To make things more clear, First Deputy Minister Semenov invited Ambassador Feki for a dinner in his dacha on May 26. It lasted until four in the morning. The main theme was an appeal to Egypt to avoid war. Semenov made it clear that the Soviet Union was neither ready nor willing to enter into any confrontations. He stressed that the Soviets had had enough suffering during World War II and that it was time for Egypt to de-escalate. President Nasser was kept informed day by day of the talks, but we noticed that there were other messages sent from the offices of the Egyptian military attaché, and by Shams Badran, to Marshal Abd al-Hakim 'Amr. I recall during our stay in the closed mansion in the Lenin Hills that the Egyptian generals who were members of the delegation were confident and relaxed, but, for the record, one member, Colonel Ahmad Fakhr, told me in confidence that he believed Egypt was on the brink of a disaster that would happen within a week. Colonel Fakhr was at that time in the military operations center.

While I was writing the summary of the talks and the assessment on our way back to Cairo, I was told by Minister of War Badran to change the conclusions on the basis of a message from Marshal Grechko [before we had left] the airport. I asked Ambassador Feki, what message? He told me, in a sarcastic way, the message from Grechko. I replied [that his words had been] only normal Russian expressions while tossing back vodka and bidding Badran a safe journey back home: "My friend, we are with you," and this type of talk. I asked Ambassador Feki on arrival in Cairo to proceed immediately to the general headquarters of the armed forces and not leave Badran alone in reporting to the president. Ambassador Feki's impression of the meeting with President Nasser was pessimistic; he told me Nasser and 'Amr were not on speaking terms. The ambassador did report to Nasser our real assessment, but 'Amr was not listening and was staying away from Nasser. I don't want to dwell any more on the Soviet position, and I think the time will come on another panel when we'll have a lot to say about Soviet policy at that time.

Between May 28 and June 5, the American Embassy staff in Cairo and the newly appointed ambassador, Richard Nolte, were trying to assess the Egyptian reaction. They felt from their talks how confident Egypt was, but they were informed that Egypt would not start the war. Upon a proposal from Ambassador Feki, Nasser sent a message to General de Gaulle informing him of his decision not to start hostilities, and this message was also given to all Western ambassadors. When the war broke out, it was only de Gaulle who issued a statement blaming Israel.

Because of misinformation and the total lack of coordination between the military establishment in Egypt and the Foreign Ministry, on June 5 and 6 we were totally misinformed about the conduct of the war. Our UN representative in New York, Muhammad al-Kony, fell into the same trap until we were told to inform al-Kony to accept the cease-fire. The reasons for Egyptian mismanagement and misperception are numerous regarding both Nasser and 'Amr. I believe it was a result of the political system initiated by both of them. That system led to a situation in which Gamal Abd al-Nasser was a hostage to the power of 'Amr and the army. It was only after defeat that Nasser was able to get rid of 'Amr and his clique. General Fawzi recalls that because he had been appointed chief of staff upon the proposal of Nasser, he was deprived (by 'Amr) of all his powers and charged for three years to confine himself to nonmilitary duties.

After the war, 'Amr declared that the defeat was Nasser's responsibility because of his refusal to implement what 'Amr termed the Egyptian defensive plan. It might be true that 'Amr pressed from the start for a war situation without the consent of the president, who one way or the other was cut off from the military establishment, especially since all commanding officers were the choice of 'Amr and under his direct orders. When the Egyptian ambassador to Washington reported that Dean Rusk had information that Egypt was going to start the war on May 29, Abd al-Hakim 'Amr wrote on the cable, "Shams, it seems there is a leak." According to an assistant in the Secretariat of the Presidency, Nasser commented on the behavior of 'Amr in these words: "Why is 'Amr upset? Does he think that we shall start the war?"

[There were signs of discord]: Abd al-Hakim 'Amr's pressure for the withdrawal of UNEF and the way it was done, and his reluctance to use the word "redeployment" instead of "withdrawal" [in the Egyptian letter of May 16 to the commander of UNEF requesting that he give orders to withdraw all these troops (which install OP's along our borders) immediately"—*Ed.*], his insistence on closing the Strait of Tiran, the way Badran handled the Moscow talks, and then 'Amr's disappointment with Nasser's decision not to start the war. All these incidents indicate how 'Amr and Badran were acting in a different way from Gamal Abd al-Nasser. Were they serious about an offensive, as they claimed later, knowing that the true state of the Egyptian armed forces did not permit or guarantee success of such an offensive? Were they planning to blame Nasser, whatever the outcome of the war, and get rid of him?

These are all questions, I think, to be added to the numerous questions already presented to us. I believe that under these circumstances the reasons behind the June War lie in a gross mismanagement of a crisis. Mismanagement includes misperceptions of a conspiracy and embarking on an adventure that led to a disaster. I may add that Gamal Abd al-Nasser fell victim to a political system that could never have been able to face this type of challenge.

Commentary

Karen Dawisha: I want to make one point and develop it because I think it is central to all three presentations that have been made, and it is reflected in the series of excellent articles that are in the spring 1992 *Middle East Journal*.

One thing that is agreed in both the presentations today and in the articles is that in Israel, in Egypt, and in the United States, both the conduct of diplomacy and the pattern of interactions leading up to the war were deeply affected by extremely important political splits within all of the leaderships. This is a given, in fact, in most people's assessments of the development of political contacts up to the outbreak of war. Yet at the same time most people assume unanimity on the Soviet side. We talk about either "the Soviets" having an interest in escalation, or "the Soviets" having an interest in de-escalation, and whichever view we hold, most observers in the past have assumed Soviet unanimity.

I think this is illogical, in light of what we know now about Soviet behavior in the Cuban missile crisis in 1962 and at the time of the invasion of Czechoslovakia in 1968. So why should we assume as a prima facie matter that the Soviets were united one year before '68 and five years after '62? We also knew from studies of other issues that the Soviet leadership was highly divided in 1967, on domestic economic reform, on the handling of the emerging dissident movement, on relations with the West, and on the best way to achieve unity in the international communist movement. I think it is therefore not logical to assume Soviet unity on the Middle East, and given even the limited information we have, I also think it's not accurate. I also think it is possible that the splits that were present at the highest levels of the Soviet leadership in 1967 actually may have exacerbated the crisis by increasing the risks that some were willing to take for political purposes. The split also undermined the credibility of moderate leadership and its efforts to de-escalate the crisis, thereby strengthening the perception of Moscow generally as an unreliable and duplicitous partner.

Soviet behavior in the run-up to the Six-Day War, as in the Czech crisis a year later, was characterized by division on this specific Mideast issue as well as on the Soviet Union's global policies and on core domestic issues. The thesis is something like this: There was a continuum of views on this issue within the highest levels of the Soviet leadership. At one end, some Soviet leaders put an extremely high priority on some or all forms of global confrontation with imperialism, as one policy; on the isolation of China, as the second; on the assertion of Soviet ideological leadership, as a third; on geopolitical ascendancy of the Soviet Union in general, and the military in particular, in the Middle East and elsewhere, as a fourth policy; and, finally, on the promotion of greater domestic orthodoxy. The leaders, I believe, in this group, although they may not have acted together or held the same views on all of these issues, were Suslov, as Vitaly Naumkin said; his deputy, Boris Ponomarev, who, although not a member of the Politburo, was a secretary in charge of the International Department and important in distilling information—he was a gatekeeper within the party; Grechko, newly appointed as minister of defense; Gorchkov, the head of the navy, who had deep-water ambitions of a primordial nature; possibly Podgorny, the president; and someone who certainly would have agreed with him on their domestic agenda, Leonid Brezhnev, first secretary of the Soviet Communist Party.

At the other end of the continuum were those who put domestic restructuring as their first priority. Cooperation with Europe and the United States was seen as possible on some issues and even desirable on others. These leaders were willing to work with the United States, and this was the beginning of the detente process and the height of the nonproliferation agreement negotiations. There were those, including Kosygin, who favored relations with Middle East states that could benefit the Soviet Union economically. In other words, they were in favor of improving relations with Iran, as evidenced by Kosygin's visit there, which was postponed by the war to March 1968, and even with moderate Arab states. This group, I believe, was led by Kosygin. It was supported by some within the Foreign Ministry and also possibly by Andropov, who moved into position as head of the

KGB only in May 1967. There is strong reason to believe that a number of his deputies were strongly in favor of accommodation with the West, particularly with the United States, and did not seek confrontation in the Middle East at that time. But it is possible, even likely, that there were major splits even within the KGB that Andropov inherited.

This latter group, I think, wanted neither war nor any significant disruption in the slow movement toward diplomatic improvement of their relationship with the United States. And I think it is significant that almost all of the diplomatic traffic with the United States went through Kosygin, since Podgorny could have been, from the protocol point of view, the initiator of such traffic. Brezhnev, politically, also could have initiated traffic, as Gromyko could have, yet Kosygin is the single voice, both in diplomatic traffic and in the negotiations.

On the issue of the warning of Israeli troop buildups, the worst-case scenario that has garnered the most credibility in the literature so far is that the Soviet Union issued the warning out of bad intelligence—and certainly there were many on the Soviet side who believed that the Arabs had the capability, given a certain amount of unity, to deflect or to defeat Israel. Apparently, they may have been encouraged in this view by people in the Egyptian military hierarchy.

But it is also a possible thesis (one that I think has not yet been decisively excluded) that some in the Soviet Union, and I formulate this carefully, needed a Middle Eastern conflict more than they needed an Arab victory. In other words, while an Arab victory might have been a favored outcome (although I think the Soviets knew from the beginning it was unobtainable and they calculated the United States would not allow it), an Arab defeat was seen as a better result for the Soviets than no conflict at all because the conflict would draw U.S. military forces away from Vietnam, and U.S. imperialism would be confronted in an arena more favorable than southeast Asia for Soviet force projection capabilities. [For the Soviets, such a conflict would also] silence Chinese criticism, torpedo the first efforts being made toward detente by members of their own leadership, and end Romanian and Polish flirtation with the new German policy of Ostpolitik, which threatened the Soviets at the core of their strategic center in Eastern Europe. An Arab-Israeli war would also re-create a psychology of embattlement, which would facilitate a domestic crackdown on dissidents in general and Jewish dissidents in particular, as the trial of Ginsberg and others was being prepared at this time. Further, Egypt had rebuffed previous Soviet efforts to station military units on its soil, as we know from Egyptian archives that were included in the book by the Egyptian naval officer Husseini; and

Gorchkov's efforts to launch a deepwater navy beginning in the early sixties would come to nothing without basing facilities.

Some in the Soviet military establishment, including some at the top (certain to have been the source of any information or misinformation about military movements), therefore, may not have seen the weakening of Nasser's military independence as a bad thing. This is an extreme thesis, but I think it deserves serious elaboration and research.

Discussion

Carl Brown: One thing that seems to come through strongly is what political scientists refer to as bureaucratic politics. Diplomacy begins at home; all politics is local politics. Each one of the four speakers has pointed out that one mustn't think of diplomacy as so many billiard balls on the table. The United States, or the Soviet Union, or Egypt, or Israel is a group of different people often in considerable contention.

I would like to see two points treated in the discussion period. One is that the 'Amr-Nasser rivalry was apparently unknown to the outside world. It came as a considerable surprise to me, and I've checked it with many diplomats who were on the spot, many Western diplomats. I'd like to be corrected if I'm wrong, but I find it absolutely fascinating that not even the CIA, presumably, knew about this rivalry. If there was such a rivalry, as Egyptian sources now emphasize, and if Nasser had the feeling that he didn't even have control of his own army and that 'Amr was an incompetent, wouldn't this have made Nasser even more prudent and cautious than he actually was?

Another thing, what in the world were all the military professionals doing? I thought one thing we surely had clear was that all of them believed Israel would easily prevail in a military confrontation. Now we are hearing indications of their assuming that this was not the case. If military professionals who were being listened to were so advising, then that changes the scenarios that many of us have.

I would also like to hear much more about the thesis the late Malcolm Kerr put so deftly in *The Arab Cold War*, that the catalyst on the Arab side was inter-Arab politics more than anything else.

Meir Amit: First, I think the Soviet strategy, as practically transmitted to the Egyptians and Syrians, was the Cuban model, namely to play at brinkmanship, to go up to a point and then retreat and gain some political benefits out of this movement. But my main point is that there was an internal feud in Russia between hawks and doves, and I would like to mention a few facts that I think are not known.

I refer to a book in Hebrew, which I recommend be translated into English, called *The Soviet Involvement in the Six-Day War*. The author is Abraham Ben Tsur, a member of a kibbutz, who did thorough research into the war. He pointed out that on March 31 Marshal Malinovsky died, and the Supreme Soviet appointed Ustinov minister of defense. The hawkish side, namely Brezhnev—you mentioned Kosygin, but Kosygin was not strong although he was on the dovish side—fought the appointment. They didn't want Ustinov; they wanted Grechko, and this fight ended after a couple of weeks with the appointment of Grechko as minister of defense. That was an important factor.

The other point is that many researchers think that the war started on April 7, when the big air battle with the Syrians occurred. The fact of the matter is that a delegation from Syria came to the funeral of Malinovsky, and they were briefed by a Russian air force general by the name of Battov, who advised them to use their air force and that's what happened. (I'm talking in headlines because I want to keep it short.) On May 19, Smitchasni, the head of the KGB, was ousted and Andropov was appointed. I don't concur with you, Mr. Naumkin, that Andropov was a dove.

Vitaly Naumkin: That was Karen, not me.

Karen Dawisha: You can disagree with me.

Meir Amit: Okay. So, I don't concur with you. The fact of the matter is that Andropov was one of the key players and one of those responsible for the disinformation and the escalation of the situation.

Now, an important fact. On April 22, the same year, there was a summit, a semisummit meeting in East Berlin—Brezhnev, Gomulka, and Ulbricht. Ulbricht's translator, whose name is White, deserted to the West and wrote a book, like everybody else. In this book he says, "Brezhnev told his colleagues, 'We've already succeeded in pushing the Americans from the area. Shortly we are going to hit them strongly.'" It was our understanding that the Brezhnev-Grechko alignment was one of the main reasons for the development of the '67 war. By the way, I told my friend Dick Helms that General Gamasy, who was [Egyptian] chief of staff in the '73 war, told us—we met him in 1978; it's a new world now, we sit together (it's one of my conclusions that if this type of meeting would have taken place before, maybe the war would not have started, because everyone has his own recollections, his own understandings of the war)—that he warned Nasser not to go for war, that they would not succeed.

My last point (maybe the one before last). The late leader of the Communist Party in Israel, Moshe Sneh, had a meeting with Ambassador Chuvakin [Soviet ambassador to Israel], an intimate, unofficial meeting. Chuvakin said, "You must understand that this war will be over in twenty-four hours and the end will be that there will be no Israel." That was the understanding of Chuvakin at the time, according to Moshe Sneh.

My last point refers to the day Nasser resigned [June 9]. He mentioned three reasons for his actions leading to the crisis that are worth repeating. (1) We have information [about the troop concentrations] from our brothers in Syria. (2) Our friends in the Soviet Union told our parliamentary mission that was visiting the Soviet Union before the war [the same thing], and warned them. (This, Nasser says. It's not me.) (3) We have figured out meticulously the balance of power—the air force and the land power, etc.— and it showed us that we can win the war. So that was his explanation.

By the way, I have a feeling that this whole conference is to kind of vindicate Nasser. To tolerate him and to say, "Well, he was not the one who was to blame for the war." But he says [in his resignation speech] "We, like anybody who was responsible, are responsible, for better or for worse." And Nasser said that it was "our" big calculation that "we" are going to win the war. It was in fact a big miscalculation on the part of the Russians. Maybe it got out of hand. They didn't intend what happened, but it was a miscalculation, a big miscalculation on their part and on the part of the Egyptians.

Richard Parker: Just one thing. The purpose of this conference is not to vindicate Nasser; it's to vindicate the United States. [Laughter.]

Georgiy Kornienko: I would like to share with you something I know, or I think that I know, about the mystery of "the Soviet warning." In quote marks or without, with my hand on this kind of Bible [the spring 1992 issue of the *Middle East Journal*], I will testify. No instructions were given to Ambassador Pojidaev to pass any information on May 12 or 13 or around those dates. I am absolutely positive on that. And, as Dr. Naumkin mentioned already, no report from Pojidaev about any talk with al-Feki, or anybody else, on these dates is in the archives. On May 16, Pojidaev was invited first by Minister Riad and the same day by Minister Badran. They invited him to talk about the situation and Badran, at least, mentioned the information received from the Syrians about twelve brigades concentrated on their borders. Both of them asked from Moscow the Soviet evaluation of their situation.

Richard Parker: Both Badran and Riad asked for it?

Georgiy Kornienko: Yes. Riad and Badran. Separately. They had separate meetings with Pojidaev. It was only on May 20 that Pojidaev, on instructions from Moscow, went again separately to Riad and Badran. The information he gave was rather general in character about the statements made by Israeli

Georgiy Kornienko, chief of the
American Department, Soviet Foreign
Ministry, 1967.

leaders and so on. But there was a short passage included in that information that, according to intelligence data which needed verification, there are up to fifteen brigades on the Syrian border. There was such a sentence in that information, but it was passed in answer, in response to the request by Riad and Badran, on May 20. None of them in speaking with Pojidaev on May 16 referred to any information delivered by Pojidaev before that. It would have been logical to say, "Well, as you informed us yourself a few days ago," and so on. No such reference. They just asked the evaluation from Moscow. The evaluation was given on May 20.

The next day, on instructions, again from Moscow, Pojidaev had talks with President Nasser. That passage about any number of brigades was not included in his instructions or talk with President Nasser. And the main theme of the talk was cautioning restraint. Now about the mystery of Pojidaev's talk on May 12 or 13 with someone in the Foreign Ministry—if there were really such a meeting and a talk. (I can just speak hypothetically.) Yes, I know that around that date information was passed by a KGB man to his counterpart in Cairo. I can imagine, hypothetically, that had Pojidaev been told by a KGB man that he had passed such and such information, Pojidaev might have decided on his own initiative—with no instructions from Moscow, I'm positive of that—to pass the same information to his counterpart in the Foreign Ministry. I did not know Pojidaev well enough to be certain now that he would have dared to do that. But speaking hypothetically, if there was a meeting, if there was such a talk, I have only that explanation. No instruction, no provocation from Moscow on the governmental level.

About information passed by the KGB man, according to my knowledge it was a routine exchange of information on just the service level. There was no special decision in Moscow taken to pass this information by this channel. The decision was taken by the intelligence service itself. There was a link and there was an exchange of information from day to day and it was done in that routine way. That's my understanding of the fact of information given by a KGB officer to his counterpart.

Again, speaking from memory but refreshed a bit by looking recently into the archives, no consultations took place between Cairo and Moscow about the withdrawal of UN forces, about the Strait of Tiran, and so on. I remember vividly how disturbed we were in Moscow when we heard over the radio about these steps. And, yes, the ministry sent cables to Pojidaev asking for information: What is going on? What is the reason? He had a talk on May 19 with Marshal 'Amr, and 'Amr explained that the purpose of sending Egyptian troops to Sinai and of withdrawing UN forces was just to deter the Israelis from attacking Syria. But there were no previous consultations on these issues between Cairo and Moscow.

Speaking frankly, I cannot take seriously all the allegations about Moscow being interested in provoking war and in involving the United States in the Middle East to create "another Vietnam." Moscow has always been scared of the United States being in the Middle East, and to think that someone was interested in involving it there isn't serious, regardless of differences of opinions among the ideologists and pragmatists and others. There were differences, no doubt, but no grand design. Grand follies, yes, but no grand designs. [See "Documents" section at the end of this chapter for follow-up by Kornienko.]

Salah Bassiouny: I just want to comment on the fact that the Soviet ambassador came to the Foreign Ministry and delivered a report consisting of five to six pages. Possibly, as you have rightly said, when the KGB liaison officer in the embassy showed the ambassador the report, they consulted with each other and the ambassador decided that he should also go to the ministry and deliver a copy of it.

Georgiy Kornienko: Hypothetically.

Salah Bassiouny: No, but this is what happened. I mean we are not talking hypothetically about a phantom that came to the ministry.

Georgiy Kornienko: I am speaking hypothetically.

Salah Bassiouny: No, there was no phantom. It was Ambassador Pojidaev who came. So, it seems, if there were no instructions from the ministry, it was an agreement between himself and the KGB man to strengthen the report that was presented the same day to Salah Nasr, the director of intelligence.

Eugene Rostow: I can add a footnote to what Ambassador Kornienko has said about the Soviet report. One day in this period, in a meeting, I think in the White House with the president, a report was made that our representatives all over the Middle East were picking up stories to the effect that Soviet officials in considerable number were spreading this story, which of course we knew was not true. It was a bit like throwing gasoline on a fire, so I was instructed to call in the Soviets and report that to them. Ambassador Dobrynin was away and his no. 2 came in. I've forgotten his name, a great big tall fellow, very cheerful.

Georgiy Kornienko: Chernyakov.

Eugene Rostow: Yes, that's right. We all liked him and got along well with him. I told him we were getting these reports and we thought his government would want to know that such reports were coming in. They were very dangerous and inflammatory and could do no good. And Chernyakov said, "Is this a warning?" Well, I thought, I had no instructions to deliver an ultimatum to the Soviet Union, so I said no—you can characterize it as you will, but it's just a friendly exchange. And if we found some of our agents doing unauthorized things of that kind, we would be grateful for any information about them, and it was left there. But this was at the official level and I'm sure that, I know that, a telegram to that effect went out all around the circuit and I'm sure that he did the same to his government. That was late in the day, and it showed that this activity, whether it was by FSOs or the KGB, had been going on vigorously for a long time.

Robert Freedman: I would like to follow up on Karen Dawisha's most interesting presentation, with which I identify almost 100 percent. It is also my theory of what happened. I would like to carry the story a little farther. Dick Parker, in his very good article in the *Middle East Journal,* argues that when he was in Moscow and had his interviews at the [Oriental Studies] Institute, the Soviets there told him that the relationship between the Soviet Union and Syria wasn't all that important and that really Egypt was the greater prize. Yet the Soviets seemed to be willing to take a major risk at the time for Syria, to preserve the regime, which was a weak one, I think we all agree, in power. So I would like our Soviet colleagues here, our Russian colleagues now, to talk in some detail about the nature of the relationship of the Soviet regime with the left-wing Ba'athist regime in Syria. Exactly what were the commitments? How far was the Soviet government going to go to try to protect this regime that was under domestic attack and also under threat from the Israelis?

Carl Brown: Mr. Naumkin, would you take hold of that?

Vitaly Naumkin: No comment.

Carl Brown: Tahsin Basheer.

Tahsin Basheer: I find in Shimon Shamir's buildup no answer to the talk that happened when Rabin went to Dayan before Dayan assumed the ministry, in which Dayan blamed him for irritating Nasser beyond any positive role, and that is the most dangerous escalation that can happen on the Israeli side. The Israeli action was planned to implicate Nasser, and that is dangerous because it is difficult to de-escalate. That's on our part.

On the part of Vitaly Naumkin and Karen Dawisha, I find absent from your answers whether Kosygin was moderate or not. The Soviet Union did not warn Egypt about blocking navigation in the Gulf of Aqaba. Egypt did not consult the Soviet Union before the act of withdrawing UNEF or blocking the passage, but no Egyptian claimed that. But once it took place there was no warning whatsoever, no friendly warning from the Soviet Union as to the danger of that act. Nor was there any information from the Soviets about what they must have heard from the Americans: that there is a certain American commitment to Israel regarding the passage. The important thing about the Soviet warning is that it was repeated twice to the parliamentary group headed by Sadat, on their way in [to North Korea] and on their way back. So there was a definite message and you cannot discount it. The double message about threats to Syria was even carried by the Soviet media. But the fact is that they picked Sadat, who they knew was irritable, was not pro-Soviet, to repeat this to, to which Sadat responded, "Well, we are primitive people, we do not have means of finding the news. You have your KGB, you have your satellites, you tell us what's happening." They never dismissed that. It is true that they warned Nasser later to exercise caution and restraint, but the facts do not in any way minimize the contacts between the Russians and us. It's only when Egypt started actively reacting that they wanted to put a stopper on it.

Now, for Salah Bassiouny. The question is, on whom is one putting the blame, Nasser or 'Amr? The issue nowadays is to be seen in the light of the Arabic term that describes how 'Amr died: the word we used is *intaharuh*, which means [in effect that] we made him commit suicide, because we don't know whether he committed suicide or acted under intaharuh. But once it happened, there was a split in the military-political elite in Egypt between those who accused Nasser of the debacle and those who accused 'Amr. The split is recounted in all the books, including a recent book against 'Amr by [Amin] Huwaydi, a minister of war after 'Amr and a former head of intelligence, who is pro-Nasser. But no matter what rivalry existed between Nasser and 'Amr they were close. Nasser never left Egypt without leaving 'Amr in charge. It was not a kill-or-be-killed type of competition. They were close. Nasser trusted 'Amr more than anybody in the leadership, but there was a lot of competition between Nasser aides and 'Amr aides, including Shams Badran. Each of them was trying to penetrate the other's operations. But the two men up until the debacle [of 1967] were very close. Nasser also opted to use 'Amr's visit to Pakistan to inform him of what the Saudi radio had said, because in the intra-Arab cold war Saudi and Jordanian propaganda was criticizing Egypt. The question is, Why did Nasser not have the patience to wait two to three days until 'Amr returned from Pakistan to discuss this matter? These radio attacks continued for many months. [Apparently this is a reference to Saudi and Jordanian attacks on Egypt for not closing the Strait of Tiran to Israeli shipping; the 'Amr visit to Pakistan referred to is presumably that of 1966.—*Ed.*]

Ernest Dawn: As for whether Israeli retaliation policy was a disaster—actually, of course, retaliation had worked well. It first convinced Jordan in about the mid-1950s to put much closer controls over the frontier. After the Suez War, the Egyptians kept control for ten years. So if you were an Israeli statesman in 1965–66, you would think retaliation was a paying proposition. However, Syria was always a different matter. That's a short frontier, heavily defended by the Syrians, with all the geographic features in favor of them. The Israelis never really attempted anything through that frontier. They lobbed shells back and forth, carried out an air strike, but that was all. Syria was the only one of the confrontation states during that ten years that actually carried out little firefights with the Israelis. And even though the raids by Fatah and others after '65 were mostly based in Syria, it was Jordan that took the retaliation, not Syria. You have to keep this geography in mind. There is no way you could hide one division, one brigade out there opposite the Syrian frontier. . . . It's hard to hide a battalion.

About the Soviet warning, I know nothing other than what I read in newspapers. But I do know well what was in Arab newspapers during that period—or I used to know it, and I've checked my notes. It is interesting that there was little information of Soviet attribution in the Arabic newspapers at that time, or on the radio. There was one report very early. Syria attempted to convert its own internal crisis into a Zionist-imperialist reactionary plot against Syria in a major way on May 7, and Tass picked that up on May 9 in a report tying the Syrian internal threat to Zionist-imperialist reaction. The Arab press picked it up on May 10. It didn't last long. From that time on, it's Israeli statements—or the alleged Israeli statement mostly based on the UPI report—that fill up the pages of the Arabic newspapers. Interestingly enough, Egypt from 1963 on had done everything that it could to keep the Israeli-Arab confrontation on the back burner. There is no question whatever about this, and Egypt, longer than any other Arab country, was silent on the Israeli tie-in to the Syrian internal crisis. Only on May 15 did the major Cairo dailies start reporting that the Zionist-imperialist reactionary conspiracy was involved in the threat to Syria.

One final word, about military competence. Back in those days I had close relations with a few well-placed, well-informed Egyptian graduate students at the University of Illinois who had relatives in the army, and I was also doing some work of my own through the newspapers on Syria and Egypt, keeping track. The interesting thing was that almost as soon as an officer in an Arab army got to be a lieutenant colonel and a battalion commander, he became a commercial attaché based in Sweden, and my conclusion was that the Arabs can't have an army. They had no battalion commanders who had learned their jobs. Without battalion commanders, you don't have an army. Anyone who thought that the Egyptian army or the Syrian army had any combat potential paid no attention whatsoever to personnel policies. It's obvious that they were shifting officers just as soon as they got to the higher rank. It was lieutenant colonels who carried out all the coups. You've got a battalion, you can take over a government building. So they just never left anyone in that position long unless he [his loyalty] was absolutely certain.

Gideon Rafael: My observations about a period in which I was actually involved twenty-five years ago may shed light on at least some of the mysteries. First, you must think about the background and the context of the events. The war broke out after twenty years of a state of belligerency with all the trimmings—hostilities, incursions, retaliation, blockade of the Strait of Tiran. Second, we should not forget that in 1966 Great Britain gave up its commitments in the Persian Gulf, which created a new situation that worried us [Israel], as well as Iran. It worried Washington, too, but the United States was involved in the war in Vietnam. A power vacuum was on the point of being created—attractive for the Soviets. Third, incursions from Syrian territory obliged us to take some action.

In November 1966, we decided on a new way, on a diplomatic way, and we submitted a complaint to the UN Security Council and asked it to intervene and to call on Syria to take necessary measures to prevent activities against us. The Soviet Union supported Syria in its rejection of the resolution. The United States and the Western countries tried to water down the resolution so that it could be accepted. At the end it was more water than a resolution. Nevertheless, the Soviets vetoed it. So, as a matter of fact, they barred the Security Council in November '66 from diplomatic action.

I would like to get, if possible, from Mr. Bassiouny some enlightenment about what happened in March 1967, when Mr. Gromyko paid a visit to Cairo and to other countries in the Middle East. We don't know what really happened. There are certain versions about this mission, but it would be important to hear the respective Soviet and Egyptian versions. In April 1967, our government felt that the situation between Israel and Syria was moving into a very tense spot. I was, at the time, in charge of these affairs in Israel, and we felt that the Soviet Union might not be aware of the dangers involved. Therefore, the government sent me to Moscow on a special mission to discuss the situation, as Israel saw it, with the Soviet government.

Karen Dawisha: When did that [Gromyko's visit] take place?

Gideon Rafael: In April 1967.

Meir Amit: It was March 29.

Gideon Rafael: Anyway, I had discussions. I feel somehow sadly amused, if I may say so, for apparently there were three Mr. Semenovs, the deputy foreign minister: one who spoke with us, one who spoke with Ambassador Feki at the dacha, and another who spoke to the late President Sadat when he was leading a parliamentary delegation to Moscow on his way to Korea. I encountered on May 1, in Red Square, this delegation led by Sadat.

Later, in the discussions in the Security Council in May '67, I said how much better it would have been if we could have explained to Egypt, and to Mr. Sadat, the intentions and the viewpoint of Israel. But it took eleven years until we had the chance to speak directly with Egypt.

What happened in my talk with Mr. Semenov? We explained that the Soviet Union was overheating the situation, that perhaps their temperature control affecting the Middle East was not exactly the temperature control suitable for the Middle East and they were fanning a smoldering flame. Whereupon, in three days of talks, like a gramophone record, he repeated, "Well it may be that Israel itself is innocent, but you have been involved in a plot by the CIA, which wants to topple the regime in Syria. This is a new regime. . . . As a regime, they are friendly to the Soviet Union. We are very interested in the regime and you would make a terrible error if you would take that assignment and act against Syria." This was the line of Mr. Semenov, as we understood it. He dismissed our assurances that we were not plotting with the CIA. All we wanted was quiet on our northern border.

The balloon went up when the Soviets, despite our explanation, launched that story of the twelve or fifteen brigades mobilized by Israel along the

Syrian border. Before I was sent to Moscow, I was asked by the government to go on an inspection tour to the northern border, and all that I saw there were two companies guarding the border. When Moscow launched the story that Israel had mobilized twelve or fifteen brigades, Israel's prime minister, Mr. Eshkol, invited Soviet Ambassador Chuvakin to go with him personally to the border and see what was happening there. Chuvakin gave the classic answer, classic in the books of diplomacy: "I am not here to observe facts in Israel, I am here to present the views of Moscow."

Robert Oakley: I want to ask one question of Shimon. Can you explain how Yariv's briefing was blown out of proportion and the hysteria which then was seen coming from Damascus and Arabic radios? We've seen how the Soviets, apparently in a number of different places, put gasoline on the flames. What did Israel do, or consider doing, or not do, to damp down the flames, including correcting the erroneous report to UPI?

Samuel Lewis: Just a quick point about communication. I am intrigued by the general assumption by my Russian friends, and nobody has challenged it, that it is only the foreign minister who sends instructions to the Soviet ambassadors abroad. Surely, another hypothesis, besides the one that he [Pojidaev in Cairo] did it on his own, is that he had a back-channel instruction from the hardliners in the Politburo or the KGB or any one of a variety of characters. I don't think anything demonstrates that there weren't any instructions from Moscow simply because the Foreign Ministry doesn't have any record of it. Certainly it wouldn't be that way in the U.S. government.

Georgiy Kornienko: An ambassador receives the orders only through the foreign minister. He cannot . . .

Samuel Lewis: Only?

Georgiy Kornienko: Only. No instruction can be sent to the ambassador through KGB channels. Never. It cannot be done for technical reasons alone, not to mention organizational routine.

Carl Brown: That sounds like the table of organization that prevails in the U.S. government and we all know what actually happens, but I leave it at that.

(Indistinct): I'm with the State Department. It is clear that there is a long chain of events leading up to the war. My question is, at what point in this chain of events did the war actually become inevitable? The discussion here has focused mainly on the events leading up to the mobilization, but it seems to me that the mobilization was not the key. The key development could conceivably have been the blockade. There was a mobilization in 1960 of Egyptian forces, which did not lead to a blockade. At what point in these events did the war become inevitable?

Carl Brown: I would like to suggest, and see if the panelists agree, that the point of no return was the announcement of the blockade of the strait, and other things were precipitants and forerunners, but war was not inevitable until that. . . .

Alfred L. Atherton: Dredging my own memory of that period, I believe I, at least, felt that the war became inevitable with the withdrawal of UNEF. That was going to precipitate a situation and it did.

Richard Parker: I would disagree. Abba Eban said there will be no war if the strait is not closed.

William Zartman: Phrases are sometimes trace elements, and Shimon was, I think, clear in tracing the phrase "the toppling of the government in Damascus." I haven't heard a trace on the phrase "ten to twelve brigades," and I think it would be interesting to hear more on that.

Richard Parker: What do you mean by "a trace on"?

William Zartman: Well, where did it start?

David Korn: I would like to ask the Egyptian participants to speak a little bit more about the war of words between Egypt and Syria and Saudi Arabia and Jordan that was going on at the time, in 1967. My recollection of this period, clearly, was that this was a powerful factor pushing Egypt to enter the war.

Janice Stein: Just a quick question to Shimon: From your reconstruction, it appears that a raid was being planned in a routine way—that such raids were part of retaliatory action. Is it not fair to conclude that Egyptian policy succeeded in the first instance, that moving troops across the canal ended the possibility of a retaliatory raid, which was, as I understand it, the initial Egyptian objective? Would that be a fair reconstruction?

Granville Austin: Dr. Shamir was talking about the Israeli policy of strengthening the governments of Jordan and Lebanon so that they could better control terrorism and cross-border raids, and of weakening Damascus. But if that is so, why was the Samuʻ raid conducted against Jordan and not against the Syrians? How did this help King Hussein's position? And, second, is there any possibility, as seen by any of the participants here, that when Nasser made the speech closing the strait, his tongue simply ran away from him? (The logical magic of language, as [Philip] Hitti used to describe Arabic.) Did people plan his speech? Was it written for him ahead of time? Was this expected, or did he all of a sudden feel enthusiastic and simply say something that led to the disaster, his disaster?

Richard Parker: You didn't read my article.

Granville Austin: Yes, I did.

Carl Brown: I'm going to take one last question now and call on the speakers to make sure they have enough time to answer the many questions.

Victor Israelyan: I don't have a question, but I wanted to share with you an episode that could perhaps enlighten the problem of the Soviet warning. But, first, in my several decades in the Soviet Foreign Office, I have not heard of or witnessed any action by an ambassador without instructions signed by the foreign minister or deputy foreign minister in charge of an issue. So certainly the ambassador acts under the instruction of the Foreign Ministry.

On December 3, 1967, before going to New York as a deputy representative of the Soviet Union, I had a talk with Brezhnev and en passant he started to pose a question to me, saying that "the Middle East is the most serious problem you have to deal with in New York." Then he said, "Look, we have decided"—"we" meaning the Politburo, the Central Committee—"to pay more attention to the Middle East. And we decided that we are changing the guard." And that's what happened. Pojidaev was replaced by Vinogradov. Barkovsky was replaced by Mukhitdinov, and the Federenko team at the UN was replaced by Malik and his team, and he explained this. I cannot say whether these changes in personnel were an expression of a dissatisfaction with Ambassador Pojidaev who did something wrong. I cannot say that, but that showed the Politburo's concern with Soviet diplomatic representation in the Middle East.

Carl Brown: Let's turn now to the responses to the several questions.

Shimon Shamir: Four questions were addressed to me, the first by Ambassador Basheer. I was looking for an opportunity to address the general point, which, I think, was also made indirectly by Ambassador Bassiouny: There is an allegation that in 1967 Israel was ready for war, was well prepared, and was only waiting for an opportunity to launch it. I talked to many Egyptians on this allegation, and they unanimously adhered to it. Most of them even used the phrase that Israel had "laid a trap for Nasser and Nasser fell into it." The belief is that the whole thing was premeditated by Israel.

In an attempt to reconstruct history, we can use for that purpose documents, articles, interviews, and so on. But there is another factor that we must bear in mind if we want to have a correct reconstruction of what happened in 1967. I am referring to the knowledge we have about the general climate that prevailed in Israel, the perceptions and feelings in Israeli society and among its decision makers. Anybody who was in Israel at the time—and there are many in this audience who were there—knows that Israel was caught unprepared. There was a deep sense of crisis in Israeli society and a deep confusion at the top. There were clashes between generals and ministers, a feeling of sudden emergency. The Israelis didn't know which fire to put out first: the blockade in the strait? the concentration of forces in Sinai? the incursions from Syria? There was a general sense of perplexity. This was not a society, and not a political elite, that had been preparing itself for this event and was now exploiting an opportunity, or even creating an opportunity, to implement its plans. The premeditated conspiracy version is simply wrong.

Regarding the point made by Dr. Dawn that retaliation, in fact, did work: If retaliation worked and if the Israelis believed that, it only strengthens my point that what the Israelis wanted to do vis-à-vis the Syrians before May 15 was another retaliation of essentially the same kind. The question itself is a legitimate historical issue, and it is being debated in Israel up to this day. There are people who hold views that are close to mine, namely that retaliation did *not* work, and there are others who have a different view. I think that a good way to examine the effectiveness of the strategy of retaliation is to take the period from '54 to '56. We had then a series of retaliation operations, mostly against Jordan, each one generating a new wave of violence. Each retaliation was followed by another, larger in scale and involving more military units. Eventually it led to an all-out war. I think this was the true dynamics of the retaliation strategy.

Janice Stein raised a serious question: If Israel was preparing eventually to launch an operation against Syria, wasn't Nasser justified in trying to do something to prevent it? This question is often asked. The answer depends on what you regard as justification. What is important here is that Nasser was trying to create deterrence in a way that was changing the rules of the game. By sending the Egyptian army into the Sinai, let alone the subsequent eviction of UNEF and the blockade of the gulf, the Egyptians were changing the rules that had prevailed in this strategic arena since early 1957. The unwritten rules laid down also how much harassment Israel could tolerate along its borders and when it would feel compelled to react. There was a certain rhythm to that. Israel did not deviate from this pattern, whereas Nasser was responsible for an escalation that could not be justified within the rules of the game that existed at that time.

Samu' was a controversial operation, and Meir Amit certainly knows more than I about it. It is quite puzzling: What could have been the intention behind the raid? Actually, many Israelis too were surprised by that operation. My view is that the choice of this target was another manifestation of the polarity in Israeli thinking on the challenge of Syria. There was a feeling that something *must* be done. The Israeli public expected it and Israeli deterrence required it. On the other hand, there was the imperative of caution and the prospect of working through diplomatic channels, created by the Syrian-Soviet link. There was reluctance to jeopardize that. The way out of this dilemma was a retaliation in Jordan, which was a way of sending an indirect message to Syria: Israel is capable of inflicting heavy blows on its enemies, and it will retaliate against Syria if all other options fail.

As for the question concerning the impact Israel wanted to make on the Jordanian government: It is indeed inaccurate to say that Israel tried to "strengthen" this government—this is a wrong expression. Israel wanted to motivate the government in Amman to increase its efforts to control the irregulars that perpetrated the hostilities across border, to adopt a firm position that would be in its interest as well. To say "strengthen" may indeed be misleading.

Concerning the Soviet Union's role in triggering the conflagration, here again we are engaged in microhistory: Who said what when, who met whom, what message was transmitted, and so on? This is an important dimension of the discussion, and there is no history without it. But there is also the macro dimension of history. I think that we have not yet looked at the general map of the Middle East and the broad strategic situation in the region. What were the essential trends of development taking place there? The Soviet Union had been engaged, since '66, in an offensive, a political offensive and a strategic offensive, promoting what was called "the Progressive Bloc," which consisted of Egypt, Syria, Algeria, the Republic of Yemen, and to some extent Iraq. Up to that time, the Soviets concentrated their efforts on developing bilateral cooperation with each country individually, but in 1966 it appears that the Soviet Union felt that the time had arrived to bring these pro-Soviet regimes together and consolidate a strategic bloc. May 1967 offered an opportunity to lead the Egyptians into a situation where they would be doing something to support the Syrians and to have the two cooperating under the Soviet umbrella. The Soviets certainly didn't want a war, but they wanted a demonstration on the part of Syria and on the part of Egypt that these two Soviet clients were reinforcing each other. They wanted to show that the Middle Eastern pro-Soviet bloc, "the Progressive Bloc" so to speak, had been consolidated and that it was the winning side in the competition against what was called "the Reactionary Bloc," namely the regimes that were pro-American at that time. So, with all due respect to the important information that we heard from Ambassador Kornienko, there did exist a Soviet concentrated effort to activate the Egyptians. There is a whole list—I think Ambassador Bassiouny mentioned it—of statements that appeared in *Pravda, Izvestia,* and on Moscow Radio, all referring to concentrations of Israeli troops and to the grave danger to Syria from the Israeli threat. This was perfectly in line with the Soviets' basic strategy, and whether their message was transmitted this way or that way is, perhaps, secondary. What we should look at is the regional strategy of the Soviet Union at the time.

Tahsin Basheer: That didn't really answer my question regarding Rabin.

Shimon Shamir: I don't know what his intention was, but I can tell you that there was no Israeli strategy of Rabin, Dayan, or anybody else that targeted Egypt as an object of an Israeli action.

Tahsin Basheer: That [there was such a strategy] was Dayan's perception of what Rabin did.

Shimon Shamir: So, he may have been wrong. The fact is that Rabin rejected the plans that were submitted to him.

Tahsin Basheer: It was Dayan who said that [about provoking Nasser— mentioned earlier by Basheer] to Rabin.

Carl Brown: Okay. Vitaly Naumkin.

Vitaly Naumkin: First I would like to agree in principle with Karen Dawisha's summation of what was going on in the Soviet Union. In principle, though, it is very difficult to simplify this split in the Soviet leadership and to portray it as if it was some kind of open political struggle. It was an underground struggle, it was not very open, and a lot of people were somewhere between polar positions. At the same time, I don't agree with General Amit's understanding of the role of Ustinov. First of all, he was not very dovish, and the reason why the military were against Ustinov's appointment as minister of defense was that he was not military. They were preferring somebody who was a general during the war [World War II]. That was the reason—not because one was dovish and one was hawkish.

Coming to the Soviet estimation of the different pro-Soviet regimes in the Middle East, I would say that Egypt was considered extremely important for the Soviet Union, much more important than Syria. Of course, ideologically the Syrian Ba'athist leadership was close to the Communist Party leadership in Moscow. But at the same time, a lot of people were scared by the extremist tendencies expressed by the leaders of Syria in those days.

Of course, the Soviet warning may have been transmitted according to Professor Shamir's explanation, but it is not important whether the official diplomatic channel was used or not. There were some other channels. For instance, sometimes the party leadership used the channels of the KGB or military intelligence to pass information. But in such cases, information was not taken seriously and did not influence the situation as strongly as when it had been transmitted by an ambassador officially. Technically the Soviet warning may have been passed through the KGB or through a KGB officer or maybe a representative of military intelligence. We know there were visits paid by generals. For instance, there was one representative of military intelligence, named Ryevsky, who came in the middle of May to Egypt and who had some meetings there. I have no information about his talks, but I think that there might have been some information passed by him.

In conclusion, I would say that this information was not so effective as to move Nasser, to push Nasser toward war. On the contrary, if there was an idea for a preventive attack on the part of the Egyptians, maybe it was Marshal 'Amr's idea, which was passed by Badran to Kosygin and then rejected by the Soviets, since the Soviet Union was not eager to take risks in the Middle East.

Salah Bassiouny: The problem regarding the sequence of events preceding the June War was that from the American side things were clear. From the outset, events were going to lead to this type of confrontation, and I believe that the Israelis were definite about this confrontation coming to a full-scale war. And they were not in need, really, of another agreement like the one with Britain and France [in 1956] because relations between Israel and the United States did not leave any doubt about what was needed for Israel. It was not a question of green light or yellow light or red light; it was an understanding that we might come to this later.

On the Soviet side, there was a special relationship of friendship formed on illusions on both sides. It was a relationship based basically on arms supplies and Soviet military experts and Soviet economic cooperation with Egypt. But it was not a real relationship. The fact is that the report was presented to us, whether with instructions or not. It is a material fact that Ambassador Pojidaev came to the ministry on the same day that the same report was presented to Salah Nasr, director of General Intelligence. But between May 13 and May 16, there were no more contacts between the ambassador and high officials. [Meanwhile, there was] movement of troops, the Egyptian Army moving with big fanfare everywhere through the streets of Cairo. There was no Soviet caution there. From May 16 until the decision to close the Strait of Tiran, as Ambassador Basheer mentioned, there was no advice or caution to the Egyptian government about the seriousness of the situation. A friend and ally should have done this, but unfortunately it did not take place.

I must also mention that when the letter was addressed by Egypt to U Thant, the secretary-general, to withdraw UNEF, there was again no effort from the Soviet government to caution Egypt on this question. In fact, the only ones who were trying to convince Nasser to postpone this decision were the Yugoslavs and the Indians, who were members of the Advisory Committee, and when they found that Egypt insisted, they ceded and became hardliners in the committee in insisting on the withdrawal of UNEF. I mention this because—as our friend Amit has said—we are not really vindicating Gamal Abd al-Nasser. I'm trying to vindicate Egypt because we, in the final analysis, were victims of a situation in Washington, which I explained, and another in Moscow. Israel understood very well the situation in Moscow and in Washington and acted accordingly, and there was no doubt of a guaranteed success under such circumstances. Why, for instance, do some say that the Soviet Union might have had the intention of getting rid of Gamal Abd al-Nasser?

How would it have been possible, as Ambassador Shamir said, to pull together the Arab countries under Soviet influence or friendly with the Soviet Union in the confrontation with the United States? In fact, that was not possible at all. Nasser's policy, Egypt's policy, was anticommunist. Communists were arrested. They were in concentration camps in the western desert, in the oases, and we know Nasser's problems with Khrushchev in '64, and he insisted on this policy. And so long as there is no Communist Party in Egypt, all communist movements in the Arab world will be in a weak position. Look at history, and you will see that the communists are hated in Egypt, they are not in a good position in Syria or Iraq or Iran or Sudan. They are really hated. So Gamal Abd al-Nasser, in this sense, was an obstacle to real Soviet ideological influence in the area, exactly, if I may add, like the Ba'ath. The Ba'ath Party tried to infiltrate Egypt. They couldn't. So the party is confined to Syria and Iraq; they are nowhere else in the region. This might be one of the mistakes of the U.S. policy in challenging Gamal Abd al-Nasser.

Still there are many questions on the conduct of Soviet policy vis-à-vis Egypt. You [the Soviets] push for such a situation, and you are not to know that the bulk of the Egyptian army is moving to Sinai. You know well the capabilities, the real capabilities of the Egyptian army, and Marshal Zakharov in Moscow, during the talks, hails the high standard of the Egyptian armed forces. Shams Badran tells him about the excellence of the Egyptian army, and the Soviet side is repeatedly telling him how great you are—you can defeat Israel, you can do whatever you want. This is a deceit. It was not honest because some of the Egyptian officers who were in the delegation knew the facts. So why, in the Kremlin or in the Ministry of Defense, does such behavior by high Soviet officials take place? Even worse, when Egypt was on the brink of war and asked for urgent military supplies, the first answer was, we will give them to you in August and September. Only after a lot of talking were limited supplies sent to us.

As for the talks between Gromyko and Egypt, the Egyptian brief of the meeting was centered on the tense situation on the Syrian-Israeli border and Israeli intentions to wage a war. As I have said, the assessment in the Foreign Ministry and, I think, in the intelligence community also was that there is going to be a war waged by Israel. It might be that this assessment determined by itself the course of events at that time.

I want to comment on the question of Nasser and 'Amr. Gamal Abd al-Nasser cannot be [absolved of] his responsibility. He was the leader, he was the president of the country and the commander in chief, and no one could give him any reason for the mismanagement of such a serious situation. But the fact is that Gamal Abd al-Nasser was consistent in informing everyone that Egypt would not start the war. As has been published by General Fawzi, Marshal 'Amr gave orders for the Egyptian units in Sinai to be on the offensive, whereas the orders of Gamal Abd al-Nasser were to be in defensive positions. General Fawzi says this is one of the prime reasons for the chaotic military situation. I think the testimony of General Fawzi by itself points to a strange situation between Nasser and 'Amr.

Karen Dawisha: Just four points of detail. One, as Ambassador Bassiouny confirmed, was Zakharov's statements that he made in the meetings in Moscow. It's important not just because he got into the spirit of things and praised the Egyptian military, but because he had been in Egypt and had witnessed maneuvers. Therefore, he was in a position to know in detail about the lack of preparedness of the Egyptian military. This is important and has to be taken into account if you are going to make a worst- case scenario. It has to be dealt with.

The second point is that once Grechko came to power as minister of defense, there was a series of meetings. I believe one of the results was that, in order to further the tasks given them by the Politburo for meeting frontal attacks by imperialism in Vietnam and elsewhere, the Ministry of Defense sought as a matter of policy to extend the forward positioning of Soviet troops outside Soviet borders. They started in 1967 to put pressure on the Czechs, who had not had Soviet troops on their border since 1948, to reinstate Soviet troops on Czechoslovakian soil. This happened at a time when the Prague Spring was just beginning to unfurl, in the summer of '67. At the same time, pressure was increasing on the Egyptian military to accept more advisers.

The third is that at some point in '67, either just before or just after the

Six-Day War, the Soviet Ministry of Defense opened in their embassy in Cairo a direct line between the military attaché and Grechko. It is not inconceivable, therefore, that the military attaché had his own direct contact outside normal embassy channels.

Georgiy Kornienko: The military attaché was not an ambassador.

Karen Dawisha: Right. I am just saying that we shouldn't assume that everything had to go through the Ministry of Foreign Affairs at that time, even in the period before the war. Normal diplomatic cables between the ambassador and the Ministry of Foreign Affairs did not represent the totality of communications between the embassy and Moscow. The KGB station chief would also have had his own channels.

Finally, on the question of Andropov, I am not arguing that he was necessarily a dove. Andropov was a secretary of the party up to May 1967. Almost his entire career had been devoted to Eastern Europe. He was a novice on the Arab world. He knew nothing about it, and I don't think that coming in, in May '67, as he did, he was in a position to push any view different from that of the Arabists in the KGB. I do not believe that he was a strong advocate for war, but all the evidence we have suggests that Arabists within the KGB did engage directly in the passage of information that I think they probably knew was not correct.

Documents

Copy of teletype, AP, McClure, from Tel Aviv, May 12

McClure 11415 Telaviv 12/5 Military force against syria appears only way to halt continued sabotage acts against israel an israeli qualified source said friday. Exactly what action envisaged notnot disclosed stop but source said there were alternatives between guerilla war against syria and invasion and conquest of damascus itself. Source said he felt that only sure and safe answer to syrian problem was to launch aye military operation of sizable strength, but he admitted that this might notnot solve problem and there still reasonable chances solution could be found short of fullscale invasion stop twas his view that egypt would notnot intervene on syria's behalf as long as there was notnot an israeli invasion into syria extended into time and area. this informed source said he thought egyptians would notnot risk war against israel unless there nono other alternative stop he cited past statements by uuaarr president nasser that time notnot yet ripe for war against israel. however added egypt notnot been able to restrain syria comma which blamed for most sabotage acts inside israel including recent mining of roads and mortar shelling of kibbutz. egyptians shaky economy and war in yemen where moren fiftythousand egyptian troops downtied held reason for nasser notnot wanting showdown with israel stop twas believed nasser had warned syria to be careful notnot getout on limb because egypt notnot going to help. source said for this reason should nasser gain control of southern entrance of redsea after departure of british from aden he felt israeli shipping would continue unmolested through straits end mcclure.

Excerpts from *New York Times,* James Feron, from Tel Aviv, May 12

Some Israeli leaders have decided that the use of force against Syria may be the only way to curtail increasing terrorism. Any such Israeli reaction to continued infiltration probably would be of considerable strength but of short duration and limited in area. This has become apparent in talks with highly qualified and informed Israelis who have spoken in recent days against a background of mounting border violence. They tend to believe that Syria cannot be dissuaded from her infiltration tactics except by direct action from Israel. According to the view prevalent here, the Soviet Union, which supplies arms to Syria, is unwilling or unable to temper Syrian actions, while Western powers have little or no influence in Damascus.

UPI, Eliav Simon, from Jerusalem, May 12

MIDEAST 5/12
night ld mideast (pvs beirut upi 100)
by Eliav Simon
United Press International

Jerusalem, Israel (upiv)—A highly placed source said today that if Syria continues its new campaign of sabotage in Israel it will inevitably provoke military action intended to topple the Damascus army regime. Military observers said such a reaction would fall short of all-out conflict but would be mounted to deliver a telling blow at the government in Damascus, which is held responsible for the renewal of harassments along the frontier.

According to these observers, the end of the military regime in Damascus might not be unwelcome to other circles inside Syria itself since nationals of both would realize the Israelis would not "come to stay."

(More)
jp1642

Georgiy Kornienko, *The Cold War: Testimony of a Participant*

The following clarification of the Soviet role in the June War comes from Georgiy Kornienko, *The Cold War: Testimony of a Participant* (Moscow: Institute of International Relations, 1994), pp. 129–33 (in Russian, translation by James F. Leonard). [It is apparent that the discussion in this panel prompted Kornienko to delve more deeply into Soviet archives on his return to Moscow from the conference.—*Ed.*]

After the Suez crisis of 1956 and up to the summer of 1967, the situation in the Near East, despite all its complexity, did not produce any particular collisions in Soviet-American relations. Then on June 5, 1967, the "hot line" between the Kremlin and the White House was used for the first time since its establishment in 1963 after the Caribbean crisis. It was being used in connection with the Israeli attack on Egypt, and then on Syria. The Soviet leadership turned to the Americans with a persistent call to take measures to halt the Israeli aggression, since it was clear that Israel could not have decided on it without at least tacit agreement from Washington. The attempts of Washington to appear surprised and to convince Moscow that the Israeli actions were for it as completely unexpected as for Moscow were in no way credible to the latter. Moreover, the then Secretary of State Rusk was quite wrong when he wrote in his memoirs: "Fortunately, they [the Soviets] believed us and did not consider us responsible for the outbreak of the Six Day War." That was not so. If the Soviet leadership at a certain point acted as if it believed the assurances of the American leadership, it was purely for tactical considerations, for otherwise the USSR for its part would have been obliged to extend much more decisive and broader aid to the victims of Israeli aggression than it was able to do. Indeed, Rusk, as is evident, was not himself fully convinced of the correctness of his assertion (contained in those memoirs) that "Israel did not receive from the US secret encouragement to start the war," since he accompanies this assertion with the very significant condition, "So far as I know." Authentic facts which have subsequently become known leave no doubt that in reality Tel Aviv in an unofficial manner received a blessing on its aggression from President Johnson, about which in fact Rusk may not have known, since Johnson had his reliable channels to the Israeli leadership, in particular through Supreme Court Justice A. Fortas.

Nevertheless, despite its lack of any foundation, a version has circulated in the West that the Near East War of 1967 was provoked by the Soviet Union, which supposedly wished to draw the US into the Arab-Israeli conflict, creating a "second Vietnam" in the Near East. I wish to recount briefly what has served as a basis for this version and what actually took place. At that time I headed the US bureau of the Soviet Foreign Ministry and I was actively involved in the events in Moscow and around the developments in the Near East.

The rise in tension began when Israeli officials in May 1967 began to threaten, in public, military actions against Syria if there was not a halt to penetrations of Palestinian terrorists and saboteurs from Syrian territory into Israel. On May 8 the Syrians informed the Egyptian leadership that they had information about concentrations of Israeli troops on the border with Syria to strike at its territory. On May 12 the American agency United Press disseminated a statement by a senior Israeli official (from various data this was either Chief of Staff Rabin or the head of military intelligence Yariv) saying Israel will carry out military operations "with the aim of overthrowing the military regime in Damascus if Syrian terrorists continue their sabotage raids on Israel." As Nasser later explained, this Israeli threat played a decisive role in the decision by the Egyptian leadership to send troops into the Sinai peninsula, so that in case Israel attacked Syria, Egypt would come to her aid in accordance with the Egyptian-Syrian treaty of mutual assistance of November 6, 1966. As a supplementary argument on the basis for his decision to send the troops, Nasser subsequently referred to the fact that information on a concentration of Israeli troops on the Syrian frontier was received by the Egyptians not only from the Syrians but also from the Soviet side.

In fact, as was later made clear, on May 13 the KGB representative in Cairo, in line with the standing practice of an exchange of information with Egyptian intelligence, transmitted to the Egyptians a communication received by him from Moscow on the existence of information concerning an Israeli troop concentration (10–12 brigades) on the Syrian frontier. This information, received in Moscow either from Syria or from Lebanon, was transmitted to Egyptian intelligence, I repeat, in a working framework following review by the leadership of Soviet intelligence without special sanction (approval) of the political leadership of the country. As was later explained by the then head of the First Main Administration of the KGB, Sakharovsky, the reliability of the information given to the Egyptians had not been confirmed by Soviet intelligence sources, but they still considered it necessary to share it with their Egyptian colleagues. In the eyes of the Egyptian leadership, the information transmitted in intelligence channels may have been given additional weight since according to Egyptian sources this information was brought to the attention of the leadership of the

Egyptian Foreign Ministry on the same day by the Soviet ambassador to Egypt, Pojidaev. Moreover, on the same day, May 13, something similar was conveyed by Deputy Foreign Minister Semenov to the members of an Egyptian parliamentary delegation headed by Sadat enroute from North Korea. This triple delivery to the Egyptians of information, which as it later turned out was not wholly accurate, about Israeli troop concentrations near Syria has been cited in the West as evidence that Moscow consciously pushed Cairo into confrontation with Israel.

In this connection, it is reliably known to me that no instruction on this matter was given by Moscow to Ambassador Pojidaev, and if he duplicated to the Egyptian Foreign Ministry the information that the KGB representative had passed, then that was done at the initiative of the ambassador himself. I believe that what took place with Semenov was similar. He had the habit before meeting with foreign representatives to inquire of our "near neighbors," as the KGB intelligence service was known in Foreign Ministry jargon, whether they had anything for him to use in his conversations.

Later, on May 16, when the Egyptian troops began to cross into the Sinai, the Egyptian foreign minister, Riad, and the minister of war, Badran, asked through the Soviet ambassador for an evaluation of the situation on the Syrian frontier with Israel. The answer that was given on May 20 also noted the existence of data on Israeli concentrations on the border with Syria, but underlined that these data required checking.

In any case, there is neither a factual nor a logical basis for saying that the Soviet Union was interested in pushing Egypt into a collision with Israel or in a broader involvement of the US in Near Eastern affairs. On the contrary, it always feared that. Furthermore, following the entry of Egyptian troops on May 15 into the Sinai, the Egyptian government demanded the partial withdrawal of UN troops from the Egyptian-Israeli frontier. The idea that this was, as supposed in the West, done with the knowledge and even on the initiative of the USSR also did not correspond to reality. I recall with what concern the news of this action by Egypt was received by the Soviet leadership. And if the Soviet representative in the UN supported the demand of Egypt, it was because that was a sovereign decision by Egypt and because of considerations of solidarity with it in general and not on this particular question.

The announcement by Nasser on May 22 of the decision (again taken without consultation with us) on closing the Strait of Tiran to the passage of Israeli ships was received in Moscow with even greater alarm, since it was clear that this seriously complicated an already complex situation.

(Incidentally, Nasser later said that he did not plan to close the Strait of Tiran, since he did not demand originally the withdrawal of UN troops from the Sharm al-Shaykh area on the shore of the Strait; but when UN Secretary-General U Thant, in response to the demand of Egypt for the partial withdrawal of UN troops from the Egyptian-Israeli border, took the decision to fully withdraw them from Sinai, including Sharm al-Shaykh, and Egyptian troops then moved in, there arose the psychologically unbearable situation for Cairo in which Israeli ships would pass through literally under the eyes of Egyptian troops.)

At the time of the visit to Moscow, May 25–28, by Egyptian minister of war Badran, as he himself acknowledged, Kosygin and other Soviet officials warned the Egyptians in every way about steps which could lead to a further complication of the situation and an increase in the possibility of war with Israel. It is true that these pertinent warnings by the Soviet leadership, according to the testimony of [Egyptian Foreign—*Ed.*] ministry representatives accompanying Badran, were to a considerable degree weakened by the following event. Defense Minister Grechko, accompanying Badran to the airport, in a toast "for the road" boldly stated that if Israel attacked Egypt and the US came in on its side, then "we will come in on your side." Considering that Grechko had become defense minister only a couple of months before and was not strong on questions of high policy, his bravado at the airport, as Grechko himself said later to the Egyptian ambassador, Murad Ghalib, should not of course have been taken seriously. All the more so since Kosygin in the talks with Badran, and other Soviet leaders in a series of messages to Nasser (May 20 and 26 and June 1), warned him against rash steps in order not to give Israel reasons to unleash an armed conflict. The Soviet leaders in this period also addressed similar warnings to the governments of Israel and the US. Rusk, in his memoirs, writes in this connection, "Inasmuch as the Soviets had stirred up the Arabs, we were somewhat surprised when in late May the Soviets began to display great concern about the possibility that war could break out." But one could be surprised at this concern only if one thought that the USSR had "stirred up" the Arabs to war, and this, I repeat, in no way corresponds to reality. Indeed, as is evident from what has been said above, Soviet representatives committed "blunders" which, if one wished, could be wrongly interpreted, but they could not serve as proof of what was not in fact the case. The USSR, neither in 1967 nor at any other point, ever gave its blessing to the Arabs for war with Israel.

CHAPTER 2

The United Nations Response

I. William Zartman

The impending catastrophe in the Middle East in 1967 placed before the
United Nations a raw challenge to its basic mission of preserving the peace.
It failed. That much is incontestable. Less incontrovertible but potentially
more enlightening are the reasons for the failure, not as an effort to find
the culprit but as an attempt to ascertain whether failure was inevitable.
Did the UN, and the individuals who represent it, do all they could do to
maintain the peace, so that the lessons of the encounter lie in the limitations
of the world body, or were there stones left unturned, pointing to new
possibilities in future crises?

As a prelude to the subsequent conference discussion, this chapter will
review the arguments on both sides of the debate. The sides of the debate
do not at all correspond to the sides in the conflict: There are Arabs and
Israelis (and their supporters) who argue that the UN was powerless to do
more, and Israelis and Arabs (and their supporters) who maintain that the
UN did not live up to its potential. In weighing these arguments, however,
this chapter will come to the latter conclusion. For specific reasons tied to
the nature of the organization, the UN failed to meet a challenge where its
chances of making a difference were real.

Over a quarter-century later, it is important to be clear about the UN
being considered. In general, peace and security issues fall under the purview
of the Security Council, or, in case of blockage, under the General Assembly.
In these cases, it is inaccurate to speak of the UN as a corporate actor; the
responsible agencies are the member states and the UN is only the place

where they meet. This "UN" was in no position to act—or at least to take the initiative—to preserve the peace in June 1967. It was hamstrung not only by great power vetoes but by the spirit of cold war competition that underlay their use. Even where the superpower stalemate could be circumvented or harnessed in the cause of peace, the states of the nonaligned movement were lined up behind Nasser's United Arab Republic (UAR), not in support of peace-making moves. In this situation, the name "UN" refers to the only corporate actor under the UN flag—the secretary-general and his advisers in the secretariat. While there have been dynamic secretaries-general—Dag Hammarskjöld and Boutros Boutros-Ghali stand out—it is not to the secretariat that the world usually looks for decisive leadership. Thus, to begin with, the subject of evaluation is not a likely candidate for a strong response in a peace-preserving role.

There is general agreement that the period covered by the UN response was the crucial moment of the impending crisis. This is not to deny the importance of previous steps in escalation—the Fatah raids of the previous six months, the massive Israeli retaliations at al-Samu' and in the air, and the vague and provocative Israeli threat in mid-May—or of the need to deal with each of them in a de-escalatory fashion. In some of these cases, the UN could have played a role, notably in condemning the terrorist raids in the same terms in which it condemned the Israeli response, had a way been found around the Soviet veto. But the week of May 16–22, between Egypt's demand for UNEF withdrawal and its decision to reimpose the naval blockade, was the last chance to stop the locomotive of war thundering down the track, and this part of the track was guarded by the UN secretariat.

The Argument

The first line of argument in defense of the UN response to the escalating catastrophe, as presented in the following discussion, was that the secretary-general did everything he could, and what he did not do he could not because of the various structural constraints. In response to the request for orders from UNEF commander General Rikhye when served General Fawzi's request on May 16, Secretary-General U Thant the same day gave his six-point answer, essentially accepting Egypt's right to demand *total* withdrawal of UNEF but nothing less. The concentration of UAR troops along the border rendered UNEF ineffective, in jeopardy, and therefore useless. This response may have been planned as a delaying or sobering tactic but it did neither; it left the divided and uncommunicating Egyptian government with a case of overcommitment that it could not escape. Over the next two days

U Thant sounded out the UNEF committee, a necessary consulting and delaying tactic. Two major contributors to UNEF, India and Yugoslavia, were already committed to following the UAR request and withdrawing their units, whatever the UN did.

The matter was not referred to the Security Council until ten days later. It ended in an accusation match between the superpowers. Even if the Uniting for Peace procedure had been followed, guiding the matter to the General Assembly, Third World support for the UAR, backed by the Soviet Union, would have merely confirmed inaction. On May 20, the day after he ordered the complete withdrawal of UNEF, U Thant announced his intent to visit Cairo to dissuade Nasser. He left two days later, and in an early morning stopover in Paris learned of the Egyptian decision to reinstate the blockade of the Strait of Tiran. The discussion in the conference brings out the fact— or at least the interpretation—that at that point the visit would have been ineffectual and that Nasser decided on the blockade before U Thant's arrival because he did not want to refuse the secretary-general to his face.

The other side of the debate, as might be expected, is more pluralistic. One strain argues that for various reasons the Egyptian decision-making machinery was running out of control and that it presented either a voluntary or an involuntary opportunity for helpful intervention. One version of this argument is that the locomotive had two conductors fighting in the cabin, that Marshal 'Amr was vying with President Nasser for control of policy (and eventually of the state), that the military was operating on its own in ordering the full withdrawal of UNEF or in their occupation of Sharm al-Shaykh, and that Nasser would have benefited from international support for a gradual disengagement from the confrontation policy. The other version is that the locomotive was chasing the engineer, that Nasser was looking for some external help to save him from the accelerating escalation, and that the UN had an opportunity to provide a face-saving exit. A third version would be that the locomotive only looked like it was moving, that the Egyptians merely wanted to be ready to counter a possible border attack but had no desire to occupy Sharm al-Shaykh, and that a partial redeployment would not have provoked the Israelis or encouraged the Egyptians.

Many agreed facts underlie all three versions. The rivalry between 'Amr and Nasser is well known; it appeared in the open after the June War, just as the gap between military and civilian estimations of the military balance in the Middle East appears clearly in the following discussions. The notion that Sharm al-Shaykh was beyond the original intentions is contradicted by much evidence, including the initial request for UNEF's withdrawal. In this context, it is clear that Nasser was caught up in a rolling process of overcommitment, although there is no evidence that he was waiting, wanting, or willing to be saved from it by a deus ex machina *UNiensis*.

Another strain, not incompatible with the first, runs through the various paths that the secretary-general could have followed. Some of them are active and counteractive—a meeting of the Security Council to examine the Egyptian request or to consider the situation as a threat to the peace, a special session of the General Assembly (more difficult to convene in the absence of a two-thirds convoking majority), an appeal to the International Court of Justice, or an earlier trip to Cairo armed with the UN Truce Supervision Organization (UNTSO) report of May 16 on the absence of an Israeli troop buildup. Others are passive and delaying tactics—less ready acquiescence to the Egyptian request or to its all-or-nothing implications, referral of the request to the Security Council or General Assembly, or use of the UNEF Advisory Committee to reaffirm the forces' mission and importance at a time of crisis.

None of these paths was easy but none was impossible. Only the use of the International Court of Justice appears to be irrelevant to the pace of events, although there was enough positive response to the suggestion of enlisting the court's aid that even the court might have provided a temporizing alternative; the United Nations Conference on the Law of the Sea (UNCLOS I) of 1958 provided little support for the Egyptian position. It is hard to see how any of the various alternatives could have led to a worse outcome than that produced in reality or how it could have exacerbated the current situation.

Remaining Questions

It is natural for those involved in an action (or inaction) to see, in the hindsight of a quarter-century, little else that they could have done. History, after all, is authoritative. It provides conclusive proof of the unique feasibility of what was done and of the counterfactual uncertainty of untried alternatives. No criticism or opposing plan has much authority behind it. It is easy to object that incalculable consequences were hidden in its folds or that supposed options simply were not there. U Thant and his advisers did all they could, and what they did not do could not be done. The locomotive was on the rails, under full steam.

But the defense of history is more airtight than convincing. The same assurance of impossibility outside of the chosen path could have been applied with equal conviction to the outbreak of the war itself, before the event. More important, it would have been equally facile to show how the many successful peace initiatives in the Middle East (or elsewhere) were impossible in the face of the locomotive of the time. There is a nagging air of mere "adequacy" in the accounts of the secretariat's activity, of meeting the challenges on their chosen level rather than rising to surmount the crisis of the moment. The third week of May in 1967 was a moment of extraordinary challenge to the world community, and the secretariat of the world organization did not show the extraordinary leadership initiatives that challenge required. As a result, it was overcome by events, run down by a runaway locomotive while doing routine maintenance.

The discussion does not help us understand all the reasons for what happened, nor are there good answers to some of the questions and suggestions from the discussants. The problem seems to have begun with U Thant's six-point response of May 16, in which he carefully convinced the Egyptian representatives that he could respond only with a total withdrawal, an argument again developed to the UAR ambassador the next day, leading to the conclusion that continued Egyptian deployments would leave him "no choice but to order the withdrawal of UNEF from Gaza and Sinai as expeditiously as possible." Both the purpose and the reasoning are hard to follow. If total withdrawal was to be a threat or a hard choice, it was a curious threat that embodied the maximum outcome that the threatened party demanded. If it was merely a consequence, it was not a logical one. Why UNEF's presence was indivisible was never communicated. If it was expressed as a response to a nonrefusable order, it was not only procedurally flawed but internally inconsistent. Since one of the six points indicated that an implied temporary withdrawal was unacceptable, U Thant obviously felt himself able to tell the Egyptians what was acceptable and what was not. Instead, he told them that lesser interpretations of their ultimatum were unacceptable; only the maximum interpretation could be entertained and must be followed. Had Ambassador al-Kony been secretary-general, Nasser could not have hoped for a more compliant response.

In addition, before the UNEF Advisory Committee, U Thant turned a divergence of views into acquiescence with the same view, that compliance with the ultimatum was the only course possible. No time was lost after that afternoon meeting on May 18 to convey the secretary-general's compliance to Cairo and the withdrawal order to Rikhye, sent that same evening. To counter the notion that UN peacekeeping forces serve at the pleasure of the host country, the subsequent discussion section brings out a view more compatible with the peacekeeping purpose: Acceptance of the host country is required for initial stationing of peacekeeping forces, but the contract cannot later be broken by one side—that is, by the host country—alone. The discussion also brings out the view of U Thant's predecessor, Dag Hammarskjöld, that peacekeeping forces were not to be removed until they had fulfilled their aims, a criterion manifestly contradicted by plans to go to war. Instead U Thant could have responded to the Egyptian demand with questions of his own, asking about Egyptian intentions, serving as a communications channel between the UAR and Israel, seeking to clarify ambiguities in the countries' actions and purposes.

If delay was not one of the secretary-general's tactics in regard to the withdrawal ultimatum, it certainly was so in regard to his own efforts to influence the situation on the ground, the third missed opportunity. Instead of making a visit to Cairo before ordering the withdrawal of UNEF, the secretary-general waited two days after he complied with the withdrawal ultimatum and then took two more days to arrange the trip. By this time, whatever his personal intentions, Nasser was so overcommitted before his military commanders that he ordered the maritime blockade so as not to have to hear out U Thant. There were plenty of other options. The secretary-general could have gone to Sinai to inspect his peacekeeping forces (had he kept them in place). He could have made a fact-finding tour of the region. He could have led an international delegation to visit the region, splitting up to touch several capitals simultaneously; it could have included some or all of the Security Council members (X, Y, and Z plus the Big Five), or the UNEF countries (Brazil, Canada, Denmark, Norway, Sweden, India, and Yugoslavia), or the UNEF Advisory Committee members, or some other group.

It was clear during that week that the region was heading for war. The world organization had a higher purpose than responding to demands or following regulations; its challenge was to preserve the peace. That meant doing everything to avoid the two prime dangers in the situation—the direct confrontation of hostile forces and the closing of the Strait of Tiran, the latter specifically defined since 1957 as a casus belli. In the broader sense, it meant slowing down the locomotive. None of the organs of the UN seemed to have this sense and this purpose in mind. The focus of this section on the secretary-general and his advisers does not exonerate other branches of the UN; the United States could have called the Security Council at any time and through it or with other allies inaugurated a range of measures from transparency and fact-finding mechanisms to the allied flotilla opening up the Strait of Tiran. It is no defense of U.S. policy to note that Washington had other policy concerns around the world, but New York did not.

In focusing on these three points of weakness in the secretary-general's response, on May 16, 18, and 20, there is of course no assurance that a different policy would have been successful, or, a fortiori, that once this crisis had been overcome another—maybe even several—would not have emerged that would eventually have overwhelmed peace-preserving efforts. But that is no argument. The point is that at a crucial moment, the major efforts required from the peacekeeping body to try to preserve the peace were not even attempted.

Panel 2

Chairman: Dr. I. William Zartman, SAIS Johns Hopkins
Speakers:
  Sir Brian Urquhart, The Ford Foundation: "The View from New York"
  F.T. Liu, International Peace Academy: "The View from the Field"

William Zartman: After our presentations and an additional note by Samir Mutawi, we will have a collective discussion. Our focus is the UN response.

The View from New York

Brian Urquhart: I was told I have come here to defend U Thant, which is not at all my intention. My intention is to get on the record what actually happened on the UN end in the summer of 1967. I won't be going into any particularly micro or macro approaches to this, nor do I intend to speculate on the motives—good, bad, or indifferent—of the various parties to this major disaster, because I think there is enough to talk about in describing the problems of the secretary-general, which were extremely large and were not as well understood as they might have been. Also, I'm going to describe this from the point of view of what we knew at the time, which was, in view of all the things that have been said here, rather little, I must say. But I don't think there is any point in trying to be clever about all the things we didn't know or might have known. I should also say that the UN does not have an intelligence service of its own and is not, on the whole, privy to the inner workings of governments and the people who influence governments, which may or may not be a disadvantage.

There was a considerable amount of illusion indulged in, both during and after the crisis that culminated in the Six-Day War. Among the few people who couldn't indulge in many illusions were the secretary-general of the UN and his principal advisers. They had good reasons. In the first place, they were stuck with the responsibility for a peacekeeping force on the ground,

UN Deputy Undersecretary General Sir
Brian Urquhart.

including its security. They could not delegate that responsibility because
UNEF had not been set up by the Security Council, where the French and
British would have vetoed the force at the time of Suez. UNEF had been
initiated by the General Assembly and set up by the secretary-general. There
wasn't any way the secretary-general could elude that responsibility.

As was not always clear, certainly in the Western press at the time, the
secretary-general has a general responsibility to all the members of the United
Nations, not just one faction. He has to take that into account. Even if he
doesn't, the way the UN works is that there are things that are decided by
the majority of members, and if that majority is not in favor of something
it will not happen.

Last, there is the cold war context. Even though we have been out of the
cold war for only three or four years, it's difficult to remember what a pain
in the neck it was for anybody who was trying to do anything about a
regional situation, the Middle East, or Africa, or elsewhere. There was no
rational debate in the Security Council on any situation according to its
merits. Everything was seen through the distorting glass of the cold war, with
really devastating results on anything the Security Council might conceivably
have done at the time.

There were a great number of comments and speculation, to some extent self-serving, both within and outside the UN at the time and later. The secretary-general, being probably more responsible than any other individual for the initial stages, namely the question of UNEF, made a useful scapegoat. Reading one typical version of what happened in May 1967 will give an idea of the illusions held by a lot of people about UNEF. I'm quoting here from Dean Rusk, as told to his son, in *As I Saw It*. It contains the most astonishing number of errors for somebody who was supposed to know something about what happened. He says, "Without even consulting the Security Council or the General Assembly, U Thant made two decisions and they were both disastrous. First, he decided that the UN could not keep forces in any country that did not want them, and, second, he decided that if part of those forces were to be withdrawn, all would have to leave. Had U Thant at least taken Nasser's demand to the Security Council, we would have had several weeks to try to stabilize the situation and work something out. As a matter of international law it is, perhaps, true that UN forces cannot stay when the host government does not wish them to stay but on the other hand those forces were stationed there by UN action. We felt U Thant ought to have, at least, referred this matter to the UN, and we were both upset and alarmed when on May the 18th, he withdrew the entire contingent from the Sinai."

Let's just examine this quote from the back end forward. U Thant did not withdraw the entire UN contingent from the Sinai. In fact, unfortunately, they were all still there on June 5, and the first casualties of the war were seventeen Indian soldiers in Gaza. The whole point was to try to temporize and get the UNEF negotiated back in. The matter was referred to the Security Council, on May 26 specifically, and a fat lot of good it did anybody. The discussion broke down almost instantly into an East-West dogfight. There is no question about the matter in international law, and if there was any question, unfortunately, the agreement under which UNEF was on Egyptian soil in the first place, which was negotiated by Dag Hammarskjöld with President Nasser, was absolutely specific that Egyptian sovereign rights to have UNEF withdrawn were a primary condition of the arrangement. In fact, UNEF wouldn't have been there at all if that hadn't been agreed to. As far as referring to the General Assembly is concerned, a two-thirds majority is needed to summon the General Assembly to a special session, and there was nothing like a two-thirds majority of the members who thought that this was even a question that needed to be discussed, because they believed that Egypt had the legal right on its side to have UNEF withdrawn, no matter what the consequences.

What were the hard facts of the situation of UNEF in the summer of

1967? In the secretary-general's office we had been relatively concerned about what had been going on for about the previous ten months—notably the incidents originating from Syria, which were new, and the reactions of Israel. In fact, U Thant had asked for an emergency meeting of the Israeli-Syrian Mixed Armistice Commission, which hadn't met for some time, in order to deal with what he thought could become a critical situation. Those meetings finally broke down after the Israeli air action against Damascus on April 7.

Of course, we were not aware of all the machinations that were occurring: the Soviet involvement, what was or wasn't going on in Egypt, and so on. The first real news we had about a crisis concerning UNEF was on May 14, when there were clearly large Egyptian troop movements to Sinai. There was no agreement that troops couldn't move into Sinai, which after all had been Egyptian territory for more than 4,000 years, but there was a kind of gentlemen's agreement that the balance would not be disturbed without consultation. Unquestionably, moving troops into Sinai would have a destabilizing effect on the peacekeeping force, which was then in Gaza and on the old international frontier through Sinai and was also stationed in Sharm al-Shaykh.

That worry became focused on May 16, when the UNEF commander, General Rikhye, received in Gaza a message from General Muhammad Fawzi, the Egyptian chief of staff. It was a puzzling communication to begin with. It requested, "for the sake of complete security of all UN troops which install OP's along our borders, that you issue orders to withdraw all these troops immediately." Right or wrong, this communication was thought, certainly by Ralph Bunche and me, to be some kind of mistake. So the Egyptian ambassador, Muhammad Awad al-Kony, was called in on the evening of May 16, but he'd never heard of the order. He was asked please to refer to Cairo and suggest that this communication be withdrawn immediately because it was an extremely dangerous game, and also to get some clarification.

After calling Cairo, al-Kony reported that there was absolutely no question of this communication being withdrawn—on the contrary, it was Egyptian policy—and that, in any case, Egypt had a perfect right to demand the withdrawal of UNEF whenever it liked. I don't know whether he was operating on the word *withdrawal* or the word *redeployment*. We were operating on the word *withdrawal*, which was the only one we heard. He then brought up the idea of a partial withdrawal, the idea being that UNEF should defend Gaza and other parts but withdraw in the middle sector of the border. Bunche explained that one of the principles of UN peacekeeping—an important

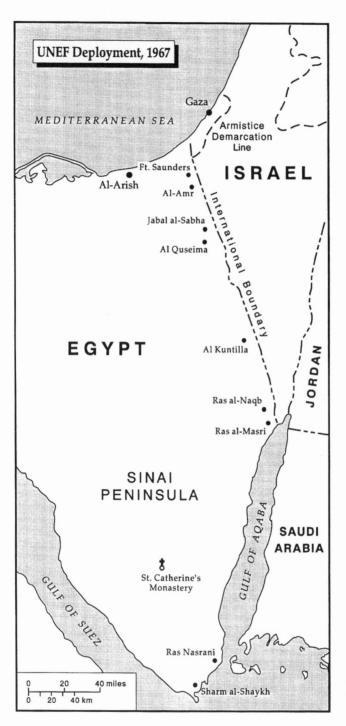

UNEF Deployment, 1967

MEDITERRANEAN SEA

Gaza

Armistice
Demarcation
Line

ISRAEL

Ft. Saunders

Al-Arish

Al-Amr

Jabal al-Sabha

Al Quseima

International Boundary

EGYPT

Al Kuntilla

JORDAN

Ras al-Naqb

Ras al-Masri

SINAI
PENINSULA

GULF OF AQABA

SAUDI
ARABIA

St. Catherine's
Monastery

GULF OF SUEZ

Ras Nasrani

0   20   40 miles
0   20   40 km

Sharm al-Shaykh

United Nations
Emergency
Force deploy-
ment, May
1967. From
Richard B. Par-
ker *The Politics
of Miscalcula-
tion in the Mid-
dle East*
(Bloomington:
Indiana Univer-
sity Press,
1993).

principle—is that it is not supposed to give any special advantage to either side in a conflict; therefore, we couldn't make any arrangement by which, effectively, UNEF would stand aside in one sector to facilitate confrontation between Israeli and Egyptian armies, while protecting Egypt's flank in the others. It was, simply, against the whole idea of peacekeeping. He also pointed out that the mandated purpose of UNEF was to prevent the recurrence of fighting, and therefore it couldn't be asked to stand aside so as to enable two sides to resume fighting. That would be a total contradiction of its basic mission.

This conversation was later ingeniously reinterpreted a number of times in several quarters to make Bunche part of whatever you'd like to call it, the Israelis' or the CIA's conspiracy to trap Egypt, or something like that. Some of you here may have dealt with Bunche, and you know he was not a devious person. It is inconceivable that he would have been involved in such a thing, and what he was stating was simply the principles under which peacekeeping forces have to operate if they are to be respected. If there was any doubt about Egypt's intentions, the events on the ground relieved that doubt; they certainly did in our minds.

Rikhye had been presented on May 16 with a demand for immediate withdrawal from al-Sabah, the main UNEF post on the old international border, and from Sharm al-Shaykh, on the Strait of Tiran. He was told that withdrawal must take place that very night because the Egyptians were going to move in the next day.

On May 17, we hadn't yet got, and were hoping not to get, a formal request for UNEF withdrawal, but U Thant thought he should warn the countries with troops serving in UNEF. So he met informally with the ambassadors of these countries to explain what had happened and to ask them what they knew about it. At that meeting, the UN legal counsel, Constantine Stavropoulos, was asked for a legal opinion, and he said there wasn't any question that if a state withdrew its consent to the presence of a peacekeeping force on its sovereign territory, it had to go. The two countries with the two largest contingents in UNEF were Yugoslavia and India, and they both strongly supported not only the principle but also the withdrawal of UNEF. We were quite surprised at this, and we only discovered the reason the next day.

On the next day, the formal request for withdrawal was received, and we then formally summoned the Advisory Committee for UNEF, made up of representatives of the countries providing the troops. Before this, in a meeting with Ambassador al-Kony, we had said that the secretary-general wished to send an extremely strong appeal to President Nasser, pointing out the highly dangerous consequences that were almost certain if UNEF was withdrawn in this way. Al-Kony, after consultation, told us for God's sake not to send this appeal, that it would be publicly rebuffed; there was absolutely no question about changing the decision, and the appeal would merely serve to make matters worse. At that point, U Thant said that he wished to restate his feelings about the probable consequences of what was happening, and he told al-Kony that he, himself, would go to Cairo to talk to President Nasser and that he proposed to take Ralph Bunche with him. After a suitable pause, al-Kony got a response from Cairo, which said, "Fine" but that it would be extremely unwise to bring Ralph Bunche, an American, since some segments of Egyptian opinion were incensed with the United States, presumably over public statements about the inadmissibility of UNEF's withdrawal.

One thing that hasn't been mentioned here is the enormous indignation in Cairo at the idea that UNEF was an occupation force that had an independent right to stay on Egyptian soil regardless of Egyptian consent. More particularly, ten years before, Israel had invoked its sovereignty to say that UNEF could not be stationed on the Israeli side of the line and nobody had ever challenged it, although Dag Hammarskjöld had made a number of unsuccessful attempts to get Israel to change its position. Statements in the Western press and by people in Congress and in various parliaments created an angry and intransigent atmosphere in Cairo, which had a great deal to do with the difficulty of reversing its course.

After withdrawal had been requested formally, U Thant met with the Advisory Committee to inform them, to hear their views, and to say that in the circumstances he had no option but to call for the withdrawal of UNEF. No one in the Advisory Committee, much as they regretted it, could think of a single good reason why that wasn't the only thing he could do. Under Hammarskjöld's formulation, if the UNEF was to be withdrawn, the Advisory Committee was to be consulted and would, if it thought fit, refer the matter to the General Assembly, which had set up UNEF. The Advisory Committee did not do this in May 1967 for the simple reason that they knew in advance that there would not be a two-thirds majority to call the assembly into session.

We also learned at that meeting that on the previous day the ambassadors of the countries providing troops in UNEF had been called into the Foreign Office in Cairo and had been told that their troops were to be withdrawn. Both India and Yugoslavia informed us that they had immediately agreed, which meant, in fact, that we didn't really have an operational force anymore. This was the first time we heard of their agreement to withdraw.

Bunche, who was a down-to-earth person and not one to try to escape into illusions when faced with a difficult situation, put before the Advisory Committee, and later on the press, the hard facts of the decision that U Thant was being compelled to take. There was a rider in this decision, which was mentioned to the Advisory Committee: While in principle the UN couldn't refuse the request to withdraw, the withdrawal would be orderly, dignified, and deliberate—ODD—and it would thus take a hell of a long time. In fact, the whole of UNEF was still there two weeks later, except for the Canadians, who had been informed by the Egyptians that they could not ensure the safety of the Canadian contingent after some of the things that had been said in Ottawa. The Canadians withdrew in twenty-four hours, leaving us without any logistics or air component.

UNEF's presence was based on Egypt's consent because the buffer zone where it operated was Egyptian territory. In 1957, when UNEF moved up to the Israeli borders and into Sharm al-Shaykh, General Burns, who was then the commander, made an unpublished local agreement with the Egyptian military authority, sanctioned by Hammarskjöld, under which the Egyptian forces would stay 500 meters away from the armistice line in Gaza and 2,000 meters away from the former international border in Sinai. It was in this space, this buffer zone, that UNEF operated. When Egyptian troops moved up to the line and filled the buffer zone, there was no space for UNEF to operate, and nobody had ever suggested in 1957, or after, that Egypt did not have the right to move its own troops on its own territory. Egypt had simply agreed that it would not move into the buffer zone, and when it did so on May 18, that was the end of the buffer zone function.

Bunche had another valid worry, a hard fact: Gaza, a volatile place at the best of times. In the UN's previous experiences, notably in the Congo, we had bravely said that UN peacekeeping forces would stay on regardless [of the host government's attitude] but had been informed that calling out the populace to harass the small UN force would end its stay because it was not allowed to use force and would be overwhelmed. The Egyptians, likewise, could call out the people of Gaza to make life impossible for UNEF. Bunche mentioned this possibility as one of the hard facts that nobody except those responsible had to face.

There was no easy solution. It wasn't possible to pass the buck to the General Assembly because you couldn't summon the assembly. U Thant felt strongly that to go to the Security Council would simply precipitate an undignified East-West dogfight, of no help in calming things down in the Middle East. In fact, when the council did take up this matter on May 26, that's exactly what happened.

While U Thant was on his way to Cairo, President Nasser made the speech declaring the blockade of the Strait of Tiran. U Thant was of two minds as to whether to go on. He did go in the end, but all of his efforts to keep the lid on, to have some kind of moratorium, did not work. He was impressed by President Nasser's determination to go ahead on the suicidal course he had selected.

Meanwhile, in New York, we tried various possibilities. We suggested, for example, a special representative to travel in the area and try to defuse some of the rumors, like that of the twelve Israeli brigades, which had led to the whole mess in the first place. That was turned down by the Israelis, though later on we got Gunnar Jarring in precisely that function. We suggested that if UNEF was inactive, we should revive the old armistice machinery of the military observers as a stopgap. The Israelis, who had denounced the armistice agreement in 1956, also did not agree to that. It was also suggested, I think perhaps quixotically, that the Israelis might take UNEF on their side of the line, and that too was absolutely refused. In fact, the Israeli representative said, "Ridiculous, Israel is not the Salvation Army and would not be willing to accept UN discards from Egypt," according to Bunche's notes on the meeting.

After U Thant's return from Cairo, it seemed as if we had exhausted anything that could be done and so had the Security Council. U Thant tried hard to get a breathing space in which no one would do anything. We tried to bring forces to bear to reinstate UNEF. UNEF troops were still there, but they simply couldn't function. On June 5, you all know what happened.

In a conversation a year later, which you [Richard Parker] quote in your book [The Policy of Miscalculation in the Middle East], Bunche asked Dr. Mahmoud Fawzi, the Egyptian vice-president for foreign affairs, how he thought this disaster had happened. Fawzi replied, "Gross miscalculations based on gross misinformation." I think that's certainly a large part of the explanation, and the other large part was the cold war context, which made it difficult to do anything sensible about the crisis.

Was there a communications problem between the Egyptians and the UN? Is it true that Egypt didn't intend to have UNEF evacuate Sharm al-Shaykh? Yes, I think there was a communications problem, because I'm not sure whom we were really dealing with or that Ambassador al-Kony knew either, and I think some of the things said this morning bear that out. I personally never had any doubt that the Egyptians intended to have Sharm al-Shaykh evacuated because they turned up and took it. That seems to me to be a funny thing to do if they didn't really mean it. Later on it was said by Dean Rusk and others that the Egyptians hadn't really meant it [evacuation], but I never saw much evidence of that. If you're not going to do something, it's best not to do it.

Could the UN have accommodated an Egyptian request for redeployment of UNEF rather than withdrawal, if that was what the Egyptians actually had in mind? Bunche felt strongly that redeployment was absolutely against the operating principles of peacekeeping forces and that if you did it once you would discredit the whole business. I think he was right. There would have been an uproar in all sorts of places if we had done that, and we would have been acting against our own principles.

Richard Parker: You said you read the word *withdrawal* as meaning withdrawal. In one of the points that Heikal raises, he says that Nasser had tried to change *withdrawal* to *redeployment*.

Brian Urquhart: Yes, but we didn't know that then.

Richard Parker: Well, would it have made any difference if he had changed it?

Brian Urquhart: Frankly, I'm not sure it would have made any difference. It would depend on what was meant by redeployment, but if we were opening up a narrow front for an attack by overwhelmingly large forces and we're protecting Gaza, which was difficult to protect against the Israelis, I don't see how any serious person could have done this while posing as an impartial, objective international peacekeeping force, and that's the whole point of the thing. Once you take sides, you're out, that's it. Nobody came back on this. The next day we got a request for a full withdrawal. If there had been a real intention of having just a redeployment, I don't think they would have taken Sharm al-Shaykh in the first place.

Another of the questions posed to us by the conference moderator was whether U Thant could have stalled on the Egyptian request. How would the Egyptians have reacted if he had? Well, of course he was, to some extent, stalling on the Egyptian request by the "orderly, deliberate, and dignified" withdrawal formula, because that was going to take several months. But I think this was academic after the announcement of the blockade of the Strait of Tiran on May 22. After that point, stalling or not stalling, the Egyptians didn't really have too much to do with what was going to happen next.

Richard Parker: Can I ask for a clarification on that point? When I said stalling, I meant that when U Thant got the letter from Mahmoud Riad on May 18 asking for withdrawal, he immediately sent a telegram to Rikhye, ordering him to organize a withdrawal.

Brian Urquhart: That's right.

Richard Parker: That's what I meant by my question about stalling. Could he have drawn the process out at that point?

Brian Urquhart: Our judgment was that already in Cairo there was enormous indignation at the implication that UNEF was an occupying force. The issue came up over and over again. There is no question that we were under two legal obligations. One was the arrangement made by Hammarskjöld with Nasser, and the other was the general principle enunciated by the legal counsel, which after all has wide application. We're not just talking about the Middle East here, we're talking about the UN presence in all kinds of places. If a UN peacekeeping force can suddenly be turned into an obligatory presence, then nobody is going to accept this kind of arrangement in the future. Consent is an important point of principle here. What U Thant and Bunche wanted to do was to say, "All right, we warned you about this" (which they did in no uncertain terms). "This is an extremely dangerous affair; we have absolutely no alternative if you insist but to accept withdrawal, but we will continue to try to find a way of renegotiating this." That was the whole object. That is why UNEF was still there on June 5. And I don't see, in the hard circumstances of the case, what else they were supposed to do.

I think you also ought to remember that the UN is a supposedly universal organization, and a large majority of the members, including the two most important members of the Advisory Committee, the ones who had the largest number of troops in UNEF, were absolutely adamant on immediate withdrawal. They had in fact already agreed to it. We learned about that only the day after they had already accepted. So we were in a mess in a different number of ways, and we had to try and figure out some way of getting out of it. We were not helped, I must confess, in this period by some of the things that were said, especially in the Western world, where there was a lot of huffing and puffing about the Egyptian dictator and how dare he, and the weakness of the UN, and so on. That made matters a great deal worse.

Finally, would it have made any difference if the secretary-general had gone immediately to Cairo or sent a senior member of his staff as soon as the first Egyptian request was received? My impression is that Nasser's resolve was so firm that it wouldn't have mattered who went.

The basis of this disaster was that UNEF was a symptom of a symbol. What we were really talking about was an unresolved twenty years of belligerency in the area, which had been kept under the rug by UNEF and which suddenly erupted. Moreover, it is impossible to overestimate the paralyzing nature of the cold war context in which all this was taking place.

Eugene Rostow: Were you and the secretary-general conscious of the Hammarskjöld memorandum that settled the procedures in 1957?

Brian Urquhart: I am sorry you asked that question, Gene, because it's a long subject. I was conscious of the memorandum because I was at that point writing a biography of Hammarskjöld and had been into his personal papers in Stockholm. U Thant and Bunche were not conscious of it because it wasn't part of the official papers at all. It was written in August 1957. When he had a little time on his hands, Hammarskjöld liked to dictate notes to himself. I don't know whether you have tried to read that memorandum, but it comes out on all sides of the question, and what it is basically is a description of his efforts to convince Nasser to have UNEF in Egypt at all. Nasser was resistant to it, I think with some reason. He had just been invaded by three foreign armies. Egypt had a long history of foreign occupation, and he wanted to be absolutely sure of the conditions under which this new lot were coming in before he agreed to it.

The procedure for UNEF was laid down in the document for the General Assembly, a report by Hammarskjöld, and the procedure was very simple: UNEF was on the Suez Canal, not on the Israeli border, which UNEF went to only in March 1957. But there was also the "good faith agreement" that Hammarskjöld had concluded with Nasser. It was a typically Hammarskjöldian arrangement which said that neither side, neither the UN nor Egypt, would seek the termination of UNEF unless they felt in good faith that its task had been completed. The task referred to was the evacuation of the British and French on the Suez Canal zone and the beginning of the Israeli evacuation. At that time nobody knew that UNEF was going to finish up on the international frontier and on the armistice line between Egypt and Israel.

Other parts of the agreement make it clear that Egyptian sovereignty and the Egyptian sovereign right to call for the withdrawal of UNEF were paramount in the understanding between Nasser and Hammarskjöld. Hammarskjöld also said that if at any time, for any reason, either the UN or Egypt wanted the withdrawal of UNEF, the secretary-general would refer the matter to the Advisory Committee, which U Thant did, and the Advisory Committee, would, if it thought wise, refer the matter to the General Assembly. That was what Hammarskjöld laid down. Lester Pearson, who was a member of the Advisory Committee in 1956 and 1957, because Canada was a charter member of UNEF, expressed at the time grave reservations about the arrangement Hammarskjöld had made. He said something to the effect that this was a fragile arrangement and one that is going to give us a lot of trouble sometime in the future. How right he was. When the '67 debacle came about, he quoted that in the Canadian House of Commons.

So the idea that in some way Hammarskjöld miraculously could have done something completely different and would have handled the whole thing better is probably an illusion. As Hammarskjöld says in the memorandum, it was touch and go whether Nasser was going to agree to this arrangement at all, and he had a tremendous struggle to get him to agree to it. I think that it is understandable why.

Leonard Meeker: A comment on the legal status of UNEF: It's right that the force could not go into place without the consent of Egypt. The force was placed there by agreement between the UN and Egypt, but that did create a new situation in which, I think, the agreement could not be unilaterally terminated, suddenly, by one party, namely by Egypt. The question does need to be raised as to what would have happened politically if the secretary-general, instead of agreeing to withdraw at once, had dug his heels in firmly and at once said to Egypt, "Well that, of course, is impossible. Naturally, I'll have to refer this to the appropriate organs of the UN who can consider your demand in this case."

The General Assembly was not in session, and it would have been difficult to convoke it at that particular time, but I think people recognized that the situation was so serious that it would have been appropriate to take it to the Security Council. The council clearly, given its powers under chapter 7, could have taken some action, which might just have averted the war. Insofar as the law is concerned, I disagree with the view of Constantine Stavropoulos. I don't think that an agreement made in the way this one was could be annihilated overnight by just one of the parties.

Tahsin Basheer: Brian's rendering of the events is correct. However, I'm not sure that the UN did canvass voting in the General Assembly. Did you meet with the different blocs to make sure of the conclusion you reached that two-thirds would not accept it? That's no. 1. You could have canvassed votes not to discuss the issue of withdrawal versus nonwithdrawal; you could have canvassed issues for a meeting to elect a group for good offices between Egypt and the whole situation. That's no. 2. No. 3, U Thant could have stalled for a longer time while saying, "Yes, I accept, but let's satisfy all conditions." Nasser was not against the idea of a moratorium. He accepted it. U Thant in the end, when they had disagreed on everything, said, "Let's cool it, let's freeze the situation as it is, Israel will not test it, you will not test it and nobody will do anything else."

But question no. 4 is this agreement between Hammarskjöld and Nasser. In the UN, you must have known, others must have known, and Ralph Bunche did know of the American commitment to Israel regarding the Gulf of Aqaba, to which Egypt was not a party. That was not highlighted to the Egyptians or to anybody else. In fact, Egypt never received any official version of that agreement until Dick Nolte was in Cairo; that was in May, after the events.

Richard Parker: The agreement was covered in the *New York Times* in 1957.

Tahsin Basheer: We don't read the *New York Times*. The agreement was never communicated or repeated by the American government during the crisis.

Gideon Rafael: I would like to give you the facts as Israel knew them. On May 15, 1967, I got a signal from Jerusalem to ask the secretary-general to inform the Egyptian government immediately that Israel has no belligerent intentions whatsoever and that the information or disinformation spread by the Soviet Union about Israeli troop concentrations was false. Ralph Bunche transmitted this information to Cairo on May 15.

On May 16, the answer came, canceling the position of UNEF on Egyptian soil. There was never any question from Nasser or the Egyptian government about the meaning of the message that we had sent, or even an expression of doubt or suspicion. The Egyptian government had decided, as is well known from documents, to evict UNEF. This became known to us on May 17, together with a statement issued by the UN and the secretary-general that the UN would have to withdraw all its forces from their positions. At that point we intervened personally again with U Thant and Bunche, telling them that this was a disastrous decision and that if the UN felt obliged to move or redeploy its forces, it must insist on keeping its forces at Sharm al-Shaykh, controlling the entrance to the Gulf of Aqaba and to the Israeli port of Eilat. I received a reply from the secretary-general that either Egypt would keep the entire UN force or he would withdraw it in its totality.

I showed U Thant the documents that were the basis for the deployment of UNEF as decided in 1957. On March 1, 1957, Israel's foreign minister declared before the UN General Assembly Israel's conditions for the withdrawal from Sinai, including the statement that the restoration or reinstitution of the blockade in the Gulf of Aqaba would evoke Israel's legitimate right of self-defense. In other words, the reinstitution of the blockade would be a casus belli. We had an argument about the meaning of the documents from 1957. U Thant was not fully aware of the proceedings at the time, although he had published, in September 1966, a report to the General

Assembly saying that should UNEF be removed from its position, it would cause the outbreak of a new war between Egypt and Israel.

In his report of June 26 to the General Assembly, U Thant stated after the war that Egypt's demand to move its forces up to the line meant an inevitable confrontation with Israel. These facts were known to the UN at the time. In May 1967 he had told the Egyptians that they should reconsider their position [on withdrawal of the peacekeeping force]. He got a negative reply, and when he contemplated sending a message directly to President Nasser he was told by Foreign Minister Riad not to do that because he would be rebuffed. So U Thant dispensed with that message.

Believing that the crisis was growing more and more severe, Israel suggested, through the good offices of the U.S. delegation, that the secretary-general visit Cairo, Jerusalem, and Damascus in a last major effort to prevent the war. As Sir Brian has mentioned, when U Thant was on his way to Cairo, he was surprised at a stopover in Paris to hear that Nasser had declared the reinstitution of the blockade. At that point I was called at night in New York and was asked whether Israel suggested that the secretary-general proceed with his mission although it seemed to him a mission impossible. I answered that he should proceed because no chance should be missed to convince Nasser to refrain from any further act that could inflame the situation or bring about a new conflagration. When U Thant returned from his failed mission, and I don't blame him for the failure, he drafted a letter to the heads of the governments of Israel and of Egypt, asking for a breathing spell of two weeks.

On May 29, while I was transmitting this letter to Prime Minister Eshkol, I got a call from Ralph Bunche, in the name of the secretary-general, to stop transmission; he had canceled that letter. As we found out—as Bunche admitted—U Thant had canceled his letter because President Nasser objected to it. So even the last-minute appeal on May 29 was frustrated.

We, on our part, did not leave any stone unturned to prevent that war through diplomatic action. Not only did we act with the secretary-general by asking him to involve the UN organs to support his view and [by arguing] that the agreement on stationing UNEF could not be canceled unilaterally. Israel also acted in the three capitals of the West: Foreign Minister Abba Eban went to Paris, London, and Washington to explain the gravity of the situation. By June 5 the Israeli government concluded that no international action would take place. There was no possibility that the blockade, the war measure, which entitled us to self-defense, would be rescinded.

Brian Urquhart: A footnote to what Gideon Rafael has said about the moratorium, which I think Tahsin Basheer also asked about, because I think that there is something that he doesn't know. When U Thant came back, he decided, among other things, as Gideon Rafael said, to appeal to both Nasser and Eshkol to exercise restraint and specifically also to Nasser to refrain from interfering with Israeli shipping through the Strait of Tiran during the so-called breathing spell. And as Ambassador Rafael has said, those letters were sent to the Israeli and Egyptian ambassadors to be transmitted. Bunche then got a call from an extremely agitated Ambassador al-Kony, who said that in U Thant's talks in Cairo, it had been agreed that the moratorium would include an appeal to all countries not to send oil or strategic materials to Israel through the strait. This was the first that Bunche or I had heard of this particular provision. Bunche told U Thant that this would mean, in fact, that he as secretary-general would be imposing and implementing a blockade on his own, without any kind of authorization, and that it simply was out of the question. The Israeli ambassador was thus asked not to transmit the letter because the Egyptian ambassador would transmit it only if it included this clause, and we didn't think that under the circumstances this clause could be put in.[1]

The View from the Field

F.T. Liu: While Brian Urquhart was in New York with the secretary-general and Ralph Bunche, exerting their best efforts to avoid the withdrawal of UNEF, General Rikhye, the force commander, was in Gaza, and I was in Jerusalem as senior adviser to UNTSO, the United Nations Truce Supervision Organization, one of the two UN peacekeeping operations in the area. Unfortunately, General Rikhye cannot be with us today, but his views are well known because he has described them in his book *The Sinai Blunder*. I have discussed them many times with him. We have some differences of view on points of detail and procedures, but on the basic issues we are in agreement. We felt, as at UN headquarters, that the withdrawal of UNEF would have extremely dangerous consequences. On the other hand, we were aware that if Egypt should maintain its request and Israel should continue to refuse to accept UNEF on its territory, then the withdrawal would become inevitable.

---

1. From Ramsis Nassif, *U Thant in New York,* the UN memorandum of the meeting between U Thant and Nasser on May 24 reads: "SG stated that he would cable Bunche tonight *if possible* to carry out consultations to persuade Israel not to send shipping through the Gulf ~~for some time~~ and other ~~countries~~ to refrain from sending strategic materials to Eilat as *required* by the UAR" (italicized items were added and those lined through were deleted by U Thant from the draft). [The Egyptians had said they considered petroleum products to be strategic materials.—Ed.]

F. T. Liu, political advisor, UN Truce
Supervision Organization, Jersualem, 1967.

At the beginning of the crisis, we were told by the secretary-general that
the matter was being handled in New York and that we should not deal
with it in our areas. We followed his order strictly. While the negotiations
were going on in New York, General Rikhye's job was mainly to hold UNEF
together and uphold its morale in trying circumstances, and he did that job
splendidly. Although their governments immediately sided with Egypt, the
Yugoslav and Indian contingents of UNEF behaved with discipline and
followed the instructions of the force commander. The Yugoslav troops,
especially, which were deployed along the Sinai border and the Sharm al-
Shaykh area, had a bad time because the Egyptian troops were moving to
the border, surrounding them. But they demonstrated discipline, dignity,
and courage.

At UNTSO we were following the developments closely, both in New
York and in the UNEF area. At the same time, we were preparing contingency
plans, because if UNEF were to be withdrawn, UNTSO would become the
only UN peacekeeping operation in the region. At that time the mandate
of UNTSO was to assist the parties in supervising the observance and application of the general armistice agreements concluded in 1949 between Israel
and its four Arab neighbors, under the auspices of Ralph Bunche, then UN
acting mediator for Palestine.

From 1956, UNTSO's role in the Egyptian sector had been greatly reduced.
In 1956, during the Suez crisis, Israel denounced its armistice agreement
with Egypt, and after the withdrawal of Israeli forces from the Sinai and
Gaza, UNEF took charge of peacekeeping duties in the Egyptian sector.
Nevertheless, we continued to maintain the Egypt-Israel Mixed Armistice
Commission in Gaza. The position of the secretary-general was that the

armistice agreements could be terminated only with the consent of both parties or by a decision of the Security Council. Since neither condition was met, the Mixed Armistice Commission was maintained, but without the cooperation and participation of Israel it became largely symbolic. Consequently, the group of UNTSO military observers in Gaza was reduced to a bare minimum of six. In the other sectors, the armistice agreements remained in force, but the performance of the three Mixed Armistice Commissions varied widely from one sector to the other. The Lebanese sector was fairly quiet and its commission worked well. The situation was more disturbed in the Jordanian sector, and the Israel-Jordan Mixed Armistice Commission could meet only rarely, in special sessions. The worst of the three was the Syrian sector. There were many incidents, and the Israel-Syria Mixed Armistice Commission (ISMAC) had been paralyzed since the mid-1950s because of the boycott by Israel.

The situation in the Syrian sector further deteriorated in early 1966 when an extremist branch of the Ba'ath Party took control of the Syrian government after a military coup. There were many incidents in the course of 1966, and on January 1 and 2, 1967, two serious incidents arose out of the dispute over land in the demilitarized zone, which had been set up by the 1949 Israel-Syria armistice agreement on the Israeli side of the armistice demarcation line. On January 15, Secretary-General U Thant appealed to both sides for restraint and urged them to meet in the Mixed Armistice Commission in an effort to settle the disputed lands. Both sides accepted, but the negotiations broke down after two meetings because of the differences over the agenda. The Syrians insisted that the negotiations should be confined to the problem of disputed lands, while Israel wanted to examine the larger problem of peace and peace arrangements.

The collapse of these negotiations caused tensions to rise again, and on April 7 there was a series of serious incidents. There have been suggestions that those incidents were engineered by Israel. I have no opinion on that, but I would like to recall the events that took place.

Early that day, an Israeli tractor appeared on one of the disputed lands in the demilitarized zone. The Syrians fired at the tractor from their positions on the Golan Heights, as they usually did. Immediately, hundreds of Israeli planes were launched to attack not only the military positions on the Golan Heights but also several localities well inside Syria, including Damascus. In a dogfight over Damascus between Israeli and Syrian jet fighters, six Syrian MIGs were shot down.

A number of ominous developments followed. During high-level meetings between Syrian and Egyptian leaders, the Syrians, who had long accused

Israeli Prime Minister Levi Eshkol visiting Ein Gev, on the eastern shore of the Sea of Galilee, April 8, 1967, inspecting damage following the border clash and air battle over Damascus on April 7. The man on his far right is Chief of Staff Yitzhak Rabin. By permission of AP/Wide World Photos.

Nasser of hiding behind UNEF, apparently persuaded him to play a more active role in the common struggle against Israel. There were troop movements in many parts of the region and inflammatory statements on both sides.

Around May 11, there were persistent rumors from Arab and Soviet sources that Israel was massing troops near the Syrian borders and was about to launch a major offensive against Syria. After inspecting the border area, UNTSO reported to the secretary-general that there was no evidence of any Israeli build-up. U Thant made public the report and appealed again to the parties for restraint, as Ambassador Rafael has said. Nevertheless, tension continued to heighten, and on the evening of May 16 the message from General Fawzi to General Rikhye set off the crisis we are discussing now.

There is no doubt that the secretary-general, Bunche, and Brian [Urquhart] in New York did everything possible to avoid the withdrawal of UNEF, and the severe criticisms leveled against U Thant were unfair. I have only two comments, with the benefit of hindsight. First, U Thant should perhaps have invoked article 99 of the UN Charter, so as to bring the matter before the Security Council. That would not have changed anything; certainly it would not have gained time, as some speakers have suggested. The result would have been the same, but the blame would have been laid on the Security Council and perhaps on the two superpowers—not on U Thant.

My other comment is that the criticism against U Thant has been especially severe because, again with the benefit of hindsight, we now know that the withdrawal of UNEF eventually led to a destructive war. But on May 18, 1967, there was no reason to believe that the withdrawal of UNEF would necessarily mean war. It would create tension, it would have dangerous consequences, but war was still avoidable.

Under the contingency plans prepared by UNTSO in case UNEF was withdrawn, we were to try to revive the Mixed Armistice Commission, but that failed. We also decided to increase the number of the military observers in Gaza and, as the first step, to send immediately twenty-five military observers from Jerusalem. That was accepted by both sides. In the meeting that I had with my counterpart, Ambassador Moshe Sasson, the director of armistice affairs at the Israeli Foreign Ministry, he told me that although the position of Israel regarding the armistice agreement remained unchanged, it would cooperate with the UN, and the twenty-five military observers could pass through the Israeli checkpoint without impediment.

He also told me that Israel would exercise the utmost restraint and would do everything possible to avoid war. But at the same time, he warned against two possible developments: an increase in terrorist activities from Gaza by

Palestinian fedayeen and, more serious, the closure of the Gulf of Aqaba to Israeli shipping. He said that such an action would be a casus belli for Israel. We, of course, immediately cabled this information to New York, and U Thant decided to visit Cairo on May 23—mainly, I believe, to persuade Nasser not to close the Gulf of Aqaba. Unfortunately, during the night of May 22–23, while U Thant stopped over in Paris en route to Cairo, President Nasser announced the closure of the Gulf of Aqaba. When U Thant arrived in Cairo on May 23, he asked Nasser, "Why did you do it? I came here to discuss this matter with you." Nasser replied, "I didn't want to say no to you, that's why I decided to close the Gulf of Aqaba before your arrival." With this decision, fate was sealed. War became inevitable; it broke out on the morning of June 5.

I recall one episode that has some significance for our discussion. On the morning of June 5, I received a call around 8:00 from the Israeli Foreign Ministry. It was Ambassador Aryeh Lourie, the director general, who was then acting foreign minister because Abba Eban had left for New York to attend the Security Council meeting. The director general wanted to see General Bull, the chief of staff of UNTSO, and me urgently. We met him at the ministry around 8:45. He told us that about an hour earlier an Israeli position had been attacked by Egyptian troops and that the Israeli armed forces had begun military action against Egypt. War had started. Then he asked us to transmit a message to King Hussein to the effect that the Israeli forces would not attack the Jordanian troops if not attacked by them. We immediately transmitted the message to King Hussein through the senior Jordanian delegate to the Mixed Armistice Commission. Despite that, fighting began in Jerusalem around noon and soon spread to the entire Jordanian front. King Hussein later said that he had received the message, but by that time he had no control over the situation because the Jordanian troops were then under Egyptian command.

Commentary

Samir Mutawi: Talking about Samu' at this point may seem a little too late. But given the question of why the raid was directed against Jordan rather than against Syria, there are some points to be made about perceptions. I think the 1967 war started partly as a response to the wrong perceptions. At the time it seemed to everybody that Israel would attack Syria rather than Jordan, because the raid that caused the reprisal against Samu' originated from Syria, by al-Fatah, which was backed by the Syrian military.

In interviews that I conducted for my book [*Jordan in the 1967 War*], one of the interpretations was that Samu' was a sign of weakness on the part of Israel. Arab public opinion had been persuaded by the Syrian and Egyptian media that Israel knew that its real enemy was Syria but was afraid to take action against it that might escalate into full-scale war; it therefore struck at a country that was militarily weak and unlikely to retaliate. Both the Egyptian and the Syrian press expressed at the time their conviction that the growth of the Egyptian army had made it a formidable force that the Israelis were scared to confront.

This is an important point because it bears, as I said, on perceptions. The Syrian press went even farther, expressing the view that Samu' was evidence of the success of the newly established defense pact between Egypt and Syria. The Jordanians interpreted this stance as a method of encouraging Nasser to adopt more aggressive responses to Israeli provocations against Syria.

Another point I recorded from those interviews was that Jordan's participation in the war later on must be viewed in the light of the experience at Samu'. The Israeli raid was supposed to be a reprisal for events undertaken not by Jordan but by Syria. The Jordanians thus concluded that one of the purposes behind the attack was to demonstrate to the Arab world that as far as the Israelis were concerned, all Arabs were their enemies, whether they were Jordanians, Syrians, or Egyptians. This interpretation of Samu' is of the utmost importance in explaining later events.

First, it heightened Jordanian leaders' awareness that Jordan's weak defenses made the West Bank a prime target for Israel. The raid thus convinced them that they needed to cooperate with other Arab nations and to seek to join them in a system of regional defense.

Second, the Jordanian leadership felt that the raid was designed to deepen divisions in the Arab world. The Israeli attack led to charges from Syria and Egypt that the Jordanian government was incompetent, unable to defend its citizens, and that its leaders were unfit to rule. Such charges hardened the rift between the Arab nations and destroyed any possibility that the Unified Arab Command (UAC) would become an effective regional defense system. According to the Jordanians, the Israelis hoped that the Arabs would be so divided that they would be unable to mount any future coordinated attack on Israel.

Third, the raid resulted in such a feeling of insecurity and panic among the people living on the border with Israel that the Jordanian army was forced to spread itself even more thinly along that border, thus decreasing its effectiveness.

Fourth, the Jordanians believed that Samu' was designed to provoke West Bank citizens to rebel against their government, which Arab propaganda had already accused of being too soft on Israel. According to this theory, unrest in the West Bank might become so severe that it could be used as an excuse by the Israelis to invade. They could claim, so the Jordanians said, that the danger of West Bank Palestinians gaining the upper hand in Jordan represented a threat that they could not tolerate.

Fifth, the Jordanians also believed that the Israelis intended for the Samu' raid to have an inflammatory effect on public opinion, which was already intoxicated by Egyptian, Syrian, and PLO propaganda against King Hussein and his government. This heat would make it extremely difficult for Jordan, and I quote a senior Jordanian military officer, "to stay out of any serious confrontation between the Arabs and Israel in the future." Certain of its military superiority, Israel would seize the opportunity to occupy the West Bank.

My final point was actually Wasfi Tel's impression at the time. Wasfi Tel had been the Jordanian prime minister in 1966, when Samu' took place. He personally believed that Samu' had been a dress rehearsal for 1967 and that the Israelis, by hitting not at Syria but at Jordan, actually wanted to entice Jordanian public opinion to rebel against the government; the government would then take retaliatory action against Israel, thus giving the Israelis the long-awaited opportunity to attack back. Because of that belief, Wasfi Tel stood firmly and stubbornly against any alliance with Egypt or Syria in the future and against any possibility of going into war with Israel.

Discussion

Meir Amit: In regard to Samu', I was shocked, really shocked [to hear Samir Mutawi's theory]. The proclaimed Israeli policy is to protect the Hashemite regime. To this day, it is the official view of the government of Israel to keep the Hashemite regime because this is the most favorable regime to us. So I cannot understand, Mr. Mutawi, the strange theory you have developed. It seems to me you worked backward. You created facts to justify a certain theory, but the truth of the matter is that we never, never wanted King Hussein to be harmed.

Carl Brown: He was reporting what people thought.

Meir Amit: Okay.

Carl Brown: Perceptions are important.

Meir Amit: I am also reporting what my perception is. My perception is that this was a wrong presentation.

Carl Brown: Your perception is important, too.

Meir Amit: Okay, so you can make up your mind afterward. But you must take into account that when a school bus full of kids is hit [by terrorists], there must be some eruption, some retaliation, something must be done— there are internal pressures. We are a democratic country; the prime minister has to take into account various opinions. But you said, Mr. Mutawi, that was a sign of weakness. I think it was a sign of restraint, because that was immediately after the pact between Syria and Egypt and we didn't want to escalate. On the contrary, we wanted not to go to Syria. Maybe in retrospect it [to attack Jordan instead] was a mistake. But to develop a theory that it was Israel's intention to topple the Jordanian regime or to create an uprising of the population against King Hussein couldn't have been our intent; it doesn't make sense to me, at least.

Let me come back to the UN. First, I think that in the whole presentation of the UN position here, you failed to mention that between May 15 and June 5 there were maybe five or six sessions of the UN Security Council. The United States did whatever it could to get a resolution to reprimand the Egyptians, but it couldn't get nine votes in favor. For us it was a questionable sign. It's not important; a decision of the United Nations is not important. We know that, but it was a sign. My last point is the remark that has been made about [the events of] April 7: that hundreds of Israeli airplanes took part. This is totally untrue. We didn't have that many planes; we used maybe two, three squadrons for the whole thing, just for the record.

My last, and maybe most important, question is, do we need the UN? Is it not better to have a direct line between opponents, to solve problems in a better way? In Israel it is a debatable question, and I think it is worth discussing. I'm not sure that this is the forum, this is the occasion, but [the same sort of hostility] goes on today. We had the Gulf war; now look at what's happening in Yugoslavia. This is not exactly the UN.

Salah Bassiouny: I want to join other comments on the basic question of why the secretary-general did not take some stalling steps in order to maneuver with Egypt. I accept, of course, all the legal aspects of the presence of UNEF in Egypt and I know how hard, in fact, were the negotiations between the legal adviser to the UN and the Egyptian government in 1957; I am not contesting that. But why not invoke article 99, present a report to the Security Council, taking into account that at the time both Moscow and Washington were taking the same position? Moscow a week later appealed to the Egyptian government not to start the war, to de-escalate, to open the Strait of Tiran for oil shipping, and Washington at the same time was sending messages to Egypt not to start the war. The international environment at that time could have been effective. But not to try and, as Ambassador

Basheer said, to just take it for granted that there would be no majority in the Security Council, no majority in the General Assembly, I think, was not a wise decision.

Samuel Lewis: I want to pursue the same question from a different angle. It strikes me as extraordinary [that during] this crucial period of forty-eight hours or so, after the letter was delivered to General Rikhye until the point that the Advisory Committee had met, apparently nobody was willing to argue, or even delay. What was Arthur Goldberg doing in this period? What was the United States doing to try to encourage U Thant to stall, to go to the General Assembly? I hear that U.S. diplomacy was probably absent; nobody seems to remember. What was the United States up to and why weren't we more of a factor in a stalling strategy that many people here seem to think would have made sense? And is it true that during the next ten days we were pushing, as Meir said, for a Security Council resolution and couldn't achieve it? Is that factually correct? It doesn't seem consistent.

Gideon Rafael: In answer to Sam Lewis's question, the United States, represented by Arthur Goldberg, along with Britain, represented by Lord Caradon, and France, represented by Roger Seydoux, made the strongest representation to U Thant not to accept the Egyptian ultimatum. Not once but twice, three times, but he said he had already committed himself to taking the forces out.

At that point, the idea of the mission to Cairo was initiated. Even after the mission ended, the three powers and Canada, which had initiated UNEF—Mike [Lester] Pearson was the initiator—gave a strong presentation requesting the secretary-general to bring the matter up in any form before the General Assembly, as had been agreed in 1957. Nobody—certainly not Israel—would have agreed in '57 to withdraw from the Suez on a unilateral condition, a unilateral decision, and, indeed, we didn't. We made it clear that this is not a unilateral act by Egypt, [not a matter of] either offering or canceling hospitality. It was a matter of far-reaching implications for the world community. First, UNEF would stay put.

As for the collapse of the armistice agreements, may I remind you that on September 1, 1951, the Security Council decided that a state of belligerence as practiced by Egypt in the forms of blockade and hostility was incompatible with the armistice agreement. Israel had tried to resurrect the armistice agreement, save the armistice agreement, and we continued [to do so] for years. Nothing changed except that the inroads and incursions made by our neighbors increased. Practically, the armistice agreements had been violated from the beginning, or shortly after their signatures. The very fact that Egypt

Arthur Goldberg, U.S. permanent representative to the UN, with deputy William Buffum, 1967. *U.S. News and World Report* photo, Library of Congress collection.

maintained a blockade in the Gulf of Aqaba and in Suez and supported armed incursions, of course, had eroded the meaning of its armistice agreement with Israel, which in its preamble states that it is a first step toward the establishment of peace. That's the armistice agreement right up to 1951.

The proposal that Israel accept the UNEF forces evicted from Egypt was made to me on May 19 by Secretary-General U Thant. I then asked him, "Is there any meaning and relevance to the continued stationing of UNEF in Egypt?" He said, no, they are—he didn't use the word *evicted*—they have to leave. So I said, "What shall they do in Israel? Are we going to be a refuge for UN forces? They cannot be meant to hold [restrain] our actions to defend ourselves. Israel is not to be defended, will not be defended by UNEF as the purpose of UNEF; rather Israel will defend itself with its own army." UNEF was stationed in order to help Egypt not return to the situation that arose in 1957 with this blockade—to help them as a neutral factor of restraint and a kind of, I would say, shock absorber between the two countries. So there was no purpose whatsoever in making this proposal unless

Gideon Rafael, Israeli permanent
representative to the UN, 1967.

the secretary-general was looking for some kind of public relations device
that would divert the attention from the collapse of UNEF into the Egyptian mud.

On May 29, King Hussein suddenly went to Egypt and signed a military
alliance. On the same day, he returned to Amman with the chief of the
United Arab Command, General Abd al-Mun'im Riad, as commander of
the Jordanian forces. For Israel, strategically, it meant that the ring was
closed: Syria to the north, Egypt to the south, and Jordan to the east. That
was a clear indication for us of moving into a military confrontation.

My last point regards the events in April 1967 on the Israeli-Syrian border.
The reason for the tension between Israel and Syria in '66 and '67 was not
only that there were marauding forces and terrorist forces and fear operating
but also that Syria had begun to divert water resources, the headwaters of
the Jordan, which was the source of Israel's irrigation program. We were,
at that time, engaged in a program to carry water from the north, the only
water resource we had, to the south via the national water carrier, and we
saw that project endangered. It was a lifeline for Israel. There was not only
a statement from Syria that it was going to divert the water. There was first
a decision on diversion at the summit meeting in Casablanca, and Syria had

started its work. Whether it would have been successful is not important. At that point in 1966, it created an enormous amount of tension, and Israel decided to remove this hazard.

Shimon Shamir: May I make some minor corrections? (Ambassador Rafael, forgive me.) First, King Hussein went to Cairo on May 30, not May 29. Second, the summit conference where they decided to divert the waters was held not in Casablanca but in Cairo.

Carl Brown: There are three other points, which are admittedly asking you to speculate after the fact, Brian Urquhart and Mr. Liu.

(1) What if, in that limited period of time, U Thant had said, in effect, "Yes, I, as secretary general, totally accept the principle of Egypt's right to ask us to withdraw" but then buttered them up a bit, evoking Egypt's long cooperation with the United Nations, saying, "We're asking you to give us a few days." In other words, I would, I guess, disagree with Mr. Meeker about the legal case, but instead of trying to threaten or forbid, what about another approach? Would it have made a difference, in your judgment?

(2) While certainly accepting the intelligence and integrity of Ralph Bunche, which is beyond dispute, isn't it possible that a fallback position along the lines of a partial withdrawal might have been a good thing? One could have said, "Look, we realize Egypt's need for a show of force in order to stop possible action on the part of Israel against Syria." As long as there can be two armies in confrontation, at least that's a sort of a stand-off, and one would hope nothing would happen.

(3) Since we are supposed to learn lessons from all of this, isn't it possible that we are perhaps paying too much attention to who did what or who failed to do what and not enough to certain structural problems? An indefinite, unending truce supervisory situation, necessarily on somebody's sovereign soil, which necessarily can be withdrawn when the sovereign power says so, is a systemic nightmare: you have a truce supervisory organization in place when you need it least, and it can be withdrawn when you are going to need it most. Isn't the answer to have sunset laws on truce supervisory groups? After a war takes place, the groups would stay sixty days, ninety days, or a hundred and twenty days and then get out, saying to the parties involved, "If you don't go ahead and move toward some kind of resolution of your problem, you'll have only yourselves to blame and you'll pay the price." I wonder what you, especially with your UN experience, think of that idea?

William Zartman: Let me add a question. Ambassador al-Kony apparently said a number of times to U Thant, don't ask for a reversal because it will be looked on as an occasion for a rebuff and for making a stronger stand.

Presumably the reversal was to be a public statement. Was there no possibility for U Thant to get on the phone or to talk more informally to Nasser?

Janice Stein: Building on a question that Sam put earlier, let me ask Brian a question and let me also ask Tahsin and Ambassador Bassiouny one. The issue of stalling is complicated because it has been discussed largely in terms of what could have been done after the initial five to ten hours when U Thant effectively agreed to the Egyptian request. It is much harder to stall when you have to get people to reverse positions, and that's precisely what President Nasser would have had to do.

A fairer formulation of the question of stalling is, was it possible for U Thant to stall in agreeing to the initial Egyptian request, as stalling would have made it much easier for President Nasser? In your presentation, Brian, you were fair. You said the Security Council meeting didn't work. That Security Council meeting was held on May 26, after everybody had already committed themselves to their positions, so it's not really the best possible test of whether that would be possible. The same thing with the General Assembly: Even if we knew that there were not the two-thirds votes there, it would have taken time to count them, to call everybody, to canvass. Wasn't there a possibility of using up forty-eight hours to provide some additional time?

Another question we've hinted at but haven't addressed: The Soviet Union was not consulted on either the withdrawal of UNEF or the blockade. Was there any possibility of consulting with the Soviets and the Americans before a Security Council meeting to see whether there was some room? If that kind of strategy was to work, it had to be done before that fast system of exchanges that took place between U Thant and al-Kony, where in fact U Thant found himself, against his wishes, committed to a withdrawal.

Tahsin Basheer: One of the problems is how we interpret events. For example, Gideon Rafael told us about the Security Council resolution of 1951. The resolution, regarding freedom of passage in both Suez and other passages, was a political decision. Why did Egypt refuse it? Egypt did not refuse it ipso facto. Egypt said that the decision was not legal, and Egypt was willing for anybody to challenge us by going to the International Court. Nobody went to the International Court from that day until today.

On the question of Israel stopping the UN armistice machinery with Egypt after its attack on Egypt in '56—that was a unilateral Israeli decision. Had Israel at any time agreed with U Thant to revive it, we would have had a mechanism for some direct communication.

To answer Janice Stein, the issue in any crisis depends on what level of escalation has been reached and how you get the parties to disengage or de-escalate or go sideways. The handling by U Thant of this one was, to me, not very apt. He could have stalled in responding by saying, this is your right, true, but let me canvass world opinion to make the thing possible. Let me see where it would lead. The United States and Britain and France took the position in the Security Council to reprimand Egypt. There will be no decision to reprimand Egypt. If you want to handle a crisis, you don't reprimand anybody, and that was another mistake. The United States was left with an embassy in Cairo in which there was no ambassador. Communication was on the secondary level, and waiting for the vice-president to go to Egypt or Zakariya Muhieddin to come to Washington created the time for Israel to take the initiative before the United States was committed. In the days of escalation, the management of the crisis becomes important, and we missed it.

Eugene Rostow: It seems to me that this discussion has gone astray because we are ignoring *Hamlet*. The most important element in the drama, or melodrama, was the intensification of crisis. It is perfectly true that we had the depressing experience, somewhere in the middle of the month—May 19 sticks in my mind—when we couldn't even get a vote of nine on a mild and innocuous Security Council resolution, the purpose of which was simply to force the Soviets to veto it. We had no expectation that the Soviets would go along; the notion that the Soviets were amiable cooperators is naive beyond words. They were pouring gasoline all over the fire at that point. They didn't want a war, but they thought the Egyptians had a better chance than in fact they had; they were pressing toward the brink and they did not want to come back. At that moment, proposals for a partial withdrawal or limited allowance of oil through the Strait of Tiran would have given Egypt a tremendous political victory without a war.

The fact of the matter was that the great powers and Egypt had agreed in 1957 that closing the Strait of Tiran was an act of war, and they went through an elaborate series of ceremonial statements to that effect. Don Bergus was my tutor on this subject. He once gave me the documents in the case, a volume of State Department documents on the Middle East with about twelve paper clips in it; the clips represented the scenario of agreed statements to be made in order, by the parties, in various places or through silences.

The casus belli in 1967 was the closing of the strait. That act was serious, as was agreed by the whole international community in 1956 and 1957. The Israelis withdrew from the Sinai in reliance on those promises. Nasser knew all about it. It was done in that peculiar form in an effort to make it easier for him. We invited Nasser to send a representative to meet with an

Israeli representative on an American cruiser in the Mediterranean. He said, no, no, I can't do that, and so the agreement was embodied in this strange and mysterious form. It was an agreement, nonetheless, and it was an agreement to which he was a party and he knew he was a party. There isn't any nonsense about it.

There were others in the United States and in the other governments who were involved in the Suez crisis of 1956 and '57. Lyndon B. Johnson was one. At the time he was chairman of the Senate Armed Services Committee. He maneuvered to get the Eisenhower resolution bill before his committee rather than the Foreign Relations Committee precisely so that he could help engineer this settlement. Of course, Rusk knew all about it, and the whole of resolution 242 derives from this story. Rusk used to go around saying that when Nasser closed the Strait of Tiran he cut our throat from ear to ear because we had brokered the 1957 agreement. This isn't a secret of history. This is a fact, and lots of the participants in '67 all knew about it. We didn't publish it a lot because we didn't want to embarrass Nasser, to stand up and tell the Arab world that he had made a secret deal with the Israelis through the United States, Britain, and the good offices of the secretary-general.

So there is nothing strange about this affair. President Johnson's position on the Gulf of Aqaba was simple; it had to be no give, no budge, that's the whole thing. So you couldn't say, we'll let oil in but not something else. That's a ridiculous sort of thing, and it misses the whole point of what this drama was about. As Gideon Rafael said, properly, this is part of the prolonged Arab war against the Jewish political presence in the Middle East. It goes back to 1922, with the announcement of the Balfour Declaration, and there's no use calling it anything else. It was our policy to prevent another big outbreak of hostilities, but not at the sacrifice of the fundamental point. That's why resolution 242 is what it is and resolution 338 is what it is.

Sam Lewis asked why we didn't do more at that point in the UN, and that is a good question. We were preoccupied at that time. We knew that the locomotive was loose on the track and heading straight for war, and we were doing our best to prevent it. But trying to get the situation, the egg, put together—Humpty Dumpty put together again—with UNEF was missing the whole point, because no solution putting UNEF on Israeli soil could have dealt with the problem of Sharm al-Shaykh. Sharm al-Shaykh was on the other side of the water, and a UN force had to be there on Egyptian soil in order to deal with this problem, which was the central one. The Soviets weren't going to cooperate because that wasn't their policy.

They did just the reverse. As the thing intensified, President Johnson invited the Egyptian vice-president to come to Washington; we were preparing talking points for that meeting, and he was determined to try it, but that's where he had to be. It couldn't be U Thant asking Nasser to reverse himself on the closing of the strait, it had to be President Johnson, who had more divisions behind him. That's the answer to your question, Sam, and we were going twenty-seven hours a day on all those things, and there were lots of them: the maritime question, the maritime declaration, the flotilla, and so forth.

Carl Brown: May I ask for clarification? I was asking and, I believe, Sam was asking about those first few hours. I would agree with you that the announcement of the closing of the strait put an entirely different face on the matter. That took place on May 22. We're talking about May 15 to 22, or even May 15 to 17.

Eugene Rostow: President Johnson made strong statements and, as Gideon Rafael has reminded us, the British and the Americans and the French made strong representations to U Thant. U Thant had purported to use his own powers as secretary-general to do what he did.

Richard Parker: But didn't these representations come after it was too late? In this first week, we didn't do anything.

Eugene Rostow: The Yugoslavs and the Indians pulled right out that morning, and the Canadians too. There was no force.

Richard Parker: At that point, it seems to me, we should have been trying to use our elbows with U Thant to encourage him.

Lucius Battle: What was it possible for U Thant to do in the circumstances after the request for UNEF troops to be withdrawn? I don't think very much. At the time that happened, almost immediately we knew that the Yugoslavs and the Indians wished to have their troops withdrawn . . . the great nonaligned triumvirate coming forth again and responding quickly. Also, if I'm not mistaken, the Swedes and Norwegians, who I think both had groups there, have policies that any time a nation does not wish to receive troops under UN auspices, they would not leave them there. So it was pretty obvious that was gone.

Where we did make a mistake, I think, is that we should have brought the UN into the whole thing earlier than we did. We had too much of a cold war approach in our attitude. If we remember the uncertainty we've had with respect to Russian intentions on the dissemination of the information with respect to Israeli troops—if you think that's perplexing today, how perplexing do you think it was in those days? No one knew what the Soviets' intentions were; we had a slight tendency to look too much to our own little Western group as opposed to the UN. An earlier role for the UN would have been more satisfactory had we gone in earlier, but we didn't. I don't know why we didn't. We had sitting in all of our sessions Joe Sisco and Pete Day [from the Bureau of International Organization Affairs] and others, but we were focusing perhaps too much attention on the armada, as we called it, and on actions that were not to be taken under UN auspices— international but not UN, which makes a difference. I think that there was a failure, and I'll sit back for the rest of my life wondering what we might have done that we didn't do.

Just one other point: I want to respond to the statement that there was no one [for the Egyptians] to talk with. We had Charlie Yost there, a distinguished diplomat. Our ambassador had not presented credentials, and I had been away since March 5, but Charlie could see anybody with the possible exception of Nasser and even that, I think, would not have been too demeaning. Nasser also was seeing, on a fairly regular basis, a lot of senior American corporate types. So there were avenues of communication. I don't think that was the problem.

Tahsin Basheer: Nasser accepted all of the terms of the businessmen who met him [a reference to Robert Anderson, former U.S. treasury secretary].

Richard Parker: I would disagree with you totally about that, Luke [Battle]. There was nobody [American] in Cairo at the time who had contact with Nasser. We had no contact, no meaningful contact at the upper levels of the UAR government.

Lucius Battle: Even with Charlie there?

Richard Parker: It was too late by the time Charlie Yost got there. He arrived on May 22 or 23, and it was all over by that time. Nolte just didn't arrive and didn't arrive, and we had nobody there.

Tahsin Basheer: And Nasser was very positive with [former Treasury Secretary Robert] Anderson in that meeting.

Lucius Battle: Yes, I remember that.

Richard Parker: But that's June 1. The war is on.

George Tomeh: In answer to Mr. Rostow on the refusal of the Arabs to accept the Balfour Declaration as of 1921, nothing is more detrimental to a real understanding of history than to mention partial history arbitrarily and not the whole history. The question should be asked, why did the Arabs refuse the Balfour Declaration? Briefly because it was illegal and immoral. It is at the root of what made the recent history of Palestine, the Arabs, and the Jews a great human tragedy. When in 1919 the Jewish population in Palestine did not exceed 50,000 to 60,000, the World Zionist Organization submitted its official plan for the creation of a Jewish state in Palestine to the peace conference in 1919. The minimum that the organization would accept for a viable Jewish state in Palestine included the following: the headwaters of the Jordan River in Syria and Lebanon, the south of Lebanon up to the town of Sidon, the southern Bekaa valley in Lebanon, the Hauran Plain in Syria, control over the Hijaz Railway from Dera'a to Amman to Maan in Jordan, and control over the Gulf of Aqaba.

Here let me ask Mr. Rostow as an American, suppose the Arab countries had the force to make such a demand on the United States, invoking so-called historical rights of 2,000 years ago, what would have been the attitude of Mr. Rostow and of our American colleagues around this table?

I was amazed when I heard Mr. Amit ask the questions, What can the UN do? Can the UN play a role? Why should the UN play a role? Some friend or colleague here said this matter demands a whole session or perhaps a whole seminar like this. And I would attend that seminar. But it is really strange for the State of Israel, which owes its existence to the UN, now to deny a role to the world.

Meir Amit: We want to talk directly to you.

William Zartman: But not during the session right now.

Donald Bergus: I want to make a historical nitpick. In those documents I sent Secretary Rostow, where everybody got up and said this was a good thing about [freedom of navigation in] the Gulf of Aqaba, Dr. Fawzi did get up and reserve his position and said nothing that other people have said here binds Egypt. That is off the record, but the fact is that for ten years Egypt acted as though it were bound by it.

Richard Parker: It acquiesced.

Donald Bergus: It acquiesced, yes.

Tahsin Basheer: That's an important point, because Nasser consulted with Fawzi before [closing the Strait of Tiran in 1967], and he said Egypt has no commitment to anybody, and the text of the UN is clear. It's ours. It's our own soil.

Richard Parker: I'd like to go back to the point we raised earlier about stalling. What would the Egyptians have done if, instead of responding, U Thant had delayed, for two or three days or a week, any response to the Egyptians and simply had prolonged the process? What would Egypt's reaction have been?

Tahsin Basheer: Whatever proposals there were to de-escalate, Egypt accepted. Nasser accepted Anderson, he accepted the vice-president [Humphrey] coming, he was willing to send his vice-president [Zakariya Muhieddin]. By withdrawing the UN force, he wanted to return to the status quo ante. He did not accept that Israel will gain any political or strategic advantage from the attack on Egypt in 1956.

Richard Parker: That means getting rid of UNEF then.

Tahsin Basheer: He accepted from U Thant that there will be a gentlemen's agreement on a moratorium that will not be tested, either by Israel or by the suppliers of oil. It's risky. He accepted that.

Richard Parker: Yes, but I'm talking about the question of UNEF, of not withdrawing UNEF. Could this have been drawn out?

Lucius Battle: May I answer that question? I've thought for a long time that what Gamal Abd al-Nasser wanted, expected, was to have someone pull them apart. I'm not sure he would have been upset about it. I don't believe he really intended going to war, and if we had come in and he'd been given a face-saver at that point, I think he might have welcomed it.

George Tomeh: I agree fully with that.

Ephraim Evron: I disagree completely.

Lucius Battle: Well, I expected you to.

William Zartman: Anybody want to spell out what a face-saver might be?

Lucius Battle: Well, something that didn't come from him; the face-saver would come from somewhere else. That's what I think he really expected.

Georgiy Kornienko: Just a few words on why the Soviet Union was not more active on this [UNEF] withdrawal and did not try to reverse the situation. The answer given by Secretary Rostow is simple, that the Soviet Union was pouring gasoline, but I am not sure it is correct. My explanation is different, twofold.

First, the situation was developing too fast for our bureaucratic machine to react properly. A second explanation may be more important. As in many other cases of this type, we would try to talk privately with the proper party, in this case with the Egyptians, cautioning, restraining, and so on. But at the same time, because of ideological, political considerations, we would declare publicly that we supported [their stance]. That was one of the major troubles in our foreign policy in those days.

William Zartman: Mr. Liu, do you want to respond to anything or make any conclusion?

F. T. Liu: About the advisability of UNEF stalling for a few days: On May 17, just a few hours after the first Egyptian request had been received and transmitted to UN headquarters, the Egyptian forces had moved to the border in the Sinai near Sharm al-Shaykh, and there were some near clashes between the UN troops, the Yugoslav troops, and the Egyptian forces. So already the confrontation had begun. How could UNEF stall when any stalling would entail loss of UN lives?

Another point: I just want to remind Mr. Amit that Israel was created on the basis of the UN partition plan.

Meir Amit: I did not refer to the UN but to the UN forces. I don't think we need UN forces. This was my point. I didn't challenge the UN.

Brian Urquhart: Of the points that have come up, the basic one seems to be what U Thant could have done that he didn't do. A second one is whether there was some face-saving procedure that wasn't tried. Let me start with what U Thant might have done. F. T. Liu has pointed out that this wasn't merely a game going on between capitals and the Security Council and the UN in New York, and so on. There were all sorts of interesting things happening on the ground. First, there was the movement of Egyptian troops, and I would remind you that, apart from the fact that peacekeeping operations were not allowed to use force, UNEF in those days consisted effectively of 1,400 lightly armed soldiers, not allowed to use force, on a 395-mile front. The Egyptian army was estimated at something like 70,000 to 90,000 heavily armed troops, on their own soil with a perfect right to move on it. So the idea of resistance is out.

Then, apart from this, we have the Gaza populace, which was a major problem, always, for UNEF. It had been a problem right from the beginning, and it was always hanging over us, and it cannot be dismissed.

Yugoslavia and India—the guts of the force, the two largest contingents—had gone, and the Nordics were not far behind. They had always said that they would not stay in a country against the will of the government, so what were they supposed to do?

Somebody asked why the Security Council couldn't have acted under chapter 7. It was all the Security Council could do to agree to have a meeting in those days, and action under chapter 7 is a recent phenomenon in its history. During the cold war period, it was inconceivable that there could have been agreement on action under chapter 6, let alone under chapter 7. Indeed, the experiences of the Security Council in this period, which Mr. Rostow referred to, do point to this. There was good reason to believe that you couldn't summon the General Assembly. In fact, the ambassadors on the Advisory Committee, including Brazil, Canada, Denmark, and several others, had actually done a poll to discover whether it was possible to call the assembly into special session. The answer was no.

The moratorium. I mentioned the rather peculiar fate of the U Thant letter to Eshkol and Nasser about a moratorium and why that came to nothing. I notice that nobody has mentioned the moratorium on Israeli action, and I don't think anybody challenged the boats going through the Strait of Tiran during those days. I think they went through, but on the other hand the action when it happened was on the Israeli side, not the Egyptian side. So, I think this moratorium thing can be a little bit overdone.

I'm not sure whether U Thant knew about the U.S. commitment to Israel [re navigation in the Gulf of Aqaba] made in February 1957. I certainly didn't, but that doesn't mean that he didn't. There wasn't any doubt in our minds of the seriousness of this situation. Ambassador Bassiouny asked, why didn't the secretary-general maneuver with Egypt? The reason is that he was told on a number of occasions, set forth by Ambassador al-Kony and in messages from Cairo and then by Nasser himself, that there was absolutely no room to maneuver. How many times does a head of state have to say it before you believe it? I am dubious about this business of maneuvering.

The secretary-general did, indeed, report to the Security Council. For example, in the May 19 report on the situation he wrote, "I do not wish to be an alarmist but I cannot avoid warning the Council that, in my view, the current situation in the Near East is more disturbing, indeed, I may say, more menacing than at any time since the Fall of 1956." In a quiet kind of way, I should have thought that was a fairly straightforward warning. The trouble was that the Security Council didn't meet on that morning. It took Canada and Denmark to get it into session nearly a week later.

I don't know what the answer is about the United States in the forty-eight-hour period, but I think Mr. Rostow more or less answered that. Certainly we were in daily, and sometimes almost hourly, consultations with both Ambassador Goldberg and Lord Caradon. It was explained to them at length what the problem was, and I think they understood it very well. Certainly neither of them, as far as we could see, was particularly anxious to summon the Security Council. They were keen for U Thant to do that, but they didn't want to do it themselves, for good reasons, in my view.

Gideon Rafael said that he couldn't accept a unilateral act by Egypt about UNEF, but the trouble was that UNEF had always been a one-legged operation. It was only on one side of the line, unlike most peacekeeping operations. Israel had never accepted UNEF within its territory on the grounds that it would be an infraction of Israeli sovereignty, and thus only Egyptian sovereign territory was involved with the presence of UNEF. That does seem to me to give Egypt a rather special position.

What should UNEF have done in Israel, supposing Ambassador Rafael and others had accepted the idea [of stationing UNEF there]? The sole idea of suggesting it was our hope, until June 5, that it would be possible, eventually, to get President Nasser to reconsider the withdrawal of UNEF. We had hoped that if we could preserve it on the ground until that time, it would be possible to reinstate it. Now this may have been pie in the sky, but that was the logic behind it.

What if U Thant had said that we accepted the legitimacy of Egypt's request for withdrawal but could we have a few days? That, in effect, was what he did. That was what all the discussion in Cairo was about. It was about a breathing spell, and that blew up on the conditions of the moratorium.

Partial withdrawal. Supposing you had withdrawn UNEF from everywhere except Gaza and allowed the Egyptian forces to confront the Israelis—large armored forces of the Egyptian army across the old international frontier across Sinai. I wonder what Israel would have said about that. When I recall what they said about the arrival of one administrative so-called governor in Gaza in 1957, I think there would have been an uproar. I think that, rightly, there would have been a great protest about a partial withdrawal, opening up one part of the front and protecting Egypt on the other pass. Obviously that was not an appropriate function for UNEF.

It is true that the armistice agreement had become greatly eroded even by 1956, in the Suez crisis, and by 1957 there was little left of it. Incidentally, Bunche, who negotiated all the armistice agreements between Israel and its Arab neighbors, never ceased to comment that when he negotiated them he had always assumed that they were a short interim stage before the settlement that the Palestine Conciliation Commission was supposed to negotiate on the basis of the armistice.

Stalling. The idea of U Thant picking up the phone and having a quiet chat with President Nasser is wildly unrealistic. Nasser was a difficult man. It sometimes took weeks even to make an arrangement for the secretary-general or for Bunche to visit him. He was not the sort of person you rang up and had a cozy chat with. Also, in those days long-distance calls to Cairo weren't so hot.

Face-saving devices. Everyone keeps saying that Nasser should have been given a face-saver. Quite honestly, for someone who wanted a face-saver, Nasser acted in a strange way. There were lots of possible face-savers. U Thant's visit was one. Nasser deliberately cut it off before U Thant even got there by the declaration of the blockade. Sometimes I wonder how long one is expected to go on trying to save people from themselves. We guessed, early on, in face of some fairly brusque messages from Cairo, that face-saving was the last thing in the world President Nasser had in mind on May 18, 1967—maybe later, but certainly not then.

Consultations (between the Soviet Union and the United States). Dream on. This was one of the worst periods of the cold war, and the Soviet Union was taking the line, what's all the bother about, what are you all fussing about, why do we need to have a meeting with the Security Council? It was maddening. There was no common ground whatsoever between the United States and the Soviet Union. If you decided to discuss things with the United States and the Soviet Union, you ceased shortly discussing the Middle East at all and started discussing the East-West struggle, which wasn't quite the point.

   William Zartman: I think that not all the questions have been dispelled, but I think the questioners haven't come up with firm alternatives as to what else could have been done. I think the questions will remain for a while.

CHAPTER 3

✄ The Israeli Response

Bernard Reich

Israel's perspectives concerning the developments in May and June 1967 that led to the Six-Day War were conditioned by its views of itself in the region and of the international community at that time. Israel saw a real threat to its existence. Whatever the perception may be in hindsight, and especially given the outcome of the hostilities, the fact remains that before the war, Israeli leaders were genuinely concerned about the threats to Israel's survival.

Israel's policies were conditioned by the view that it should retaliate in response to continued Arab hostility and specific attacks. This, in turn, might convince the Arab leaders not to attack Israel and caution them to restrain their acts against Israel. But retaliation did not prove wholly successful.

The Arab world context of 1967 was one of anti-Israel summits, water diversion schemes, radicalization, terrorism, and inter-Arab tensions. Israel was beleaguered and surrounded by hostile states supported by an unfriendly superpower that gave unlimited aid and comfort to Israel's adversaries. It saw itself as a biblical David surrounded by the modern equivalent of Goliath. In its solitude it faced a negative environment in which it was supported, albeit not fully or wholeheartedly, by the United States. Thus, as it contemplated the developments in May and June, as well as those earlier that spring, the central question remained the reliability of the U.S. commitment and its willingness to take action in support of its reassurances to the Jewish state.

The central questions for Israel revolved around two issues: the seriousness of the potential Arab threat and the role of the United States in the event of a serious threat. Were President Nasser of Egypt and the leadership of Syria bent on war, or were they simply making another feint in the long process of confronting Israel? Israel's perception and response changed with Nasser's announced blockade of the Strait of Tiran on May 23. The question then became whether the United States would honor its obligations and take action in support of its 1957 pledge to Israel concerning freedom of passage through the strait to and from the port of Eilat.

The second question derived from the special relationship between the United States and Israel. In 1967 the special relationship had not yet attained the levels of later years, when there was a significant popular American commitment to the security and survival of Israel. Thus, for Israel the question was whether the United States would be reliable in meeting its perceived commitments and obligations. What would the United States do in response to a challenge posed by Nasser's announced blockade and military mobilization? What were the constraints on President Johnson? Did he use Congress as a pretext for inaction, or was he seriously concerned about the need to go to Congress to secure support for his actions?

Other issues emerge: What was the extent of the U.S. knowledge of and support for the Israeli preemptive strike? What color light did the United States give to Israel? Was it green, red, or yellow? Affecting these questions was the issue of Israel's military capability and its military balance with the Arab world, especially with its likely adversaries. The likely outcomes of conflict were not nearly as certain in 1967 as they were in retrospect. Among the questions of particular concern was the potential level of Israeli casualties.

Israeli policies reflect several clear conclusions.

This was not a war in isolation. It was another episode in twenty years of belligerency by the Arab world and the third major war (1948–49—Israel's war of independence; 1956–57—the Suez war) since the declared independence of the state in 1948 at the termination of the British Mandate of Palestine.

The UN was ineffective. The UN Emergency Force failed in its primary task; it departed at Nasser's request. The UN had been unable to prevent incursions from Syria in the spring (and earlier) and was unable to prevent, or even substantially slow, the escalation to conflict.

Although Lyndon B. Johnson was a central player and the United States was the main external factor, the Middle East was not yet a major focus of American policy making and policy makers. Johnson and the U.S. government were preoccupied elsewhere. Although Johnson and others were concerned about what would happen to Israel, it was clear that the Middle East was not a high priority, and it was unclear what the United States would or could do in the event of the threats to Israel.

Israel had access to the highest levels of the U.S. government, reflecting the special nature of the relationship, but further indications of this connection (e.g., economic aid or military supply) were not yet consequential.

The United States and Israel were not linked in a conspiracy; there was no U.S.-Israel collusion to bring down President Nasser, although there was an American assent to Israeli action to do what it must. As both Meir Amit and Richard Helms noted, their meeting was a straightforward one, comparing notes on the regional situation, not a clandestine session to give Israel a light of any color. Israel believed that the United States was positively inclined but that it was unprepared and had inadequate planning to deal with a crisis of the sort that was developing. Israel had questions about U.S. policy and responses to the developing situation. Israel was not always certain about the alertness of the United States or of its assessment of the situation or of its probable responses.

There was a developing Soviet-Arab and especially Soviet-Egyptian connection and consequent threat. The Soviet Union had been active in providing military and economic-technical assistance to the Arab states, especially Egypt, since before the Suez crisis and war, while Israel by contrast felt endangered and isolated, a perception that prevailed until the 1967 war. In addition, by the spring of 1967 the mood in Israel was growing problematic. There was therefore an asymmetry of Arab and Israeli positions, perspectives, and statements. Nevertheless, in the spring of 1967 Israel's military intelligence assessment was that there would be no full-scale war before the 1970s. Israel did not prepare to go to war—it had no such intention or plan. Its Eshkol-led government was considered one of the most moderate in Israel's history, and Eshkol himself was seen as a moderate and noncharismatic leader unlikely to take decisive actions. Instead Israel reacted, cautiously and slowly, to the actions of the Arabs, especially Nasser. Ultimately Eshkol's public image and the growing concern of the strategic planners among Israel's generals led to the pressure on Eshkol to replace himself as defense minister with Moshe Dayan. There were also domestic pressures deriving from economic problems and the general feeling that the government must "do something" about the deteriorating situation, which put the future of the state at stake.

Israel's first reaction to Egypt's mobilization in May was one of calm, expressing the view that this was a show of force and a reassertion of the

Egyptian role as leader of the Arab world. The announced blockade of Aqaba changed the Israeli interpretation. Concern became the paramount Israeli position, although there were doubts that Nasser's real intention was to go to war. An immediate Israeli response was expected, since Israel maintained that the strait was an international waterway and should be open to Israeli shipping and that a blockade of the Gulf of Aqaba was an aggressive act. After the 1956 conflict Israel had agreed to withdraw its troops from the Sinai Peninsula only after having been assured that freedom of navigation in the gulf would be maintained. Major factors in Israeli calculations were the American *aide mémoire* of February 11, 1957, which noted that the "Gulf [of Aqaba] comprehends international waters and that no nation has the right to prevent free and innocent passage in the Gulf and through the Straits giving access thereto," as well as U.S. decisions concerning its obligations and the measures it might take in support of them. Between 1957 and 1967 Israeli shipping utilized the Strait of Tiran and the Gulf of Aqaba to reach the Israeli port of Eilat. This passage was assured, in part, by the presence of UNEF troops in the Sinai Peninsula, particularly at Sharm al-Shaykh.

Israel's response to the blockade of the Gulf of Aqaba was to send Foreign Minister Abba Eban to the United States to inquire into the American position. En route he met with President Charles de Gaulle of France and Prime Minister Harold Wilson of England. During his discussions with President Johnson, Eban explained the Israeli view that the Gulf of Aqaba was international waters and that Israeli flagships must be allowed to traverse the strait. He probably spelled out that Israel was ready, willing, and able to utilize military force in support of this position should that be necessary. Eban questioned the American position and asked what support Israel might expect from the United States. Johnson urged restraint and suggested that Israel wait for the exhaustion of diplomatic efforts to open the gulf. The immediate response of Eban and the Israeli Government was to wait and see whether the various options available to the United States in support of freedom of navigation at Tiran would be exercised to assure Israeli passage through the strait. Israel placed no deadline on the requirement of free passage, but it seemed likely that an indefinite postponement of meeting the requirement would not be tolerated, since time would work to the advantage of the Arab position by allowing for the full mobilization and coordination of Arab armies. Eban indicated that the time expanse was a matter of weeks, not months.

Israel held the position that it would allow the United States and the other maritime powers sufficient time to try to use the offices of the UN and other international agencies to support this position of free passage. During the course of these attempts, Israel would maintain its national armed power at a level of full readiness and would attempt diplomatic maneuvering of its own, including presentation of its case to the UN. Once the United States and England were seemingly making little headway in their attempts to ensure freedom of navigation, public pressures in Israel were exerted to include Moshe Dayan in the government as minister of defense. His co-option to the government indicated that the time for diplomacy to prevent war was short.

Israel's views were influenced by its historical memories. In 1967 the surrounding region was still unwilling to accept its existence or the realities of the international system. As Shimon Shamir pointed out, "Israel was subjected to harassment throughout the whole period from the establishment of the state on, for a period of about twenty years." Israel responded with retaliation. The Arab infiltrations and incursions "were seen as a real danger to existence." The government believed that response and retaliation, desired by the public at large, were appropriate policies to pursue. Israel felt, in the words of Ephraim Evron, "extremely isolated and endangered" at the time of the 1956 crisis, and that feeling lingered on.

At the beginning of May 1967, Israel had not expected war, despite regional clashes. Ambassador Evron saw Israel as making decisions "in response to actions and decisions made by Egypt." Nor is there any evidence to suggest an Israeli "plan" to goad the Arabs into war to achieve various [nefarious] purposes. This was not 1956 all over again—there was no collusion with great powers (especially the United States) to "deal with the Arabs (especially Nasser)."

Israel was not sure that the United States would be able to act in its behalf for a number of reasons, including the preoccupation of the United States elsewhere (basically Vietnam). The United States also urged restraint on Israel not to provoke Nasser. Nevertheless there was a feeling that the United States would somehow live up to its commitment under the 1957 pledge. There was, however, a contradiction or asymmetry between this promise of commitment and actual behavior. As Ambassador Evron comments, Johnson was seen as "a friend of Israel" and "it seemed totally inconceivable . . . that in a time of great danger and a great need he would leave us in the lurch."

The United States, for its part, had not yet established the security of Israel as a central theme of its policy, despite some assertions to that effect by a number of American presidents.

Israel was under U.S. pressure not to take actions to provoke Egypt but also sought to get the United States publicly to reaffirm its commitments under the 1957 aide mémoire.

It should be clear that the Soviet report that Israel had concentrated troops along the Syrian border simply was not true. This is a fact, although there continue to be suggestions that this report was accurate. The evidence against the report is overwhelming. There were Israeli warnings but no Israeli plans to move ahead with an attack.

Were there preparations for war? Clearly Israel was not preparing to go to war; its mobilizations and other actions were responsive to those actions taken by Arab adversaries, especially Egypt and Nasser.

There was no American conspiracy with Israel, and the Israeli Embassy in Washington sought to prevent Eban from coming to the United States to avoid any such appearance. The Israelis who met with Johnson came away with some uncertainty but seemed to conclude that in the final analysis the United States would be helpful. But Israel remained under heavy pressure not to do anything. There was also internal pressure from the military, which argued that with each day that passed the cost of the war (casualties) for Israel would go up. The generals put pressure on Eshkol in a discussion suggesting that Israel was making a grave mistake by simply sitting like a "dead duck." And there were public pressures to take some action.

The U.S.-Israel special relationship was not yet clear and obvious in regional and international systems. In the assessment of the threat, and even in the various cold war overlays, U.S.-Israel collusion is not a factor or fact of consequence.

Indeed, it is clear from the various Israeli participants that they were not wholly certain of the timing or extent of potential American actions. "Israel alone" seems to be the basic understanding of the relationship, despite close and friendly ties with the United States, especially with key decision makers.

Meir Amit, then head of Mossad, was clear about "the color of the light" signal from the United States to Israel. Amit said Israel sought and, he noted unequivocally, received "not a green, neither a yellow nor any other light." Amit went to Washington "in the ordinary course of business to compare notes with the CIA" and to ensure that the facts were clear. He also sought to find out if anything was being planned to open the Strait of Tiran. The act of war was the closing of the strait. Amit also suggested that he would tell the Americans that he was going "to recommend to ask our government to strike," and he wanted to sense the American response. In Washington, he found that both countries had similar understandings of the situation. He also concluded, "I found no trace of anything specific that is planned."

The conclusion was that Israel was "alone." But he also developed the impression that the United States would not object if Nasser was defeated.

During the crisis buildup, Israel was under pressure from the United States not to act. There was a constant urging of restraint. Israel, by contrast, expected the United States to live up to its 1957 pledges and commitments and kept seeing an asymmetry between its 1957 promises and its 1967 delivery. Nevertheless, there was also the view that President Johnson would never leave Israel in the lurch, and many were convinced that the United States would implement its 1957 pledge. Nevertheless, the signals from Washington were ambiguous. There was a belief that in the end Israel could act. It would "stand alone," but it was suggested that Israel would know how to act, and the U.S. response remained ambiguous.

Among the conclusions that can be drawn from the perspective of Jerusalem is that Israel did not seek to provoke conflict but instead was responding to the various actions (casus belli and other) emanating from Egypt and its partners. The failure of the United States to deal with the Gulf of Aqaba issue in a meaningful way (from the point of view of Israel, by reasserting the right of free passage), and thereby to honor its 1957 commitment, played an important role in Israeli thinking. The Israelis seemed to believe (but it was not clear) that they had no less than a yellow light (and some perhaps believed there was a green one) for ultimate action, even while there were strong pressures for restraint prior to the hostilities.

Nevertheless, in the case of Israel, there are some relatively clear factors that might have been successful in preventing conflict.

If the continued escalation by Egypt had been stopped and later reversed, whether by self-action, UNEF and United Nations, or the United States and its allies, there would have been an opportunity to prevent the escalating Israeli response and ultimate preemptive strike. The Israelis were not seeking conflict but responding to Egyptian actions (and other Arab and Soviet machinations). Had these actions not escalated and had they not included the casus belli—the blockade of the Strait of Tiran—there probably would have been no resort to hostilities.

Had the United States met its 1957 obligations to keep open the Strait of Tiran to ensure freedom of navigation to the Gulf of Aqaba, there would have been an opportunity to reverse the situation to the status quo ante, and this likely would have prevented the escalation to conflict. In part this would have been accomplished if the United States had reassured Israel concerning its commitment to Israel's survival and security, which would have eliminated the ambiguities generated in various discussions between American and Israeli interlocutors at all levels. There would have been little room for doubt about the commitment and will of the United States, up to the level of the president.

Clearly, ambiguity can be destructive as well as constructive. Israel's uncertainty about U.S. commitments and willingness to support them raised major questions about U.S. responses and actions and in a sense contributed to the probability of conflict.

Intelligence remains an inexact and imprecise art rather than a science. Israeli intelligence seemed rather confident about the relative stability of the region only weeks before the Six-Day War altered the Middle East landscape for the decades that followed. In attempts to assess the U.S. position, different Israeli interlocutors reported different findings and assessments from different meetings, and some even reported different findings from the same meetings. Clearly, the same facts often were subject to different assessments at different levels and in different arenas. For example, compare Eban's and Evron's reactions to their meetings with Lyndon Johnson and compare Amit and Shamir concerning Amit's "light" from Washington.

The crisis of 1967 provides useful insight into the will and the ability of the UN to function in the cold war era, when the Soviet Union and the United States were aligned on opposing sides of a controversy. UN helplessness and lethargy suggest the real limits imposed by the cold war on that international body (as well as on the larger international community).

Does any of this suggest mechanisms for conflict avoidance? Perhaps there is the basic observation that clear positions are significant in preventing misinterpretation that may lead to incorrect decisions.

Panel 3

Chairman: Dr. Bernard Reich, George Washington University
Speakers:
   Ambassador Ephraim Evron, former counselor of the Israeli Embassy in
      Washington: "The Israeli Decisions"
   General Meir Amit, former head of Mossad: "Israeli Perceptions"
Comment: Dr. Janice Stein, University of Toronto

The Israeli Decision

Ephraim Evron: I'll just give a general outline of the policy pursued by Mr. Eshkol and his associates. This presentation will go back and forth in time. It's difficult, in today's world, to imagine the events that we lived through twenty-five years ago. I, for one, never thought that in my lifetime I'd visit Egypt as an official representative of the State of Israel or that I would welcome in my own homeland the president of Egypt as the official guest of the president of Israel. I didn't think that I would live to see the Soviet Union disintegrate.

I'll refer briefly to things as we saw them and felt them in Israel. A lot has been said about the fact that all President Nasser wanted was a return to the pre-1956 situation. It was a simple request. It seems very justified. Why not?

But what did it mean? In 1956 Israel was faced with very grave problems. There were the ongoing attacks of the terrorist groups, the fedayeen, that created havoc inside the country. The Arab economic boycott was in full swing. The Egyptians had blockaded the Suez Canal and the Strait of Tiran. We watched Egypt's massive rearmament and preparation for war. We watched the West whole-heartedly support part of the world, while at the same time the Soviet Union supported the other part. The United States and Britain cold-shouldered Israel at that time, which in turn weakened her politically and militarily. We felt extremely isolated and endangered. At the same time, the Arab world, with President Nasser leading it, seemed convinced that Israel's doom was achievable in a relatively short time. That feeling, which was echoed in many non-Arab capitals as well, prevailed until the Six-Day War.

At the same time, because of the deliberate policy of the Syrian government, we faced serious problems in the north. Much has been said about statements made or not made—some of them were pure inventions—by Israeli leaders and generals in the days preceding the Six-Day War. And you will see a sign of the asymmetry of the whole conflict if you compare these statements with others made by leaders of our neighbors at the same time. I'll cite just two quotes, one made by President Atassi of Syria on May 22, 1966. They are important because they point to the general policy that his government was following. He told the Syrian troops in the Golan Heights, "We arrange the slogan of the Peoples' Liberation War. We want total war with no limits, a war that will destroy the Zionist State." General Asad, who was at that time the defense minister, followed up two days later, saying, "We say we shall never call for nor accept peace." I'm glad to note that he has changed on this one. "We have resolved to drench this land with our blood, to oust you aggressor and throw you into the sea for good." No responsible Israeli could ignore such statements.

In spite of all of these forebodings, Israeli military intelligence, in presenting its annual report to the defense minister and the chief of staff in the

Ephraim Evron, minister counselor of the
Israeli Embassy, Washington, 1967

spring of 1967, concluded that an all-out war was not expected before the
1970s. So much for intelligence forecasting. The accepted view in Jerusalem
was that President Nasser would enter a war only when several conditions
were met: when there was a commanding Arab military superiority, when
Israel was in the throes of some kind of a domestic crisis, and when there
was a favorable international situation that would ensure Israel's isolation.

Now a few remarks about President Nasser's behavior. There have been
previous discussions about whether he wanted war or did not want war
and about the Soviet initiative in provoking the war. But it is my view that
between May 14 and June 5, Israel was reacting to Nasser's initiatives. The
decisions of the Israeli government were basically in response to actions and
decisions made by Egypt.

Another factor in Israel's decision-making process was the American pressure on Israel not to take any initiative, and we had in Israel at that time
the most moderate government in Israel's history. Prime Minister Eshkol
was no Ben-Gurion or even President Nasser in terms of his charisma—
his public speaking capability. Throughout the crisis, he faced tremendous
pressure by the general staff, the people who were responsible for Israel's
defense and security, and the opposition included not just the eternal peren-
nial opposition of what today is called the Likud but also people like Ben-
Gurion, Moshe Dayan, and Shimon Peres, who were his political enemies
at that time. Although Israel was going through an economic recession and
the general mood was not high, in spite of all that he found the strength,
supported by Foreign Minister Eban, to resist all internal pressures, all
domestic pressures, to take the initiative, the military initiative, in the face
of the mounting crisis. It is in stark contrast to the behavior of President
Nasser, who was far more in control of affairs in Egypt. I remember Luke

Battle when he came from Cairo talking about whether there was a possibility for peace, and he was of the view that only President Nasser would bring about peace. He told me then that the president could change the opinion of the Egyptian people within forty-eight hours, and yet we heard yesterday of a man who was somehow carried away, who had no control of the events that led him to war.

I disagree with this view. I think that at least beginning on May 17, when the decision was taken to withdraw UNEF, Nasser—maybe not in the first few days when he was pulled into the crisis by the Soviets, but from then on—acted with deliberation, carefully calculating his next move up to and including June 5. It's not only his speeches, his public speeches, that testify to that, and one cannot ignore the importance of public speeches anywhere in the world, certainly in the Arab world. His private conversations with foreign dignitaries and emissaries who came to see him indicated a determination and a deliberate conviction that he could face Israel on the battlefield and destroy it. He probably thought, and miscalculated, that it would not come to that, but if it did, there's no doubt, as one reads it—what he said to U Thant, what his people said to Ambassador Yost, to Bob Anderson as the crisis mounted—that he was well aware of what the stakes were. I quote from a letter that Mr. Khrushchev sent to him in April 1959: "Knowing your impulsiveness we feared that our unlimited support of your belligerent sentiment might have prompted you to take military action which we have always regarded as undesirable." But in May 1967 Mr. Khrushchev had been sent to green pastures and his successors acted otherwise.

Now I come to a point that is sometimes difficult to explain: the position of the U.S. government in the period between May 14–15 and early June. I had the pleasure and honor of working closely with some people who are sitting here today—Gene Rostow, Luke Battle, and many others in the State Department and in the White House—and I looked at the documents in the archives. I was given the privilege by Mrs. Eshkol of looking at his [Eshkol's] private papers and a diary that he kept throughout. I wonder how naive we could have been in the embassy, at least part of the time, because one thing was clear from the beginning. Although the U.S. government did not have a clear policy or a contingency plan on how to deal with the departure of UNEF, as I looked through the papers I noticed that what dominated the U.S. activity was restraint on Israel—don't do this, don't do that, don't send the ships through the strait, don't test the blockade, don't provoke Nasser. That was the view that prevailed at the same time, and after all, you would say, how foolish could you be, just accepting that and letting things deteriorate? They also, in an effective manner, made us feel that this administration was somehow, somewhere, sometime going to live up to its commitment under the 1957 agreement.

That was a theme that we carried in all our talks, particularly with my friend Gene Rostow, and with everybody in the administration. There seemed to be a certain contradiction, or asymmetry, between this promise of commitment and actual behavior. We didn't quite react to that and for good reasons. President Johnson was a friend of Israel, and I say it clearly. He was also a party to the 1957 agreement, indirectly, but as leader of the Senate. Somehow it seemed totally inconceivable to us that in a time of grave danger and great need he would leave us in the lurch. Second, he was an enigmatic person, as those who knew him well know, and one felt that even when he seemed that he was most clear, after you left him you had a sense that somehow there was something missing there. And with your permission I will describe a conversation that he initiated with me quite unexpectedly on May 26 that was throughout—and Mr. Eban fell victim to this—I wouldn't say double-talk, exactly, but there it was.

So I want to refer briefly to the 1957 arrangements because they are the core, the heart, of that crisis and certainly of our relationship with the United States at that time. I was surprised, Sir Brian, to hear that the UN Secretariat didn't know about those arrangements. That aide mémoire from Secretary Dulles to Ambassador Eban was made public by the State Department on February 17, 1957. The president of the United States spoke to the nation publicly on February 20, 1957, and the speeches at the General Assembly by Prime Minister Golda Meir and Ambassador Cabot Lodge are in the public record, and they were the basis of those agreements. We were convinced until much later that the president and his administration were going to implement those commitments. It seemed inconceivable that they wouldn't, not only because of what it meant to us, but because the credibility of the president of the United States and his administration were on the line.

After all, this is what he told us Vietnam was all about, and therefore, as many people said to us—including the vice-president—if the president went to war over Vietnam, surely he's not going to leave you in the lurch. So what was it? In that aide mémoire, of which you have a copy, Secretary Dulles said to Mr. Eban in writing, "With respect to the Gulf of Aqaba, and access thereto, the United States believes that the Gulf comprehends international waters and that no nation has the right to prevent free and innocent passage in the Gulf and through the Straits giving access thereto. The United States recalls that on the 28th of January 1950, the Egyptian Ministry of Foreign Affairs informed the United States that the Egyptian occupation of the two islands of Tiran and Sanafir in the entrance of the

Gulf of Aqaba, was only to protect the islands themselves against possible damage or violation and that 'This occupation is being in no way conceived in the spirit of obstructing in any way innocent passage through the stretch of water separating these two islands from the Egyptian coast of Sinai.' It follows that this passage, the only practical one, will remain free as in the past in conformity with international practices and the recognized principles of the law of nations."

Nothing could be clearer. The United States, says Secretary Dulles, "on behalf of the vessels of United States registry is prepared to exercise the right of free and innocent passage, and to join with others to secure general recognition of this right." It doesn't say that the United States will act only in conjunction with other nations. The commitment, the assurances are that the United States will act, and also with others, but it doesn't condition the American exercise of this right on the exercise of this right by others. "The United States believes that the UN General Assembly and the Secretary-General should as a precautionary measure seek that the UN Emergency Force move into the Straits area as the Israeli forces are withdrawn." In other words, the presence of the UN force in the Sinai is part and parcel of these general assurances. The president in talking to "Face the Nation" on February 26 repeats it and says clearly that this aide mémoire was sent to Israel on his instructions. He repeats the commitment on the freedom of the gulf and says, "We should not assume that if Israel withdraws Egypt will prevent Israeli shipping from the Suez Canal or the Gulf of Aqaba."

On February 24, Mr. Eban met with Secretary Dulles to verify and amplify this memorandum. There the secretary told Mr. Eban that the United States would recognize that interference, and I quote, "By armed forces, with ships with the Israeli flag exercising free and innocent passage in the Gulf of Aqaba and the Strait of Tiran, will be regarded by Israel as an attack entitling it to exercise of its inherent right of self-defense under Article 51 of the [UN] Charter and to take all such measures as are necessary to ensure free and innocent passage of its ships." [This precise wording does not appear in the U.S. record of the February 24, 1957, conversation between Dulles and Eban, and the source of the quotation is unclear. The substance, however, is correct. Dulles said that he "saw no inherent obstacle to U.S. recognition of" an Israeli declaration regarding its right to use force under Article 51 in the event of an attack on Israeli ships exercising the right to innocent passage through the Strait of Tiran.—Ed.] I want to underline the fact that this wording is that of Mr. Dulles. The Israeli draft was a little different, but the final wording is that of Mr. Dulles. With concurrence of the U.S. government, Mrs. Meir included it in her statement to the UN General

Assembly, and this is therefore on the record. The next day the president, in a letter to Prime Minister Ben-Gurion, said that he knew that the decision was not an easy one, but he believed "that Israel would have no cause to regret her withdrawal."

We tried during those days [in 1967] to get the United States to restate these assurances. Eshkol decided, in spite of the pressure, to follow the course of diplomatic activity and to lower the tone in public responses. He also instructed his associates, once UNEF was withdrawn, not to make any references to the Gulf of Aqaba or to the Strait of Tiran in order not to provoke President Nasser. What he did keep asking for the next two weeks was for the United States to reaffirm these commitments publicly, so as to leave no doubt in the minds of all concerned—the UN, the Soviets, the Egyptians, and the Israelis—about its public position. We did not succeed until May 23 in getting the U.S. government to state that the closure of the strait constituted an illegal act.

For me, one of the most dramatic meetings that I had in Washington was on May 22, at midnight, when Gene Rostow asked me to come and see him because the ambassador was out of town. The State Department at midnight, with the lights dimmed, is not the most cheerful place to be, especially when we had by then learned that the strait had been closed by Nasser. In the outer office of Mr. Rostow, I met a dear friend. I would like to say a few words about him, Rodger Davies [then deputy assistant secretary for Near Eastern Affairs and South Asian Affairs, killed by Greek assailants while ambassador to Cyprus in 1974—Ed.]. He was one of the most honorable persons with whom I have ever had to deal and for whom I had the greatest respect and personal affection. Although I don't think that we agreed on anything at all, we still had this wonderful relationship, and it is a tragedy, an irony, the way he was killed and by whom. While waiting to see the secretary, Rodger said to me that as far as he could see the situation, war was inevitable and he couldn't see any way out of it. He said it with a broken heart.

I was asked by Mr. Rostow to tell our government to hold our fire for forty-eight hours and that in the meantime the United States would get in touch with the Soviets, the Egyptians, the Syrians, and all concerned. In the [Israeli] cabinet discussions that followed, the prime minister, who advised accepting the U.S. requests, also stated that in fact the first shot in the war had been fired; an act of aggression had been committed, and Israel felt obliged, in fact it was its duty toward its citizens, to act when the time came in accordance with article 51 of the UN Charter, as had been recognized by the United States. We asked the United States, we asked the president to make all that publicly clear.

I won't go over those terribly frustrating events of May 23. First we received a draft of the president's statement, which put us on the same level as the Egyptians; then finally he came out with the declaration that an illegal act had been committed and that there was danger of an escalation of the crisis, and he called for both sides to exercise restraint. On that day the Israeli government decided on total mobilization. It was then decided to send Mr. Eban to Washington to find out what the American position really was and what they were going to do about implementation of their commitment. I might add here that Ambassador Harman advised against sending Mr. Eban to Washington. His argument was that it would tie our hands if we did want to act later; if there was anything the U.S. government did not want, it was to appear to be in collusion—conspiracy—with Israel, and Eban's appearance in Washington would make the government of the United States even more wary as to what to do.

In retrospect, I believe that trip contributed greatly to the world's understanding of Israel's position and to the understanding that Israel was doing all it could in exhausting the diplomatic route. Before meeting with Mr. Eban, when I made the arrangements with Mr. Walt Rostow [then the national security adviser in the White House] for that meeting, President Johnson asked to see me. I was completely taken aback by this. It was unusual that in such a situation, a critical situation, that the president would speak to the DCM [deputy chief of mission]. He obviously felt it was important, otherwise he wouldn't have done it at that time, and therefore I listened carefully to what he had to say. Again the message was done in Texan terms, but it was more clear than the statement that he made later to Mr. Eban, where he used the papers prepared for him by the State Department. When he talked to me he was talking off the cuff.

He started by telling me in great detail about his visit to Ottawa. He had just returned from a meeting with Lester Pearson, who was one of the key designers, planners, of the 1957 arrangement. He wasn't complimentary (I use diplomatic language), in his description of the Canadian position, of Mr. Pearson personally, of the way he had been treated there. I got the impression that he did not get what he wanted. Obviously there was no clear Canadian support for whatever the president wanted. Then he went on to say, "I, Lyndon Johnson, have to get congressional approval if I want to act as president of the United States. Otherwise I'm just a six-foot-four Texan friend of Israel." (That description stuck in my memory.) "But you

Israeli Foreign Minister Abba Eban calling on President Lyndon Johnson, May 26, 1967. Secretary of Defense Robert McNamara is on the left; Assistant Secretary of State Joseph Sisco has his back to the camera; and Israeli ambassador Avraham Harman and Minister Counselor Ephraim Evron are on the right. Courtesy of Lyndon Baines Johnson Library; photo by Yoichi R. Okamoto.

and I, the two most powerful people in Washington, are going to get the Congress to pass another Tonkin resolution." Then, knowing a little about the Tonkin resolution and the mood in the United States at the time, and what they felt about the president and the way he got his resolution, I thought, he's telling me that Congress is never going to give him permission to use military force.

He then used the words "Israel is not a satellite of the United States." But so as not to make me feel too important, he added, "Neither is the United States a satellite of Israel." And we agreed on both. He then said that Israel—here he was quoting from memory from that rather enigmatic memorandum prepared by, as I know now, Dean Rusk, which was repeated to us time and again during the coming week—would not be alone unless it chose to be alone. And it could be interpreted in different ways. But in case I felt that maybe he was telling me that we were on our own and could act, for obvious reasons—and I felt strongly for him, sympathized with him—as if we were free, he made it clear that this was not what he meant, that we should go the United Nations route and go through the maritime countries' plan, but in the end, don't worry, everything will turn out well. I must confess that when I left him to find Mr. Eban and tell him where the meeting would take place, I wasn't the happiest man in town. His meetings with Mr. Eban have been described in great length, but there too, Mr. Eban had every right to understand that the president in the end promised him that the United States, if everything else had been exhausted, would act to implement it [the U.S. commitment regarding the Gulf of Aqaba].

I'll quote two short sentences from that memorandum of conversation [with Eban] that I saw in Jerusalem. At one point in the conversation, the president says, and this is again Texan, "At this moment, I do not have one vote or one dollar for taking action before threshing this matter out in the UN in a reasonable time and trying to work out some kind of multinational group." But then, in direct answer to a direct question, the Israeli record shows that he said: "You can tell your cabinet that the president, the Congress, and the country will support the plan to use any or all measures to open the strait to the ships of all nations." I also believe that Mr. Eban was completely right when he reported this to the cabinet. He said that there was a presidential promise, if everything else failed, for a unilateral American action to open the strait. You all know that it wasn't easy for the prime minister and the foreign minister to get the cabinet to accede to the president's request to wait another two weeks, but they finally did it, on the condition that it would be made clear to the president that it was this commitment by him that made Israel wait. It's interesting to note, though, that the president, according to your testimony, Gene, and others, had a feeling that he had failed in conveying to Mr. Eban, in persuading Mr. Eban, not to act, for the simple reason that he felt, apparently, that he didn't give him the kind of commitment that was necessary.

I believe that this was at the heart of the president's decision the next day to send a stern message to Israel not to act, following a message that he had just received from Mr. Kosygin. He didn't want, under any circumstances, any Israeli action to follow immediately from Eban's visit. During the week that followed, everything began to unravel. As the days passed, it was clear that nothing was going to happen and that we were on our own, and we had to decide whether we were going to accept strangulation or, as Mr. Eban once said in his own inimitable way, "National suicide is not an international obligation." The Israeli cabinet on June 2 decided that they had exhausted all possible routes and had to go to war.

I hope that later on, Mr. Chairman, I'll be given an opportunity to refer to some of the myths involved, including the role of Justice Fortas, which

General Meir Amit, Mossad director, in the Sinai, June 1967.

is exaggerated and out of place, as well as the so-called meetings that I never had with Mr. Angleton and others, as well as the lessons we must draw, we Israelis, from the war.

Israeli Perceptions

Meir Amit: My goal in this meeting is to give an answer to the simple question whether I, Meir Amit, got a green, yellow, or any other light from the American authorities to wage a war, especially from my friend Dick Helms. I want to say now, before I start, the answer is no. Not a green, not a yellow or any other light. To convince you, I have the original report that I wrote on June 4, 1967. This is copy number two out of eight. This is written here and whoever reads Hebrew can read it.

To start where Eppy ended, we thought that we had exhausted all other means, and my mission was to go the States and find out exactly, because we were in an unclear situation. Everybody told a different story. But before starting to describe my mission, I must make a few background remarks.

First, it is a big danger to sit twenty-five years after the fact and discuss things that happened twenty-five years before under different conditions. The Soviet Union existed; now it doesn't. People tend to weigh things according to what happened then. This is a human and natural thing. Please remember this and keep it in mind. Don't translate the existing prevailing situation to those days. It was a different time altogether.

Point two: In answering Ambassador Evron's remark about intelligence, I have to defend intelligence. In 1960 the Egyptians put forces into the Sinai, from January to March, and we thought that 1967 might be another such exercise in the first two days. By the way, intelligence affairs [agencies] are not prophets, because the way things operate, when you move it is not a one-sided game. When I'm Nasser and I'm making one move, it depends what is the response on the other side, because wherever you get to a cross-point, you have two or three options and then you act accordingly.

In our particular case, I think Nasser was dragged along in the first phase by the Russian mingling [involvement] we discussed yesterday. In the second stage, he was making one move without predicting the next move. This is the way he operated. If the UN had acted differently, he would have acted differently. So you cannot predict exactly what will happen and don't ask intelligence to give all the answers. We can give you a picture but not a precise answer.

Then, when nothing happened after the first stage and after the closing of the Strait of Tiran, he started to move forces, and we were worried. He moved, for example, the Shadhli force [a division-strength mobile task force under the command of Saad al-Shadhli (el-Shazli), later chief of staff during the October 1973 war] from the north to the south, and we were worried, concerned that the Egyptians would cut off the southern part of Israel and create what they called a link, a terrestrial link, to Jordan, to the other side. If you sit like a dead duck and do nothing, you are bound to be surprised and you cannot predict what will happen. And that's why we, at least some people in Israel, advocated doing something. By the way, just for the sake of comparison, during the Gulf war I had the same feeling: we are sitting like dead ducks, being shelled by Scuds, and we cannot do anything. Our hands are tied. I have here documents where I personally was warned, not on the diplomatic level but on the professional level, not to do anything until the last days.

Now the third point, before I come to the description of my mission, is a list of events in the Arab world. How we observed it since the 1964 summit number one, summit number two—the decision to divert the Jordan, Egypt in Yemen and all the consequences, the radicalization of Syria, the revolution, the second or whatever revolution of the Ba'ath that became extremist. They backed the terror, the escalation of terrorist activity. And then of course you have to add to it the struggle between the two big powers.

So these are a few opening remarks before I start to describe my mission.

Maybe one more word. You must understand that the government of Israel was under pressure. External pressure as explained by Ambassador Evron—an effective pressure not to do anything. But there were also internal pressures by the military people who counted every day, every minute, and said that every minute that goes by we'll have to pay more casualties. Every day that elapses. And there was the famous generals' rebellion, so to speak. Not a rebellion, it was a high-level discussion trying to describe to the prime minister and his aides the consequences of sitting like a dead duck and doing nothing and waiting for somebody else to do the job for you. And we had no sign. And I don't want to repeat what Eppy Evron said, although he didn't say enough about the confusions that were transmitted to us by different people: that we have a task force; we have an armada; the navy forces will come and open up the strait. All kinds of stories we heard, but we didn't have hard evidence, and this caused a lot of confusion. Of course, in addition to the military there were the people in the streets. There was a famous phrase, that the merry wives or women of Windsor, whatever you call them, went out to demonstrate, the women on the streets, so the prime minister was under pressure.

We recruited, we mobilized most of the armed forces. The economy was on the verge of standstill and we could not go on like that. It was an either-or proposition: Either you do something or else you lose face. And it's not a matter of face; you are putting at stake the future of the state. That was the situation on May 30. We had a daily meeting with the prime minister where we discussed it, and we said we couldn't go on like that; something had to be done. Either we give up, or we do something. So at the suggestion of General Yariv, who was my deputy and afterward head of military intelligence, who participated—we were five people in this meeting—he said, maybe you should go to Washington and try to find out if all these stories that we are hearing are true. You are in a position to sit informally and find out the facts.

Here I want to use parentheses, because people here don't know how intelligence works. Intelligence is a big racket. There are close relations between the services—not only with the CIA but with everybody who is more or less friendly. Of course there are all kinds of relationships, but when there is an accusation that there was a collusion between the United States and Israel, between the CIA and the Mossad, to topple Nasser, it is really ridiculous. It was just the ordinary course of business that we used to have with any other service. We could sit with the British, with the French, maybe not at that time but there was a time. In intelligence, you know, there is a corridor, a living room, a bedroom, and the question is how far you let your ally or your colleague go inside. There was a time in 1956 that the French went into our bedroom, and ever since then we regretted it because once the Algiers thing stopped, then we'd had it.

So, what I'm trying to say is that my mission to the United States was in the ordinary course of business to compare notes with the CIA and to let them know our reading of the situation. We were not sure that the Americans knew the exact facts. What was their perception of the situation? And that is simple: You compare notes and you tell them, this is the picture, how do you see it? Before I left I had three objectives in this mission. One, to compare notes—namely to explain to the Americans the exact situation and what's going on and to find out whether they knew it or not. Two, to find out if anything was being planned to open the strait, and by the way, at this stage the closing of the strait was just a casus belli. On May 22 that was it. The war started and we knew that there was no way back. But we wanted to know if they were doing something to open the strait, although that was not the case. The case was that the Sinai was full of seven divisions, mechanized units that we were concerned about. My third objective was to tell the Americans, I, Meir Amit, am going to recommend that our government strike, and I wanted to sense what would be their response, their attitude toward that.

On May 31, I flew into Washington and spent a day and a half there, June 1 and half of June 2. First, I met with, I would say, the professional level. They're not politicians. The professional level keep track of what's going on, and I told them what our picture was. My impression was that their conception did not differ much from ours, from our understanding of the situation. There was some divergence, some differences on the number of tanks; they said that we are taking into account self-propelled guns and things like that. So we had a little more than they had, but basically my reading was that the Americans had the right picture—professionally, not politically.

The second stage was to learn what was on the minds of those involved in the decision-making process, namely that they must know what the Americans or the naval forces were going to do. Who would be in the task force? To my great sorrow, I found no trace of anything specific that was being planned, and later on we found that President Johnson had a lot of difficulty arranging for these kinds of operations, which are complicated. Eppy Evron mentioned some of the difficulties.

Now, my third point was, after I found out there was no task force, only the president, the secretary of state, and the secretary of defense, I said, "Okay, let me meet any one of them." They agreed and made arrangements for me to meet McNamara, who was secretary of defense at that time. I told Mr. McNamara, "Mr. Secretary, first of all, I want to be clear from the beginning. I am not on any official mission here. You must understand how things are working." Mr. Evron, although we are good friends and we were in direct touch all the time, belongs to a different hierarchy. Gideon Rafael was in the UN. I did my best to brief them, but I was not in this hierarchy and I made it clear that I came from the outside, informally. I made it clear from the beginning. I told him [McNamara] I was in touch with the late Ambassador Harman and also with Mr. Evron and with Gideon Rafael.

The second thing that I told Mr. McNamara was, "Mr. Secretary, I know that you are not in a position to answer or to react or to tell me anything, so please listen and I don't want you to answer. I just want you to listen." And I told him three things. (1) I gave a short description of the military situation. (2) I told him—and I knew his background—our economy is at a standstill. We can't go on living like that. (3) I told him that I'm personally going to recommend that we take action, because there's no way out, and please don't react. He told me it was all right, the president knows that you are here and I have a direct line to the president.

All of a sudden somebody came into the room and handed him a piece of paper. And then McNamara stood up and said, "General Dayan has been appointed minister of defense. I admire this person. Please give him my regards." That's all. He asked two questions, only two questions. He said, "How long will it take?" And I said, "Seven days." That was our assessment. And then, "How many casualties?" Here I became a diplomat. I said less than in 1948, when we had 6,000. That's all; I think the whole meeting lasted forty minutes or so.

I didn't get a green light or a yellow light. I told McNamara what I thought, what I was going to recommend, that was it. And all this is written here in my report. All the other stories that are heard—hundreds of pages that have been written about the mission—are twisted in one way or another.

Before I went back to Israel on June 2, I came back to the embassy for a couple of hours. Eppy Evron shared my views; Ambassador Harman was very, very undecided. I would say he was leaning toward waiting, not doing anything, so I told him, you're coming with me because we are going, I'm going, to recommend and I want another voice to be added, not just mine. Both of us went back to Israel on an empty plane Friday night from New York. By the way, at Kennedy Airport we met with Gideon Rafael and we briefed him.

Gideon Rafael: I told him, "Tell the prime minister that we are alone, alone."

Meir Amit: You didn't have to tell me. That was my perception; you just strengthened it. I went back, and we had a meeting of what we called a committee for defense and security, the ministerial committee for defense. I reported, the ambassador reported, and the decision was to go ahead. I was a little bit lenient; I said, let's do something before, let's send a ship, it would take a few hours and let them shoot first, let them fire the first shot. Dayan said no, if we are alone, we have to do it alone, we cannot be dependent on any chance that might or might not happen and we should start right now. That was Saturday night. Sunday morning there was a cabinet meeting, where I again reported. There were two people from the left-wing Mapam Party who were more or less against, but they abstained, nobody was against, and first thing Monday morning, the war started.

Bernard Reich: I know what it feels like now to be the prime minister of Israel trying to preside over an Israeli cabinet, but we'll leave the discussion between the two gentlemen till later. We have now Professor Janice Gross Stein of Canada.

Commentary

Janice Stein: I think it's probably useful to stay away from the issue of the green light, red light, and amber light until tomorrow, when this subject is formally on the agenda. Let me pose a series of questions to both Eppy Evron and Meir Amit that were not answered in terms of assessing the Israeli response. I think the critical question for us here is, from May 22 until June 3, when the decision was made, was there any alternative to war, was war in fact inevitable?

There were certainly voices around the table yesterday saying that there was nothing the crisis managers could do once the blockade was announced and that war was inevitable. I think if we look at the record between May 22 and June 3, we have a far more complex picture. There were deep divisions within the Israeli cabinet throughout this period. There are interesting similarities to what we saw in the Soviet position and the American position. But these were not political divisions in the normal way we think about them. The divisions about what to do did not overlap consistently with party or ideology. It was really an argument about what the problem was. When you look at the record throughout this whole period, the Israelis were not agreed on what the primary problem was that confronted them. That came out in the two presentations we heard this morning.

One group argued strongly that the problem was the blockade and that if the blockade could be addressed, the primary problem would be resolved and the crisis could be managed. The second group argued, especially as the Egyptian forces began to move quickly into the Sinai, that the problem was no longer the blockade and that the issue was twofold. First, the failure of deterrence could put in jeopardy Israel's future relationship with its Arab neighbors and second, there was a growing and acute problem of defense. And from this perspective, all the discussions that occurred in Washington were irrelevant. Until the end, they really did not deal with that issue; they dealt with the proposed multinational fleet, which wouldn't address the second problem. Much of what happened in this critical two-week period was an argument about how the agenda was going to be shaped in Israel, and that's where I think the critical divisions were. Within that context, there was a struggle to assess intentions on three levels. The first one is, of course, assessment of Egyptian intentions and, to come back to Meir's comment on intelligence, it's difficult; you can't impose unfair criteria.

But I think there are two interesting incidents that we haven't talked about. First was the intelligence prediction from Israel on May 25 that an Egyptian attack was imminent. That came directly from what Salah Bassiouny described yesterday, when 'Amr ordered Egyptian troops to prepare for an attack. Clearly the Israelis intercepted that order but didn't get the countermessage and therefore anticipated that an attack was imminent. That message came through to Evron and Eban when they were in Washington, yet the cabinet nevertheless voted against preemption. They asked the United States for a declaration that an attack on Israel would be considered as if it were an attack on the United States. But even under that tremendous pressure, they waited. And that actually should have been the most dangerous moment in the crisis.

One thing hasn't come out, although Meir alluded to it: the estimates of casualties. What was the Israelis' estimate if the Egyptians in fact struck first? What was the Pentagon's estimate? I've heard various figures informally around the table here, but they differ. Clearly the outcome of the war was not in doubt, but there were significant differences in estimates of casualties. Without naming names, in the discussion yesterday I said to one of the Americans, what were the casualty estimates? He said, I don't remember, they weren't important to me. Now I understand that, but they were very, very important in the Israeli cabinet discussions, where casualties are a crucial political issue. It would be interesting if people could address that.

The second question of course is the assessment of American intentions. The crucial issue here was twofold. Was there going to be a blockade? Was there going to be a fleet that would break the blockade? That's what we focused on. But the second part of the issue is what I think began to dominate discussions in the last few days. What would the United States do if Israel took matters into its own hands? That's where we get the question of green, red, and amber lights. For the record here, and here's a question for Eppy, in my reading of the notes on the discussion of those critical meetings in Washington, that second question in the aide mémoire, which recognized Israel's right to act in self-defense, did not come up until the end of May, and I think you were the first one to raise it in talks with American officials. There is a puzzle here. The Israelis were in Washington talking about the appropriate response to the crisis. Once the initial alarm about May 25 had passed, discussions focused exclusively on the fleet, and Eban did not raise with Johnson on May 25 what the consequences would be if that second part of the aide mémoire became the dominant political issue. There was a big gap between what was going on in Washington and what was going on in Israel in the discussions at that time.

The third and last question is how Israel's assessment of Jordanian and Egyptian intentions changed at the end of May. What we know, again from people who participated in the meeting that Meir described when he went back [to Israel], was that there was an assessment that an Egyptian attack was likely sooner or later. If it wasn't imminent in the sense that it was going to be on June 4, 5, 6, or 7, the feeling was that Nasser would have difficulty keeping his generals under control, and that's not inconsistent with what was said yesterday about the tension between 'Amr and Nasser. There was also the feeling that King Hussein's trip to Cairo cemented Jordan into a military relationship with Egypt. And much of the discussion that morning took place within the framework of an intelligence assessment that said war [an attack on Egypt] is coming.

We know in fact that that assessment was not correct, given Nasser's views. He was determined to sit back and wait to provoke an attack because of the diplomatic consequences that would flow from having Israel strike first. So here's a hypothetical question for both of you gentlemen. Would the response have been different if you had appreciated that Nasser's strategy was one of provocation rather than one of attack? I think in the answers to those three questions will come some conclusions to the question of whether war was inevitable.

Bernard Reich: I might point out that this afternoon we will look in some detail at the U.S. response, and I think we will hear some of the reactions. Tomorrow morning we will come back to the conspiracy theory, which deals with some of the rest. Bill Quandt has asked to speak first.

Discussion

William Quandt: [Let's pursue Meir's] account of his visit here and his report back a bit farther, to complete the record. There are accounts of your report to the defense committee, I think, in the book that is based on [General Israel] Lior's diary, which Mr. Cockburn drew to American readers' attention, and I believe that there are other accounts that suggest that you made a comment something like the following (forgive my poor translation): You had reason to believe that the United States would not object if Israel took action that would crush or destroy—some strong word—Nasser. I am interested in whether you did in fact say something to that effect, and if so, what that statement was based on, in terms of your conversations with anybody in the United States, because you've made no reference to the objectives of the Israeli military actions and what American responses might have been to the prospect that you were going to war.

Meir Amit: The answer is yes. Within my report, I included my impressions. Maybe I failed to say that I take all the responsibility, and I didn't have any hard-core evidence to present that the Americans will back us or do nothing or whatever. It was my interpretation, it was my impressions. I had a chance to talk here in Washington, within a day and a half, with maybe twenty-five, thirty people on different levels. We have a Hebrew saying, to "sit shiva"—when somebody dies you sit seven days in mourning. I used this phrase, that I believed that the Americans will not sit shiva if we do this. This was my expression word for word. And again, I take all the responsibility, all the blame, everything upon myself. This was an interpretation, an impression from my talks with many people. You get the feel of how they think, and that was my impression. By the way, Mr. Lior's book is not accurate (although this is beside the point); there are a few things that I know he didn't invent but "developed." At least according to my reading, it was not exactly correct. Did I answer your question?

William Quandt: You implied that you did say something like pressing Nasser, not just defeating Egypt, but a personalization—getting rid of Nasser, something like that.

Meir Amit: No, no, I must, I must . . .

William Quandt: Breaking into pieces, shattered . . .

————: Breaking into pieces is mentioned in several books.

Meir Amit: I didn't use this phrase, never. I will just refer to one question of Janice's about the dilemma of either opening the strait or dealing with the whole complex. Now, as I said before, the strait was just a casus belli, but the real threat was the filling of the Sinai with seven divisions and more, and that's what concerned us. So as a matter of fact, when I described the situation I referred more to the big complex or the whole complex rather than to the mere tactical thing of opening the strait. We had to refer technically to this particular issue because that was the thing that we were fed all the time. Here, wait, wait, wait, we are going to open the strait, but to be frank that was not our main concern. Our main concern was that the Egyptians are practically wiping out all the 1957 agreement. And I'm not going to elaborate on that.

Carl Brown: Let's get more precision on that important point you're giving us. You say, "If we do this. . . ." What is "this," what did you say in your report?

Meir Amit: I said that we have to strike, and we had a contingency plan that I was aware of—don't call it the Six-Day War, call it the three-hour war—and I must take pride in the intelligence. Intelligence is, I think, a boring thing. You work six years, ten years in order to create a picture. It's a mosaic. You put one piece to another. I, of course, cannot discuss it here openly, but I think that our intelligence did a remarkable job, not in one day but maybe over years, because of the confrontation. And we were very, very confident (a) about what will happen and (b) about the pictures, in which you could even distinguish between a real airplane and a dummy plane, a false one. This was exactly what I was referring to. I was referring to the strike and what will happen afterward. Nothing else.

Salah Bassiouny: After listening to this exposé, two exposés, and looking to the level and depth of contacts between Israel and the United States at that time, and comparing also at the same time the Egyptian level and depth of contacts with the Soviet Union, it came to mind that there is a crucial question while we are discussing U.S.-Israeli relations or Egyptian-Soviet relations. What is the definition, in your opinion, of Israel as a friend of the United States, Egypt as a friend of the Soviet Union? I think that if we reach the definition, the proper definition, of this friendship we might be able to sort out a lot of things.

Ephraim Evron: I couldn't tell you about how it feels to be a friend of the Soviet Union. We never had the opportunity of being one, so that's up to you; you describe to us how it expressed itself on both sides. We have never had any formal agreement with the United States. It's a unique relationship. I heard President Carter, who on a scale of one to ten as a friend of Israel would not be ten, say in a press conference in Haifa that he was asked this question in Damascus. When asked why is it that the U.S. government, so powerful, is giving in to a pressure group of a minority, his reply was that it had nothing to do with pressure groups of a minority, that the president was responding to what he believed was the general feeling in the American people, not just in the Bronx or in New York or in Brooklyn, but throughout the country. [The relationship] had its ups and downs. It was never, as I said, formal. I don't think we were ever given anything on a silver tray. There are friends of ours here who know it. We had to fight hard for everything, whether it was a supply of guns or support in the international community.

But I think there was a sense of sharing the same values, respect for each other in spite of the vast difference in size and the different interests. Israel has only one interest and that's survival. The United States has many interests, some of them conflicting, certainly some in connection with this. On that very crisis, there were people in the State Department and others writing in newspapers who were saying that it was not in the interest of the United States to appear to be the sole supporter of Israel in the crisis that was developing. If you ask me to give a clear definition in concrete terms as to what this friendship means, I find it terribly difficult, only I know that it's there. Even, even today.

Shimon Shamir: I would like to add a few words on an important issue raised by Eppy Evron and Meir Amit, looking at it from the perspective of that time's military intelligence. Evron and Amit held then senior positions in the hierarchies of their respective institutions, while I occupied only a junior post. But I served at the hub of the intelligence assessment system, and I believe I was knowledgeable on most of the important issues.

The evaluation of the military intelligence after the closure of the Tiran Strait was that a green signal from the United States allowing Israel to strike was given. Not *would be* given, but *had* already *been* given. The evaluations submitted by intelligence on this question were unequivocal. The reasoning behind that evaluation was the following. It was commonplace that the United States wanted to avoid confrontation with the Soviet Union. This was the most important consideration for a superpower in the realities of the cold war. Accordingly, we felt that the United States could not allow itself to give a green signal to a friend, or client if you wish, to strike at a Soviet client without implicating itself and risking a clash with the Soviets.

I remember a discussion of this subject in which we analyzed the problem deductively. We asked ourselves, suppose the United States *did* want to give a signal to a country like Israel to start a war or carry out an extensive military operation against a target within the Soviet sphere of influence, how would it formulate that green light, given the constraints of the cold war and the need to prevent confrontation with the Soviets? We came up with something similar to what Ambassador Evron described. We said that in all likelihood we would get a message loaded with various insinuations and vague phrases, and perhaps even concluding with a few pious words cautioning Israel against taking unilateral action. But the Americans transmitting this signal would trust the Israelis to read between the lines. This was the ground for the belief that the green light was already there.

Naturally, the various intelligence branches worked energetically to provide corroborating evidence. Meir described the painstaking work that went into it. Every few hours somebody would come up with a small piece of information that seemed to support this evaluation: something like a report on what an American military attaché in some European capital said in passing to an Israeli diplomat, which could somehow be interpreted as indicating the existence of a green signal. This information would be rushed to the top. Naturally, intelligence can reach the cabinet directly, there are papers of all kinds of colors—the details don't really matter. The fact is that intelligence flooded the decision makers with information pointing in the "green light" direction.

Consciously or unconsciously, intelligence was not entirely unbiased on this question. What influenced military intelligence was exactly what Meir Amit described: the feeling that Israel must strike and it must strike now. As I mentioned in my paper, the military had little faith in the diplomatic option. They were skeptical about Eban's mission to Washington. They thought that politicians delude themselves, are indecisive, and waste precious time. They felt that at stake was Israel's credibility as a state capable of defending itself and, therefore the matter had an existential importance. It was believed that every day that passed would bring more losses when the war eventually and inevitably broke out. I recall, for example, the charts that were prepared showing the pace of training of new tank crews in Egypt. The Egyptians had received at that time a large number of Soviet tanks for which they lacked crews, and they were frantically training their soldiers to use them. The charts showed how many more tanks could be manned and would become operational with each day that passed.

We all had a deep sense of commitment to this evaluation. This included, by the way, the representative of the Ministry of Foreign Affairs, Shlomo Argov, who identified with our point of view—although he represented what was for military intelligence at that time almost the enemy camp. He strongly believed that the road was clear for action, and that it was disastrous to delay it. I remember him at one point, when Eban was in Washington, pacing the room and murmuring, "We must bring him home immediately; he's feeding the government with wrong impressions."

The interpretation of the American signal to Israel was a mirror image of our own interpretation of the Soviet signal to Egypt. Our reasoning was this: The information that the Soviets fed the Egyptians about the massive concentration of Israeli forces was so far-fetched that the Soviets must have known that the Egyptians would realize that it was not a genuine mistake but a deliberate lie. We interpreted this as a green signal for action. We felt that the Russians were in fact telling the Egyptians, "We are giving you this information. You know it's not correct. We know that you know that it's not correct. But this is our way to tell you that you can take action now. Do something demonstrative to prevent an Israeli operation in Syria." The explanation for this indirectness was the same as with the United States: A superpower cannot give a full-fledged signal to its client without involving itself and risking a confrontation with the patron of its client's adversary.

The lesson from this is a confirmation of the old dictum that perceptions are influenced by objectives. The military wanted very much to go into action, and this influenced its evaluation of the kind of signal received from Washington.

Tahsin Basheer: Ambassador Evron, your quotation from Khrushchev is interesting. You didn't put it in context. The context was Nasser taking the Soviet Union and Khrushchev to pieces for trying to make Egypt a satellite or to influence Egypt with communists. And he put that, he attacked Russia . . .

Ephraim Evron: I was only referring to his reading of Nasser's character, that's not the context.

Tahsin Basheer: No, no, but his reading of Nasser's character was again the speech of Nasser attacking Kruschchev, the Soviet Union, and the communists. That's one point. A second to Amit. The interaction is interesting, but I want to learn from you certain things. First, did the Israeli committee of defense estimate that the Egyptians wanted war? The situation was dangerous. There was deception of friends. Did they estimate that the Egyptian army was put in a tactic of deploying as if going to war? Second, was there at any moment anybody assessing the Egyptian army or the Jordanian or whatever forces as a real threat to Israel? It was always, to my reading, an American-Israeli assessment that Israeli forces could take on the Arabs, and there was no doubt about that. Third, what was the estimate of casualties by Israel and by your fellows in America, whether in the CIA or political intelligence and the rest? Absent from all of this talk about an impending war were discussions about what to do after the war.

Raymond Garthoff(?): I found it intriguing that Ambassador Harman had advised against the Eban prescription in part for fear of what Eban might hear, yet Mr. Amit decided to tell McNamara what he intended to recommend, not out of fear of what McNamara might respond to. This is curious, whether the Foreign Ministry and the Mossad had made their assessments of what they would do if the Americans had said no—not with what Amit was looking for, which was whether the Americans were going to do something, but simply an answer of no: "We don't want you to go to war at this time."

Leonard Meeker: I was most interested by one element in General Amit's exceedingly clear presentation, and that was his statement that on his return to Israel on June 3 he recommended as a first step that a ship should be sent [to transit] the strait to see whether it would be fired on and that that was the right way to go about it. From the point of view of international law, that was a sound recommendation. That sort of attack on an Israeli ship would clearly have been an armed attack, [calling] into play the right of self-defense. As it was, Israel did something else. It followed the Dayan prescription of going all out, which obviously solved Israel's problem, but it went far beyond that, and I think it has to be considered greatly out of proportion to the needs and terms of international law.

Ernest Dawn: Was there any discussion in the Israeli policy-making echelon of what the United States would do if Israel preempted in the face of an American no? What did you think the United States could do, cut off your supplies if you needed resupplies? My impression is still that you were mostly a French-armed army. Was there any real discussion as to what the United States might do in case you preempted without U.S. approval?

Gideon Rafael: I would like to sum up in a short way the position, as I saw it, that the United States had adopted in the decisive last days of May and the beginning of June.

The United States did not want to take responsibility for direct military involvement. It gave Israel to understand that it was entitled to break the stranglehold. The United States wanted to avoid any misunderstanding that Israel could count on a military involvement of the United States. When Mr. Eban on May 25 had his talk with President Johnson, mentioned by Eppy Evron, an authorized source contacted me in New York before Eban embarked to return to Israel. He said he wanted me to make it clear to Mr. Eban that the president had stressed the point of congressional consent, which meant, if translated into clear language, that he could not make any commitment but that he definitely did not want to deflect Israel's necessity and purposes. I communicated this point; apparently it did not sink in enough, and I was called in again by a most responsible representative of the United States. He asked me to send a telegram to Mr. Eshkol, and the bottom line was, "You must understand that you stand alone and you have to know the consequences." It was added, on a personal note, it is understandable that if you stand alone you will know how to act. This was sent to Mr. Eban, and I repeated it to General Amit when we met at the airport on the day of his departure.

On the other hand, the United States, disappointed of course by the futile proceedings in the Security Council—U Thant was paralyzed by the impending Soviet veto—and disappointed in the helplessness of the secretary-general under the circumstances nevertheless did not want to interrupt the diplomatic effort. Therefore, encouraged by the United States, I made a last appeal on June 3, 1967. This was the last Security Council meeting before the outbreak of the war, and I presented a five-point plan. I stated that if it were accepted by the Security Council and consented to by the Arabs, it would prevent the war. I said that it is not too late for reason to prevail if five immediate steps are taken in the present crisis: all inflammatory statements and threats against the territorial integrity and political independence of any state should cease; the charter obligation of nonbelligerence must be strictly complied with; the armed forces should be withdrawn to their positions held at the beginning of the month of May; all forms of armed incursions, acts of sabotage, and terrorism should cease, and the governments concerned should take all steps to prevent their territory from being used for such hostile acts; there should be no interference with any shipping in the Strait of Tiran and the Gulf of Aqaba. If these steps were taken promptly, the deep anxieties of the hour would be lifted and the present dangerous tensions would subside. This was our last diplomatic intervention. On June 5, the war started.

William Quandt: Mr. Ambassador, could you confirm for the historical record that your authorized source is Ambassador Goldberg? He has said as much in his own oral interview.

Bernard Reich: On the microphone his head was shaken in a positive manner; we don't have video, just audio in this case.

Gideon Rafael: One minute about the head shaking: Churchill in Parliament, listening to a speech of the opponent, apparently an outrageous speech, did nothing but shake his head. The speaker was apparently taken aback, and he said, "Mr. Prime Minister, I'm only expressing my opinion," whereat Churchill answered, "And I am only shaking my head."

Meir Amit: Number one: In any democratic state there are differences of opinions, views, different parties. And the same holds true for Israel. Second, to answer the question if it was unanimous, if it was a consensus: Not always even a consensus, but I would say an overwhelming feeling, but with differences of views regarding tactics, etc. I don't want to elaborate. To the question of whether after May 22 there was an option not to go to war, the answer is no. According to my reading, at least, that was sine qua non. I didn't believe that [was possible] after the closing of the strait, which as I said was not the cause—it was just the casus belli. Number three, whether there was a disagreement in the government regarding the opening of the strait: I think we don't have to repeat that in the government at a certain meeting—I don't remember what date it was—it was nine for and nine against.

Janice Stein: May 27.

Meir Amit: That means that there were differences. Why? Because they said wait, somebody else will do the job for you. Why should you do the job for yourself? Other people said it was a dream. These were the differences, but not more than that. So everybody was in favor, but some people said let's wait and wait and wait. Some people say in our country, when you ask about casualties, every day that goes by, that elapses, will bring about more and more casualties. I'll come to that in a moment.

Then, how we appraise the Egyptian intentions. I think that it is not a clear-cut case. At the beginning Nasser was swept into it because of Russian interference, so to speak. He then made some movements and waited to see what the reaction would be. If there was no reaction, he made another move, and so forth. Basically, there was somewhere in the back of his mind, for sure, not a grand design, but a kind of a grand feeling that he must do it. But I think he was a good diplomat, a good, maybe, planner, and he didn't want to eat a larger chunk as long as he didn't know the consequences. So he did it his way. We thought the Egyptians were moving toward staying in the Sinai. Some people, even in Israel, say if you had not waged a war, they would have stayed in the Sinai, nothing would have happened, and that's all. I don't buy it. Because, according to our reading, they moved forces toward the south—from the north, from the Rafa area, to the south—in order to cut off Eilat and the southern part of Israel, which is vulnerable, and establish a bridge, a land bridge to Jordan. This was our reading, and that was my understanding of what would have happened if we had not done anything.

You asked about the casualties. Again, I answered in part because there was no clear-cut answer. The [answer depends on] when we would have started to do something. If we would have waited more and more, there would be more [casualties]. Our estimate was that there would be hundreds of casualties, hundreds. But I cannot say, maybe Shimon was sitting and counting. I was on a different level. I didn't count.

I want to answer a question that I was asked yesterday about the difference between the '56 war and 1967, and what would have happened if the Egyptians had struck first. I say that there is a big difference between the

'56 war and 1967. I was chief of operations at the time [1956]. I was number two to General Dayan, and I know the exact operational scene. We were not prepared because of the connection with the British and the French, and they were going slowly, and we could not match their tempo, their rate of activity, and nobody knew. I have a note written to me by the chief of the staff of the southern command on the eve of the war: "Can we say that the war starts tomorrow?" I said, "Yes, but if." Until the eve of the war, we didn't know for sure that it would happen, because we were not operating on our own. I will come to it in a moment, about Dayan's pushing for doing it now.

There is a big difference between the '56 war, when we were not ready, and the '67 war, when we had three weeks' time to prepare, to dig, and when the thing started it was like a striking fist. So if the Egyptians would have started first—I think we should always try to do it before.

Ephraim Evron: I believe that the breaking point came on May 30 and 31 when King Hussein joined the joint command. It was clear for us, I think also for you here in Washington, that the last act had been played. For us in Israel, I had mentioned the letter that Eshkol had sent to the president, which said that we decided to wait because of his firm commitment to Eban that in the end the United States will act, if necessary unilaterally. When the president received it, I understand, he hit the ceiling. He asked Walt Rostow to call me in, and in a most unpleasant manner I was told that the president had said nothing of the sort. He said he would do everything within his power, and his power was limited by the constitutional process. When I cabled that back home, and I think General Rabin in his memoirs mentioned it, that was the last thing to convince the Israeli decision makers that we were on our own. In answer to your question, it should be remembered—somehow it is not now—that the day the war broke out the United States imposed an embargo on Israel, on all the countries in the area, but it affected us mainly. For the next few months I used to knock on the door of Mac Bundy to try to have some of the most elementary necessary pieces released, but there was until October, I believe, or November, a full embargo as far as the United States was concerned.

And last, a footnote to history. On May 24, Ambassador Harman called on former President Eisenhower to solicit his support for the president's [Johnson's] statement about the illegality of the closure of the strait. President Eisenhower said that of course he would do it when asked. He firmly believed that this was the case. And then he added that on reflection he felt that he may have made a mistake in 1956 or '57 in the policy that the United States then followed vis-à-vis Israel, France, and Britain.

CHAPTER 4

◢ The Other Arab Responses

C. Ernest Dawn

Syria was the focal point of the 1967 Arab-Israeli crisis, as the participants proclaimed at the time. Syria retains this position in the expositions presented in this panel. Ambassador Tomeh, presenting the crisis in the precise terms that he did as Syria's ambassador to the UN during the crisis, confines his remarks to charges of Israeli and Zionist aggression against Syria, the Palestinians, and the Arabs. Perceived Israeli aggression figures prominently in Dr. Mutawi's depiction of the sources of Jordanian action in the crisis, which emphasizes the Jordanian decision makers' belief that Israel was maneuvering Syria into action designed to invite Egypt to provide a pretext for Israeli occupation of the West Bank. Some of the Jordanians also believed that the United States was Israel's co-conspirator. Ambassadors Bassiouny and Basheer espouse the same thoughts, and the latter adds Jordan to the conspirators. Dr. Mutawi, however, while stressing the importance of Jordanian perceptions of Israeli action, agrees with the panel chairman in laying stress on Syria's role in inter-Arab relations and the politics of Pan-Arabism as a major cause of the crisis and war.

As proof of Israel's aggressive expansionism, Ambassador Tomeh adduces (1) Zionist pre-state terrorism, (2) pre-mandate Zionist claims to the head-waters of the Jordan, (3) Israel's obvious initiation of hostilities, and (4) Israel's military success. The first two charges are true but immaterial; the advocates of terrorism and territorial expansion had been a decided minority in both the mandatory and state periods until 1967. The second two charges, also true, do not prove aggressive intent. They depend on the unacceptable proposition that the successful belligerent is necessarily the aggressor. Israel claimed that it was exercising the right of self-defense in response to aggression by Syria and certain Palestinian organizations and to threats from Egypt.

Israel's intentions have been hotly debated. The Soviets and the Syrians at the time, and since, charged a massive Israeli troop concentration against Syria and pointed to alleged public threats by Israeli officials. There were undeniable public threats by Israeli officials of strong military action. The UPI dispatch that was published widely on May 12 may have been overdrawn, but it was not created out of whole cloth. But public threats to act and a massive concentration of troops on the frontier are entirely different things.

There is general agreement in the sources that on May 13 Egypt received intelligence from the Soviet Union that Israel had concentrated a large number of troops on the Syrian frontier. The intelligence before this time, however, is still problematic.

The Egyptian sources agree that the intelligence was received from both Syria and the Soviet Union, and the evidence indicates that the Syrians were the first informants. There is conclusive evidence that the intelligence was false, even though it was very specific. The assertion was not that Israel had the capability to mobilize rapidly or that Israel was planning to attack; it was that there was a concentration of eleven to thirteen, or at least ten, or up to fifteen, brigades on the Syrian frontier. "Concentration" in military usage means the assembling of troops in position to commence operations without additional preparation. The first meaning in this case would be positioning in the area immediately adjacent to the Syro-Israeli frontier. It is impossible that a force of such size could have been deployed in the specified region without detection.

Israeli infantry, paratroop, and mechanized brigades had a strength of 4,500, armored brigades 3,500. Ten brigades would have had a personnel strength of about 42,500 and would have included 450 tanks, at least 900 half-tracks, and 1,200 additional half-tracks or equivalent wheeled troop transport vehicles. At the other limit, 15 brigades, the total strength would have been about 61,500 personnel, 750 tanks, at least 1,500 half-tracks, and 1,200 additional half-tracks or equivalent wheeled transport vehicles. Also, there would have been some tanks and artillery and some service units assigned to brigades or to divisional units. A figure of 30,000 to 40,00 men and 2,000 to 3,000 vehicles for 10 brigades is undoubtedly closer to what the Israelis would actually have mobilized at the time. No such force could have been concentrated on the Syrian frontier undetected. In fact, even one brigade could not have been moved into the frontier area undetected, and there is conclusive evidence, which space does not permit me to describe here, that there was no Israeli troop concentration opposite Syria on or before May 13.

Although Ambassador Kornienko's sources said that the intelligence was transmitted to the Egyptians by the Soviet intelligence service as a routine service matter, Egyptian sources assert that it was passed to Anwar Sadat by high-level Soviet political figures and that is not a routine service matter. Consequently, it is difficult to avoid the conclusion that both the Syrian and Soviet governments knowingly transmitted false, or at least unverified, information to the Egyptians for political reasons. A political rather than military origin and purpose for the reports is also suggested by the circulation of such reports by both the Syrian and Soviet governments and media a number of times before May 1967.

The pre–May 1967 charges of Israeli troop concentrations originated in Syria in response to the problems of the regime. In the first case (August 1963), the charge was solely, and in all others first, circulated by the Syrians. In the twelve months preceding May 1967, the Syrian and Soviet governments had cooperated in a campaign that made great use of the charge of Israeli troop concentrations. The purpose of the campaign was to bolster the Syrian Ba'athist regime against its internal and external enemies, Arab as well as non-Arab, and give it strength to carry out its mission of restoring Arab unity by liberating the Arabs from western "imperialism," which was operating through Arab "reaction" and through Zionism. As the two associates viewed the situation, the great threat to Syria's mission was Israeli military strength, which encouraged and promoted Arab "reaction" inside and outside Syria. A spectacular Israeli raid, it was feared, might prepare the way for a successful uprising by Syrian dissidents aided by Jordan. Charges of Israeli, and Jordanian, troop concentrations had the potential of undermining the Syrian opposition and the conservative Arab regimes, as well as favoring the Ba'athists over Nasser. The charges, especially if made by the Soviets, also might contribute to restraining Israel by encouraging Israeli opposition to Israeli policy and blocking any possible Security Council acceptance of Israel's argument that its military action was justified by Syrian behavior. The charges, finally, might persuade or goad Nasser to take action that might deter the Israelis.

The perception of danger was intensified by the spectacular Israeli air action of April 7, 1967. The usual Syrian and Soviet public statements, a Syrian charge in the Security Council of troop concentrations, and a Soviet warning to Israel were made once more, but anxiety persisted. The Soviets and the Egyptians were uneasy. Both thought that the Syrians were in the grip of "nervous tension that would lead to behavior conducive to aggravating the situation," as the UAR air force chief said in reporting on his talks in Damascus on April 10–11 (Mohamed Heikal, *al-Infijar*, p. 434). The Soviets believed that the Syrians needed reassurances that would "calm the nerves of the regime" and "set them to behaving with balance" (ibid.).

Apparently, the Egyptians and the Soviets were fearful that Syria might act in the way that Syrian and Soviet statements said Israeli military action was intended to provoke them to act, that is, by a military response that Israel would use as justification for a large-scale attack. Thus, seemingly they hoped that reassurances would calm the Syrians sufficiently for them to forgo such action. Such hopes, if held, were not justified by statements regarding the roles of regular war and a popular war of liberation that the Syrians made publicly and privately. Instead, support from Egypt might encourage the Syrians; the revival of the joint defense agreement certainly had not calmed them sufficiently. There is some evidence that the Syrian civilian leadership, at least, if not the military, believed that the frontier with Israel was so well fortified as to be impregnable. Dr. Naumkin says that the Soviet military in Syria thought that the Syrians did not believe that Israel was about to attack. Perhaps, as the Jordanians believed, Syria was attempting to maneuver Egypt into action that would provoke a war with Israel in which Egypt and Jordan "would pay the price," while Syria was immune to serious damage.

The Soviet military estimate, apparently, was different. According to the discussion in panel 1, the Soviet military in Syria believed that Syria alone could not defeat Israel but that a unified Syrian-Egyptian-Jordanian force would not be defeated. There seems to have been a common Arab and Soviet belief that Egypt and Syria would be able to continue on the defensive for a number of weeks, during which time the UN would intervene. Effective Syro-Egyptian military cooperation, the Soviets might have thought, would not only preclude an Israeli victory but would also deter a major Israeli retaliatory raid that would provoke a Jordan-supported reactionary movement in Syria. Such a raid, which was the objective attributed to Israel publicly by the Syrians and Soviets, not an all-out Israeli invasion of Syria, was probably what the Syrians and Soviets feared. Accordingly, on April 19 and 20, Deputy Soviet Foreign Minister Semenov told the Egyptian ambassador that Egypt must reassure the Syrians. Semenov and Kosygin repeated these remarks to Sadat on April 29–30 (Heikal, 442–44).

Desire to induce Egypt to take action was most likely the primary purpose of the May intelligence reports of Israeli troop concentrations. The Soviets, according to General Abdul Muhsin Murtagi, commander of the Egyptian ground forces in Sinai, fearing Israeli retaliatory action that would sweep away the Ba'athist government and believing that Egypt might deter the Israelis, "foisted" the intelligence on the Egyptians (Murtagi, p. 55). That both Syria and the Soviets desired Egyptian action seems clear. It seems highly probable that the Syrians and the Soviets consulted on the matter. It was perhaps thought that the simple charge of troop concentrations that had always been used previously was not sufficient to influence the Egyptians, so this time the intelligence specified a large number of brigades. Since it is unlikely that either intelligence service had confirmed the intelligence, although both could easily have done so, the intelligence was deliberately passed on to prod the Egyptians. Both the Syrians and the Soviets, however, probably genuinely expected a major Israeli retaliatory raid. The Soviet report to Egyptian military intelligence, according to Murtagi, advised "readiness, watchfulness, and caution and at the same time self-control."

To sum up, the perceived threat of a conservative coup in Syria and the intensification of the conflict between Egypt and the conservative Arab states created a need for Egyptian action that would answer the taunts of the conservatives. The removal of UNEF met the need; it had long since been contemplated but had been thought to be too dangerous. The Soviet endorsement of the Syrian claim of a massive Israeli troop concentration provided the justification for the desired action and a means of pressuring the Soviets for support and assistance.

King Hussein and the Jordanian authorities interpreted Israel's actions, especially after the raid on Samu', as designed to manipulate Syria in order to provoke Egypt to action that would provide Israel with a pretext for occupying the West Bank. On the morning of June 5, Israel sent a message to assure the king that Jordan would not be attacked if it refrained from opening hostilities. Dr. Mutawi regards the assurance as insincere since it was not given earlier. Although the man from Mars would surely agree with Ambassador Evron's response to Mutawi, "Do you mean that we should have warned the king that we are attacking?" the Jordanian state of mind was not unreasonable. Ambassador Rafael also states that his declaration of Israel's lack of aggressive intentions, which was sent to Nasser on May 15 through U Thant, was also made available to Hussein. Moreover, on May 23, Israel, directly and through the United States, urged Hussein to stop goading Nasser. Israel clearly was not enticing Jordan into the war. Nevertheless, charges have been made that purportedly Egyptian messages to General Riad, who was in command in Jordan, messages that falsely claimed spectacular Egyptian success, were in fact of Israeli origin, sent in order to create a pretext for the occupation of the West Bank by drawing Jordan into the war.

The charge of Israeli fabrication of Egyptian radio messages to Hussein has been made in a report attributed to a former senior Israeli military official cited by Ambassador Garthoff. The most detailed version of the charge appears in Anthony Pearson's *Conspiracy of Silence* (New York: Quartet Books, 1978). In his account, the false radio transmissions are an important element in an elaborate story of American collusion and conflict with Israel. The United States, the story has it, conspired with Israel to overthrow Nasser but was opposed to attacking Jordan. The United States also was concerned with preventing Israel's use of nuclear weapons, which might have brought in the Soviets. To this end, the USS *Liberty* and a nuclear submarine were stationed off Sinai to monitor the Israelis. To frustrate the United States, Israel attacked the *Liberty*.

Neither of Pearson's two chief sources, who are clearly described, possesses adequate credentials. Neither is likely to have been privy to either the intelligence or the policy they are claimed to have had knowledge of. One, a British military man with intelligence experience in southern Arabia, strongly suggests that his story is the result of speculation in the regional intelligence service. The other, an unnamed general at the Pentagon, is given no further credentials.

Moreover, the alleged U.S. policy is not consistent with some documented aspects of American policy. The United States at the time did not believe Israel had nuclear weapons, and such villains of the collusion thesis as [National Security Council member] Robert Komer and Walt W. Rostow regarded good relations with Nasser as an important U.S. interest. In addition, the feat is an impossible one. To carry it out, the Israelis would have had to jam all Egyptian transmissions to Jordan for three or four hours while transmitting their own false messages, without either the Egyptians or Jordanians being aware of the Israeli action. It cannot be done. Moreover, the contents of the two telegrams from 'Amr to Hussein were repeated by Nasser in a telephone call to Hussein at about 12:30 that day. Egyptian publication and broadcast of official communiqués making the same claims as the questioned messages is beyond dispute.

Israeli use of radio communications to deceive the Arabs was the subject of press reports soon after the war. A respected Israeli military correspondent, for instance, has reported, presumably from official sources, that Israel did broadcast false orders to Egyptian units. This is possible, but far from the impossible actions described by Pearson and the source cited by Ambassador Garthoff.

Jordan's participation in the inter-Arab propaganda war is a legitimate object of debate. Jordan had long been privately chiding Nasser about UNEF, and the accusation that he was hiding behind that force was the central feature of the public propaganda exchange in 1966–67. That this campaign influenced Nasser to order the withdrawal of the force is a reasonable belief. Moreover, the closure of the Tiran Strait may be ascribed, at least in part, to the continued taunting of Nasser by Jordan, Saudi Arabia, and Tunisia. It is difficult, however, to see an alternative for the Jordanian government. Since the mid-1930s, Palestine had been the preeminent Pan-Arab cause, the measure of the Arabism of every Arab politician. The Jordanian government was by far the most vulnerable to attack on this issue, given Jordan's large Palestinian population, as the aftermath of the Samu' incident demonstrated. Ba'athist Syria, the prime mover in agitating the Palestinian cause, frustrated every attempt to downplay the question. King Hussein, correctly sensing that Syria's action would probably lead to war between Egypt and Israel, tried to warn Nasser as early as May 2, but the warning was held up by Field Marshal 'Amr until noon, May 14. The delay, however, was probably without effect, because the crisis was the result of many factors.

The Arab response to Nasser's act left Hussein with no alternative. Throughout the Arab countries, wild enthusiasm greeted Nasser's blow at Zionism and imperialism. Dr. Mutawi is doubtless correct in describing the king as a sincere Arab nationalist who acted from genuine commitment to Arab solidarity. The same can be said, of course, about his grandfather, as well as about Nasser, the Ba'athists, or any other Arab leader, all of whom, like statesmen everywhere, claimed to be the sincerest and most competent advocate of the higher interests of their people. Like all statesmen, Hussein's vision of the higher interest was closely connected to his view of his immediate situation. Dr. Mutawi convincingly relates Hussein's decision to join Egypt to his immediate problems. If Jordan had not joined Nasser, the internal threat, especially from the Palestinians, would probably have been greater than that arising from Samu'.

Even if the internal threat could have been contained, the Jordanians were convinced that Israel aimed at seizure of the West Bank. The belief can easily be dismissed as not well founded, but it was not irrational, and the Israeli statements of May 11–13 did nothing to dispel it. Accordingly, since Jordan, it was believed, faced war with Israel, it was wise to have an ally before the war began. Nevertheless, Hussein's agreement with Nasser was not made until May 30.

The suggestion that if Israel had attacked Egypt before the Egyptian-Jordanian treaty was signed Jordan would have stayed out of the war and the West Bank would not have been occupied by Israel is highly plausible. If the Israeli victory had been very, very quick, Jordan might have refrained, but even a six-day war would have created irresistible internal pressures. In either case, Jordan's abstention from the war would have intensified its internal problems astronomically. In fact, the internal problem appears to have been uppermost in Hussein's mind. He later explained, according to Dr. Mutawi, that he had intended to make only a symbolic show of force that would not have invited Israeli retaliation. It is doubtful if a mere symbolic action would have had the desired effect on the Palestinians.

A radically different view of Hussein was presented by Ambassador Basheer. In this view, the king was concerned only with securing his person, family, and regime. He consequently, this interpretation runs, refused to accept Iraqi and Saudi forces in Jordan, as provided for by Unified Arab Command plans, unless Egyptian forces joined them and Egypt removed UNEF. The reason was that Hussein knew that such action by Egypt would provoke an Israeli attack on Egypt, with the approval, Basheer suggests, of the United States. This interpretation, though lacking documentation, is plausible, but no more so than the one supported by the documents. The Jordanians always insisted that the presence of other Arab forces in Jordan would provoke an Israeli attack on Jordan and that such forces could not be introduced until the Arabs were ready for war.

Jordan was neither maneuvered into war by Israel nor a party to an American plot against Nasser. Hussein, believing that war was inevitable, decided to ally with Egypt. He did not expect the Arabs to win the war. On the other hand, he did not foresee a quick, overwhelming Israeli victory.

Retrospective Jordanian criticism of the Egyptian alliance does not include Jordanian abstention as a course of action. Instead, the criticism is that Jordan accepted, without question, Egyptian command. The Egyptian conduct of the war was incompetent, the Jordanians believe. What Jordan should have done, the critics say, was to follow the plan agreed to by Hussein and Nasser on May 30, that is, to maintain a static defense and to open hostilities on a limited front only. Such action, it is believed, would have demonstrated Jordan's fidelity to Arabism without providing Israel with an excuse to attack Jordan. This, the Jordanians say, is what Jordan would have done if their forces had not been under Egyptian command or if they had known the true extent of the initial Israeli successes. That this strategy would have worked is highly improbable.

Any kind of Jordanian action, even the most limited kind, almost certainly would have provoked a major Israeli response. Revisionist Zionism, aiming at Greater Israel, was always a strong minority in Israel. The Labor government probably was sincere in desiring Jordanian neutrality and in accepting Jordanian control of the West Bank as the best Israel could hope for, given the international realities. Jordan's initiation of hostilities, however, by placing responsibility on Jordan, removed these restraints and rekindled long-suppressed hopes of uniting Jerusalem at least—even of regaining the entire Land of Israel. Such views were combined with confidence that complete military victory would enable Israel to force the Arabs to make peace. It is probable that only total Jordanian abstention from hostilities could have prevented the Israeli seizure of the West Bank. It may be that the Jordanian critics are correct in believing that if the Jordanian army had not been under Egyptian command, Jordan would have prevented the complete conquest of the West Bank. The rapid collapse of the Egyptians and consequent release of most Israeli forces for employment against Jordan, however, strongly suggest that nothing could have prevented the actual result. The Israeli numerical superiority was too great.

Panel 4

Chairman: Dr. C. Ernest Dawn, University of Illinois
Speakers:
   Ambassador George Tomeh, former Syrian UN delegate: "The Syrian Response"
   Dr. Samir Mutawi, Jordanian author: "The Jordanian Response"

Ernest Dawn: I have been asked to present a brief discussion of the Pan-Arab nationalist dimension of the 1967 crisis. Nasser and his associates in their younger days were members of organizations that acted in the belief that the liberation of the Arab nation from Western imperialism and its unification required the overthrow, by violence if need be, of the Arab ruling elements, who were perceived to be reactionary feudalists and collaborators with the imperialists.

These beliefs became more widespread and influential after the Palestine war of 1948–49. In the 1950s, especially after 1955, Nasser became the real hero of Pan-Arabs everywhere because of his great success. He was the personification of the Arab left, the progressive forces that were going to unify and purify the Arab nation. But with the Iraqi coup in 1958, Nasser soon found himself between the Arab left and the Arab right, and this intensified with the rise of the Ba'athists to power in Syria and in Iraq in 1963. By this time, of course, Nasser was involved in the Yemen and South Arabia, as well as in his semipermanent conflict with Arab reaction. The new Ba'athists, especially the Syrian Ba'athists, carried on a bitter propaganda campaign and also a campaign of subversion in the various Arab countries.

Nasser did succeed in 1964 and 1965 in actually cooperating with the conservatives through the summit conferences, trying to put inter-Arab relations on a more stable basis and above all to keep the Palestine question quiet.

Nasser did not want to be forced into a war, and he wanted to keep Palestinian irregular activity to a minimum, so he created the PLO under Ahmad Shuqayry. This, of course, stimulated the growth of the other element within the Palestine movement, which mostly took the form of Fatah, the organization headed by Yasir Arafat, which appeared in 1965. Syria then began to support, for the first time since the Suez crisis was settled, various raids into Israel.

All the while, Nasser had been trying to settle the South Arabian question, and he thought he had done so in 1965 with King Faisal, but the settlement came unbound before it was actually tied up because there was no real agreement. The Ba'athists immediately attacked the agreement. Nasser was so afraid of the conservative "Islamic Pact" that he had to start the war against the reactionaries all over again and line up with the Ba'athists. As 1966 opened Nasser was firmly back in the leftist camp, with no pretense of cooperation with the conservatives, and competing with the Ba'athists, especially the Syrians, for leadership. This is why the crisis that erupted in 1966 over the fate of the Syrian government soon turned into a propaganda contest.

My own belief, from what I can say about Nasser's other public statements leading up to the June War, is that he was acting to save the Syrian government. He did not intend war, but if the Israelis struck they would regret it. All the other Arab governments followed that general pattern, "we will fight the Israelis if they strike." Now the problem was that even if the Arabs did not intend to strike, they could not control the Palestinians, who kept up their activity, and above all they could not control the propaganda war. The Jordanians, the Tunisians, and the Saudis immediately ridiculed Nasser's remilitarization of Sinai as a pretense—he wasn't going to do anything. Even Jordan called for the act of liberation to begin. The Syrian government radio, and then government spokesmen, began a long campaign, and I think that Nasser, as you can see from his public statements, was forced to go farther and farther. The Syrians especially took the lead.

I'd like to read only one statement, which seems to sum up a lot, by a high-ranking Syrian officer, General Ahmad Talas, on June 3. "The UAR and Syria can destroy Israel in four days at most. We will follow a strategy of pinpricks towards our enemy Israel. That is, of slow deaths which will compel Israel to commit a new folly, which will be a direct face basis for eliminating its existence." So while they were saying that they would not start a conventional war, they were all saying that we must keep the Palestine movement alive . . . and ultimately Israel will react and will be destroyed.

The Syrian Response

George Tomeh: I must say you [Ernest Dawn] have already made my task rather difficult; you presented a point of view as chairman and, with all due respect, the chair is supposed to be neutral in the debate.

To really understand and assess the whole situation in the Middle East would be impossible without knowing the background and especially the mental atmosphere in which the peoples of the Middle East, and the Arab people in particular, have lived through this crisis. Our work so far seems to me to be an effort within history and it has a historical context; that's an honorable task. But when there is a rewriting of history with a definite inobjectivity, then I disassociate myself from such an endeavor. I will start with facts that were referred to yesterday by Mr. Urquhart and Mr. Liu and other speakers. I was in the battle that was taking place in another field, the UN.

On Sunday, January 15, 1967, Ralph Bunche, the undersecretary-general of the UN, called me at home and said, "In a very brief time a message from U Thant will be coming to you and he wants you to send it to your government." I received the message and sent it to Damascus immediately. It was an appeal from U Thant to [Syria to] attend a meeting of ISMAC, the Israel-Syria Mixed Armistice Commission, which had not met since 1951. At noon the next day, I got from the Syrian government the answer to this appeal, saying that they gladly accept and would attend the meetings of ISMAC, and I carried it to the secretary-general. To make all things doubly sure, after delivering the letter to U Thant, I went to the press room of the UN and read to the press the answer which I delivered to U Thant.

That evening, and this is part and parcel of the tragedy of the Arab people of the Middle East, during the "Huntley-Brinkley Report" on NBC, Brinkley said that U Thant had sent an appeal as I described it and that Israel had accepted but Syria refused. I was upset because this was a clear-cut case of misinformation. I objected. I tried to see the representative of NBC at the UN but to no avail. I only mention this to tell you that difficulties such as I am meeting or will meet today are not new and that, unfortunately, misinformation has played a biased role in adding fuel to the fire.

The escalation of 1967 that led to the war of June 5 actually started in the demilitarized zones between Israel and Syria. Yesterday Ambassador Rafael mentioned Israel's 1966 complaint to the Security Council against Syria. During the debate on that complaint, which lasted over one month, and upon a request from myself and the ambassador of Jordan, who was a member of the Security Council, U Thant issued two reports, dated November 1 and November 2, 1966. The title of the reports indicates their contents: "Report by the Secretary-General on the Present Inability of the Israel-Syria Mixed Armistice Commission to Function and the Attitudes of the Parties Thereof."

Let me read a paragraph: "Since 1951 Israel has taken the position that the Mixed Armistice Commission is not competent to deal with issues pertaining to the DZ, asserting that these issues should be dealt with by the Chairman of the Mixed Armistice Commission and that he should contact the Israeli delegation with a view to their settlement." I believe that it would be good for the understanding of our case and of the whole issue if these reports could be circulated to those attending this meeting.

The second report is on the present status of the demilitarized zones set up by the general armistice agreement between Israel and Syria. In it, the secretary-general shows how the majority, the largest areas, of the two or three DZs were actually occupied by Israel; that fortifications were erected there; and that there were reports from the chief of ISMAC showing that the armament by Israel in the DZ contravened the armistice agreements. I quote paragraph 16 of the report, which states: "The part of the central sector of the DZ which is on the eastern bank of the Jordan River is a narrow strip of land generally controlled by Syria, while the western bank generally controlled by Israel is a large area. On the western bank Arab villages have been demolished, their inhabitants evacuated. The inhabitants of the villages of Baqqara and Ghanname returned following a decision taken by the Security Council, but they were later driven away."

Besides these two reports, I would like to mention four books by the chiefs of the Mixed Armistice Commission: *Arab-Israeli Conflict (1951–1955)*, by Commander E. H. Hutchinson, 1956 (American); *Between Arab and Israeli*, by E. L. M. Burns, 1962 (Canadian); *Soldiering for Peace*, by General Carl von Horn, 1966 (Swedish); and *War and Peace in the Middle East*, by General Odd Bull, 1973.

On April 7, 1967, a large air battle took place over Damascus between the Israeli air force and the Syrian air force, which lost six MIGs. As a result of it, attention was brought time and again to the fact that Israel was preparing to strike at Syria. But then came all the declarations that we heard yesterday and the able explanation given by Mr. Shamir about the article in the *New York Times* of May 12. In connection with that declaration, I wish to refer to the *Jerusalem Post* of May 12, 1967, in which an article titled "Eshkol Warns" quoted Eshkol as saying, "In view of the fourteen incidents in the last month alone, we may have to adopt measures no less drastic than those of April 7." He made this declaration at a meeting of leaders of the Mapai Party in the club called Yahdov. I have with me here exactly eleven declarations by members of the Israeli government and army. First Menachem Begin, minister without portfolio: "In June '67 we again had a choice. The Egyptian army concentrations in the Sinai approaches do not prove that Nasser was really about to attack us. We must be honest with ourselves. We decided to attack them." Already we heard from Mr. Amit today that that actually was the case.

I'm not going to read all eleven statements, but two of them are relevant. General Mordechai Hod, commander of the Israeli air force, said, "Sixteen years of planning had gone into those initial eighteen minutes. We lived with the plan, we slept on the plan, we ate the plan, constantly we perfected it." And no less than a leader here at this table, General Meir Amit, the former head of Israeli intelligence, who was head of Mossad in '67, said, "There is going to be a war. Our army is now fully mobilized, but we cannot remain in that condition for long because we have a civilian army, our economy is shuddering to a stop." He also said, "We don't have the man-power right now even to bring in the crops. Sugar beets are rotting in the earth. We have to make a quick decision. If we can get the first blow, our casualties will be comparatively light."

"From my mouth do I condemn you, O Israel." This is a sample of what Israeli leaders said. So on May 13, after the appearance of the article in the *New York Times* and these statements, I asked to see Mr. U Thant and showed him the *New York Times* article. U Thant issued a statement refer-ring to this and previous threats.

We have a clear picture about what was taking place then. Following the debate yesterday and today, there is a clear-cut conclusion that Israel had decided to strike on June 5 and that careful planning was behind it. Another question arises. Did Syria and Egypt really threaten Israel before June 5? The consensus of world public opinion is that they did not constitute such a threat when Israel attacked on June 5. The statements that I brought here can attest to that. The results of the war of 1967 support the fact that the Arabs were not preparing for aggression against Israel. Meir Amit said today that actually it was the first three hours that were decisive. Let us also remember that before June 5, there was a change in the government of Israel. Moshe Dayan, known for his belligerency, was appointed minister of defense and had the upper hand in the army, another proof that Israel was planning aggression.

We have heard, we hear today, that the Arabs, the terrorists, have been the cause. Mr. Chairman, I want to tell you that the party that introduced terrorism to the Middle East was Israel and the Zionist fighting militias such as the Haganah, the Irgun Zvi Leum, and the Lehi, or the Stern gang. There is no literature in the world that contains as many books on terrorism as there are on Zionism and the State of Israel. To mention a few, in *The Revolt* (New York: Henry Schuman, 1951) by Menachem Begin, there is a chapter titled "Descartes said, 'Je pense, donc je suis,' but I say we fight, therefore we are." And could you find in any literature in the world a book such as *Memoirs of an Assassin: Confessions of a Stern Gang Killer* by Benjamin Zeroni (New York: Pyramid Press, 1960)? There is a third book, *The Edge of the Sword* (renamed *Israel's War of Independence*) by Netanel Lorch (Jerusalem: Masada Press, 1968) that describes Operation Nachson that led to occupying Arab lands outside the partition plan, and how thousands of Arabs were driven out of the lands—how many Arabs were killed, how many operations and suboperations were involved. We again hear that the terrorists are coming from various parts of the Arab world, but in spite of the optimism expressed around this table yesterday and today, I find that the situation is parallel to what it was in 1967 and that Israel is always ready to wage official terrorism.

To complete the picture, it is vivid in the mind of every Arab that there is a map produced by the World Zionist Organization, a map of Israel, which I respectfully request to be distributed. When I heard Ambassador Evron say that he doesn't like to look at maps, I can understand his fear of facing reality. But every Arab, every Arab, cannot forget that the area of Palestine under the mandate was 10,500 square miles. The area of Israel under the partition plan was 5,765 square miles. The area of Israel in 1948 was 7,592. The map you are looking at now is the 1967 map. When President Johnson was asked by Prime Minister Eshkol to guarantee the borders of Israel, Johnson asked, "What borders do you want me to guarantee, the '47, the '48, the '67, or what?" So at least this should be clear. Together with these figures, let us remember: Jewish landownership in 1947 was 5 percent of all Palestine; Jewish ownership in Israeli-held territory was 7 percent; Jewish ownership in the Negev was one-half of 1 percent; Jewish ownership in the Jerusalem area was 7 percent. No wonder that Begin said, "We want to get Jerusalem." Israel attacked on June 5 and got all that it wanted from its surprise attack and quick victory.

I want to bring to your attention the following resolutions of the Security Council: resolution 233 of June 6, 1967, 234 of June 7, and especially 235 of June 9. Why? Because Israel attacked Syria on June 9, and a resolution was adopted by the Security Council that unanimously notes the statements made by the representatives of Israel and Syria (Ambassador Rafael and myself); confirms its previous resolutions about an immediate cease-fire and the cessation of military action; demands that hostilities should cease forthwith; and requests the secretary-general to make immediate contacts with the governments of Israel and Syria to arrange immediate compliance with the above-mentioned resolution and to report to the secretary-general. But Israel continued its advance, and I remember well and certainly Ambassador Rafael should remember, the long, late hours, until three and four in the morning, when we continued debate. In fact, I was reminding Ambassador Rafael today of how, when the Israeli army kept advancing, suddenly there was a flurry of literacy and he starting quoting books and poetry until one of the permanent members of the Security Council reminded him that that [behavior] was not proper at the time.

Anyhow, Israel continued its advance into Syria, and on June 11 the Security Council voted resolution 236, which does the following: (1) condemns any and all violations of the cease-fire, (2) requests the secretary-general to continue his investigation and to report to the council as soon as possible, (3) affirms that its demand for the cease-fire and discontinuance of all military activities includes—please pay attention—a prohibition of any forward military movement subsequent to the cease-fire, and (4) calls for the prompt return to the cease-fire positions of any troops that may have moved forward subsequent to 16:30 GMT on June 10. This is a clear-cut resolution by the Security Council requesting that the Israeli army go back to the lines that they had gone beyond on June 10. Needless to say, this resolution is still awaiting application, and perhaps the new international order will improve its credentials if these resolutions are respected and implemented.

We come to the present hour. Before finishing my statement, I want to recall that today Ambassador Evron, in justifying the surprise attack by Israel, referred to article 51 of the UN Charter, which gives any member of the UN the right to self-defense. But article 51 says, "Nothing in the present Charter shall impair the inherent right of individual or collective self-defense if an armed attack occurs against a member of the UN until the Security Council has taken measures necessary to maintain international peace and security." So what is the condition here for the application of article 51? It is, if an armed attack occurs. If the Security Council is [asked to consider] the complaint or the problem, no action, no individual action by one individual state, should be accepted or tolerated. Therefore, to invoke article 51 in order to justify a blitzkrieg against three Arab states is insulting the intelligence of the Arab people and the world community.

Ernest Dawn: We turn now to Dr. Mutawi, who will speak on the Jordanian position.

The Jordanian Response

Samir Mutawi: Before I start, I'd like to make an observation that the 1967 war may be the subject of debate today, twenty-five years after, but to me it means two things: the loss of Jerusalem, my hometown, and five years of extensive research for my book on Jordan's role in the 1967 war. It is therefore a privilege to be given the opportunity to speak and to listen to what my distinguished colleagues here have to say on the subject. I thought I'd restrict myself to answering the four questions that relate to Jordan from the list of questions submitted to all of us by Richard Parker.

The first question in that list relating to Jordan is, did King Hussein have any realistic alternative to entering the war? The true question is not whether he had a realistic alternative to entering the war, but whether he should or should not have allied his country with Egypt and Syria. Having known well in advance that in any war with Israel the Arabs could not hope to win, this alliance seemed at the time particularly significant. I should like to begin by quoting King Hussein describing his dilemma: "The atmosphere that I found in Jordan, particularly in the West Bank, was one where frankly we had the following choice: either to act at the right time, with no illusion of what the results might be but with a chance to do better than we would otherwise, or not to act and to have an eruption occur within, which would cause us to collapse and which would obviously immediately result in an Israeli occupation of the West Bank. This was really the reason why I went to Egypt to meet Nasser, to his surprise."

It is not unrealistic to conclude from this quotation that King Hussein had no alternative other than to participate in the war, because the civil turmoil that would inevitably erupt if Jordan stood aside would provide Israel with the excuse to occupy the West Bank. As critical as such an eruption might have been, it was not the king's only dilemma. For if Jordan failed to participate in the war, King Hussein would find his subjects so antagonistic to his role that his fall would be inevitable. If the war ended in an Arab defeat, it would be attributed to his failure to participate. He would be branded as an imperialist tool and a traitor to the Arab cause. If the war was successful, his failure to participate would have an equally destabilizing effect because he would be accused of failing to support the principle of Arab unity and the cause of Palestine. In either event, public opinion would be so antagonistic to him that civil war would be inevitable.

The view that Israel was anxious to capture the West Bank and was only waiting for the opportune moment was central in Jordanian calculations all the time. It was matched by Jordanian leaders' knowledge that they could not defend it on their own. King Hussein confirmed this to me, saying, "Always in our minds, and in my mind in particular, was the fact that the West Bank was the most important target as far as Israel was concerned." If the Israelis were to implement their plans to settle comfortably and extend beyond the area of Palestine, then obviously the first objective would be Palestine itself. Therefore the most important area apart from Jerusalem was the West Bank. King Hussein's fears of Israeli expansionism and his recognition that for this reason it was essential for Jordan to belong to a wider defense structure, his commitment to Arabism, as well as geographical considerations all made him anxious for that defense structure to be Arab.

The reasons for Jordan's participation in the 1967 war can be found in four main areas: Jordan's commitment to Arab unity and cooperation, its commitment to the cause of Palestine, domestic pressures, and external pressures. I am now certain that the most important of these four areas was Jordan's commitment to Arab unity and cooperation. The remaining three can be related to the pursuit of this idea.

As for the view of some observers that Jordan joined the Arab war effort either as a result of a mistaken belief that the Arabs would be victorious or because it had no choice, I wish to stress that at no point did King Hussein really believe that there was a possibility of overrunning Israel. Instead, he sought to preserve the status quo that was a strategic objective in Jordanian calculations. The king believed, however, that he could not stand aside at the time when Arab cooperation and solidarity were vital, and he was convinced that any Arab confrontation with Israel would be greatly enhanced if the Arabs fought as a unified body. The plan of action devised at his meeting with Nasser in Cairo on May 30 was established on these bases. By forcing Israel to fight on three fronts simultaneously, King Hussein believed that the Arabs stood a chance of preventing Israel from making territorial gains. He decided that for this reason the wisest course of action was to bring Jordan into the total Arab war effort. This would ensure that his army would be provided with two elements that were essential for its defense of the West Bank: additional troops and air cover.

The second contention, that Jordan joined the Arab war effort because it had no choice, is misleading. There is no doubt that Jordan faced a dangerous situation in the months preceding the war. Arab propaganda had whipped up feeling within Jordan in favor of war and had cast doubt on the Jordanian government's commitment to Arabism and to Palestine. Although the riots that followed in the wake of Israel's raid on Samu' were well contained, popular feeling in favor of war was still strong and King Hussein was forced to take that into account. He believed that if he failed to contain this feeling, he ran the risk of civil war. However, King Hussein had faced many similar situations and had not given in to the popular mood if he perceived it as detrimental to the survival of Jordan. For this reason, his decision to enter a defense pact with Nasser must be seen in terms of his commitment to Arabism.

This commitment is borne out by the fact that the king was prepared to place the Jordanian army under the direction of Egyptian commanders. There is no evidence to suggest that this was imposed on him against his better judgment. Instead, the evidence suggests that he freely consented. Such an action can be understood only in terms of King Hussein's determination to operate in harmony with his Arab brethren. If he had merely wanted to still the clamor of his Palestinian population, he would not have gone as far as war. Further evidence of his primary motivation is provided by comparing Jordan's actions during the war with those of Syria. When asked to go on the offensive, Jordan did not hesitate but responded whole-heartedly, even though Jordanian officers had serious misgivings and this action had not been agreed upon during the Cairo meeting on May 30. Syria, on the other hand, took only limited action, despite the plight of the Jordanian army and the pleas of Egyptian leaders to support Jordan.

The second question on the list: How much control did the Jordanians, as opposed to Egypt's General Abd al-Mun'im Riad, the nominal commander, have over military operations? The universal feeling amongst the Jordanian political and military leaders who were actively involved in the 1967 war was that their major mistake was to rely on the help and leadership of other Arab nations. King Hussein confirms this, saying, "In my view, our first error was the fact that we did not organize our military operations on the basis of our own plan and according to our own capabilities. . . . If we had not depended on the potential of outside support, war with Israel would undoubtedly have taken a totally different course."

The king elaborated on this point: "When one expects the air cover that I expected, it was imperative to act the way I did. If our men had known from the beginning that they could not expect support from either Egypt, Syria, or Iraq, our strategy would have certainly been different." Put simply, by accepting Egypt's leadership the Jordanians placed Arab interests above

King Hussein of Jordan and President Nasser signing a defense agreement in
Cairo on May 30, 1967. By permission of AP/Wide World Photos.

their own and subjected their fighting strategy to requirements unrelated to
their needs. Having placed their armed forces under the leadership of their
Egyptian allies, they reaped disastrous results. During the war the Egyptians
were caught up in the events taking place on their own territory and paid
little attention to what was happening in Jordan. This is reflected in the fact
that Nasser took twelve hours to reply to King Hussein's desperate telegram
on the morning of June 6 asking for advice on how to deal with the rapidly
deteriorating situation in the West Bank.

On the operational level, the Jordanian military commanders are extremely critical of the way General Riad conducted operations in the West
Bank. They can make a long list of tactical and strategic errors attributed
to General Riad's lack of understanding of Jordanian defense requirements,
on the one hand, and false information passed to him by his superiors in
Cairo, on the other. After having claimed that 75 percent of the Israeli air
force had been destroyed, Field Marshal 'Amr ordered Riad to launch offensive operations along the entire Jordanian front on the morning of June 5.
Later that morning 'Amr sent a second message claiming that his ground
forces were on the offensive and had penetrated into Israel through the
Negev. At noon Nasser called King Hussein and repeated 'Amr's claim. He
then asked the king to "quickly take possession of the largest possible
amount of land in order to get ahead of a UN cease-fire."

This same morning another instruction came from 'Amr to move the Sixtieth Armored Brigade south to Hebron to provide support to an Egyptian division advancing toward Beersheba in the Negev. The Fortieth Armored Brigade near the Damiya Bridge in the northern sector of the West Bank was to replace it in its positions in the hills west of Jericho. According to this message, the northern sector of the Jordan valley, which the Fortieth Brigade was vacating, would be protected by a Syrian brigade as instructed by Cairo.

On learning of these orders, the Jordanian officers were horrified because the orders signified a complete departure from the planned strategy and put Jordan on a dangerous course of action that stood little chance of success. They could not understand the orders' military logic. They had no plans to open hostilities along the entire Jordanian front and no strategy for the capture of Israeli territory apart from Mt. Scopus and the encirclement of Jerusalem as part of an old tactical operation plan. The officers also pointed out that it had been agreed upon at the signing of the joint defense pact in Cairo on May 30 that Jordan would not enter the active phase of operations until all agreed conditions were met. These conditions were the arrival of all promised reinforcements from other Arab nations and their deployment on Jordanian territory, receiving positive and satisfactory news from the Egyptian front, and the provision of air cover. The officers tried to bring to the attention of their Egyptian commander through Brigadier Atif Majali, Riad's Jordanian director of military operations, two vital points. One was that if Israel defeated the Egyptians on the southern front, the Jordanians' only achievement would have been to provide Israel with an excuse to launch a full-scale assault on their territory. The second was that if Arab reinforcements were late or failed to arrive before the Jordanian forces went on the offensive, they would find themselves hopelessly outnumbered.

Although the Jordanians were against seizing Israeli territory, they argued that if it was necessary the best strategy in the Jerusalem area would be to implement Operation Tariq. They told Riad that the Jordanian army was fully prepared for it and stood a good chance of success. If they could take Mt. Scopus and encircle Jewish Jerusalem, it would place them in an excellent position to bargain for the return of any land Israel might have seized. However, Riad did not agree with his Jordanian officers' advice. His view was that the first Jordanian objective should be not Mt. Scopus but al-Mukabbir Hill, south of Jerusalem. Mt. Scopus lay in northern Jerusalem, and Riad believed that it was the southern sector that would be the most strategically vital area.

The reason for this belief was the information passed to Riad by general headquarters in Cairo that Egyptian troops were advancing north in the Negev. He therefore concluded that the main axis of operations would be Beersheba–Hebron–Bethlehem–southern Jerusalem. Hence he believed the Egyptians would need the Jordanians to conduct an offensive operation along the frontier in southern Jerusalem and Hebron rather than in northern Jerusalem. Accordingly, Riad must have felt that if Jordanians occupied al-Mukabbir, they would offset any attempt by Israel to advance into the area and provide a much needed armored support to the supposedly advancing Egyptian forces in the Negev.

The occupation of al-Mukabbir Hill was debated at length in the operations room while staff officers, Egyptian and Jordanian, quarreled and insulted one another. The Jordanians were equally horrified at Cairo's request for the Sixtieth and Fortieth Armored Brigades to be moved south. The location of these brigades had been carefully planned and was essential to protect the strategically vital areas of Jerusalem and Nablus and the expected axis of Israeli advance. The movement of the Sixtieth Brigade to Hebron made it impossible for the Jordanians to conduct Operation Tariq, which required maximum strength in the area of Jerusalem.

The information passed by Egypt to Jordan was one of the reasons for the sense of panic and confusion that characterized operations on the Jordanian front. Because they were acting on false premises, the Jordanians were completely unprepared for the strength of the Israeli offensive both on land and in the air. They were also implementing activities for which they had no prearranged plans. Order was followed by counterorder, which created a great deal of confusion and chaos. This sense of confusion was increased by the air bombardment of the Jordanian troops by the Israeli Air Force. It was all the more stunning because of the Egyptian claim of having destroyed 75 percent of Israeli fighter planes, which made Israel's air supremacy incomprehensible to the Jordanians.

The early issue of the order to withdraw from the West Bank on the evening of June 6, surrounded by confusion, was one of the most crucial mistakes made during the war. Most Jordanian military commanders expressed the view that they should have attempted to regroup their forces in certain areas and to press for a Security Council cease-fire resolution before contemplating total withdrawal. In fact the Security Council resolution did come at the end of the second day, but only after Riad had issued the order for withdrawal. Tragically, although the Jordanians realized that the orders coming from Cairo did not make sense, and in some cases were incomprehensible, they still carried them out because they believed that the need to cooperate with their allies and participate in a concerted Arab effort overrode all other considerations. Because the Jordanian army was acting as part of a joint Arab defense force, the Jordanian general headquarters officers were under the command of the Egyptians and were virtually mere observers of the war.

The third question on the list: Would the Jordanians have begun firing if they had known the truth about what happened to the Egyptian air force in the first hour of the battle? The key to an accurate answer to this question lies in a fresh attempt to reexamine the plan of action for the Jordanian front agreed on during discussion in the Cairo meeting between King Hussein and President Nasser on May 30. It was agreed that in the initial stages of war on the Egyptian front, Jordan's role would be to maintain a static defense posture and open hostilities on a limited front, with the aim of neutralizing a portion of Israel's forces that otherwise would be deployed on the Egyptian and Syrian fronts.

This limited engagement was to be expanded only after the fulfillment of three other conditions that I mentioned earlier: the arrival of Arab forces and their deployment on Jordanian territory, positive information from the Egyptian front, and air cover. Only when these conditions had been met were the Jordanian forces to extend operations along the front and enter into the active defense phase of operations. It was envisaged that a concerted effort of all three Arab armies would at least prevent an early Israeli victory and allow enough time for the superpowers to intervene and impose peace. For the Jordanians, joining the war on these conditions was both an opportunity to demonstrate their commitment to the Arab cause and a calculated act designed to increase their chances of fending off what they believed would be the inevitable Israeli march into the West Bank.

Instead of waiting for the fulfillment of these agreed conditions, the Jordanians followed all commands coming from Cairo. As a result of these commands and the false information passed to them, claiming fantastic successes, grave tactical and strategic errors were made, including the occupation of al-Mukabbir Hill, moving the armored brigades, and, most important, failing to implement Operation Tariq. Hence, when asked, King Hussein replied that had he discovered the true state of affairs on the morning of June 5, the Jordanians would not have embarked on what he described as the suicidal course they followed. They would have engaged in limited action on the basis of the prearranged strategy, which would have demonstrated their adherence to the Arab cause but would have fallen short of providing Israel with sufficient excuse to invade the West Bank. Most Jordanian commanders express similar sentiments: [if only] they had been given the opportunity of twenty-four hours to assess the validity and truth of reports emanating from

Cairo, given the fragile nature of Jordanian-Egyptian relations until only a week before.

The fourth question on the list: Is it true as claimed in Heikal's book *1967 — Al-Infijar* (pp. 435–47) that King Hussein informed General Riad on May 1 that he had reason to believe that a trap was being laid for the UAR and President Nasser by the Syrian leaders? As the story goes, the message that the king wanted Riad to convey to Nasser alone outlined the following information: "The group in Syria are planning to ignite the situation along the Syrian front to compel Egypt to come to their rescue. By doing so Egypt itself becomes the target to be hit." Heikal confirms that although King Hussein's meeting with Riad took place on May 1, Riad's report, submitted through Abd al-Hakim 'Amr, was not delivered to Nasser until May 14, only after Riad pleaded with Heikal to find out whether it had been delivered. Would it have made any difference if Nasser had received this message sooner?

Ever since the signing of the Egyptian-Syrian defense treaty, the Jordanian leaders were convinced that the Syrians had laid a trap for Nasser from which it would be difficult for him to extract himself. A reference to this trap is made in almost every interview I conducted with the Jordanian leaders during the preparation of my book. Their conclusions were based on the assumption that the treaty increased the likelihood of an Arab-Israeli war, because it spelled the end of Nasser's moderate and cautious approach to Arab-Israeli relations.

In most interviews the Jordanian leaders stressed their theory that the Syrians were actively trying to involve Nasser in war with Israel, not to revenge the injustices done to the Palestinians but in order to gain supremacy over Nasser as leader of the Arabs. According to their analyses, by forcing Nasser into a war with Israel, the Syrians would be victorious no matter what the outcome was. If the Arabs inflicted defeat on Israel, the Syrians could claim that the initiative had been theirs. If the war ended in defeat for the Arabs, Nasser could be held responsible and would be forced to resign. Even if he did not resign he would find his dominant position greatly reduced.

While that failure to have this important report delivered as urgently as King Hussein requested may have been deliberate, it is just as hypothetical whether expeditious delivery would have made any difference. The problem faced by Nasser was that, as leader of the Arab masses and champion of the Palestinians, he was vulnerable to the Syrians' accusations that he was failing to act on the Palestinians' behalf. If he was to maintain his dominant position, Nasser had to prove that he was serious about confronting Israel.

He could not allow himself to be outdone by the Syrians in this regard. Consequently, by calling into question Nasser's sincerity about the issue of Palestine, the Syrians were able to push him into an increasingly belligerent position toward Israel.

For this reason, Jordan's decision makers regarded the signing of the defense treaty between Egypt and Syria with great apprehension. Although they believed that Nasser hoped that a close alliance with the Syrians would enable him to restrain their aggressive attitude toward Israel, he had in fact been outmaneuvered and had entered a volatile situation that seemed certain to get out of his control. The Jordanians point out, for example, that army intelligence had revealed no evidence of a buildup of Israeli troops on the Syrian border. In fact, as mentioned yesterday, General Muhammad Fawzi, then chief of staff of the Egyptian army, himself reached the same conclusion on his visit to Syria on May 14.

The theory of a trap for Nasser was seen by the Jordanians in broader terms as part of a general Israeli strategy to draw the Arab world into a war for which it was not prepared. They therefore felt that the Israelis were manipulating the Syrians in order to lay a trap that would spell disaster for the Arabs. Shortly after the Israeli raid on the border village of Samu', King Hussein met his officers at the army general headquarters and conveyed his thoughts to them. According to General Amor Khammash [the Jordanian chief of staff], the discussion reflected a fear that Israel was plotting something big and that it was provoking Arab radicals into providing it with the excuse to act. King Hussein believed that Samu' was the perfect psychological preparation to help set the trap, and unfortunately the Arabs (he meant the Syrians) played into Israel's hands.

Discussion

Raymond Garthoff: I would like to ask about an unconfirmed report attributed to a former senior Israeli military officer to the effect that one or more of the key messages from Cairo to General Riad on June 5 in fact originated not in Cairo but were Israeli fabrications using the appropriate Egyptian codes and so on. This was disinformation on alleged Egyptian military successes intended to provoke Jordanian entry into active hostilities in order to provide a pretext for occupation of East Jerusalem and the West Bank. I would be interested in any information that would indicate whether there is anything to that report.

Meir Amit: A few remarks. First, when you present something you must present the whole picture and not part of the picture, and unfortunately the picture that was presented here, especially by Ambassador Tomeh, was not a complete picture.

He omitted the whole subject of the terrorism that was launched from Syria and backed by Syria. And second, the [attempted Arab] diversion of the Jordan that was a source of a concern, a big concern to us, and that makes things very different.

The proclaimed policy of Israel was to protect the Hashemites, or not to let the Hashemite regime fall. Because of the "Jordanian option," as we call it in Israel, we are concerned to solve the Arab refugee problem. By the way, the direct talks that have started now, and I hope will continue, are an important factor in this area. We think Israel is a democratic country. There are all kinds of people. Every Jew has a different view, but I would say the majority would like to see a solution. Mr. Mutawi, you said strongly that one of the problems, the internal problems, of Jordan is the Palestinians and that the king cannot just overlook them. This was one of your four considerations. What we think, most of us, is that one way or another, the Palestinian problem should be solved in conjunction with Jordan. We think King Hussein is an essential factor in this direction. So I don't see any reason why Israel should attack Hussein or push him to fall.

My answer to the question is that we had warned Jordan before the first shot not to enter the war. Maybe Mr. Mutawi explained that they were dragged, they were deceived by the Egyptians, things like that. But I want to say clearly on our part that we had warned Jordan that if they will not enter the war, not participate in the war, nothing will happen to them. All the stories about Israeli's intentions to conquer Jordan are baseless.

William Quandt: First, in response to what General Amit said. I once interviewed the American ambassador who was in Amman in 1967 [Findley Burns], and I believe he was at least one of those who conveyed the Israeli warning to King Hussein that if you don't enter the war you won't be attacked. [Burns] confirmed that he was asked to deliver this message and that he did so shortly after the Jordanian forces had opened fire. So it may not have served any effective purpose as a deterrent. That's not my question—just an observation of what I heard.

Referring to Mr. Mutawi's interesting presentation, there is one thing that he left out that I would like to hear more about: the whole Jordanian propaganda war with Nasser in the period leading up to the closure of the strait. Why was Jordan so intent on making Nasser's life miserable by taunting him for hiding behind the skirts of UNEF and not standing up to Israel? Didn't you realize—not you personally—didn't my friends in Jordan understand that they were playing with fire? How do you account for what appears to be in retrospect an extraordinarily reckless policy, because if Nasser had been inclined to do what he was being asked to do by Jordan, certainly the chances of war would go up astronomically?

There is a second thing that I think in the interest of historical truth we're bound to ask, even if it's unlikely that we'll get an answer. We have learned through subsequent episodes that Jordan and Israel had over the years a special kind of relationship that didn't have to be mediated through the United States or anyone else. I think it would be interesting if anyone could shed light on whether this direct relationship between Jordan and Israel was used to try to defuse the crisis, other than this last-minute communication: Don't enter the war and you will be left alone. There were several weeks leading up to the outbreak of war; can anyone, will anyone, tell us if there were direct Jordanian-Israeli talks, contacts? Because twenty years after the fact we always find out that there had been. On this occasion we haven't heard anything about them, either because no one will talk about them or because they didn't happen. Either would be interesting to know even if it were that they didn't in fact happen.

Ephraim Evron: On May 23, the prime minister informed the cabinet, when the decision was taken to accede to Mr. Rostow's request for forty-eight hours, that he had contacted King Hussein and asked him to stop, to cease needling and goading Nasser over the strait.

Richard Parker: And the Israelis also made a *démarche* to us at that point to do the same thing. Whether we ever got through to Amman, I don't know.

General Amit, you didn't answer Ray Garthoff's question. Did you people cook up a message from the Egyptians to the Jordanians using the Egyptian codes to confuse?

Meir Amit: I have the message here. We intercepted it. I gave it to Ambassador Basheer. This message has two main points. One, this misinformation, untrue information that we are winning on all points. . . . Nasser or Hussein, you asked?

William Quandt: They asked if you cooked it, not whether you intercepted it.

Meir Amit: We didn't do this thing. We did not cook anything.

Ernest Dawn: Mr. Quandt asked a question about Jordanian propaganda. Again, other people have answered, but we'd like to hear your answer.

Samir Mutawi: My answer? Well, at that time the prime minister was Wasfi Tel, known to be vehemently opposed to Nasser. He simply did not agree to any rapprochement with Nasser, because he felt that Nasser was playing the policy of brinkmanship and that it would spell disaster for

Jordan. But obviously, as influential as he was, the decision was finally not his.

But referring to the propaganda war campaign, at that time you must remember that the Jordanian propaganda machine, compared with the Egyptian, Syrian, and PLO machines, was small and ineffective. Egypt was broadcasting from Radio Cairo, from Sawt al-Arab, and from many other stations, with wave lengths reaching nearly every part of the globe, while the Jordanians had a small radio station. And the Egyptian press reached everywhere in the Arab world. The Jordanian press reached nowhere, and in the campaign that was mounted against the Jordanians, that they were traitors, Nasser was even saying that Wasfi Tel was a spy for the British and the CIA. The Jordanians were being branded all the time as imperialist tools, traitors, spies. This continuous and severely hostile campaign affected the stability of the regime and its very survival.

So they had to reply. They devised this method of trying to show that it's not they who were allies of Israel and imperialist tools but that he [Nasser] was not actually serious in wanting to confront Israel or in being the real champion of the Palestine cause, because he was shielding himself behind UNEF. Of course many people, many wise people, in Jordan realized that indeed this was playing with fire, because it would push Nasser into taking action which they knew was detrimental to the Arab cause. But there was no way, or no other way, let me say, of defending themselves against the charges that were pouring out against them day and night from the Egyptian and other Arab propaganda machines. And I do say in my book that indeed this propaganda campaign was one of the indirect reasons for igniting the war, for causing the war to happen. I am not trying to apologize for the Jordanians but only trying to explain why they have launched that propaganda campaign against Nasser which unfortunately led to the result that we all know about.

Your [Garthoff's] point was about the message, whether it originated in Cairo. I'm interested particularly in answering this point because I tried to follow this line in my investigation and to find out whether the message was doctored on the way, and the only evidence I could find was secondary published material—the book by Edgar O'Ballance [*The Electronic War in the Middle East* (Hampden, Conn.: Archer Books, 1974)], if I remember correctly. But, anyway, the Jordanians were not in any position to confirm this to me—whether it was true. They did of course complain that at certain moments during the war their communications were difficult. For example, General Salim, who was commander of the West Bank operations, said that some of his brigade commanders were able to communicate with general headquarters when he was not and that this was an indication of the difficulties he faced as far as communications were concerned. But whether it indicated that the Israelis did interfere with the Jordanian-Egyptian communications, there was no one who could confirm it to me.

Meir Amit: I will tell you that we were in favor of King Hussein right from the start.

Samir Mutawi: But again, as I was saying to Mr. Shamir, you launched Samu', which was detrimental to King Hussein. It did not help him. Anyway, the point is about whether this message was doctored; I can't tell. The only thing I could find of interest was the messages that General—what's his name, the commander of the central command?

———: Narkiss.

Samir Mutawi: Yes. Narkiss in his memoirs said he sent several messages to his headquarters to send the Israeli Air Force to deal with the Jordanian Sixtieth Brigade because the Jordanian tanks were superior to his, and therefore he was worried about the Sixtieth Armored Brigade, but, regrettably, I found no primary evidence that the message was doctored to get these tanks out of their hiding so that they could become easy targets for the Israeli Air Force. I cannot claim that I found any hard evidence to support that point.

As for the [Israeli] message delivered to King Hussein on the morning of the war, General Amit and Mr. Quandt, I think, mentioned it. I myself believe that this was really a camouflage. It was not sincere. Ambassador Evron said that on May 23 there was another message. I haven't come across that message at all, and I have investigated every single document that exists in Jordan, so if it was communicated to the Jordanian government on May 23, I cannot claim to be aware of any message of that sort. But what I'm interested in is the message on the morning of the war, because General Amit said that the Israelis were interested in the well-being of the Jordanian regime. Therefore, if indeed the Israeli authorities were sincere in convincing the Jordanians that no harm will come to them if they don't participate in this war, you don't deliver a message at the last minute. There were many channels through which such a message could have been delivered well before the war. I mean, they knew that the Arab world was heading toward war with Israel.

Ephraim Evron: You mean we should have told the king, we are going to attack on the morning of the fifth, but please don't be alarmed?

Samir Mutawi: I beg your pardon?

Ephraim Evron: You said we should have warned him long before the war. Do you mean that we should have warned the king that we are attacking?

Samir Mutawi: You should have warned him, don't enter the war and no harm will come to you. Jordanian calculations were based all the time on the assumption that Israel was waiting for the moment to occupy the West Bank. So if Israelis were really sincere about conveying a message that "if you don't participate in the war, no harm will come to you," it might have changed the course of history. I'm not saying that it would have, but I'm saying it might have.

Tahsin Basheer: The reconstruction of the events by Mr. Mutawi is interesting. The first conclusion I can see is that King Hussein calculated his personal security and his regime, which is his family, above the interests of the Palestinians and the Jordanians. He never sacrificed his own self to take the risk, but he was willing to sacrifice his country to be on the throne. That's clear from your analysis.

Samir Mutawi: Is it?

Tahsin Basheer: Whatever you quoted from Heikal is correct. But Heikal said more than that. He said that King Hussein kept insisting in the contacts at the Arab summits that before Jordan would accept Arab contingents as the plan of the general Arab command stipulated—that the Iraqis and Saudis get in [to Jordan]—Egypt had to nullify the work of UNEF. And when Nasser said, at Casablanca, I think, that UNEF is not a constraint on the Egyptian army going to Sinai, that's what we agreed to; there was an insistence that UNEF should stop giving protection to free passage in the strait. Now, if any Arab would know the international calculus of the agreement between America and Israel, King Hussein must have known it. The insistence of Jordan's line of propaganda was exactly on that point for month after month, even after the Arab summit tried to clear the Arab atmosphere and decided at Casablanca not to indulge in Arab cold war rhetoric on the radios.

The question becomes, what was the game of King Hussein? Why was he insisting on the Egyptians going to Jordan? He is the one who chose the last minute to send a special, important message to General Ali 'Amr with five conditions, telling him that the clique in Syria was planning a trap and that he [Hussein] would not allow the Iraqi or Saudi forces to go into Jordan until the Egyptian forces were there and until he got clearance from Egypt that UNEF was not a constraint and that passage through the strait was stopped. The king must have known that whatever trap was made in Syria, it would mean a casus belli, that Israel would attack. What was his interest in putting it to brinkmanship of his own? Was he a party, as parts of Heikal's book say indirectly—that Hussein was also part of the conspiracy of Israel, that by pulling Egypt in he wanted to get rid of Egypt? Another book by a

Tahsin Basheer, member of Egypt's UN
delegation, 1967.

CIA agent in the Middle East [Wilbur Crane Eveland], *Ropes of Sand,*
mentioned in passing, as a matter of fact, that the king made sure that Egypt
was involved, and by asking, by signing the agreement with Egypt he sealed
the deal, that Egypt would be targeted. To what extent is that valid?

Samir Mutawi: Well, I think you seem to be on the verge of moving Arab
propaganda from the sixties to the nineties and into this room. I was not
in any way propagating what the Jordanians said or did. I was merely being
a historian. I was conveying history. This is what happened. The perception
that the Jordanians had about the Syrian regime's tactics of trying to attract
Nasser into a situation where it would become difficult for him to extricate
himself is a perception of that period. We cannot change it. It happened
and it was conveyed to the Egyptians because it was felt that the Unified
Arab Command had been destroyed at the moment the Syrians and the
Egyptians decided to sign a joint pact. The Unified Arab Command was
supposed to be a pact for all the Arab confrontation states. From the moment
that Syria and Egypt chose to sign a joint defense pact, together it meant
that the Unified Arab Command was finished.

Tahsin Basheer: King Hussein chose to contact the United Arab Command, which you say was defied by the Jordanians.

Samir Mutawi: I said finished, but as General Amit said earlier, referring
to half the truth doesn't represent the picture. Heikal was talking about
King Hussein developing a special friendship with General Riad and that's
why he asked for him personally [to convey the messages to Nasser]. And
he [Hussein] felt, and he's saying that in many places, deep in his heart,
that he was a party to that agreement signed in the first summit conference,

that is, the Unified Arab Command, irrespective of the fact that it was not functioning at the time. So when he felt there was a danger, because of the nature of relations between Jordan and Egypt at that time, there was no way of communicating this message to Nasser except through someone who is trusted, by the Jordanians as well as by the Egyptians. General Riad seemed to have been that person. The campaign against Egypt regarding the strait or its closure or hiding behind UNEF was an unfortunate episode, but as I mentioned earlier, many Jordanians realized that they were playing with fire. But the point that you [Basheer] mentioned about their insistence that they would not abide by the UAC's decision unless the Egyptians made certain to them that UNEF would not be an obstacle. . . .

Tahsin Basheer: No, withdraw UNEF. That was the condition.

Samir Mutawi: Okay, withdraw UNEF.

Tahsin Basheer: The Egyptian answer was, UNEF is not an obstacle.

Samir Mutawi: Okay, fine, but you're referring to decisions taken during the summits. I was talking about the period immediately before the war, when King Hussein went to Cairo to sign a pact with Nasser.

Tahsin Basheer: No, I'm referring to the period in the crisis when King Hussein started saying, there is a threat, and Ali 'Amr wrote to the common command to help you. We'll send the Iraqis and the Saudis. . . .

Samir Mutawi: Okay, but when was that?

Tahsin Basheer: That was in April.

Samir Mutawi: Yes, but you must remember that the Jordanians have always maintained that the entrance of Arab forces into Jordan would provide Israel with a casus belli to attack Jordan or the West Bank because the Israelis have always made clear that they will not accept the entrance of Arab troops into Jordanian territory. So the Jordanians have always said that if there was going to be a war with Israel, the Jordanian army should be able to defend Jordan at the beginning and call on Arab troops to come to its aid, but not to station Arab troops in advance. So they were taking into consideration different calculations, not just the fact that the Unified Arab Command has imposed on them the bringing in of Arab troops so that they would immediately fulfill what was required of them. They had to make clear to the Unified Arab Command the other conditions, the restrictions, the pressures from the other side, the constraints from the Israeli side, and indeed when war became inevitable, the king came and asked for these troops himself.

Tahsin Basheer: A bit too late, huh?

Gideon Rafael: Was King Hussein informed of Israel's good intentions? The message that I had the privilege to send on May 15 through U Thant to Egypt, that we had no hostile intentions whatsoever, was made available to King Hussein. We know that King Hussein knew that Israel would not attack Jordan because he knew that his political and strategic reinsurance was deposited in Jerusalem, in Israel. It was no problem at all to give him the message earlier or later. To make sure, on June 5, when the war had actually broken out, he got the message.

The second point is this. I don't want to revive my historical discussion with my colleague from Syria, who was my neighbor at the Security Council when we dealt with these problems exhaustively—also to our mutual exhaustion at the time. But there is one point he made that I think of actual importance for peacemaking now. Ambassador Tomeh referred to the last cease-fire resolution of June 11, 1967, relating to the deployment of forces as mentioned in the adviser's report. The cease-fire was agreed upon by Israel on the tenth and coordinated with the UN representative, General Bull. It entered into force at 2:00 P.M. GMT. The Syrian army and the Syrian representative at the UN were nervous about the deployment of our forces on the cease-fire line, and they believed that despite our commitment to cease fire, we had moved our forces forward. The nervousness I fully understand, because after all there was not much distance between our forward position and Damascus, so any move could be dangerous. Therefore Ambassador Tomeh called for an urgent Security Council meeting. At that meeting not only did I assure that there's no forward movement, but the UN truce supervisor's representative stated that what Syria had regarded as forward movement was nothing else than Israel straightening out its positions, to place the forces into the line that had been agreed to form the forward line. From then on there was no forward movement until the Yom Kippur war in 1973.

George Tomeh: The resolution adopted by the Security Council on June 11 states in its fourth working paragraph the following: "Calls for the prompt return to the cease fire positions of any troops which have moved forward subsequent to 16:30 GMT on 10 June." I want also to remind you that when this resolution was adopted, and the records of the Security Council are there to consult, that paragraph took into consideration the reports that were submitted to the Security Council by the UN group that was there [ISMAC observers].

You say that there was a zigzag line and that you wanted to make it straight. Well, this is an advance. . . .

Gideon Rafael: The truce supervisor of the UN had certified the line on the map and that remained the line until October 6, 1973.

George Tomeh: Mr. Chairman, may I be allowed to answer the other questions that were raised by General Amit?

Ernest Dawn: Go ahead.

George Tomeh: First, with regard to the diversion of the Jordan River, I wish to ask General Amit, who knows geography better than I do, [to recall] that on the map that represents the point of view of the World Zionist Organization before the establishment of Israel, or even before the Balfour Declaration was embodied in the League of Nations mandate, the first quest was for the headwaters of the Jordan River in Syria and Lebanon, and the Litani is also mentioned elsewhere.

In the early 1950s President Eisenhower sent a representative, Eric Johnston, and the Arab League took a decision to accept the Johnston plan [on division of the Jordan waters among the riparian states]. The party that did not accept the Johnston plan and did not want to discuss it with the Arabs was Israel. This question is so critical and is [so much] a part of any aspect of a Palestine problem and the Arab-Israeli dispute that it might be advisable to have a seminar to study this particular problem and follow it on the map. Without that, any discussion would be insufficient.

With regard to terrorism, it surely is a common problem. But what about the terrorism of states? The answer is to be found in a book by [Meir] Mardor, a commander in the Haganah, published in the United States as *The Haganah* [New York: New American Library, 1966]. In it there is the following sentence, speaking about the work of his group and himself in various parts of the Arab countries: "We were conspirators outside the law but obeying what to us was a superior law." That statement about the superior law established by man is, I believe, a travesty of any law.

Most of our deliberations so far have been directed toward the past. As I said, delving into history is a normal task if the truth is to be obtained. But looking into the future is as important as looking into the past. Here I want to put on record that one of the obstacles to peace is occupation, which is against the UN Charter. No matter what words could be found, the charter does not accept war as a solution to existing problems among members of the UN. It is forbidden basically by the charter. Occupation is a continuation of war and a result of war. To annex the Golan Heights, to annex Jerusalem, which is sacred to all of us, whether Jews, Christians, or Moslems, is a violation, indeed a great violation, of the law. Therefore, if we are looking into the future, and the present is laden with the past and big with the future, we have to take all these points into consideration— the unacceptability of occupation.

Richard Parker: Could I make two historical points? One on the Israeli assurances to King Hussein: I don't think he believed them. The record that I gave to Dr. Mutawi from Ambassador Findley Burns's oral history records his constant meetings with King Hussein on the eve of the war and King Hussein saying, "They're going for the West Bank." He was deeply suspicious of Israel's intentions.

Another point, with regard to the Johnston plan. I was one of the low-level people involved in those negotiations, and I remember them well. There was agreement at the technical level among the engineers from Israel, Jordan, and Syria as well as Egypt on the division of the waters of the Jordan Valley. It was sabotaged by the Lebanese at the meeting of the Arab League Political Committe in October 1955. Israel did not reject the Johnston plan. The Arabs did. A lot of arm-twisting from people like Don Bergus got the Israelis on board.

Karen Dawisha: I want to ask Ambassador Tomeh a question about his role in the UN in the month or two before the war. I think that you've accurately portrayed the psychology of the leadership of that time. I was interested to hear, when you were talking about the meetings that you had and your own actions, your own frame of mind, that the words "Soviet Union" never passed your lips. Yet we are led to believe that the Soviet-Syrian relationship was an important calculation, at least for the Soviets, and I'm wondering if you would be able to give us any information about your own personal relationship with the Soviet ambassador at the UN.

For example, I wonder if you have a memory of how you heard about the brigades. I certainly recognize the point about Israeli militarization of the demilitarized zone, but it is also a separate point from the whole question of the brigades. We heard yesterday that Eugene Rostow spoke to the Soviet number two, saying we're picking this [information on brigades] up all over Europe. Did you hear it from the Soviets in the UN or did you hear about it in a cable from Syria? How did you hear about the brigades first?

George Tomeh: Well, everybody who spoke [here] spoke about the book that he is writing. I will also say that I'm writing a book, and maybe the answer will be in it. But besides that, there is [another] aspect to the problem. If you mean by [your question] the mobilization in the demilitarized zone or the existence of any Israeli troops in the demilitarized zone, we have to remember that Israel was always able to mobilize in twenty-four or forty-eight hours, and exercises to that effect take place whenever Israel wants to wage a war. So that a brigade was seen or not seen is not really important in this particular situation.

With regard to any statement about the existence of a brigade, I was not party to that. But I would like also to add that, with regard to our relations with the Soviets, I had close working relations with the USSR delegation to the UN as well as with the United States. For instance, during the last three years of my service at the UN—when President Bush was the permanent U.S. representative—relations between Syria and the United States were not so good, but personal relations among the colleagues were very good.

Karen Dawisha: But just let me push you a little bit on the question that I asked you. When you look back, let's say in the month and a half prior to the outbreak of war, do you have particular memories of as close a working relationship with the U.S. delegation as you had with the Soviet delegation? Do you have a perception that the Soviet delegation was urging caution—I mean, do you have memories of meetings [where that occurred]? Were they using the position at the UN to try and ratchet down to cool the rhetoric that was coming out of the Syrian delegation, or did they urge you on? What do you think the Soviets' own objectives were in that period?

George Tomeh: There was no rhetoric coming from the Syrian delegation or the Syrian representative.

Karen Dawisha: Oh, there was rhetoric coming out of all delegations.

George Tomeh: From all delegations. That makes it a little more accept-able, especially since basically I'm a student and a teacher of philosophy, and usually that particular field makes us careful about how to pick our words. But to answer your question on the relation with the USSR delegation, at no time, no time, did they encourage, tacitly, implicitly, or explicitly, any, so to speak, provocative situation. On the contrary, they were always keen on advising or—I wouldn't use the word advising—of preferring a moderate course, and I had meetings with the Soviet delegation on a high level. For instance, Deputy Foreign Minister Semenov was mentioned yester-day. One evening at a family dinner in my apartment in New York, we stayed up until three or four in the morning and he was very, very clear that the only means that should be followed was one of negotiations and understanding and the avoidance of war in every sense of the word. And also at a very high level, together with the Syrian foreign minister and president, we met with Kosygin and Gromyko when they came here to meet with President Johnson, and the same course of being reserved, quiet, conciliatory was recommended by Kosygin and Gromyko. They did not encourage any adventurism in relations.

Ephraim Evron: That was after the war.

George Tomeh: I said before the war and after the war.

William Zartmann: I hope I can get a quick answer to a short question. Ambassador Evron had said that on May 23 there was a message from the

Israeli cabinet to Jordan, giving assurances of nonattack. Mr. Mutawi had said that that didn't exist. Which one didn't exist?

Ephraim Evron: No, these are two different matters. The matter about nonattack went on the day the war broke out, and that isn't referred to. I was talking about a message by the prime minister to the king to stop needling [Nasser] and . . .

————: Goading Nasser.

Ephraim Evron: And goading Nasser over the strait and over Israeli shipping and so on.

CHAPTER 5

✍ The View from Washington

Donald C. Bergus

The decade following the jerry-built settlement of the Suez crisis of 1956–57 saw a series of challenges to the peace and stability of the Near East. One difficulty followed another: the beginnings of breakdown in the delicate balance of Lebanese internal politics, a process temporarily halted by the intervention of American troops; short-lived but unsettling experiments in Arab unity; an Iraqi revolution that took the country out of security arrangements aimed at deterring Soviet physical expansion into the area; the growth of Soviet presence and influence, bringing significant economic assistance and massive arms deliveries; Iraq's first challenge to the integrity and sovereignty of Kuwait; the overthrow of the monarchy of Yemen; Egypt's armed intervention in the Yemen and the Saudi-American response, to name but a few.

Nevertheless, the Suez settlement held, and Egyptian-Israeli hostilities were avoided. The UN Emergency Force operated effectively despite being stationed only on the Egyptian side of the 1949 armistice line. The Suez Canal remained closed to Israeli shipping, but Israeli commerce passed through the Strait of Tiran without challenge.

The final months of the Eisenhower administration saw the beginnings of a rapprochement between the United States and Egypt. This was enhanced when the Kennedy administration made no effort to exploit the blow to Egyptian prestige resulting from Syria's abrupt departure from the United Arab Republic in 1961. President Kennedy hoped that President Nasser would concentrate on the economic development of Egypt. Nasser's response was sufficiently encouraging to prompt the input of large amounts of American economic aid, particularly in the form of food shipments under U.S. Public Law 480, but the U.S.-Egyptian relationship began to deteriorate after Egypt's massive intervention on the antiroyalist side in the Yemen civil war in the latter half of 1962. A further decline followed the death of President Kennedy in 1963.

At best, the relationship required careful tending, substantial economic resources, and recognition of longer-term interests that were not readily apparent. The increasing involvement of the United States in the Vietnam conflict, as well as the decline in U.S. agricultural surpluses and the perceived threat posed by Egyptian activity in the Arabian Peninsula to Free World access to vital petroleum resources in that region, brought into question the worth of trying to maintain the American policy toward Egypt. That policy was neither convincing nor particularly effective, as seen by American legislators and by governments in the Near East and elsewhere that were traditionally friendly to us. Nasser and his government did not seem desirous, and perhaps not even capable, of recognizing the problems in the relationship and attempting to address them. Instead, Nasser fell victim to the prevalent political disease in the area and seemed increasingly convinced that the United States was mounting a conspiracy against him. The U.S. government endeavored to set up a process whereby top policy and intelligence officials from Egypt and the United States would jointly and carefully examine the basis for these misapprehensions with a view to resolving them. Nasser waved away these efforts. Moreover, Nasser concluded that the United States might try to humiliate him by terminating food aid in a public and dramatic fashion. In other words, he feared a repeat of the 1956 withdrawal of the offer of U.S. assistance in putting together the financing of the Aswan High Dam. Acting on these bitter feelings, Nasser sought to preempt the situation by publicly withdrawing any outstanding Egyptian requests for U.S. Public Law 480 assistance. It was clear from his public behavior from March until June 1967 that the United States stood near the top of Nasser's "enemies list."

The degree to which this factor and his serious economic difficulties and loss of prestige in the Arab world contributed to his reckless behavior in May and June 1967 is difficult to estimate. But against this background, the process of diplomacy, the painstaking search for mutual interests, became almost impossible. Nor were the prospects for diplomacy enhanced by the vacancy in the post of American ambassador to Egypt from March 5 until May 21. The result was that an inexperienced ambassador-designate arrived in Cairo at the heart of the crisis. His initial contacts with the Egyptian authorities did not engender hope that the colossal obstacles to mutual understanding between the United States and Egypt would quickly be removed. Two other American emissaries were sent to Cairo: Retired Ambassador Charles Yost journeyed to Cairo as a publicly announced representative of the secretary of state, and former Treasury Secretary Robert B. Anderson, who had a history of dealings with Nasser, made an unpublicized visit to Egypt at the request of President Johnson.

Neither Yost, who had a number of conversations with Foreign Minister Mahmoud Riad, nor Anderson, who met with Nasser, came away from their meetings with the impression that the Egyptians would undo their actions. The deployment of Egyptian troops in the Sinai Peninsula would be maintained; the declared blockade of the Strait of Tiran would not be modified; and no effort would be made to reinstate UNEF on Egyptian territory. The American emissaries did hear statements that Egypt would not initiate hostilities and that Egypt would not object if Israel chose to refer the Strait of Tiran question to the International Court of Justice. Agreement was reached on the possible usefulness of further high-level discussions. It was understood that Egyptian Vice-President Zakariya Muhieddin would arrive in Washington on or about June 7 to explain the Egyptian viewpoint. In summary, it could be said that there was nothing in the U.S.-Egyptian conversations before June 5, 1967, to indicate that anything like a meeting of the minds had been achieved. At best, what took place was a series of ambiguous arm's-length transactions resulting from American initiative.

These American efforts at quiet diplomacy with the Egyptians took place against a background of increasing public tension and belligerence fostered mostly by the words and actions of Nasser himself. The professions of support for Nasser's actions coming from many parts of the Arab world revived memories of the days when his leadership was largely unquestioned. Again it was demonstrated that hostility toward Israel was the major impetus for aspirations of Arab unity. This heady process climaxed with King Hussein's "journey to Canossa" on May 30, when he totally reversed his position toward Egypt, flew to Cairo, and put himself and his armed forces under Egyptian command. On paper at least, three out of four of Israel's Arab neighbors were now mobilized and committed to altering the status quo in the area to Israel's disadvantage.

There was the closest consultation between the United States and Israel throughout the crisis. This process reached a higher stage with the arrival in Washington of Israel's Foreign Minister Abba Eban on May 25, two days after Cairo's announcement of the closure of the Strait of Tiran to Israeli vessels and third-country ships carrying strategic cargo to Israel.

The Washington that received the Israeli foreign minister on May 25 was a different place from the Washington of February 11, 1957, when Secretary Dulles had handed his historic memorandum to Israeli Ambassador Eban. The Dulles document, which spoke confidently of American readiness to exercise the right of free and innocent passage through the Strait of Tiran, was the product of a government secure in its support by a large majority of the American people and certain of its purposes and policies. The major factor, by far, that had changed the Washington scene was America's deepening involvement in the war in Vietnam, which was accompanied by increasing public opposition to that war. There was little appetite for policies or actions that might result in America's waging another war, alone, in an area far from our shores. This was particularly evident in Congress. In earlier times, one might have expected almost a knee-jerk reaction from Congress, which had hitherto strongly supported Israel with rhetoric and appropriations. Now, however, congressional attitudes had changed to the degree that President Johnson ruled out any unilateral American military action to come to Israel's assistance.

Moreover, while the Washington intelligence community, civilian and military, had estimated for years that Israel could effectively defend itself against any possible coalition of Arab military forces, President Johnson was not confident as to the accuracy of such estimates. He had been burned too many times by overoptimistic estimates of the military situation in Vietnam. The president appeared to have been reassured about Israel's military strength within a few days. He was not to be moved, however, from his position that the most the United States could do, militarily, was to join in a "Red Sea regatta" of warships of friendly Western powers to force, if necessary, freedom of passage through the Strait of Tiran.

Eban's mission, naturally, was to determine the extent of the American commitment to Israel. His opening gambit was to cite an Israeli intelligence report that the Egyptians were about to strike at Israel. He asked that the United States make an official statement that an attack on Israel would be considered an attack on the United States. American intelligence agencies, however, said they could not confirm the Israeli report. The American side confined itself to warning the Egyptian ambassador to Washington against attacking. The Israelis were told that it was most unlikely that President Johnson would be able to meet Israel's request for a broad public statement.

Donald Bergus, chief of the U.S. Interests Section of the Spanish Embassy, at his office in Cairo in 1967, following the break in diplomatic relations between the United States and Egypt as a result of the Six-Day War.

President Johnson, in his meeting with Eban on May 26, confirmed his reluctance to give a broad commitment involving the use of force to open the Strait of Tiran. He said the United States was working on the multinational naval force proposal. He then uttered the Delphic statement: "Israel will not be alone unless it decides to go alone."

Eban returned to Israel to report to a cabinet equally divided on the question of going to war immediately. The United States continued its efforts to assemble a multinational naval force but with almost total lack of success. The British, who had launched the idea, walked away from it. The Pentagon, with so much of the American fleet committed to the Far East, did not try very hard to conceal its lack of enthusiasm for the proposal, while the defense bureaucracy planned its implementation. Only the Netherlands firmly volunteered participation.

It was against this background in Washington that King Hussein dramatically joined the Syrian-Egyptian coalition. This action represented a fundamental change in the situation. Again, Israel sought to probe the American attitude, this time sending General Meir Amit, Israel's chief intelligence officer, for discussions with, inter alia, Richard Helms, director of Central

Intelligence. Amit returned to Israel with the clear impression, justified or not, that the United States would not actively oppose Israeli preemptive attacks on the Arab coalition.

Once hostilities began, the United States did not, as in 1956, call for an immediate cease-fire and a withdrawal of warring forces to previous positions behind the armistice lines. The Soviet Union pressed hard for such action in the Security Council but had to content itself with U.S. insistence on a simple cease-fire in place. Tensions between the United States and the USSR reached their apogee during the final two days of the fighting, when Israeli forces invaded Syria and reached a point only forty miles from Damascus. The Soviets threatened direct military participation to defend the Syrian capital and regime. The United States moved units of the Sixth Fleet to the eastern Mediterranean. Israeli forces halted their advance and accepted another cease-fire in place. The end of hostilities saw Israel occupying the entire Sinai Peninsula, all of Jordan west of the Jordan River, and the Syrian Golan Heights.

The outcome of the fighting was extremely popular in the United States. Friends of Israel were delighted that Israel's strategic position had improved as hostile forces were driven behind more defensible barriers. It was generally felt that the USSR had suffered a major setback in its plans to expand its influence in the area. There was gratification that the Israelis, unlike the South Vietnamese, had been able to resolve their national security problem on their own. President Johnson, in private at least, did not share in this euphoria.

The president went on to proclaim a major shift in American policy toward the Arab-Israel dispute. In 1956–57, the American objective had been the withdrawal of forces and the restoration of the armistice regime. On June 19, in a hastily arranged speech in Washington, the president stated that withdrawal should take place only in the context of a formal negotiated peace between Israelis and Arabs. This pronouncement came as a surprise, at least to those in the working level of the U.S. government who had been directly involved in the crisis. Like Athena, the new policy seemed to have sprung fully armed from the head of Zeus.

Twenty-five years later, formal peace between Israel and Jordan, and between Israel and Syria, had yet to be established. Innumerable questions arise from a study of these crowded events. Many of them are speculative and cannot be answered on the basis of materials presently available to us. Examples: What was the Soviet objective in precipitating the crisis? Why were the Syrians so lethargic in responding to the Soviet warnings? Would

Nasser, using Zakariya Muhieddin's visit to Washington as a vehicle, make possible the dispelling of the crisis and return to the status quo? The oral history presented at our 1992 Washington meetings cast little light on these and many other questions.

Why was there such reluctance on the part of the "Free World" as constituted in 1967 to follow the U.S. lead in creating a naval force to apply the doctrine of innocent passage to the Strait of Tiran? Was it purely timidity, or reluctance to associate with a United States so bogged down in a questionable and unpopular war in Vietnam? After all, many of our friends and allies depended on their merchant marine for their well-being and prosperity to a greater extent than the United States. Perhaps it was because the U.S.-Israeli case was not all that compelling from the viewpoint of international law. A close reading of the Dulles memorandum of February 11, 1957, shows that its conclusions regarding Israel's right to innocent passage depend upon the restoration to force of the Israel-Egypt armistice agreement of 1949. That agreement had been denounced by Israeli Prime Minister Ben-Gurion at the outset of the Suez war of 1956, and no successor Israeli government had found it politic to re-adhere to it. From 1956 until 1967, Israel did not participate in the work of the Egypt-Israel Mixed Armistice Commission. Moreover, the 1956 UN General Assembly resolutions establishing the UN Emergency Force called for UNEF to be stationed "along the Armistice lines." Despite this, Israel did not permit UNEF to operate on Israeli-controlled territory. Finally, although Israel had reason to assert that free passage through the strait was a vital national interest, the use of the strait by Israeli-flag vessels during the decade 1957–67 was minimal. In short, were the matter to be adjudicated in an international tribunal, Israel might have been coming into equity with something less than immaculate hands.

Viewed from a political rather than a strictly legal standpoint, the U.S. position as set forth by President Johnson on June 19, 1967, was much more tenable. As Brian Urquhart noted, those who painfully put together the 1949–50 armistice agreements never imagined that they would not have been supplemented by formal peace agreements after nearly two decades. The interest of the international community, indeed, the interests of the parties to the conflict, cried out for something better than a return to an intrinsically unstable status quo. During the long summer and most of the autumn of 1967, a consensus was reached between the United States and the USSR, a consensus shared by most of the international community, that the time had come to move forward to a lasting peace in the Middle East.

Twenty-five years later, it is commendable that the two major protagonists in 1967 have found that peace. The rest of the region has yet to achieve it, but even here none dares to deny that peace remains the common goal.

Panel 5

Chairman: Ambassador Donald Bergus
Speakers:
  Prof. Eugene Rostow, U.S. Institute of Peace: "The View from State"
  Dr. William Quandt, Brookings Institution: "The View from the White House"
Comment: McGeorge Bundy, the Carnegie Corporation

Donald Bergus: These events took place against a background of U.S.-Egyptian relations that were not only deteriorating but in many respects rapidly disappearing. A relationship that had been created during the administration of President Kennedy, despite the wishes of a good many on both sides, began to slip shortly after his death. I think this was basically true because of the tendency in the area to personalize relations between states. I recall that after President Johnson took over (I was in the embassy at Cairo at that time), on our urging he wrote a letter to President Nasser that was to continue the correspondence that had been going on between President Kennedy and Nasser, which had made a significant contribution to our relations. The letter duly came, and all of us in the embassy thought it was a good letter. It was delivered, and we got word back that Nasser thought the letter was cold. Now the fact is that that letter was drafted by the same people who drafted the earlier ones. But it wasn't the letter, it was the image that stood behind the letter, that had changed, and this affected Nasser's attitude. Moreover, in the relationship that we had developed with the UAR, Nasser depended to a large extent upon a ready supply of U.S. surplus foodstuffs, but a series of droughts and poor crops in the United States meant that this mountain of wheat and other commodities that we were eager to get rid of—that we, in some respects, pressed on the Egyptians—was disappearing.

The other big cloud on the horizon was the Yemen problem, and I certainly don't want to go into detail here. But one particular thing came out of this problem: a growing together, not consciously or overtly, but the coming together of the positions of two major public opinion groups in the United States—to wit, the friends of Israel and the American oil industry. They both began to share a jaundiced view of Nasser, whereas in the past one group had to an extent balanced off the other.

Then, in the world of intrigue and suspicion, we got messages from several channels that Nasser was convinced that we were out to do him in, by fair means or foul. We did our best to try and nip this thing in the bud. We made an offer, with the advice and consent of the CIA, that we would sit down together, his people and our people, and we would really go through and ransack the cupboard and try to get at the root of this thing. Nasser's reaction to that was a sort of grinning and saying, "Gee, I sure could never believe that [the United States was out to get him]." But it was obvious that he did believe it, so we didn't get through on that point. It was against this background that on that warm morning in May we woke up to the alarming news that was coming out of Egypt.

I'd like to ask Secretary Rostow to give us a picture of the view from State of these events.

The View from State

Eugene Rostow: I'll take my thesis from a remark one of our colleagues made yesterday about the Security Council's legally binding decision in 1951 that, under the 1949 armistice agreements, no nation has the right to claim or to exercise rights of belligerency. That ruling, one of our colleagues said, was political, not legal. The point I want to start with is to the contrary: that every political judgment, especially about responsibility for a threat to the peace, a breach of the peace, or an act of aggression, necessarily rests on and is derived from a prior legal judgment that the conduct in question was or was not a violation of article 24 of the UN Charter; and that peace among the nations, like peace among the citizens of any state, is a political condition ordered by the principle of fidelity to the law. I think that's an idea of particular importance in this long, intractable, and bitter conflict, one episode of which we're examining in this series of meetings.

In this case of the Six-Day War, I would say that the papers we've received in preparation for these meetings, and our discussion yesterday, fully confirm—except in the minor details—the judgments on which were based the policies pursued in 1967 by the government of the United States, its Western allies, including France, and most other countries around the world. In other words, the judgments on these points on which our policy rested at that time—an active, vigorous policy, duly embodied finally in UN resolutions 242 and 338—are supported, and fully supported, by what we've been reading and hearing. And what are they?

First of all, that Syria was indeed primarily responsible for a crescendo of breaches of the peace in its steadily escalating campaign of guerrilla attacks on Israel from its territory.

Undersecretary of State Eugene Rostow and President Lyndon Johnson, June 1967.

Second, that the Soviet Union did actively spread false reports of an impending Israeli attack on Syria and did urge Egypt to rally to Syria's defense. Those actions have been explained, especially by some of our Russian colleagues, in various ways, but no one has denied that such activities occurred.

Third, that Egypt did respond to changes in the circumstances, to Soviet incitement, to the corresponding statements emanating from radios and newspapers in other Arab countries. It moved its own troops and those of other Arab countries into the Sinai desert and formed a unified command, ordered UNEF out of its positions between Egypt and Israel, and proclaimed a holy war to destroy Israel, finally closing the Strait of Tiran to Israeli shipping, fully aware of what those moves meant in terms of the international agreements of 1957 that ended the Suez campaign.

We read and discussed a good deal about whether Nasser really wanted to do what he did, whether he was eagerly seeking a way out of the dilemma that he himself had created. I want to remind you here of another legal proposition, the distinction that law makes, and has to make, between objective and subjective intent. I'm not an expert on Nasser's unconscious mind, and from the point of view of the functioning of a legal system, it doesn't really make any difference. The legal system operates, except in rare and extreme cases, on the assumption that people intend the natural consequences of what they do. So, I think, fascinating as those theories of conspiracy or hidden purpose are, they're not really relevant here. These events occurred, we saw them occur, they had certain legal consequences, political consequences, military consequences, and we put together a program for responding to them as best we could.

What follows from this judgment, we thought then and I believe most of us think now, is that the time has come for the Arab states to make peace with Israel as Egypt did in 1979 and that until that step is taken, Israel can administer the territories that it occupied in the '67 war. This is the famous package deal of resolution 242, which was made legally binding by the decision of resolution 338. We're still living in the world framed and structured around those judgments, based on the evaluations of the conditions that began to develop and emerged in the fall of 1966 and the spring of 1967 in the Middle East, eventuating finally in the Six-Day War and then in the diplomatic struggle that's gone on ever since.

I came to the State Department in the fall of 1966, as the Syrian phase of the subject was warming up. After some months at the post, I was made chairman of a control group, which was LBJ's way of organizing interdepartmental cooperation on issues that were approaching a crisis level. He would have an undersecretary chair a group representing other departments at about the same level, other departments interested in the conflict, and that group was charged with preparing positions to be proposed to the president and then carrying out the president's decisions in relation to that policy. Later on, in Kissinger's time, that function was taken over in considerable part by the National Security Council, but in those days it was done through a looser coordination effort headed by an undersecretary, and I was in charge of the work with regard to the growing crisis in the Middle East.

Events went through four phases of gradually ascending intensity. First, the Syrian phase, where attention was focused primarily on attacks in Israel and elsewhere, emanating from Syrian territory and therefore the responsibility of Syria. Then the Strait of Tiran phase: the elimination of UNEF, the closing of the strait. Then the mobilization phase, when the Egyptian troops and troops from other Arab countries—from Algeria, from Iraq, from Saudi Arabia, and so on—began to move into a threatening circle around Israel to the accompaniment of ominous military music in the background. And then the phase when Hussein joined in the mobilization and put his troops under Egyptian command.

In the final stage before war broke out, the United States and others made an effort to head off the war by opening the Strait of Tiran themselves.

Despite many statements to the contrary that you'll find in the literature, some of them echoed today, I think we can say that there was a State Department view, indeed that there was a U.S. government view, of policy toward this conflict. There were differences, of course, within the executive branch and sometimes considerable differences among the participants, but there was an active procedure for overcoming and reconciling these differences. There was active participation at the top level by the president himself, by Secretary Rusk, Secretary McNamara, Cyrus Vance, Averell Harriman, and, of course, the assistant secretaries of state, Joe Sisco, Luke Battle, and their friends and colleagues. Mr. Bundy was present for a time. My brother was national security adviser in the White House at that time.

In addition to working within the government and keeping in touch with congressional committees and groups, we made a special effort to examine, to reexamine, our policy toward this part of the world pretty thoroughly. Julius Holmes, retired ambassador to Iran, was asked to do a study for the department, I think in the fall of '66, about Soviet penetration of the Middle East—Soviet policy toward the Middle East and what it implied for the United States and the Western powers. He produced a strong and clear study that commanded a great deal of respect within the government. We kept in close touch with our NATO allies. I went, and some of the assistant secretaries went several times, to meetings in Brussels to brief the permanent representatives there and to keep them fully acquainted with the evolution of this crisis. We were aware of it as a serious matter from the beginning. And I think we can say that, partly owing to those efforts and partly to luck, it's the only time in the history of the Arab-Israeli conflict that we achieved and sustained pretty much a united NATO position. It's interesting that in every previous conflict on this subject, including of course the original ones in 1948 and '56, there was division among the Western allies, but here, except for the partial separation of the French, which was overcome, we had a united Western position. I think that the fact that we had achieved that united Western position made it possible in the end to obtain resolution 242 and then 338.

Similarly, we were active in the UN. We had a strong representative there, Arthur Goldberg, and for six months or more Joe Sisco was in New York working full time with him. We had an especially close relationship with the United Kingdom, and there we were lucky in having George Brown as foreign secretary and George Thompson as deputy foreign secretary. That was not only helpful substantively, but also—as those of you who knew George Brown at all would know—entertaining and lively. With the Soviet Union we also remained in close and active touch all through this period and had many, many, many talks with Ambassador Dobrynin and his staff in Washington.

This whole period of preparation and study resulted in pretty much common positions for recommendations to our secretaries and to the president. There were active preparations for the postwar period, whatever it was going to turn out to be, whether (or not) there would be any opportunity to head off the war and to get back to the policies of seeking peace. You can see that in the policy that the president announced at the outbreak of the Six-Day War. Relying on the whole history of discussion within the department, the president committed himself to a policy of seeking peace. This time, he said, it will not do to go back to uncertain armistice, but we must go beyond that and make peace the goal of our diplomacy. While this sounds like a cliché in the history of the Arab-Israeli conflict, it is not one at all. It's a major step, going beyond the cease-fire and the armistice agreements that we've had, and to a large extent still have, as the only basis for ordinary day-to-day rule.

Late in the fall of '66, I think November, in my first close touch with Middle Eastern policy after coming to the department and before my control committee was set up, there was an episode that was mentioned here in which the Israelis had been attacked from Syria and were seriously considering, and we were seriously expecting, a major reprisal. The United States tried hard to persuade the Israelis not to do that but, instead, to go to the Security Council in the hope that we could get the Soviet Union to go along with the resolution condemning what had happened.

We negotiated hard with the Russians and got the resolution watered down through a series of compromises until it was pretty weak, and then the Soviet Union vetoed it. That was a salutary lesson for us, but a bit brutal, about the nature of Soviet policy in the area and what we could expect from direct negotiations. That didn't stop us from trying, but it chastened us a good deal.

As the Egyptians became more active and put more and more troops into the Sinai and attracted troops from all over the place, we ran into the question of the relevance of the agreements of 1957, which we've discussed here a good deal. Ambassador Evron came in one day with a copy of a key memorandum on the subject (I think he read part of it this morning). We looked all over the department, but we couldn't find our copy of it. When Don Bergus looked at it, he said, "Oh, yes." I saw there were emendations in John Foster Dulles's handwriting. Don Bergus identified it as part of a package, and he explained it to me as part of the scenario for the settlement of 1957. Luke Battle and I resolved we would never leave the building of the State Department until its files were put on computer so that this wouldn't happen again.

My brother asked me to say that he thought the key elements in the president's attitude in that final dramatic phase were former President Eisenhower's confirmation of the fact that the agreement [of 1957 on the Gulf of Aqaba] was what we were told it was, or what it seemed to be, in 1957, and [his saying] that he would back the president in whatever he decided to do. The president had sent Colonel Goodpaster [from the White House] to Gettysburg to see Eisenhower, and Eisenhower's response was important in President Johnson's mind. King Hussein's submission to Egyptian command was also much in the forefront of his mind. The British had proposed a scheme for defanging the crisis by organizing an allied flotilla to convoy vessels throughout the Strait of Tiran. Secretary Rusk and I were strongly in favor of it, and I think all our colleagues were, with perhaps varying degrees of enthusiasm. In any event, the State Department was very eager to see that experiment tried out, but we ran into two difficulties. One was that the Department of Defense was not so eager to get involved in more hostilities whose outcome was difficult to predict with precision.

A lot of people in the readings we've been presented with talk glibly of how obvious it was that the Arabs would be defeated quickly by the Israelis. The U.S. government was not so sure, and it had been through Korea and Vietnam, when the air force and other military forces promised quick and cheap victory, only to find that it was something else. So we were skeptical and deeply concerned, as everybody else was, by that prospect, and certainly our policy was to prevent the war from breaking into a stage of active hostilities.

The war began, as has been said here, when the Strait of Tiran was shut. That was an act of force, justifying the use of proportional . . . whatever force is reasonably required to cure the violation of international law. I disagree, a little, with what Ambassador Meeker said this morning about Israeli use of force being excessive in relation to the closing of the Strait of Tiran from the strict point of view of international law. I don't believe that for a simple reason: The geography of the place means that to take Sharm al-Shaykh and to maintain it, you have to deal with armies in the desert. There's no reasonable way, that I can see, of saying that the Israelis were confined in their rights of self-defense to sending a few gunboats down to Sharm al-Shaykh and overcoming the garrison that was there. I don't think that's what the law is. In any event, the war occurred. But the point I want to make, simply, is that Ambassador Sterner was right when he said the other day that the first shot in this war was the closing of the strait.

Now, were we going to do it [reopen the strait]? We ran into [the second set of] difficulties in Congress, a strong feeling on the part of some congressmen and senators that we had our plate full in Vietnam and [we should] let the Israelis do it. Finally my control group agreed to send a memorandum to the president, which the secretaries approved, saying he had only two options in this conflict. We could open the strait ourselves, through the use of this allied naval force that was being assembled just south of the Suez Canal, or we could in effect unleash the Israelis. There was some suggestion at the time the paper was drafted that we ought to put in a third option—going to the Security Council with the help of Ambassador Goldberg, who was there at the time and in the group, but the experience we had with the Soviets all through this period both on the Middle Eastern conflicts [and elsewhere did not make that look promising]. I would just say with regard to the point made by Ambassador Evron this morning, [to the effect] that the United States had abandoned commitments it made in 1957, on the basis of which Israel withdrew from the Sinai—he didn't put it as bluntly as that, but he said that the perception was that they were not going to be fulfilled—the president put great stress on the fact that he had asked for and received a promise from Prime Minister Eshkol that he had two weeks in which to fulfill these promises and open the Strait of Tiran. And the explosion occurred within that two-week period.

We could understand it. Anybody could understand it under the circumstances. The [Israeli] armed forces, in one of my brother's memoranda, were referred to as being like a coiled steel spring. They couldn't stay where they were indefinitely, and the armed forces of the Arab states were coming up from all over the Middle East, and we had knocked down previous alarms of immediate war, and there were several of them. I believe, despite the difficulties created by the Vietnam War and Congress, the president would have gone ahead with the naval force. I argued at the time that a new congressional resolution was not needed. Secretary McNamara argued very strongly that it was essential to have a new congressional resolution. I said that the 1957 resolution, the Eisenhower [Doctrine] resolution, was authority enough, putting the Congress behind the presidential decisions in this area. Of course, the Israelis thoroughly understood they were dealing here with one of the most sensitive areas of American constitutional law, exacerbated by the Korean and Vietnam experiences. But I believe that LBJ would have done it, whether Congress acted or not, with the understanding of the leadership. But that's a matter of, simply, faith. All the issues that were put before you so well this morning, I think, are genuine. All I can tell you is that during the only interview I ever had with Golda Meir—I went in to pay a courtesy call, and she kept me for about two hours, a wonderful talk—at the end when she was saying goodbye to me, she said, "You know, I will go to my grave believing that President Johnson would have done it." And my view is the same.

Donald Bergus: Our next speaker is Bill Quandt, who will give us the view from the White House.

The View from the White House

William Quandt: To dispel any misapprehensions on this score, I was not in the White House in 1967, nor was I anywhere near it, so my analysis is that of a scholar who has looked at as much of the evidence as he can, but I don't have any investment in the policy. I don't feel I need to justify it, but I do want to try to explain what I think it was and give, as best I can, an analysis of how things looked from the perspective of the president. I'm convinced that Johnson was the key player on the American side and that the Israelis were certainly more attentive to his views than to anyone else's in the U.S. government. Without belaboring the point, it's necessary just to say that Vietnam and the memory of Suez were powerful background elements in the American thinking in the 1967 crisis. Vietnam was a preoccupation for obvious reasons. The president was beginning to experience a strong domestic reaction to his Vietnam policy. Congress, which had supported the Gulf of Tonkin resolution, was turning against the war, and over and over again Johnson referred to Congress and what happened in Vietnam. There's even a phrase in one of the documents about "Gulf of Tonkinitis" as a kind of disease that has infected the Congress.

The Suez crisis of 1956 was on many minds in 1967, certainly on the Israelis'. There was a straightforward question: If the Israelis go to war, will the Americans treat this as another Suez and deprive them of the fruits of their victory? I don't think anyone in Washington thought Israel would not win militarily, but the question was, will the Americans this time support Israel's holding onto the territory until peace is achieved?

The Israelis had reasons to think that Johnson might be sympathetic since he opposed Eisenhower in 1956, but it was terribly important for Israel to know for sure what position Johnson would take. Suez did not come up much in the American discussions, but one suspects that the Americans didn't want to look like the British and the French, and some of the Americans in Arab posts who were reporting back and recommending what the United States should do had Suez much on their minds. The United States, they argued, should not put itself in a position of appearing to be co-conspirator with Israel against Egypt. So there was pressure, surprisingly, from the

Arabists not to do anything—don't get involved, because otherwise you'll look like the British and French, and you know what happened to them after 1956.

Let me say a word about what evidence exists on the American side. Obviously we don't have all the information we would like, but we have a lot more than our Soviet colleagues have to work with. The Johnson library has released several thousand pages of documents. I have a small portion of them with me, but they cover most of the crucial meetings that took place at the National Security Council, Johnson's meeting with Eban, internal deliberations—all that has been available. I don't have much that other people have not been allowed to see, but few people have bothered to look.

In addition, I've interviewed most of the living participants, starting in 1969, so I have a long record of having talked to people about this crisis; I have had access to a few documents that I came across when I was in government, and I have some notes on those that I will refer to where appropriate. Basically, what I want to do is put as much on the record as I can in a short time. My article published in the [Spring 1992] *Middle East Journal* is a fuller elaboration, with footnotes.

There has been a school of interpretation that says that throughout the crisis the United States was trying to prevent the outbreak of war. I will call this the red-light thesis. If you read President Johnson's memoirs, basically the argument is that time ran out and the Israelis took action on their own. But right up to the last minute we were supposedly trying to prevent war from breaking out. That is Dean Rusk's view according to his memoirs. I think it's Walt Rostow's view. Gene Rostow has given us his own view, which I think is close to that.

There is a different view that I call the "green-light view," of which Stephen Green was the first American proponent. Mr. Cockburn uses a version of it that implies that the United States was egging Israel on, that we wanted the war to happen as a way of cutting Nasser down to size, perhaps even getting rid of him.

I have developed an alternative to both of these views that sees an evolution of American policy from being serious about a "red light," [meaning] don't go to war when the crisis first erupts, to a more acquiescent policy—there's nothing we can do, you're on your own; we've given you our assessment of the risks, but we can't tell you not to do what we think you're planning to do.

Now for the evidence. First, I find nothing in any of the documents to suggest before May 12, 13, 14, before the onset of the crisis, any prior U.S.-Israeli collusion to bring down the Nasser regime. If it exists, it's not in any record that I've ever seen, and I don't think we've heard any evidence of it here today. That doesn't mean that Lyndon Johnson or Dean Rusk or anybody else was a great fan of Gamal Abd al-Nasser, with all the problems that Don Bergus mentioned about the Middle East. But the Middle East was not high on the American priority list as far as I can tell. Vietnam was such a big obsession that problems in the Middle East were not being dealt with as presidential problems. I don't see any reason to believe that before the crisis began there was any policy to trigger a crisis for any purpose.

Perhaps the most difficult phase of the crisis to explain is the first phase—from the time the Egyptian troops go into Sinai to the time Nasser announces the closure of the strait. A full week passes, which, depending on how you look at it, can be a long time. In a crisis or in history, it may not seem long at all. But a full week passes during which it becomes clear that a major crisis is developing. According to a certain stereotype of President Johnson, this strong, sometimes impulsive figure might have reacted strongly and said that we've really got to do something to prevent this war. The thing that I found most surprising is that the stereotype of Johnson, the kind of glandular figure who can hardly control his emotions, doesn't fit his behavior in this crisis at all.

On the contrary, he comes across as reflective, cautious, eager to listen to advice from a variety of perspectives, and almost always asking the tough questions when people give him reassuring answers, which is exactly what I think a president ought to do. During this period, he seems to have been almost excessively cautious. When the Israelis want strong reaffirmation that the United States will say the Strait of Tiran is an international waterway and it will live up to its 1957 commitments, they have a hard time getting Johnson to respond. Why? Because of his obsession with making sure that Congress is on board with anything we do, because Congress doesn't want American unilateral action.

That comes through in the first American discussions: Congress won't support unilateral actions, so we need a multilateral framework for action. So, surprisingly, in this first week of mounting crisis, up to and through the removal of the UNEF troops and the closure of the strait, there is no strong *démarche* taken to the Egyptians warning them not to go farther. The first letter that reaches President Nasser is drafted on May 22 and reaches him after the strait has been closed. Why is that the case? I can't answer for sure. There's nothing in the record that suggests a reason. The only thing I can think of is that some people had memories of a prior incident in February 1960, when Egyptian troops had gone into the Sinai. War had not followed. It had been a limited exercise, and there was no desire to fan the flames early on if this was just a limited operation. Indeed, the Israelis didn't overreact in the first few days, perhaps for the same reason.

After the strait was closed, alarm bells did go off in Washington and we entered a different phase of policy making, with intense internal deliberations and a complete record of discussions, whereas there was not much to go on in the first week. This is the period when the United States wanted to buy time, to see if we could come up with an alternative to Israeli action. We asked the Israelis not to react initially for forty-eight hours, and then we asked for another two weeks or so. In this period the recommendation from the State Department, which came in a memo on the twenty-sixth, was, indeed, to give the British alternative of a multinational fleet a try. It's phrased in a rather mild form. The first option described by Secretary Rusk is to let the Israelis decide how best to protect their own national interest in the light of the advice we have given them, in short, to "unleash" them. Rusk recommended strongly against this option. This was Rusk's position at the time; I believe it was his position right up until the last moment. The second option was to take a positive position, but not a final commitment, on the British proposal. The British cabinet was to meet on the plan the next day. This option was a kind of half-hearted endorsement of the fleet idea, but it is what the National Security Council recommended to Johnson and what he signed on to.

Just before the important meeting that Eban had with the president, Eppy Evron met with the president. Preceding both meetings, there were two serious internal deliberations that we have records of, and they are the only two that I know of. One was a full-scale National Security Council meeting on May 24, of which we have virtually the entire record—a little bit has been deleted. In that record, Johnson, when he intervenes in the discussion, is insistent on trying to make sure that there are others in this with us, that we won't do this unilaterally. But he also says these multilateral plans have a way of falling apart, and we have to figure out what we will do if this multilateral effort fails.

There was also an interesting meeting at noon on the day that Eban and Evron had their meetings with the president, but for it we have only a perfunctory version of the notes. It was never fully written up, but I have access to the notes. This was the fullest discussion of alternatives. And the president had not only his top advisers, he had people like Justice Abe Fortas, George Ball, and Clark Clifford joining the discussion. Luke Battle was present, as was Ambassador Helms. One gets the impression that LBJ went around the room and asked people what they thought and then would ask questions of them.

At a certain point the president signs on to the idea that we will try to use this multilateral fleet as what he calls "my hole card" with Eban: "I will try to persuade him not to go war by saying we'll do this for you, we'll reopen the strait." A number of people express strong views that there is no pressure on the Israelis to act: They can wait. They're going to win the war if it happens, whether they start the war or whether they're attacked. General Wheeler [chairman of the Joint Chiefs of Staff] said something like that.

Some people express the view that if the Israelis initiate an attack, they'll be on their own, that we will have no obligation to help them, and Johnson voices some concern about these overly optimistic views that the Israelis can handle it completely on their own. He seems to have a skepticism about military advice, and it's not too hard to guess where that would come from, given what was going on in Vietnam, and he keeps saying, "What if it doesn't work out this way, what are we going to be able to do if they get in trouble?" Johnson seems to be saying to himself, What if all these things I'm being told—that the Israelis can take care of themselves, that it'll be over in six days—what if they are not true? They're going to ask for our support and we can't do anything.

In the course of this discussion, in response to one of the opinions that Israel will be on its own if it strikes first, Justice Fortas says, that's not realistic. The only way we can prevent a war is, either we have to be able to take action that will solve the problem in the strait or we have to let the Israelis do it on their own, and we can't take the attitude that we can stand back if they don't take our advice, that they're on their own. It's not a realistic position to take.

And I think this was the major alternative that Johnson heard. If you can't use force yourself, you Americans, then you have to let the Israelis do it on their own, but you can't just wash your hands of the outcome. When Johnson asks Fortas in this discussion what he thought we should do, Fortas says, we should tell the Israelis that we're prepared to use force if necessary to reopen the strait. Johnson says, impossible, we can't do it. Congress will not allow it, they just won't allow it. In which case, Fortas says, you have to let them act on their own.

Fortas's advice was not taken by LBJ for use in the discussion with Eban. Eban was told, in a somewhat enigmatic phrase which Rusk had written in his own handwriting, that "Israel will not be alone unless it chooses to go alone." That was Rusk's handwritten version. Johnson added to that and used it in his discussion with Eban. Right after saying "Israel will not be alone unless it decides to go alone," Johnson added, "We cannot imagine that it will make that decision." That's Johnson's addition. I don't know why. I don't know whether he was really trying to say, "Give me more time, this fleet thing has to be tried," or what else, but anyway that was his addition.

Johnson told Secretary Rostow and others right after the meeting with Eban that he thought he had failed, that he hadn't given Eban enough to stay the hand of the hawks in Israel. In this interesting discussion, when Johnson, at noon on the twenty-sixth, says, okay, we're going to try the idea of the fleet and see if that will keep the Israelis from going to war, he also says, "I wonder if I will regret on Monday not giving the Israelis more today." That's when he left the meeting—a very reflective person, I might say.

From May 28 on, Johnson had asked for two more weeks to put together the fleet, and this became an interesting period—to see whether this fleet idea would materialize or simply die. There were differences of opinion over how good an idea it was. I'm persuaded the Pentagon thought it was a lousy idea and was not interested in doing much about it. The only reference to the fleet toward the end of the crisis, just before the war, is a leisurely memo from Rusk and McNamara that just recently has been declassified—the operational plan. They said, we can put the fleet together within a matter of a week (this is on about June 2) from the moment that we get the word that you want to do it. But Wheeler said that we needed antisubmarine capability—and that would take weeks to get there. The Pentagon was doing little to put this together. And so during this last week of May, the prospect of having an alternative to the use of Israeli force began to fade, and I think Johnson understood that.

Curiously, Johnson disappeared from Washington over the long Memorial Day weekend (May 27–30), which you might think was a fairly crucial one. If you were really determined to prevent war, you would be there, like George Bush, picking up the phone and calling everybody, seeing what could be done. Nothing of the kind. Johnson left town, went to the ranch, and, I can only infer—he was in touch, he got messages, some discouraging messages—it was during that period he concluded there was nothing the United States could do and that the only way this crisis could be resolved was for Israel to act on its own. Exactly who helped persuade him, I can't say, but he had no foreign policy people with him at the ranch, although he was getting messages. He got a discouraging report from Ambassador Charles Yost in Cairo, based on preliminary contacts there. Yost said, Nasser cannot and will not retreat, so the idea of a diplomatic backing down by the Egyptians was pretty much ruled out.

By this time the Israelis are not so much interested in whether the fleet is going to materialize, because they know it's a dead issue, or pretty close to it. But what would the United States and the president think if, in fact, Israel were to take action on its own? Can we be sure this is not going to be Suez all over again? General Amit has told you of his efforts to determine that, and he talked to the converted. McNamara didn't think there was any alternative. He thought the Israelis could take care of it by themselves.

But the real question is, did the president share that view? Evron went to the White House on June 2, a little before noon, to meet with Walt Rostow to propose an alternative. The way it came through on the American side, and I don't think too many people were aware of this at the time, was that time was running out. There was nothing sacred about this two-week period. Evron was asked, "Do we still have until June 11?" And he said, well, that was the original understanding, but there was nothing sacred about it. So time is running out, and he said what would you Americans think if there were a probe by an Israeli ship and the Egyptians opened fire and then we had to strike back? Would you recognize that we are exercising our legitimate right of self-defense under article 51 of the UN Charter? That's the other part of the 1957 commitment. Walt Rostow said, I can't give you my answer, but I will make sure the president hears about this immediately.

There is no record of what the president said about it, but there is an intriguing tidbit. A letter prepared on June 2, from the president to Prime Minister Eshkol, repeated pretty much the same things that had been said to Eban, including the whole Rusk phrase "Israel will only be alone if it decides to go alone and [Johnson's addition that] we cannot imagine that it will make this decision." Johnson then concludes the letter, which was drafted at State, by referring to conversations with Mr. Evron. Then at the last minute on June 3, just before the letter is sent, Johnson insists that a sentence be added to it. He calls Hal Saunders and says to add, "We have completely and fully exchanged views with General Amit." And Eppy Evron can tell you the impact that had on him. That meant the message that time has run out and we're going to act on our own had gotten through. That's the closest Johnson ever came to giving a green light.

The other strand of American policy, represented by Dean Rusk, was rather different. He continued to say right up until the end, if you Israelis fire the first shot, it's going to affect our attitude, and we don't want you to do it. As [Israeli] Ambassador Harman left town on June 2, Secretary Rusk met with him and reiterated the disadvantages Israel would incur if it initiated hostilities and indicated that a test of the strait by the American side could take place within a certain period of time. Rusk throughout said it matters who fires the first shot.

Sometime around May 30 or 31, Johnson, as I have said, apparently gave up thinking that there was any way of restraining Israel. Probably the Jordanian alliance with Egypt had some impact on his thinking, but also he had sent two people to Cairo to see if Nasser was in any way prepared to back down. Ambassador Yost did not see Nasser but he saw Mahmoud Riad, the foreign minister. His report was discouraging. Yost basically said we should stay out of it; we should not become the British and French in another Suez, or the whole Arab world would be against us. Let the Israelis settle the problem on their own, they can do it. Robert Anderson did meet with Nasser on June 1. The message, an eyes-only message to the president from Anderson . . .

Carl Brown: Whose channels?

William Quandt: State. Which means only a hundred other people have read it. But it is addressed to Secstate, info to the White House from the American Embassy in Lisbon, eyes only for the president and the secretary of state from Robert Anderson. Anderson goes through his discussion with Nasser, where he keeps saying, could we go to the UN and try to find a solution there? Nasser says no. Could we go to the World Court? Maybe, but we can't take too long, I don't really know, I don't have an opinion, I'll get back to you later on it.

And then Nasser expresses his view of what's going on—this is on June 1. Anderson says it's very likely that if Israel feels she's virtually alone, she might be motivated to strike first in order to secure a strategic advantage, and that so long as she felt she had friends she might be restrained. Nasser replied that this was a risk that he would have to accept and that he thought the first Israeli target and main thrust of Israeli offensive would be against Egypt and Cairo. He said that elaborate plans had been made for instant retaliation and that he was confident of the outcome of a conflict between the Arabs and the Israelis.

Anderson goes on further, probing Nasser's attitude. Nasser says, don't worry, this time it's not going to be Suez all over again. We are prepared; we've got the Jordanians under our control; we've got the Iraqis and others lined up. He says the only thing that's worrying him today is that the Syrians are not under his command, and they may try to provoke something to instigate a war prematurely. Anderson says, in that case, what would you do? What if they do launch a war? Would you stand aside? He said, no, of course not. We would have to fight, and we are prepared to do so.

There is nothing in the discussion from Anderson that would have led Johnson to ask the Israelis for another week to see whether Vice-President Muhieddin, who was at that point scheduled to come to Washington on June 7, might have something in mind to unravel the crisis. And, if one needed a final nail in the coffin, after all the many other nails had been pounded in, it was, I think, Anderson's report to the president. It was after receiving that message that LBJ changed his stance on "unleashing" Israel. The "red" light turned "yellow."

In my article I make reference to another channel that had some importance in persuading the president not to try to dissuade the Israelis. I refer to Supreme Court Justice Abe Fortas. The president was on the phone to Justice Fortas frequently. Fortas had made the case for letting the Israelis act on their own unless the United States was prepared to use force, and I have some information from Foreign Minister Eban that the conversation that Fortas had with Eppy Evron helped to persuade him [Eban] that the United States would tolerate and look favorably upon an Israeli strike. I think Eppy doesn't feel it was that important. There are other messages that Fortas conveyed to Ambassador Harman that reinforced the message, Johnson is not going to hold you back or hold you responsible if you go to war. I don't want to imply that Fortas was the main channel or the only channel, but he was a supplementary channel for indicating that the United States had no plan and this would not be Suez all over again.

Someone asked earlier, what does it mean for Israel to be a special friend of the United States? I think the operational definition was that in the last crucial forty-eight hours before the Israelis made the decision to go to war, they were able to have access at the highest levels of American government to find out if their reading of American policy was correct. Not too many other countries enjoy that kind of access. In this case, I think, they [the Israelis] read correctly that the president had nothing to offer and would not hold them responsible. That's a little different from saying that he egged them on; certainly he didn't give them a green light. Throughout the crisis, Johnson shows a suspicion that military solutions won't solve political problems. And on the second day of the war, when it is clear that Israel is winning and there's a certain amount of euphoria on the part of some of the Americans in the discussions, Johnson says, don't be so excited about the military victory, these things have a way of not solving problems, and we may look back on this and wonder whether the Israeli decision to go to war was so wise.

Commentary

McGeorge Bundy: I should begin by explaining that I was not there during all the events that we've been discussing. I joined the war after it had begun. Lyndon Johnson called in a bunch of elderly cold warriors and members of former administrations, and after that meeting he said, we need somebody. Walt's got a war. I want somebody else to handle the second war, so you stick around. And that meant that I spent the summer there [at the White House], although I really didn't do much. You've just had from Bill Quandt an extremely sensitive and perceptive description of Lyndon Johnson as counsel taker and decision maker, and I think he's absolutely right that the crucial decisions in this affair do take place in that head and heart. I'm not sure how much I can add to the helpful description that you've had of the intragovernmental process from Gene Rostow and of the process in the president's head from Bill.

It is certainly true that the relations between Israel and the United States are not a bit like those that the United States has with most other countries. If I were a citizen of an Arab country, this relationship would puzzle me and distress me. This is a deep-seated reality, not unlike the relationship that existed between the United States and Great Britain in, shall we say, the years '41 onward, for as far as you want to carry it. The British think it's still there. I don't think the Americans do. The closeness between the Israelis and the Americans is best understood, I think, in that way—not between the two formal governments but among thousands, hundreds of thousands, even millions of people in both countries. The reasons for the closeness are many and deep.

I entirely agree with Bill that it is not to be explained in terms of the sentiments of one sector of Brooklyn, important as they may be in any particular case. It's a much deeper and a much wider process. It's one that is not the same from one administration to the next, because it depends, in considerable measure, on the degree of sympathy and concern that the man in the White House has. Lyndon Johnson happened to have a warm place in his heart for Israelis and for Americans who cared about Israel. And that's an important element in this story.

One of the consequences, of course, of the friendship and of the connections is that when one gets mad at the other fellow, one gets very angry indeed, and there's some of that in this story. We've seen edges of it along the way. I think that the Israelis came to understand, intellectually and politically, that the fleet was not going to sail in a hurry. I, myself, having acquired wound stripes in the war over the multilateral force, have the broad feeling that fleets invented in the Department of State never sail. But that's partly because I helped to sink one. It was the best available device but it wasn't good enough, and it did have to be multinational for Lyndon Johnson's reasons. The U.S. Navy would have taken a direct order; it all could have been done, but it broke down along the way for a variety of reasons.

I think the simplest illustration of the depth and strength of the American feeling about Israel is the phenomenon that comes from the period later on. I think that there has never been a higher approval rating for the general behavior of another country than there was in the U.S. polls about Israel at the end of the Six-Day War. This war was, from the point of view of the great American public, a righteous, well-fought, and enormously successful enterprise, and it was greeted with almost unanimous applause in the United States. I'm not, for the moment, saying right or wrong; I'm only trying to describe the sentiments. Nonetheless, the crisis before the war began is a clear-cut illustration of how hard it is for good close friends to understand one another when the issues are as large and the choices as difficult as they were for both parties. It was a process of coming to understand what each side would and would not really, truly do.

I agree with the view that the most important point for the Israelis was that there should not be a repetition of Eisenhower over Suez—that is to say, an operational and politically damaging disapproval of Israeli action. That assurance I think the Israelis got because of their ability to sound opinion deeply and at all levels. I think that the Americans, for their part, had to come to terms with the fact that the Israelis would go. I think Bill Quandt is correct in emphasizing Lyndon Johnson's conclusion that he had not dissuaded his Israeli visitors when Eppy and Eban were there, and I think, therefore, that there was some degree of American-Israeli understanding of the coming of the war. The war had to come, and the Americans and the Israelis did pretty well on the whole in understanding each other and their respective roles and responsibilities.

Although he [Nasser] has had relatively little of our attention in the last two days, that doesn't make either the Americans or the Israelis, either by open action or by conspiracy, the agent, the people, who started the war. The fellow who started the war is named Nasser, and he did it deliberately. His estimates of his reasons for doing it may or may not be as wildly off the mark as his comments to Bob Anderson, as Bill has just quoted. But it is Nasser's decisions, Nasser's acceptance of risks, Nasser's organization of

Pro-Israeli demonstrators at the White House, June 8, 1967. *U.S. News and World Report* photo, Library of Congress collection.

what had to be to the Israelis a conspiracy to encircle and destroy, that brought the war on, and it doesn't seem to me that any of us gains by neglecting that reality. Nothing quite like it has happened since. It contrasts most strikingly with the entirely different, prudent, careful, and successful decision on the use of force by Sadat later on. And we shouldn't get so focused on details of other people's behavior that we leave out the principal agent of this particular historical event. Hussein was foolish. The Syrians— we haven't really heard much about Syrian decision making. We had a good deal of Syrian opinion about the misbehavior of other people, but that's not quite the same thing, with all respect. I think we have to think about what was done on the Arab side, especially by Nasser, more than the time devoted to it in our discussions so far would suggest.

In the deeper sense, however, I would put forward a still larger proposition: If you look at all the unfinished business, hopes, and fears on all sides in that part of the world in 1956—leave aside the particular decisions, leaders, steps, and even duck the question that I just addressed of who's really in the end more responsible than anyone else—I think you have to conclude that of all wars, at least that I have direct experience of, this was the one that was, more clearly than any other, somehow waiting to happen. It's not easy to write the Middle Eastern history on an alternative path from 1967, supposing there had been no crisis in that winter, without having a war somewhat like this, somewhere, in the twenty-five years since.

Discussion

Richard Helms: On May 23 or 24, President Johnson at breakfast turned to me and said, "Arthur Goldberg has been chewing me up about Israeli concern about their predicament, and what is the matter on our side and what's the problem all about?" Before I had a chance to respond, in the course of the day the Central Intelligence Agency received a report of a briefing by the Israeli intelligence community to the chief of station of the agency there, and he was reporting on what these intelligence officers had to say. There was an immediate written reaction from the agency group that dealt with Arab-Israeli affairs; the reaction was ready when President Johnson returned that day, I believe it was May 25, from opening the American exhibit at the Montreal Expo exhibition. This document was simply an appraisal of an estimate of the Arab-Israeli crisis by the Israeli intelligence service that had arrived that day. It [the agency reaction] disagreed with some of the points in the Israeli document and made this comment: "We do not believe that the Israeli appreciation presented to our chief of station was a serious estimate of the sort they would submit to their own high officials. We think it is probably a gambit intended to influence the United States to do one or more of the following: (a) provide military supplies; (b) make more public commitments to Israel; (c) approve Israeli military initiatives; and (d) put more pressure on Nasser."

The rest of the [agency] document simply dealt with minor differences in the military estimates of the strength of the Egyptian army. The last paragraph of it was devoted to the Israeli concern that if the Free World was not careful here, the Soviets were liable to take over the Middle East. Now it was not the first time that this had come through Israeli intelligence. As a matter of fact, General Amit had sent me in 1966, I've forgotten the date, a document that also dealt with this subject and that pointed out Israel's concern at the time about Soviet intentions in the Middle East and the possibility of their taking over the area.

I was particularly appreciative of Bill Quandt's efforts to put this whole thing in historical context because, remember, this was twenty-five years ago and circumstances were very different. A lot of what I'm saying sounds kind of silly in retrospect.

When President Johnson got back that afternoon, we had been waiting for him down in Walt Rostow's office. Secretary Rusk had turned to me and said, "Do you agree with this paper that your people have turned out?" And I said, yes, I did. To which he said, "Well, I just want to tell you this. In the words of Fiorello LaGuardia, if this is a mistake, it's a beaut." Anyway, we went on upstairs to see President Johnson. He read the paper. It was then that he turned to General Wheeler and me and asked to have this scrubbed down, which was his rather indelicate way of saying that either we could be more precise, or we could examine the whole situation more carefully, or we could do any of a number of other things, but he wanted another paper. That paper was produced in short order. And there is no question about where we came down: If the Israelis attacked first, it was going to be a short war; if the Egyptians attacked first, it was going to be a longer war, but there wasn't any question about who was going to win it, at least as far as the estimate was concerned.

At the end of that week—and I might as well say now for the record—Meir Amit came to see me on June 1 at nine-thirty in the morning, and we did indeed have the conversation that he is talking about.

And an answer to Patrick Seale and his book: I just want to say that I did not give General Amit the green light. He knows I didn't give him the green light. We didn't even talk about lights. And this jargon, unfortunately, is imprecise, particularly when you get in that amber area that covers almost anything. So let's lay to rest once and for all that there was collusion here or that there was backhandedness or anything else. We had a perfectly straightforward conversation about the situation. That weekend I sent an eyes-only memorandum to the president—I think about a page long—which ended by saying that we had no doubt that the Israelis were going to attack in a short time. I think that takes care of the points I wanted to make now.

Lucius Battle: Most of the points that I wanted to make have just been made either by Dick Helms or by Bill Quandt. I wanted to be sure that the two estimates that you referred to—I think the range of differences was simply a short versus a long war—were a difference between twelve days and six days. Is that right?

Richard Helms: The papers are not quite that precise, because they all look at this from the standpoint of who starts the war and just how it's fought.

Lucius Battle: The JCS [Joint Chiefs of Staff] was precise about how accurate they had been after the war was over.

Richard Helms: Luke, all I want to say is that it has been improved with time.

Lucius Battle: That may well have been. I'm not sure that any of us have improved much with time, Dick. At any rate, there are a couple of comments I want to make with respect to Gene Rostow's presentation. First thing, the matter of the control group and the Armada: I said the other day I felt we should perhaps have given more time and should have been working on diplomatic-UN–type solutions a little earlier, and less on the fleet. Gene suggested that there were differences of view within the control group. I had absolutely no problem with the conception of a fleet, initially. The idea of the ships sailing in grandly with flags waving, many flags of many nations, was rather appealing, a lovely way to challenge him [Nasser]. But the truth is, we were not garnering the sort of international support that one might have expected and hoped for. The fleet was not waiting in Suez to come in, Gene—it wasn't even formed. And it was not located; you really had no commitments; you had a couple of maybes. You were down to the U.K. and maybe the Dutch.

————: Australia.

Lucius Battle: Well, maybe Australia, but nobody had any ships anywhere near the locus in which they were going to be needed.

Eugene Rostow: I thought the *Intrepid* was down there.

Richard Parker: I think that we only had the Dutch signed up.

Lucius Battle: I think so. It was a small fleet by the time we got—so then the question . . .

————: No Brits?

Lucius Battle: The British backed down on the fleet entirely. They stayed with us on the maritime declaration but not on the fleet. But one of the other things that began to trouble me as people fell by the wayside was the inadequacy of our own planning for the consequences of this act. I had one conversation in a meeting with Buz Wheeler, and I said, if we go in, by ourselves with one other nation, perhaps the Dutch, and we're fired upon, what happens then? Buz pounded the table. "Luke, it means war." I said,"I know it means war, Buz, but what happens?" I said, "Do we take off and bomb Cairo at that point?" Well, it was perfectly clear to me after that session that we had no plans that covered such a possibility as this one. So the appeal of the fleet and the armada got less and less as time went on, as the size of the fleet went down and the dangers to the United States of running the thing alone, or with only one other participant, became more evident.

Now the last thing I want to do is get into a defense of Gamal Abd al-Nasser after that elegant statement by my friend Mac Bundy, but I do think that there's a little bit to be understood about it in the perspective of history. [Before] the last telegram I sent from Cairo, I had spent two hours with Abd al-Nasser on March 4. I left on March 5. And, incidentally, that night I had been at Heikal's house to dinner. It was the only time I ever met Marshal 'Amr. He came to dinner with Anwar Sadat and Mahmoud Riad, and we stayed late, drank a good deal, and had long involved discussions. The next day I sent a message back. It was my last message, saying that Egypt is in terrible shape, and Nasser is in horrible condition, and he's going to do something really quite drastic. I said, I think he has three options. One was to heat up the Yemen, aimed at getting more help financially because his economic straits were terrible; he knew he was already in trouble with the Yemen, but he had ways of heating it up one way or another. The second alternative was Libya, where money still existed. King Idris was still in power. Nasser still had something like 18,000 schoolteachers, Egyptian schoolteachers, over there [in Libya] that he could use as some sort of asset in some sort of action around there. And third, and least likely, I thought, he might heat up the Arab-Israeli war, not because he wanted a war but because he wanted to reestablish his own place in the sun, and he would hope and believe there would be some effort made to pull him back from any disaster. I think that those were the motivations as far as he was concerned.

I agree with you completely on his behavior. I think it was atrocious. He was responsible for exactly what happened to him, and he deserved every bit of it. But I do say, I still believe that had there been a way for a face-saving option that did not originate with him, in which he was not involved, it might have pulled him back before the thing took place. But that I will never know, any more than I will know whether Lyndon Johnson would or would not have forced that strait.

Eugene Rostow: I don't disagree with the judgment that the fleet proposition, initially very promising, was fading fast, which I think was Bill Quandt's phrase. I think the primary force that killed it was the Vietnam reaction in Congress when the proposal was vetoed, and the dubiousness in DOD [Department of Defense] and elsewhere in the government. It was a temporizing thing and the hope simply was—not that it would be permanent, of course; that was one of the objections: what happens if you escort military convoys through and then you have to do it for the rest of eternity? But it was a way of defusing, the only way we had, as you know, of hoping to defuse a crisis that was threatening to blow sky-high.

Donald Bergus: Speaking of the congressional attitude, I remember Kay Folger [from the Bureau of Congressional Relations] bursting into NEA [the Bureau of Near Eastern and South Asian Affairs in the Department of State] one of those afternoons saying, "I need twenty speeches for Congressmen tomorrow morning." And the thrust of those speeches was a resolution to tell the president to tell U Thant to work harder.

Lucius Battle: On the matter of congressional approval, on the day that the war began, I was booked fairly quickly to testify to the House Foreign

Affairs Committee first and then go to the Senate thereafter. The Senate Foreign Relations Committee invited all members of the Senate, and we had over a majority of the Senate crowded in and miserably unhappy, standing up for the most part. In the middle of all this, I got a note from the president saying that I should come back to the White House immediately when this was over, and he obviously wanted to find out what responses I was getting from the Senate. It was extremely negative in what they didn't say publicly but said to me privately. And it was: keep us out of this thing, don't get us mixed up in it, that was the line absolutely clearly.

Samuel Lewis: I'd like to raise a question that hasn't really been addressed at all, about the second phase of the war. How did it come about that the Israelis decided to go all-out against the Syrians, which of course wasn't part of their plan for the first part of the war? Indeed, the decision was taken only after the war was nearly over. It wasn't part of the initial combat. Now, think about the consequences of this war; that was not a necessary part of it. In fact, there were people in the Israeli government who were opposed to it. For example, Dayan was reluctant. The question is how that codicil, if you will, to the main event took place. It has cast some long shadows over history ever since. Was there any American involvement at all, and what was the Israeli debate all about? That's a question that somebody might want to speak to.

[I also want to raise an] issue: This whole crisis seems to me characteristic of the way the United States deals with crises. If you look at the history of the last thirty or forty years, I would wager that we have often delivered the same message, not only to the Israelis, but also to a lot of other people, whenever there is the possibility of real trouble erupting: "Please be restrained, hold off, give us time"; restraint, that's the standard American message.

In hindsight, one might conclude from this history we've been discussing that the decision to hold Israel back for a couple of weeks, even after the casus belli occurred, ironically ended up by producing an outcome that has complicated the world's handling of the Middle East enormously. Had the United States reached the same conclusion on May 24 or 25 instead of June 2 or 3, and had the Israeli cabinet gotten that "we're-by-ourselves" message earlier and moved earlier, before Hussein had gone to Cairo and locked himself into the coalition, perhaps there would have been no West Bank–Jordanian dimension to the war at all. We all understand how different the world and the Middle East would look had the Jordanian dimension never taken place. So the issue is: Is it always a good idea to try to slow down crises and stretch them out?

Meir Amit: I'd like to answer the Syrian question. Sam, you've known Moshe Dayan personally. Moshe Dayan had a few weak points. One of his major obsessions was not to fight on two fronts at one time. By the way, this was also Ben-Gurion's philosophy, so to speak. The Syrian problem was maybe, even from a practical point of view, not a potential. The Sinai was a potential problem for the future. We didn't have settlements in the Sinai. We didn't have forces, etc. But on the northern front we had settlements; we had people suffering for years not only from terrorism but also from Syrian shelling of villages, and it seemed natural that the least we could do was to go on the Golan Heights. Those of you who have visited the Golan Heights can understand. It controls the valley below, the Hula Valley. You cannot live there without being shelled every day and every night. Children were living in shelters for weeks. So that was a real problem. The one who delayed the operation against Syria was Dayan, only because he didn't want to fight on two fronts, on three fronts. And I remember also—Ambassador Rafael reminded me—that the other obsession of General Dayan and Ben-Gurion was not to irritate the Russians too much, and he knew that attacking Syria meant a direct involvement of Russia, or at least the danger of such an involvement.

I remember missions, delegations, friends from many villages coming to Dayan when we were sitting together. Dayan resisted these delegations. Some of the people who came were his personal friends. The one who really pushed was Yigal Allon, who represented the villages, the settlers. When Dayan finished, more or less, the war on the southern front, he then decided to move to the Golan Heights, and at this stage something strange happened. When he decided that, he overlooked the chief of staff and gave a direct order to the commanding officer of the northern command. That was also typical of Dayan. He didn't care for bureaucracy, or order, or anything like that. He used to tell us, you clean in the afternoon what I spoil in the morning.

That's exactly what happened, and there was no American involvement. I don't see how there could have been an American involvement. If, Sam, we would have gotten an American warning not to do that, I don't think that it would have had any effect because that [occupying the Golan] was crucial. It was delayed only because Dayan, as minister of defense, from the tactical or operational point of view wanted to do it this way.

Eugene Rostow: I'll answer the question from the point of view of the U.S. government. The attack on Syria came as a surprise and President Johnson's immediate reaction was the Soviet dimension. When the news came, there was a meeting of the group that he had assembled to deal with Middle Eastern questions. After the news was discussed for a while, he

[Johnson] turned to McNamara and said, "Where's the fleet?" McNamara went over to the telephone and called up and reported back that the fleet was divided into two parts, one near Malta and one near Spain. He [Johnson] said, "Order the fleet to head straight for Syria, both parts of it. They'll understand that." That was his contribution to the first phase, the diplomatic phase, of the thing. After a day or so, he began to put great pressure on Israel to stop and accept the cease-fire because he was concerned about the threats coming from the Soviet Union.

Alfred Atherton: We've heard a lot from the high-level policy point of view. I have a few observations about the American response from the working-level point of view. When I say working level, I mean that I was then director of Arab-Israeli affairs and had been for a few months. I ended up being head of the task force up in the Operations Center, which meant I was really insulated from almost everything and spent most of my sleeping and waking hours up there. Mac Bundy made the comment that this was a war waiting to happen, and the point I want to address myself to is, why were we all so surprised when it suddenly broke out as a full-blown crisis somewhere around the middle of May? In retrospect, you can say it should have been predictable in April. Some will say, and I think both Dayan and, interestingly enough, Mahmoud Riad in their books say, that they traced the war to just after the Samu' raid, in November 1966. My recollection is that most of us were not really expecting a full-blown war until it was only a few weeks away.

I had just come back from a trip to the area. I'd been to Egypt, Jordan, Lebanon, Syria, Iraq, I think, and Israel and had done the usual report, probably through my boss, Luke Battle, about impressions of the trip. I can remember clearly saying that in all of the Arab countries I went to, with the exception of Syria, people never got around to raising the problem of Israel or the Arab-Israeli or Palestine issue with me except in rather a pro forma way toward the end of these conversations. They were talking about either problems among themselves, between Egypt and Yemen, Egypt and its other Arab neighbors, and in Iraq, in particular, I remember a great deal of concern about their attempts to get their economic development program going. It was only in Syria that there was a preoccupation with the Palestine question and, obviously, very much so in Israel because of the border problems.

Trying to reflect on why we didn't see this more clearly sooner, I think it was because we tended, perhaps, not to factor in enough. We were so preoccupied with the Soviet aspect and, obviously, with the Israeli-Arab aspect that we really didn't factor in enough what was happening in the internecine warfare within the Arab world. And we didn't understand the extent to which that became a major factor driving Nasser to do what he did, because of the proddings from Jordan, the proddings from Syria, and so forth. We simply didn't give that enough weight soon enough, or we might have seen this coming. Whether that's a lesson for the future, I don't know. I hope not, because I hope we won't face this situation again.

On the point that Sam Lewis has raised, again I will speak from the working-level point of view. Bill Quandt, in his article, speaks of the "unleash Israel" option as one that was pretty much discarded until late in the game, and the question comes up, why? Again from the working level, I know I felt, and I think a lot of my colleagues had the same impression, that once Nasser asked for UNEF to be withdrawn, we said, this is going to lead to another step, this is probably the beginning of the road toward war. It was almost irreversible already, not just after the closure of the strait, because that was going to follow. If Nasser got up to the strait and UNEF pulled out, he was going to have to do something, and the next step was to close it, and that would surely be a casus belli. Even at that point, some of us were saying, knowing the intelligence estimates—that Israel was clearly going to come out on top, particularly if it was able to make the first move— why not at that point unleash Israel? Why not say Israel is going to do this? It's going to happen anyway. We're confident that Israel is going to prevail. We're not walking away or abandoning Israel, but we're not in a position— our judgment was, and it turned out to be right in the end—to stop it. Why not? Why wait? Why delay it?

Eppy made the point in his comments this morning that there were some people who felt that the more the United States could put some light between itself and Israel during this crisis, perhaps the better in the long run. That was not the prevailing view, but I think some of us at the working level— not because we didn't care what happened to Israel but because we felt Israel was going to do all right anyway—said we had to look beyond the war to position ourselves to influence the postwar situation. [We should] not be seen to be fighting right down to the wire to try to find ways to help Israel, which was going to help itself in the end anyway. So I think there's a valid question. When you can't stop something like this, isn't it better, perhaps, to do it sooner, to disengage sooner, rather than later and live, if you will, to have a little more freedom of action on another day? I'd be interested in hearing whether this got any more serious consideration at the policy level.

Donald Bergus: I would say that the biggest inhibitor to that would be the risk of losing Saudi Arabia. If we had deliberately, openly sided with Israel at that early stage, I think we could have lost Saudi Arabia.

Alfred Atherton: Oh no, I'm not saying we should have sided with Israel. That's quite the opposite.

William Quandt: You didn't answer your own question, Roy.

Alfred Atherton: I'm looking for somebody else to answer it. I want to know whether, at the policy level, this really did get more consideration than it seemed was the case.

Samuel Lewis: With Rusk's position so strong, it wasn't considered. Is that the answer?

Donald Bergus: I would guess. I wasn't there.

William Quandt: I think Rusk's position was strong. Hal [Saunders], incidentally, raises this option in a memo. He said why not just let them do it early, and he raises it again later in the crisis as an alternative. But my guess is, from Johnson's comments, that he was still worried that the optimistic intelligence assessments weren't right and that Israel might get into trouble, and then we would have to get involved but we weren't prepared to do so, and if war could be avoided, on the whole it would be better. If he had known what the outcome was going to be. . . . Sure, it's easy to play the record back and say, it would have been better if it had all happened on May 24 instead of June 5, but I think you can't play history back that way and assume that you know the outcome. I think that on May 26, when they decided to try to restrain Israel, they weren't at all certain what the war's outcome was going to be.

Eugene Rostow: I think Roy's option [to unleash the Israelis early in the crisis] was considered a lot, not formally on an agenda or in a meeting but discussed often, along with the question of whether our interest and the Israeli interest were somewhat different. Clearly the best interest of Israel was to do what it did, and with that kind of outcome in terms of establishing a long-term relation with the Arabs. . . . I think the fruit of that was Sadat's peace, going to the Knesset and all that. But from our point of view of relations with the Arabs and the oil and so forth, it was risky, or it seemed so to us, and therefore it was considered an area where we might have a deviation of interest between us and the Israelis. [If] our interest was to prevent [war], although the Israelis had a perfect right legally to do it, maybe it was better to find a diplomatic solution, or whatever solution we could think of.

————: I'd like to follow up on something that you said that intrigued me: that if we unleashed Israel early on, we would lose Saudi Arabia. Why Saudi Arabia?

Donald Bergus: Because, despite the serious differences between them, the idea of Arab unity still had enough power that I don't think the Saudis, Faisal, would have run against that current. If you recall his attitude after the June War, when he had every reason to be delighted that Nasser was taken, he was one of the first to join up in helping to finance him. There was still that much substance to Arab unity at that time.

Ephraim Evron: On the war with Syria, Meir Amit has described in full what prompted it. I might add that the only time here in Washington when I felt a growing American concern about our operations was during this phase of the war, in particular during the last day of the war. From that morning, when the president got worried, and now I understand why, the pressure was on to put an end to the war, and obviously the president was concerned with Soviet moves.

I share Sam's reflections on what would have happened had we struck earlier. In fact, I talked about it to a few friends. I'm of the opinion that had we not had your pressure on us until early June, we would have struck on, let's say, May 25, because total mobilization took place on May 23 in Israel. [In that case] the whole Middle East would look different today. That was long before King Hussein aligned himself with Nasser; it was long before Prime Minister Eshkol was forced to take into his cabinet Menachem Begin; and the war would have ended—it's nothing but a thought, I can't prove it—with King Hussein still in control of the West Bank and East Jerusalem today.

I want to make a point for the historical record, since mention was made of it by Bill in his brilliant presentation. I'm doing it at the risk of cutting myself to normal size. I'm going to shoot myself in the leg. I've been described in some books and articles, so I'm told—I haven't read all of them and I would invite those who wrote them to send them to me—as some kind of person who single-handedly got the United States involved in the war. [Supposedly, this person] had a friend named Jim Angleton, and between them they got this war going. I want to say for the record that nothing is more untrue than that. I did, of course, meet Jim Angleton during my long years in Washington. I never had any professional connection with him. Meir Amit wouldn't have permitted it, nor would Dick Helms. Throughout the weeks and months before the Six-Day War, I didn't meet him even once.

Another point is the special channel of Justice Fortas. I had the great pleasure and honor of knowing the justice and talking to him from time to time. I can say with great conviction, knowing the facts—and I think that I reflect also the opinion of Ambassador Harman, who met with him even more than I did—that we didn't look at Justice Fortas as a channel to the White House for the simple reason that we didn't need another channel. Too many channels sometimes will get you confused, and we don't do that deliberately. But the justice was judicious in his conversations with us and never once reflected, or made us think that he reflected, the views of the president. He said only what *he* thought, and even that he communicated circumspectly. Since I was the one who talked to him during that last day and I know what he told me, I feel it important to his memory to put this record straight.

Tahsin Basheer: I have to go back to Gene Rostow. I'm glad that when Eppy Evron came to you with the text of the memo, you didn't have the memo in the State Department. You couldn't find it; maybe today you'll find it. But if you assume that the State Department with its elaborate classification did not have it, how do you assume that the Egyptians ever had it? That's a big question. We never had it. Second, your very good legal defense as a lawyer . . .

Gideon Rafael: There is an error in the whole story; the memorandum was sought, and we found it at two o'clock in the morning on the twenty-fifth. We had been meeting . . .

Tahsin Basheer: Rafael, you are interrupting me! Listen to me first! Listen to me, I don't like to be interrupted.

Donald Bergus: Good!

Tahsin Basheer: Okay. Second, your good defense of the '57 agreement regarding passage in the strait and all international waterways: How come you or Israel never took Egypt to the international court, as was our repeated stand? Neither the United States nor Israel ever took Egypt to the international court for stopping what you called innocent passage of Israel in the waterways. Had you had a good case, you would have taken [the matter to court] a long time ago.

Third point, [the agreement of] '57 was not concerned with stopping passage in the Tiran Strait only, [but also with] stopping passage in the Suez Canal, and you never raised the issue of stopping passage in the Suez Canal legally. You raised it politically. Egypt answered, take it to the World Court, but you never obliged.

But having said that, I'm getting a feeling of the game. You know, very interesting. All the discussions in the White House, in the State Department, with the CIA, were about who can hit who militarily. And you were sure that the Arabs would be knocked off. There was no concern at all in all these discussions about what happened to the people in the Middle East. When references to the Middle East are made, they are made to Hussein, to King Faisal, to Nasser, never to the people of the Middle East. And that never changed until Carter's days.

Eugene Rostow: I don't think that's really fair to American policy or to Lyndon Johnson. I myself kept the PL480 [food supply] programs for Egypt going despite the Six-Day War, and I received a personal thanks, a special message of thanks from President Nasser . . .

Tahsin Basheer: He stopped [the programs] in '66; that was one of our problems.

Eugene Rostow: . . . for having testified. No, no, we kept the flow of aid going, didn't we, Luke?

Lucius Battle: It was all suspended in my last meeting with Nasser on March 4. He withdrew a request. He had fouled it up himself. We were in the process of clearing with the Senate Foreign Relations Committee; Senator Hickenlooper was the holdup, and right in the middle of that meeting with Hickenlooper, a copy of one of Nasser's speeches came on the AP ticker and was taken in to Hickenlooper, and that settled it. But a couple of days later Nasser withdrew the request, and so there was . . . continuation of all [outstanding] agreements that were still going, but there were no [new food aid programs]. By that time we were finished with the wheat.

Eugene Rostow: I think it was American charitable contributions of the Catholic organizations, and other religious organizations, that I had in mind. I remember testifying for some of that, and of course you couldn't give President Johnson a draft of a speech without his dealing with development. The draft of the famous speech of June 19, 1967, which he made here in Washington just as the General Assembly opened, had an eloquent passage about making the deserts bloom. He put it into the draft himself, as we knew he would. So there was great concern about development processes and about war interrupting those processes, not only in our rhetoric but, I believe, in our actions as well.

As for the International Court of Justice, I remember that we were greatly concerned in the last week before the war that you [Egypt] were going to propose going to the court, and that would have presented a serious problem for us. But, of course, we didn't have the confidence in the court—as later events dramatically demonstrated—that some people had. I think we were content with the Security Council decision, which was never implemented, although it was a decision, and with the statement on international waterways produced by the Law of the Sea Conference in the 1958 convention.

Andrew Cockburn: We've heard a lot from the American policymakers about considerations of unleashing the Israelis, letting them do it, letting them go, letting the war carry on, [but] I got no picture at all of what was thought would happen next. We hear about estimates of how long it would take, six days if the Israelis started the war, twelve if the Egyptians did, but what was visualized in Washington?

Eugene Rostow: Peace.

Andrew Cockburn: Well, peace, but I mean did . . .

Eugene Rostow: Peace is a very big thing.

Andrew Cockburn: Well, wait a minute. Did you imagine that Nasser would survive this six-day or twelve-day operation? Did you imagine, did you assume, that Jordan would or would not be part of the war? Did you imagine that Israel would or would not attack Syria? Were these all part of your considerations at the time?

Eugene Rostow: Sure, of course they were.

Andrew Cockburn: What conclusions did you come to?

Eugene Rostow: That the goal, or the broad goal, of the government policy should be peace. The president agreed with that. Peace as compared with an armistice or a cease-fire.

Andrew Cockburn: Peace with an [Israeli] occupation or without? Did you imagine what that would entail, would Nasser still be in power, or the West Bank . . . .

Eugene Rostow: No, that was a question left iffy, I think, in all our discussions.

Andrew Cockburn: That was not part of your considerations? You didn't stop to think whether Nasser was the problem?

Eugene Rostow: No, [we thought] not that Nasser either would or wouldn't be in power but that somebody would be in power in Egypt, and there would be a government to deal with. The idea of [resolution] 242 and an occupation as a pledge for peace was discussed before the war, yes.

Andrew Cockburn: So just the last half—just have peace. There was no sort of estimates of what peace?

Eugene Rostow: No, no, no.

Richard Parker: I would like to make a couple of comments from the viewpoint of someone who was in Cairo at that time. One, as to why we didn't predict the war. One reason was because Egypt was tied down in Yemen. One-third of its army was there, and it was in no shape to take on Israel. Nasser repeatedly said, publicly and privately, that Egypt and the Arabs were not ready for war with Israel. Two, the fact that the Palestine problem was qualified by mutual agreement as being in the icebox and hadn't come out. In retrospect, it is easy to see today that we were on the road to war, but it certainly was not apparent in April 1967.

On the other hand, we were in the middle of a terrible crisis in our relations with Egypt. We were going rapidly downhill. It was not all Nasser's fault. I think it's our responsibility in many respects: our position on aid to Egypt, our efforts to use food aid as a political weapon—this was the ultimate proof of the disastrous consequences of doing that; the fact that we had chosen to back Faisal against Nasser in the Yemen, and this was clear; the various Egyptian requests we had turned down; the fact that Luke Battle left on March 5 and Nolte didn't arrive until May 21, two and a half months later, in spite of our pleas that we were in a crisis. We got no reaction out of the department. I don't hold *all* of you gentlemen responsible for that. But [there was] no reaction: Nolte arrives, and the press meets him at the airport and asks, "Mr. Ambassador, what do you think about the crisis?" And he says, "What crisis?"

We were pretty frazzled out there. And we did not think that we were getting the sort of support from the Department of State, from the White House, from the government, that we needed in our relations with Egypt. This was an important factor. If you read Nasser's May Day speech of 1967, a third of it is devoted to an attack on the United States, and when this crisis erupted, it was clear to those of us in Cairo that the United States was as much an object of the crisis as anyone else. Nasser was going to destroy our interests. He took nine days to respond to LBJ's letter of May 22, and he responded only because Yost, when he got out there, said to Mahmoud Riad, "You haven't answered LBJ's letter." There was no apparent interest in a dialogue with us at that time, and we had absolutely no credibility. We can blame a lot of this on Nasser—certainly an enormous miscalculation on his part—but I think we bear a certain responsibility.

Robert Komer: I have a comment on the subject of parochialism. During the discussion this morning, I was stunned to see that in the Israeli presentations of what the U.S. attitude was going to be and in the Arab responses, there was no discussion of Vietnam. Let me tell you that by May 1967 we had 500,000 men in Vietnam, a half million. If you want to know where the fleet was, it wasn't in the Red Sea; it was over there on Yankee Station off Hanoi. So in the eyes of the president, who spent twenty times as much time on Vietnam as he did on the Arab-Israeli fracas, even at its height, there was no possibility of the United States adopting a military rule or intervening militarily or providing a great deal of support. We were fighting a war already, and we're rather reluctant, for reasons that have somehow escaped me, to fight two wars at the same time, [but] no one mentioned the Vietnam War as a factor in American calculations.

William Quandt: Yes, we did. I started by saying that.

Robert Komer: Yes, this afternoon Gene Rostow and you said a good deal about it. I have no complaint.

Ephraim Evron: But I did mention it.

Robert Komer: I'm sorry, I must have been asleep—my regrets.

Raymond Garthoff: I'd like to pick up the earlier question about the changed situation with the Israeli campaign in Syria, just to note that this reactivated the potential of an American-Soviet confrontation. In fact, on the morning of June 10 the hot line was used for the third or fourth time during the war, which by the way was the first time the hot line was used in an operational setting. But in any case, there was a message in by, I think, 9:48 on the morning of the tenth from Moscow warning that an attack on Damascus would create a great danger and that the Soviet Union could not remain indifferent in that situation. I think there were two or three of the usual kind of Soviet follow-through personal contacts. I know there was at least one, because it involved me.

A member of the Soviet Embassy, a known KGB officer with whom I was in continuing occasional contact at that time, called and tried to reach me the night [of the ninth]. Then I saw him on the morning of the tenth, and his message was simple: namely, that this was a new war from Moscow's standpoint; that it now involved questions of the continuation of the Syrian government, which posed a different set of considerations to Moscow; that they had changed their instructions to the Soviet military advisers with the Syrian forces, who previously had been told not to engage in any combat operations or put themselves in positions where they might be captured. They were now told that they could assist in the military defense of Damascus to the extent they were able.

But more important was the strong implication—although of course I don't know whether it would have been followed through—that the Soviet Union would have to think in terms of military intervention to prevent the fall of Damascus. It was also made clear that this [intervention] did not involve any suggestion of Soviet military action beyond that. Again, whether they would have followed through or not, this was the message they were putting out. Of course, this all came just about the time things were settling down. While we were talking, the cease-fire actually came into effect, but it was already becoming clear at about the time we got that message that the Israeli army was not going to move on from the [Golan] Heights to Damascus. Nonetheless, this message did briefly, if only potentially, reintroduce into the equation the question of the possible direct Soviet role and of a possible Soviet-American confrontation.

Donald Bergus: I recall that famous night; that was my night as a member of Roy's task force to be upstairs in the operations room, and we had the television on. A little after four A.M. the secretary called. I took the call, and he said, "I see the Security Council on the television. Is that live?" And I said, "Yes, Mr. Secretary, it is."

Janice Stein: I think Sam Lewis raised an interesting issue that we don't like to think about a lot but that nevertheless is worth considering sometimes: under what conditions the use of force might be appropriate.

There's another issue here, too. What happened during those two weeks gave us the worst of all worlds; we got a wider war than if the decision had been made on May 23 or 24. We also sent a strong message to the Israelis, and the language, I think, is crucial here: you are alone. In some sense I suspect that message, "you are alone," is also a lasting legacy in terms of peace arrangements in the Middle East. This was a case where, from the Israeli perspective, there was a commitment—not a commitment that involved American participation but nevertheless a clear commitment—that the United States would recognize the right of self-defense. That was as much on the table during these two weeks as the other issues.

In a sense, the way the strategy was handled left a legacy that makes it more difficult to persuade leaders and peoples in the Middle East that a commitment of that sort will stand up when the going gets tough, and that's the only time you need that kind of commitment. At the same time, that long-drawn-out process led to a wider war.

Samuel Lewis: In the eight years that I was in Israel as ambassador (in another era), failure of the United States to carry through on the 1957 commitment was the most persistent single factor in our discussions with Israelis of all sorts about America's reliability in lots of different situations. I think Janice is absolutely right. This had a lot of later consequences— [including] the way we played out the scenario in 1967.

Salah Bassiouny: I think that this type of commitment is one of the main features of the U.S.-Israeli relationship. Even when the Camp David accords were signed, Israel did not sign before getting a comprehensive political and economic commitment from the United States which covered different aspects, including a reconfirmation of the '75 commitment about no dialogue with the PLO and another commitment not to take any position in the Security Council without prior consultation with Israel. Again, when the peace treaty was signed, other commitments took place. These types of commitments are a main feature of U.S.-Israeli relations, and I don't think the United States was absent-minded about the '57 commitment—in fact everything was later based on it.

There is another point: We talk too much about innocent passage in the Strait of Tiran. Yes, there is paragraph 4, article 16, of the 1958 Convention on the Law of the Sea, which was drafted specifically for the Strait of Tiran. But under this convention, the innocent passage applies only during times of peace. So long as there's a state of war, paragraph 4 of article 16 doesn't apply. The Suez Canal Convention gives Egypt the right not to allow passage for states that are in a state of war with Egypt. The Convention of the Law of the Sea, paragraph 4 of article 16, applies only in times of peace.

Eugene Rostow: The Security Council has ruled that the armistice provision says that there's no state of war.

Salah Bassiouny: I don't know if you are applying now the Security Council or the convention itself as the international law. I'm talking about the convention.

Eugene Rostow: But there's no state of war, you see, legally.

Salah Bassiouny: At that time, in '67, there was no state of war?

Eugene Rostow: No, there were active hostilities and the state of belligerency, which is the state of fact, but not a legal confrontation.

Salah Bassiouny: The Israeli government abrogated in '57 the armistice agreement. Egypt did not recognize that.

Eugene Rostow: It's not so easy to get out of—no, no.

Ernest Dawn: In a state of war, does one side have rights that the other does not have, or do all parties to a state of war have the same rights to carry on hostilities?

Eugene Rostow: That's [the latter is] right.

Salah Bassiouny: That's how things occurred.

Donald Bergus: Ambassador Rafael would like to make two factual comments, and then Ambassador Tomeh.

Gideon Rafael: On the myth of the missing file: We had a night meeting at the State Department, a long dinner with Mr. Eban and Mr. Rusk and his colleagues. In the course of it, in anticipation of Eban's meeting with President Johnson, we discussed this situation as it evolved. Secretary Rostow was also present. We raised the point of the guarantees on free passage through the Strait of Tiran. Our State Department colleagues would not deny it, but they could not find the documents. The reason was understandable. That point was raised after midnight, and it could not be anticipated that the archivist would [not] be available to find the right file. Anyhow, to the credit of the State Department, I want to say that the file was produced at two o'clock in the morning and was exactly the same file, the same memo, of which we had presented a copy.

Second point: Why did Israel not proceed on the Suez Canal with litigation in any form? Because it was not necessary. The case of the Suez Canal had been adjudicated by the Security Council on September 1, 1951. [The Security Council] reconfirmed in October 1956 that the blockade of the Suez Canal and of other waterways was illegal in terms of the convention of Constantinople and in connection with the armistice agreement.

And the third point: The Soviet threat on June 10 was communicated to me; it was a request to the Security Council to announce immediately the cessation of fire. The reason was not, as explained to me, that this threat was creating anxiety in Washington, because they were absolutely sure that the Soviet Union would not take military action. What the United States wanted to avoid was that the war should be ended upon the Soviet threat, because the representative of the Soviet Union at the Security Council was about to make a statement announcing such a threat. Washington thought it wise to forestall that statement by Israel's announcement of the cessation of fire. I received the necessary instructions in time and made that announcement on June 10.

Raymond Garthoff: At one point I was a little confused about what Bill said. He said that—given President Johnson's caution about the intelligence reports, about the assurance that Israel would not lose—there was some kind of assumption in the course of this debate that if Israel did not win, then the United States would inevitably be pulled into this, would come to Israel's assistance. Is that right? It sounded as if this was an understood factor, but I didn't quite grasp what that element was. Could Dick answer that question?

Richard Helms: Yes, sure. Almost all of these people wanted Lyndon Johnson to give assistance, to come out publicly in support of Israel.

Raymond Garthoff: What kind of assistance—military assistance?

Richard Helms: Military assistance. That was the mantra, largely. Obviously everybody, as is usually the case in their personal relations with the president, had their own particular agenda and their own particular slant on this. But if you look at the record, the number of people he talked to who addressed this topic through the course of that week is up in the scores, and what they all . . .

Raymond Garthoff: They weren't all the vice-president.

Richard Helms: [Hubert] Humphrey was careful not to be specific about what he wanted the president to do, but he was weighing in constantly on the side of "let's get this problem behind us by coming out and identifying with the Israelis."

Raymond Garthoff: Not just some statement of support but actually some commitment to go to Israel's military assistance if needed?

Richard Helms: That's right, yes.

Raymond Garthoff: And Goldberg endorsed that as well?

Richard Helms: I assume so.

George Tomeh: I'm not going to speak about politics. Basically, I'm not a politician. The greater part of my career has been in diplomacy. But what kind of diplomacy? There are people who live on the borders of two cultures or two civilizations, and the tragic situation of such people is that they spend a lifetime trying to interpret one culture to the other, without ever succeeding in having their world fully understood. Of course, when we look at diplomacy from this existentialist corner or perspective, it becomes difficult to know what is the relationship between the two. If we can't answer this question, I cannot explain it.

Mr. Chairman, I listened very carefully to all the statements, especially in this session, and I regret, I'm sad to say, that the basic minimum of objectivity—with few exceptions—of legality, of humanity, was completely lacking. Especially when the great of the world think about the problems of the poorer side of the world, what do you see? Unbridled pride, cynicism, no consideration whatsoever for the suffering of humanity. I'm not against American culture. I studied at the American University in Beirut and later taught at it, and at one time I was dean at that university. I also graduated from Georgetown University, so you can't say that I'm prejudiced against Western culture. But I'm certainly prejudiced against injustice and inhumanity. In our part of the world, we have witnessed and still witness a tragedy that does not find an end, simply because the great of the world who perpetuated such a tragedy are completely absent from what really happened in the field.

All this is of the past and a result of the past, but what about tomorrow and next year and the year after? I'm sorry to say that this unhappy situation that obtains in one of the most sensitive parts of the world—the Middle East—will go on. It will go on because the minimum requirement to understand other people's problems was completely absent in almost all the statements that were heard this afternoon. So, with great hesitation, I want to tell you that I really feel this meeting to be falling into this pattern.

You can see Mr. Helms laughing at my words, which is really . . .

Richard Helms: I'm sorry, Mr. Ambassador, I was laughing at the note I just got. It had nothing to do with your words.

George Tomeh: I can never understand. Anyway, I'm sorry to say that I feel a deep regret for having attended this session and this seminar. I say so because I felt completely out of place. There was no dialogue this afternoon. There was only a monologue, on one side. So, while wishing all of you the greatest success, I cannot be part of a monologue with the purpose of rewriting history.

Eugene Rostow: I would like to say how much I regret the way Ambassador Tomeh feels. I have nothing but respect for him and his long distinguished career. And of course the subject today was the view from the American side, so naturally the concerns of the American government predominated. But this program, which has been organized by Ambassador Parker and his colleagues, it seems to me, was comprehensive in its scope. It gave full opportunity, both in the papers that were presented and in the speakers who were brought forward, to speak about the concerns of the people of the area and about the problem of poverty and humanity.

I started my prepared remarks this morning by talking about the importance of law and the fidelity of the law in the quest for peace and the political arrangements approximating peace, and there's no escaping it; the element of law which makes it law, as distinguished from many other kinds of codes, is a concern for justice. So I want to say how much I regret your statement. I understand whence it comes, and it seems to me that our considerations tomorrow and at other meetings will offer a chance to redress the balance.

William Quandt: There is one point left that I'm not entirely happy with, and that's the notion that the United States somehow didn't live up to its 1957 commitments. I've tried to read through what those commitments were, and if I understand them correctly, I don't think we did so badly. First there was a commitment to recognize that the strait was international waters. We were slow in stating it publicly, but we've lived up to that one. Then there was a commitment to exercise our right, alone or with others, to keep the strait open. Well, we didn't do it quickly, and we might not ever have done it. But, quite frankly, the period of time in which we had to test that, given that we were bogged down in Vietnam, was not very long. We never said we will not do it; we simply said we've got a laborious process to go through, trying first to get others to go with us and going through the exercise of getting congressional support, which is inherent in any commitment that runs the risk of using force.

And that's why there was the long discussion in 1957 about what if you can't open the strait for us or don't open it for us. Do you at least recognize our right, if the strait is closed by force, to act on our own? We said yes, and when the time came, we lived up to that promise. It's not a brilliant record. We were slow to reaffirm the international status of the strait. We didn't immediately undertake measures to reopen it when it was closed, but we might have [done so] eventually, or we might at least have made more of an effort. And the fallback was always that we would recognize Israel's right to act, and we would not call Israel an aggressor if she used force to reopen the strait, if it was closed by force. You can't say we didn't live up to that.

CHAPTER 6

⚓ Conspiracy Theories

Richard B. Parker

That the Egyptians were victims of a plot in June 1967 is widely believed in the West as well as in the Arab world. The details of that plot vary according to one's interlocutor, but the broad outlines of the three basic scenarios can be summarized as follows.

(1) The Americans were out to get Nasser and plotted with the Israelis to bring him down. The Israelis fomented trouble along their northern border to create a pretext for threatening Syria, knowing that Egypt would have to respond, thereby providing them with grounds to strike at Nasser. The United States aided in this conspiracy by, among other things, deceiving the Egyptians into thinking it would oppose a military strike by Israel, by providing Israel with massive arms shipments and "volunteers" to fight against Egypt, by flying reconnaissance missions for Israel, by providing air cover to Israel at the time of the June 5 strike, and by intercepting and corrupting radio communications between Egypt and Jordan.

(2) The crisis was provoked by the Soviet Union, which was, depending on the source, seeking either to discipline Nasser and make him more dependent on it; or to make him come to the aid of Syria, which was in trouble; or to make him withdraw his troops from South Arabia. To this end, the Soviets deliberately gave the Egyptians false information that the Israelis were concentrating troops on the Syrian border and were going to strike on May 17, knowing Nasser would have to respond militarily. The Soviets did not expect him to go as far as he did, however, and the situation got out of hand.

(3) The Syrians were seeking to provoke another Arab-Israel war and to this end cooked up the story of the Israeli troop concentrations and fed it to the Soviets, who passed it to the Egyptians.

The subject of a possible conspiracy was put on the conference agenda with a view to ventilating it in the presence of former senior officials who might be able to shed some light on it. In particular, we thought that it would be useful to have the comments of Richard Helms and Meir Amit, since they would presumably have been principal actors in any conspiracy scheme involving the United States and Israel. We did not expect to get any clarification from the Syrians regarding their role, but we hoped the Russians and Egyptians might be able to throw some light on the subject from their perspectives.

The Russian clarifications were given in Panel 1, but they still leave unanswered the principal question: Why did the Soviets give the Egyptians the false warning? Although they questioned the reported role of the Soviet ambassador in the affair, the former Soviet officials did not question the fact that the warning was passed by the Soviets to the Egyptians in one form or another. They offered plausible explanations of Soviet motives, but no hard information as to the genesis of that report or what the Soviets expected the Egyptians to do about it.

We know a good deal more about the actions of the Americans and the Israelis, thanks to the memoirs of various former officials and to the declassification of documents in the United States. The Israeli documents remain to be declassified. Judging by what has been released so far, we will eventually know considerably more than we do today, but we may never know the entire story about intelligence activities by any of the parties. We are unlikely ever to know, for instance, whether the Israelis engaged, as some have claimed, in a disinformation campaign directed at Syria that gave rise to the report of troop concentrations on the border. The Israelis deny such a campaign (Shimon Shamir said it was "not Israel's style"), and there is no direct evidence to support it, but it is a tantalizing idea that does not die because it would explain much.

Some doubtful points will undoubtedly be clarified as various state archives are made available to researchers, but much of what went on in all the governments concerned was never put down on paper or was done so incompletely. We will thus be reduced to researching the memories of the participants, a notoriously unreliable source.

Tahsin Basheer began the debate in panel 6 by saying that he did not believe in conspiracy theories, a number of which he described, but if we used words such as "planning," "preplanning," "contingency plan," and "communication," there was no need to speak of conspiracies. The U.S.-Israel special relationship described by McGeorge Bundy had led to a "conspiracy of misleading," in Basheer's words.

In a similar vein, Salah Bassiouny commented that from the outset the U.S. and the Soviet Union had warned Egypt against starting hostilities, and the Egyptians had given assurances they would not fire the first shot. Then there was an exchange of information between the Israelis and Americans that confirmed Israel's military superiority. Priority in striking was the key to victory. Israel was unleashed while Egypt was under pressure not to fight, and the United States had failed to tell Egypt four or five days before the war began that it was in danger. Ambassador Bassiouny asks how one explains or describes such a situation? If it was not a conspiracy, what was it?

Similarly, Andrew Cockburn said in his statement that, given the exchanges General Amit had in Washington and the impression Amit conveyed to the Israeli cabinet that the Americans would not oppose an Israeli attack on Egypt, he did not know why there was a need to argue about collusion. Janice Stein, on the other hand, citing the example of Soviet foreknowledge of the Egyptian-Syrian attack in October 1973, said it would be inaccurate to charge that the Soviets had conspired or colluded with either of those two states; she commented that we need some criteria of evidence in discussions of this nature.

In his statement, Richard Helms denied categorically that there had been any U.S.-Israeli plot in 1967. He dismissed as nonsense the idea, mentioned in Andrew and Leslie Cockburn's book *Dangerous Liaison,* that the CIA's James Angleton would have colluded on his own with the Israelis to bring down Nasser. He also commented that there was no substance to the accusation contained in Stephen Green's book *Taking Sides,* that a U.S. reconnaissance squadron had flown missions for Israel during the war. Neither Helms nor Robert McNamara had ever heard of such missions, which would have been impossible without the knowledge of either of the two.

General Amit commented only to say that the main thrust of Israeli-U.S. intelligence liaison had been exchanges about the Soviets. He apparently felt that his earlier comments in panel 3 had answered the conspiracy allegations.

William Quandt had noted in panel 5 that he had found nothing in the numerous documents he had examined that indicated any prior U.S.-Israeli collusion to bring down Nasser. He added in panel 6 that he had heard nothing from the people close to the decision-making process that would indicate that the purpose of U.S. acquiescence in the Israeli attack was to bring down Nasser. He then made the pertinent observation that we should distinguish between conspiracy or collusion, on the one hand, and other forms of cooperation or attempts to manipulate or influence a friend or ally, on the other, the latter being normal and legitimate in international politics.

The question of what constitutes conspiracy was perhaps where the discussion in panel 6 should have begun, because it was critical to the dialogue. Does consultation and the exchange of intelligence constitute collusion? Later in the discussion Eugene Rostow explained that the legal definition of conspiracy was a contract to achieve illegal ends by legal means, or legal ends by illegal means. *Webster's Third International Dictionary* defines conspiracy as "1a: an illegal, treasonable or treacherous plan to harm or destroy another person, group, or entity . . . b: an agreement manifesting itself in words or deeds and made by two or more persons confederating to do an unlawful act or to use unlawful means to do an act which is lawful . . . 2: a combination of persons banded secretly together and resolved to accomplish an evil or unlawful end."

Intent seems to be the key to a finding of conspiracy. In this case, was a deliberate decision taken to harm Egypt? We cannot speak for the Soviets and Syrians, but no hard evidence of such a decision by any of these states has been produced to date. The undeniable consultations between Israelis and Americans do not appear to have gone beyond the normal sort of exchanges described by William Quandt.

On the other hand, while one must be careful about attaching too much significance to the choice of words that are used in open discussions of this sort, it was remarkable that the participants in panel 6 did not cavil at various mentions of the United States "unleashing" Israel. That act seemed to be an option everyone regarded as realistic—that is, being within U.S. capabilities. That proposition should be examined more closely.

Nor did anyone contradict the views expressed in panel 5 that the United States, in the person of Lyndon Johnson, had assented, however reluctantly, to the attack on Egypt on June 5. Such assent is far different, however, from plotting to bring about such an attack.

The Israelis evidently wanted to believe that they had American blessing for what they did, although they probably would have attacked without it, judging by various accounts of the June 3 kitchen cabinet meeting in Jerusalem at which the decision to strike was taken. We have, for example, Shimon Shamir's striking description in panel 3 of how the Israeli military persuaded themselves that the Americans approved of what they were doing but could not tell them so directly. While this sounds like a classic case of self-intoxication, the Israelis could be pardoned for finding confirmation after the fact in American complaisance toward what they did and in U.S. diplomatic support at the UN and elsewhere once the war started. The U.S. record is not as spotless and unambiguous as President Johnson's autobiography would have us believe, but acceptance of the inevitable is one thing, and scheming to help it occur is another.

The Egyptian contention that the United States misled Nasser rests on several claims made at various times: (1) that the U.S. was slow to respond to the crisis and did not warn Egypt sufficiently of the dangers it faced; (2) that it did not inform, or remind, Egypt of the 1957 U.S. commitment to Israel regarding freedom of navigation in the Gulf of Aqaba; (3) that Nasser agreed not to strike first on the assumption that the United States would restrain the Israelis, as he was being restrained by the Soviets—in particular, Heikal maintains that Nasser agreed to a two-week moratorium on action in the gulf on the understanding that the Israelis had accepted a similar commitment; and (4) that the United States failed to honor its repeated assurances that it would oppose aggression from any corner in the Middle East.

With regard to the first accusation, it is true that the United States was slow off the mark in responding to the crisis, and that was unfortunate, but it was a reflection more on U.S. competence than on U.S. intent. Along with the Israelis and many Egyptians, the Americans diagnosed Egypt's initial moves as saber rattling and were slow to grasp their full significance. So were most other governments. As soon as the United States realized what the crisis was about, however, the Department of State instructed its chargé d'affaires in Cairo, David Nes, to inform the Egyptians that Israel was not massing troops on the Syrian border. Nes did so on May 16. By their own accounts, the Egyptians dismissed the denial as untrustworthy. By this time, the request for withdrawal of UNEF had already been drafted by the Egyptians, and the messenger was on his way to Gaza to present it to General Rikhye, the UNEF commander.

When that request became known, the United States should perhaps have warned Nasser via a stern presidential message not to go farther and close the Strait of Tiran, but by that time the Egyptians had the bit in their teeth, and it is unlikely that such a warning would have had much effect, given the anti-American climate in Cairo and the Egyptians' illusions about their own military preparedness. It would have been perceived, as President Johnson's May 22 letter to Nasser and a U.S. *note verbale* to Foreign Minister Riad, also of May 22, apparently were, as designed to protect Israel and as a sign of panic in the face of Egyptian armed strength. There is also a bit of folk wisdom about the folly of telling children not to stuff peas up their nose. Closure of the Strait of Tiran would clearly be so dangerous, and so out of character with what was understood to be the Egyptian position, that it would have been reasonable to decide against a warning as being suggestive of the possibility of closure.

In any case, the Americans should have managed to get a presidential message to Nasser soon after the request to remove UNEF was known. The fact that it took six days to generate such a message does not speak highly of the efficiency of the Department of State and the White House. Meanwhile, however, officers of the American Embassy in Cairo made repeated efforts to warn Egyptian officials that they were running a terrible risk, but the American representatives were assured repeatedly that the Egyptians knew what they were doing. Indeed, the Egyptians' overwhelming self-confidence was a source of considerable puzzlement to the embassy, which commented at one point that they acted as though they had a secret weapon of some sort.

The 1957 U.S. commitment regarding navigation in the Gulf of Aqaba was raised elsewhere by Tahsin Basheer as a fact that had not been conveyed officially to Egypt, with an implication of sinister intent. This accusation of failure to communicate is not supported by the facts. The commitment was contained in an aide mémoire of February 11, 1957, given to Foreign Minister Abba Eban by Secretary of State Dulles. There was no secret annex or understanding that went with it. It was published in the press on February 17 and was commented on repeatedly by both President Eisenhower and Dulles in public. On March 1 Dulles discussed it with the Arab ambassadors in Washington, including the Egyptian, and on that occasion and others he stated categorically that there were no secret assurances to or understandings with Israel that lay behind the withdrawal from Sinai. He said the same thing publicly in a news conference on March 5: there were "no private assurances to anyone which go beyond or which are different from what is set forth in public documents."

The U.S. commitment was furthermore conveyed in writing in a statement delivered to the Arab chiefs of mission in Washington on June 27, 1957 (American Foreign Policy 1957, Document 287). The U.S. delegate to the UN, Henry Cabot Lodge, also discussed the commitment with Dr. Mahmoud Fawzi, the Egyptian foreign minister, on March 4. As Donald Bergus noted in panel 2, Dr. Fawzi reserved Egypt's position, but he was certainly aware of the U.S. position, as were many members of his ministry. In 1967 Fawzi, then vice-president for foreign affairs, was consulted by Nasser, but according to Heikal they did not discuss the American position on the Gulf of Aqaba. Did Nasser overlook the American commitment? Perhaps, but that is a reflection on Egyptian competence, not American intentions.

The contention that Egypt had agreed to the two-week moratorium proposed by U Thant is erroneous. As explained by Brian Urquhart in panel 2, the Egyptians withdrew their agreement when they discovered that the U Thant version of the moratorium would permit oil to be shipped to Eilat.

On the other hand, it is a valid complaint that the United States did not honor its repeated reaffirmation during the crisis of its commitment under the U.S.-British-French Tripartite Declaration of 1950 to oppose forceful changes of border in the region. Dean Rusk commented in *As I Saw It*:

> For twenty years, since the creation of Israel, the United States had tried to persuade the Arabs that they needn't fear Israeli territorial expansion. Throughout the sixties the Arabs talked continuously about their fear of Israeli expansion. With the full knowledge of successive governments in Israel, we did our utmost to persuade the Arabs their anxieties were illusory.
>
> And then following the Six-Day War, Israel decided to keep the Golan Heights, the West Bank, the Gaza Strip, and the Sinai, despite the fact that Israeli Prime Minister Levi Eshkol on the first day of the war went on Israeli radio and said that Israel had no territorial ambitions. Later in the summer I reminded Abba Eban of this, and he simply shrugged his shoulders and said, "We've changed our minds." With that remark . . . he turned the United States into a twenty-year liar.

Rusk does not say why, if he felt that way, he did not take a stronger position on the territorial issue at the time but went along with a U.S. policy that acquiesced in indefinite Israeli retention of the occupied areas. The issue of U.S. abandonment of its traditional policy of opposing forceful changes of borders in the area was discussed briefly in the final panel and is a subject that deserves further study.

There were a number of interesting comments made in this panel about the dangers of the "rational actor" approach to government decision making. Brian Urquhart's description of the unenlightened views of the British government on the necessity of maintaining a UNEF garrison at Sharm al-Shaykh, for instance, and his comments on the nonavailability to the UN hierarchy of the intelligence and general information available to the member-state governments, illuminate the sort of operational considerations that are often overlooked and that can lead to serious misjudgments. He expressed the hope that the conference would lead to a look at the importance of international institutions and remarked that while he was all for discussing conspiracies, in his view 70 percent of disasters are the result of miscalculation, 15 percent arise from misinformation and manipulation, and bad luck is responsible for 10 percent. That leaves 5 percent that could conceivably be the result of some kind of conspiratorial idea.

Panel 6

Chairman: Ambassador Lucius D. Battle, former assistant secretary of state
Speakers:
   Ambassador Tahsin Basheer, member of the Egyptian delegation in 1967:
      "Deceit and Deception"
   Andrew Cockburn, author: "Collusion or Not"
Comment: Ambassador Richard Helms, former director of Central Intelligence

Lucius Battle: Today we start on a new topic, conspiracy theories. Many of you will say that's what we've been talking about all the time, and it has been in large measure, but I think there are some slightly different angles and twists and there's a large range of activity that's possible, according to your own imaginations. We often think that the Middle East is the center of all conspiracy and that's where it was born, but if you look through what's happened in our own country—Watergate, Irangate—you see that the Middle East has no monopoly on conspiracy. All international affairs and all domestic affairs in some measure, at least, rest upon it.

Deceit and Deception

Tahsin Basheer: I don't believe in conspiracy theories, but the modern Middle East started with the Sykes-Picot agreement—a huge conspiracy hatched in the British and French embassies in Cairo. It was only revealed when the Russian revolution took place, and only then the Arabs knew that the West was dealing with them under a double standard. On one hand, they supported the unity of the Eastern Arabs; on the other, with Weizmann they issued the Balfour Declaration. These two claims have never been reconciled. Conspiracies continued, but today the word itself is meaningless. If you use instead *planning, preplanning, contingency plan, communication, parallel communication,* then we don't need *conspiracies.*

The relationship between the United States and Israel, and the phenomenon of Israel itself, is unique. Yesterday, I think, McGeorge Bundy said that the relationship between Israel and the United States is like the relationship between the United Kingdom and the United States. I disagree with him. The UK was not created, artificially or not, by an act, a resolution of the UN General Assembly. It was not subject to *aliya* [immigration] that never stopped. Now we have the aliya of Russian Jews to a country. It's a unique phenomenon—the creation of the State of Israel on May 15, 1948, with the help, endorsement, and support of America the government and America the people. Now, there is nothing wrong with unique phenomena, but they are shocking unless you continue the square or you round the whole ball.

The UN in '47 and '48 never created a machinery to implement the partition plan. No one expected the Arabs—the Palestinians or the rest of the Arabs—to accept that their country be partitioned. The Arab refusal is not only logical; it's natural. If you're not convinced, go and ask Israel, now, to cede one inch from its territory beyond the partition plan, and you'll see their resistance.

[The Israelis] will argue that this was given to Abraham from our God. We will argue that we are the sons of the firstborn, Ishmael, and then we get into this ridiculous endorsement—legitimation—that each side uses to [validate] a modern political claim. Be that as it may, unless the Arabs and the Israelis are helped to create a cake that is Israel and that is Palestinian—a cake that is Arab—and [unless] these two cakes in their existence, today, despite the trauma of partition, will be synergistic, will be helping each other ten, twenty, thirty years from now [and a] new generation of Arabs in Palestine and a new generation of Jews in Israel will feel that their existence and their cooperation are beneficial, then we will have trouble, and we will always continue to have conspiracies. Right now, in light of the peace between Egypt and Israel, to talk about conspiracies is difficult. But, difficult or not, we have to put the [situation] of twenty-five years ago in the correct historical and psychological setting.

Now, let me use two words used in our discussion: "unleash Israel," as if Israel is an unguided missile to be unleashed like dogs against Nasser, to put him in his place, or to cut him down to size, or to tell the Arabs. [Another phrase that comes to mind] was not repeated yesterday, but it appears in the literature: "turkey shoot." Now, the first [news of the] unleashing of Israel comes to Nasser early in '66, told to him by a man he respects a lot, a friend, Mr. [Eugene] Black of the World Bank. Nasser was told that there is pressure on Johnson to unleash Israel against him. This was repeated to Nasser in 1966 and '67 by a number of world leaders: by U Thant—al-Kony reports that someone told U Thant, I think Goldberg told him, [that] unless Nasser behaves, there is this possibility; by Bhutto from Pakistan—he came to Egypt and said, "Mr. President you are targeted." Nasser felt all along that the United States was after his head. I spent a lot of hours yesterday reading the documents of the State Department and the White House, and Nasser's fear of being targeted by America is repeated even there. So that goes on and on.

The biggest conspiracy to me is not a dark-room conspiracy but rather two wavelengths, the communication, the kinship or friendship, of understanding, of care, of support between America and Israel and between the Arabs and America. This I will call the conspiracy of misleading. The Arabs were misled all along. Anyone who reads this [the volume of *Foreign Relations of the United States* dealing with the post-Suez period] finds that the official U.S. communications to the Arabs dealt only with incremental, marginal issues.

The major issue: America saw the Middle East through the lens of how to reshape Arab policy to fit an acceptance of Israel by the Arab regimes. [The Americans] never cared about the Arab people. Had they tried to reshape the Arab people to accept Israel, the policy would have been different. Then there was oil, and oil was not a big issue because the Arabs cannot drink it; they have to sell it, and they sell it mostly to America. That is the key. The key is the failure from '48 on to find an acceptable permanent [solution]—something that is acceptable; it's not just, but something we can live with and Israel can live with, without scaring each other.

Now, as to the theories of conspiracies regarding '67, I can find at least seven games of conspiracies. I don't subscribe to them, but they hold a lot of sway among many people.

There is King Hussein's official document—communicated to Nasser in May '67—that the clique in Syria, which is infiltrated, penetrated by Israeli intelligence (Eli Cohen, an Israeli spy, was important in the higher echelons of the Ba'ath party in Syria), is trying to create tension to entangle Egypt. That will pull the leg of Egypt, and Israel will have the execution of a war that will finish the whole thing. That was written from Hussein to Nasser.

Second, you have a mixed conspiracy. It's more than one. Conspiracies can be rich and colorful. Heikal repeats Hussein's idea, but he raises a question, an insinuation, that maybe Hussein, also, is party to that conspiracy. Knowing of it, he wanted to entangle Nasser and that's why at the last minute—what kind of military planning [is it if] you go one week before the events and say, I'm with you, we'll kiss and forgive, and there is no military planning? You ask for an Egyptian commander and that's a nice cover. And in fairness to Nasser (and Heikal), it was not only Nasser (and Heikal) who said that [but also] an important CIA operative, Wilbur Crane Eveland, in his book *Ropes of Sand* [New York: Norton, 1980]. Eveland was a CIA operative in the Middle East, in every country in the Middle East. He says on page 323: "Angleton concluded that General Abdul Nasser was responsible for the West's only problem in the area. If Nasser could be eliminated, the Egyptian Army defeated without overt major power assistance, the Arabs would be left with no alternative to making peace with Israel." The same man accuses King Hussein of being party to the conspiracy because it's Hussein signing with Egypt that made Johnson decide that no one can do anything.

The third one is Dayan's. Dayan accuses Rabin of humiliating Nasser and pushing him and, by overreacting in the case of Syria and of Jordan, inviting Nasser to react and . . . creating a situation of escalation that was explosive.

There is a Soviet [conspiracy theory]. Until now, even in this meeting, we remain without full understanding of their double game. The Soviets, on one hand, encouraged the Egyptians, saw to it on many levels that there was a concentration, an intention to escalate, [then] at the right moment told them, don't strike first. What was the game?

There are theories about this game, more than one conspiracy. One is that Nasser, not America, was the only force in the Middle East that stopped the communists and stymied the extreme fascists and stopped the radical Islamic movement. There was no hope for the Soviet Union to have clients in the Arab world so long as Nasser was there with this thinking in mind. The Soviets were friends to Nasser, but they were not friends to the Arab ideology that Nasser was trying to push, and Egypt without Nasser would at least give them room [to have clients].

There is another theory that they [the Soviets] were supported, at least in the Communist Party, by some of the rhetoric [of] Zu'ayyin and Atassi and the extremists, the three doctors who ran Syria at the time, who thought of a war of national liberation. They had juvenile thoughts of copying Vietnam and Ho Chi Minh and the rest, and they thought they could give a blow to Egypt that would not totally defeat Egypt but would cut it down to size.

This other ideology is based on mobilization of the masses—and the Russians always told us to mobilize, mobilize the masses. I visited Moscow . . . between the June War and the October War, and all I get from Pono-marev is, "What are you going to do about this?" He said, "Mobilize." I asked, "Mobilize what?" He said, "The masses." Mobilize the masses? They wanted to recruit a party that is based on popular control, and that will be the key. Part of the fight between Ali Sabri and Nasser, when Nasser got rid of him, was that Ali Sabri was playing up to that idea. Even during that time, we had to have an avant-garde party. So the Soviet double game was that.

It was nice to hear yesterday a lot of indignant, self-righteous attitude about American democracy and the rest at the time when America, including McGeorge Bundy, was involved in Vietnam, and tricks used in Vietnam were not only key in politics. They use [the word] *democracy,* but the word

Ambassador Lucius
Battle and UAR Foreign
Minister Mahmoud
Riad, Cairo, 1966. USIS
Cairo photo.

liberty is never used lest it suggest the ship *Liberty,* which is still without openness, without transparency, and without freedom, 'til today. These are some of the theories of conspiracies.

Now there was a closeness between America. . . . Mr. Helms is quoted in one book as saying, whatever facts related to Israel in America, at whatever level, be sure that Israel knows it 100 percent. I won't bore you with details.

Now 1966, 1967, what was the fight really? The fight was an Arab fear, since '64, about Israel eating up the demilitarized zones. Between the 1949 armistice agreement and the '67 war, and aside from the '56 tripartite attack on Egypt, the game was that Israel was trying to take the land of the demilitarized zones to annul or inactivate the armistice agreement between the Arab states and Israel and to expand incrementally. In 1964, Israel started planning and [implementing] its water carrier. Because of the failure of the Johnston plan and many others, and before it the [Gordon] Clapp plan, the Arabs became afraid that the water was being siphoned and that if you take water out of the Jordan, the Palestinians will not have a recourse on the land left to them to build a solution to the refugee [problem]. That happened at the time when the United States gave up on a total settlement between the Arabs and the Israelis and concentrated on finding [a] piecemeal solution through crisis control and not crisis resolution.

During that time, [the UN] had in Lausanne the Palestine Conciliation Commission, which is still on the books of the General Assembly, with the United States, Turkey, and France trying to conciliate. A lot of work, a lot of statistics, a lot of things about the refugees, but no progress. We left the problem to fester and it [became more] complicated. Israel felt that it could expand because while Israel was building, the Arab world was undergoing its own revolutionary change. Unlike Israel, which was helped by America to have aliya . . . to build a new society, to build a strong army to defend itself, the Arabs were not helped to create in the Arab body what now is allowed in Europe, in the former Soviet Union, in Yugoslavia, in all of the nations that are allowed to speak. Until today we don't allow the Palestinians to speak. We only support what is an American-Arab relationship; it's a relationship between the American government and Arab regimes—Faisal, Nasser, Hussein—as if the Arab people do not exist and they are not party to the equation.

To me that is an old conspiracy, a new conspiracy, an ongoing proposition that is worse than conspiracy because it refuses to face reality. Unless we deal, as we dealt in Israeli-Egyptian peace, to find at least a peace that we can live with, that we can build upon, where we can find that the existence of Israel does not impinge on Egypt, and vice versa, then we will be in trouble. Because the problem is not symmetrical. It's massively asymmetrical, and we have to do something about that.

The culprit in this is not really the special relationship between America and Israel. That is taken for granted. And it is not a question of the two schools—of those who say it's strategic asset [and those who say it is not]. There is a lot of humbug in this. Or the lobby asset. That too is exaggerated. After World War II, America and the Western world expressed their morality in reaction to the holocaust by giving Israel a state, even if it [inflicted] pain and harm on the Palestinian Arabs and on the Arabs as a whole. I would have accepted that [if it had been] limited to what Weizmann and Sharif Hussein of Mecca had agreed to originally: that the Arabs will accept . . . a Jewish state, provided the Israelis help the Arabs have, at least to the east of Egypt, a unified Arab state in what used to be a unified area under the Ottomans in Arab Palestine, Syria, Lebanon, and the rest. That was one area until 1917. The partition of the Levant was new, and it was not done at the demand of the people. It was imposed from above.

Now, who is the culprit and how do we deal with it? The United States, having a low opinion of the Arab people and Arab leadership, attended only to Israeli needs and sensibilities and sensitivities, and that's fine. What we need is a comparable, not exactly the same, but a comparable sensitivity to Arab needs, not only to the Arab governments' needs. That will become even more important today not only for the Arabs but also for the security of Israel.

Let me take one minute to defend Nasser. I think he miscalculated badly, but he defended the area against atomization; he defended the integrity of the area against any foreign intrusion. Nasser never had ambition over one inch of any Arab territory outside of Egypt. He accepted the independence of Sudan, which until January '56 many Egyptians considered to be the southern border [province] of Egypt. When, under [the] unity [agreement] Nasser had the legal right to fight the [1961] secession of Syria, he did not fight it. Nasser helped save Kuwait when Abd Karim Qasim wanted to swallow it [in 1961]. He accepted the right of Arab states to exist. Nasser was seen during all these crises as an enemy. An enemy who would do what? Look what has happened [in the period] since Nasser until today. You have Saddam Hussein, you had Khomeini, you have the Ba'ath in Syria, you have all kinds of extremism. If you compare them to Nasser, he looks benign. We have to create another Nasser to moderate the politics of the Middle East.

Nasser tried for a solution somewhere between the partition plan and Israel as it is. But in 1955, when Eden tried to find a compromise between the status quo as it obtained in the '49 armistice and the status quo in reality, and the partition of the status quo, Nasser was the only one in the Middle East who agreed to negotiate on this. Ben-Gurion refused utterly.

What happened in '67? I think Nasser felt, as soon as Johnson came to power—and I have here letters of Johnson in his committee in Congress intervening with Ike, two huge letters supporting Israel, trying to change the policy—felt that, unlike the administration of President Kennedy, Johnson and the people around him had as their aim encircling and getting at him. It [Nasser's alienation] happened at the time when Israel was trying to divert the [Jordan's] water. It happened at the time when Israel shifted its source of military supplies, in both the technology of war and arms, from Europe to America. Here we find in the documents how Israel got Sherman tanks or certain airplanes from America. The United States under Johnson would use a trick to say the deal was with Germany, and part of the deal would be to finance this. But above all, it was a time when Israel started developing further its nuclear power. And unlike under Kennedy, when for the first time the United States told the world about [the Israeli nuclear facility at] Dimona, under President Johnson there was no active attempt to inhibit this [development]. At the same time, the Arabs were all the time until today told not to do it, not to indulge, and we accepted the NPT [Nuclear Non-Proliferation Treaty].

There is in the relationship a certain syndrome, and I don't think it is the work of any one man or anyone we can accuse. It came out of a development that in the end no one could control. The United States wanted to restrain Israel in times of crisis, to stop Israel from preemption. After the United States ensured that Israel quantitatively and qualitatively was stronger than any one Arab state or even the Arabs combined, the issue became how to stop Israel from preemption in time of crisis, particularly against friendly Arabs. The exception, of course, was '67.

In a memo before Eshkol's visit to America in May '64, Mr. Komer wrote to President Johnson that the Israelis would have to be reassured from time to time of U.S. intentions if U.S. interests in the Arab world were to escape the military manifestation of Israeli anxiety. Because Israel had such an upper hand and because the Israelis suspected [had no confidence in] American deterrence, Israel had to be reassured. If it was not reassured, then Israel could act alone. That led always to a syndrome of giving more arms. But every time Israel got more arms, it became more independent of American suasion. In the absence of a total solution, as in the Camp David agreements, or such as the United States is now trying to achieve in the multilateral/ bilateral talks, the syndrome continues. The reason is that Israel manages with this syndrome to delink American aid to Israel—whether military or informational or intelligence or economic, and the economic aid is unique in this respect—from Israel's responsibility under the law of international organizations and the UN to do something for the Palestinians. Right now, for example, you find Israeli settlements because the American position erodes. In 1967 [the U.S. spoke of] minor rectification; [UN Security Council resolution] 242 means minor rectification. Israel did not buy that. Then the settlements are [declared] illegal. Then the settlements are [declared] an obstacle to peace.

During the last thirty to forty years, definitely from '67, this policy did not buy us stability or acceptance of Israel or cooperation in the area. It was only during a temporary success in '73, when Sadat had the vision to turn this unending stalemate into something creative, that we started on the road to peace. Now we need linkage on the Arab side and on the Israeli side to correct this syndrome of helping Israel, and only then can we stabilize this problem. In the absence of this, whether you call it conspiracy or different wavelength or lack of understanding, the asymmetry will be great and any great asymmetry explodes.

Lucius Battle: That was a good vigorous beginning. We now hear from Mr. Cockburn.

Collusion or Not

Andrew Cockburn: I was thinking yesterday that I should have given a shrill yelp of protest when Ambassador Parker told me that I was going to be on the conspiracy panel, since conspiracy theory is always deemed to be less than respectable by the normal sort of scholarly analysts. Nevertheless as Ambassador Basheer was pointing out, when you come to the Middle East, conspiracies are usually the only way to interpret events. If anyone looks at the 1967 war and reflects on the precedent of '56, where we had one of the better documented conspiracies of recent history in operation, I think it's reasonable at least to think about conspiracies.

I would like to think about what we've been hearing over the last few days, in particular the notion that I've heard coming from all quarters that somehow Israel and the United States were simply reacting to events. I think Ambassador Evron said that they were dashing around trying to put out fires, that all these things kept happening. . . . There was trouble in the north and then there was the occupation of Sinai, and it all came as a complete surprise. And I get the impression that Israel really played no active role until June 5, when, of course, their role became extremely active.

In the United States, again, I get the impression that nothing much . . . you know, bad news is coming in by the hour. The United States at times made efforts to stop, to reverse the crisis, and took such notable initiatives as sending Charles Yost to Egypt and Robert Anderson. Again, this sounds low profile on the part of the United States. I would suggest that we can't really talk about the events of April, May, June '67 without going back a couple of years and looking at the cold war context in the Middle East at the time. As we've been told many times, in the now happily distant days of the cold war all international actions took place against that backdrop, and the Soviet Union was seen as having active and evil designs on the Middle East, aided and abetted by its ally Nasser.

As we know, the relationship between the Soviet Union and Nasser was not as close as it might have been perceived at the time, nor was Nasser as strong as he might have seemed from the outside. But at a time when Nasser had 70,000 troops on the southern borders of Saudi Arabia, at a time when the British had announced their intention of pulling out as traditional guardian of Western interests in the Persian Gulf, at a time when an apparently pro-communist regime was taking over in Syria, it might have seemed to the jaundiced observer that the Soviet Union and its proxy Nasser were sweeping all before them. Indeed, we have good reason to believe that that was the view held by some in Washington. Although the bulk of official Washington's attention was focused, of course, on Southeast Asia, some who were concerned with the Middle East, particularly I believe in the Central Intelligence Agency, were worried by what was going on there. They were certainly hearing an amplified version of that worry from Israel.

Ambassador Helms mentioned yesterday that General Amit, in a visit in 1966, talked about Soviet gains in the area. I believe that this message was constantly repeated and that there was, if not a consensus, certainly an understanding of the Israeli view that they faced an escalating problem of gains by the Soviets and by Nasser in the area. We come now to the onset of the crisis, which I think we can certainly date from the Samu' raid, for which I have yet to hear a convincing explanation. If the main Israeli policy objective with regard to Jordan was to strengthen the Hashemite regime, I think we can agree it didn't do that. I don't understand the motivation unless it was to weaken the Hashemite regime and cause trouble on the West Bank. Perhaps we can be enlightened here.

On the Syrian border, yes, there was terrorism from the infant Palestinian groups, al-Fatah and others. Yes, there was a lot of bellicose rhetoric coming out of the people who had taken over in Damascus. But I think it's worth recording or reminding ourselves that in the view of many people on the scene at the time, the provocations on the border as often as not came from the Israelis. General Von Horn in his memoirs, published in 1966, said as much. Indeed, in the last couple of days I had occasion to talk to a number of former UNTSO [UN Truce Supervision Organization] observers stationed in the area at the time. As one of them put it, they all concluded—even those who had arrived with the opposite view—that nine out of every ten shooting incidents were provoked by the Israelis. He also said that the Israelis were rather sharper than the Arabs, being careful to record every Arab violation and complain to the UN, whereas the Syrians didn't bother, so when the written record was looked at in New York it seemed clear that the Arabs were principally to blame.

It was, I believe, on April 3 that Israel announced that it proposed to cultivate all the demilitarized zones, an activity that had always caused friction in the past. On April 7, as we heard the other day, they sent an armored tractor into the demilitarized zone, which predictably was followed by Syrian shelling and the famous air battle. I don't want to go day by day through what happened on the Syrian border, but I think it's worth pointing out who had the initiative here, who was controlling events and who was reacting to them, and if we're discussing who pushed the crisis in various directions, I think we ought to think about that.

What happened in terms of Israeli threats or moves against Syria in the early part of May? Everyone seems to agree that there was no Israeli mobilization in the north. It's obviously ridiculous to suggest there could have been ten or twelve brigades involved. But Ezer Weizmann said in 1972, "Don't forget that we did move tanks to the Golan [Galilee] after the downing of the aircraft on April 7." Was the notion of escalation in Israeli preparedness in that area made out of whole cloth by the Russians and the Syrians? I don't know, but there may have been something to it.

On the question of whether General Rabin said anything of a threatening nature on a radio broadcast on May 11, again, I think I heard someone say or suggest that I might have made this up, which I certainly didn't. If he didn't say it—and it's true there is no record in FBIS [Foreign Broadcast Information Service], which is lamentably thin on all Israeli pronouncements for that period—it's interesting that so many people thought he did.

On May 13, for example, the Syrian Foreign Ministry issued a strong complaint about successive threats made by, I paraphrase, "various Israeli leaders and Israeli military personnel which are merely new means to prepare world public opinion and to camouflage the forthcoming Zionist aggression and provocative actions against the Syrian Arab Republic. This is clear from the statements of Zionist army chief of staff Rabin." The Churchills, Randolph and young Winston, in their book on the Six-Day War, which could hardly be described as unsympathetic to Israel, seem to think that Rabin made a statement of this kind. Again this is just to say that things get rapidly explained away. "Oh well, you know there was no buildup. Rabin didn't say anything." I think it's curious that so many people thought he did.

We come to the interesting period when the crisis shifted south. Again, although we've heard a lot of microdetail in the last few days of who said what to whom, who phoned whom, who visited whom, the overwhelming impression I've always had is what about the dog that didn't bark?

Why did the United States do so little? Why was there no real reaction in the time between Nasser's move into the Sinai and the closing of the strait? This is the United States of America, you know, with a large and well-endowed national security operation. Are we really to believe that Lyndon Baines Johnson didn't want to pressure a small country or a larger country or make out as if he couldn't do it? Again, I've had no convincing explanation of this.

The other curious thing we've heard about is the accuracy, how well informed everyone on the intelligence side seems to have been about what was going to happen in the forthcoming war, how the CIA's estimates were accurate to within a day of what was going to happen, with General Amit's word for it that the Israeli estimates were in full agreement. In fact, we know from Israeli memoirs of the time that that was indeed the assessment. But why is it that no one else [outside the American and Israeli governments] was let in on that?

I think everyone remembers the sort of mood worldwide, the belief that there was going to be a second holocaust, that Israel's survival was at stake, that Israel was about to be overrun. The short biographies of the panelists says Andrew Cockburn was at Oxford at the time. What I was doing at Oxford was trying to persuade my Jewish roommate that perhaps it would be a good idea not to skip his final exams and go off to volunteer in Israel. I said, maybe you should wait a week. Our room was plastered with pictures of Moshe Dayan, and we listened to every radio broadcast. We all thought that Israel was about to go under. Certainly in Israel people thought so. The *people,* I mean to say. There was panic. People were clearing out the shops, digging air raid shelters, and . . . yet we discover that, inside, there was this mood of breezy confidence, certainly among the generals. As we know from the record, their mood was simply one of impatience toward Eshkol and Eban and the rest for not letting them get on with it. You know, let us do it now.

As for the nature of the U.S.-Israeli relationship, I was interested in what Ambassador Helms was saying yesterday about the way that what we can variously describe as channels of communication, or lobbyists—in the form of the vice-president of the United States, the justices of the Supreme Court, the U.S. ambassador to the UN, not to mention the redoubtable Mr. and Mrs. [Arthur] Krim—were all pestering or, perhaps that's not the word, certainly plying Lyndon Johnson with this erroneous information. I'm interested to hear if the Israeli Embassy in Washington knew of the assessments of the Israeli intelligence in Tel Aviv that Israel militarily was in no threat of going under, under any conceivable combination of circumstances. Why was there this sort of collusive effort among public statements in Israel, and statements to the press, and statements made by influential Americans to the president [to establish] that indeed this was the case and Israel desperately needed military help? Why was it that Israel felt the need, as we heard yesterday and before, to misinform the CIA station chief in Tel Aviv as to the actual military balance at the time? I think we were told that this was not a briefing that would have been given to the Israeli superiors.

It seems to me that, if not conspiracy, we have collusion on various levels, and I also think we must really keep central in our minds something that I think Ambassador Basheer has mentioned: just how much the Americans hated Nasser. At that time Nasser was maybe public enemy number two in Washington, after Ho Chi Minh. There were congressional resolutions every day of the week denouncing Nasser as an enemy to peace, an enemy to Israel, of course. He was in people's minds here, you know, a real enemy. He had people frothing at the mouth. There was a hysterical situation about Nasser, reminiscent, indeed, of the feeling in Britain, which I can dimly remember, in 1956.

We have confirmed again that the chief of Israeli intelligence, General Amit, was able to come to Washington, compare notes on intelligence estimates with the Americans as to what was going to happen, and answer some questions about the number of casualties expected by Israel and how long it would take. He was able to receive the best wishes from the American secretary of defense for the new Israeli minister of defense and able to go home and get the reaction, from within the high command, good, now we can go, or words to that effect, on the basis that the Americans had given their assent to an assault on Nasser. I don't know why . . . there's a necessity to argue about collusion or not. Just think about it for a second. If we were hearing from an Egyptian head of intelligence who had gone to Moscow, compared notes with his opposite numbers at the KGB and the Soviet ministry of defense, come back, and then Egypt launched an attack, we'd assume there had been some sort of collusion.

So, to hear people indignantly deny that there was any kind of collusion or cooperation—whatever word you want to use to dodge around *conspiracy*—I find kind of bizarre. I have talked to former intelligence people, including one in particular I quoted in my book. It's a blind source so it can't be checked and I don't make a huge deal of it, but it was a reasonably high-ranking fellow from the NSA [National Security Agency], speaking in an "everyone knows" kind of voice, who said everyone knows that Jim Angleton had been talking to the Israelis for a couple of years about what was going to happen, about how to get Nasser.

I find it interesting that it [such a claim] has also been repeated by Wilbur Eveland, who of course wasn't with the CIA at that time, but there's another CIA memoir that repeats the same thing. It does seem to be a notion that's around.

Finally, I think we ought to spend a minute thinking about the other wars that broke out—I mean the war with Syria and the war with Jordan. We have heard in exhaustive detail about the discussions with Washington concerning the attack on Egypt. The question of the attack on Syria was raised briefly yesterday, but why was it that, whereas the attack on Egypt was cleared in advance with Washington, with everyone agreeing on how long it would take and how many casualties and so forth, the attack on Syria seems to have not been [so treated]? In fact, there were a number of high-ranking officials on record, including Ambassador Helms, that the attack on the [USS] *Liberty* [by the Israelis on June 8, 1967] was—I think we ought to discuss the *Liberty* a little—a deliberate attack in order to make it harder for the Americans to find out what was about to happen on the Syrian front. So we have a question of collusion, or conspiracy if you can call it that for one part of the war, the attack on Egypt, and in sharp contrast a brutal move for another part of the war, a move made to stop the Americans from finding out what was going to happen in part two.

Commentary

Richard Helms: Just exactly how I deal with the two speeches this morning I'm not sure. It reminds me of that age-old story in the Middle East of the little mullah who was brought in when the town was in terrible trouble, who was brought in three different times, to talk to the people, and the last time the crowd asked him, "Master, what are you going to say?" And he said, "Those who know, tell those who don't know." There are several individuals in this room who know a great deal more than I about relationships between Washington and Egypt, who can deal with various points that Ambassador Basheer made with respect to American foreign policy. I was no policymaker in my government. I was simply trying to deal with the facts.

Let me put to rest one or two things. First, books like Miles Copeland's *The Game of Nations* [London: Weidenfeld and Nicolson, 1969], Eveland's *Ropes of Sand,* and others: The Central Intelligence Agency has had the misfortune to have had certain former employees who have written mischievous books, not necessarily based on fact, a lot of it just plain fiction. I would suggest to Mr. Basheer that if he wants to make a good case in Washington for anything having to do with his country, he lay off quoting those books because they're not going to convince anybody of anything.

A second myth to lay to rest: I don't think there's a single chief of state or chief of government in the world who does not expect to be attacked or assassinated by someone. This mythology that leaders who are told so-and-

Richard Helms, director,
CIA, 1967.

so is out to get you, are suddenly terribly frightened and upset by this is just not plausible. Look at the way the president of the United States travels around with two limousines and God knows how many Secret Service and so forth, and still the last two presidents who have been shot were surrounded by their protective guards. I can't believe that Mr. Nasser was upset by the fact that somebody was probably going to try to kill him. But that it was the policy of United States to kill him is not true. And there was no conniving with the Israeli intelligence or anybody else to get Mr. Nasser. The description of the distaste that a lot of American policymakers and public opinion had for Mr. Nasser and his behavior is probably correct. But to translate that into a definite plot to kill him is simply not true, and there are a lot of gentlemen in this room who will attest to it as well.

Let me go off onto something else. Every nation acts as it believes is in its own self-interest. At this conference we've been trying to sort out a myriad of facts, and I'm sure the scholars will try and work out which ones sound the most reliable and which are the least reliable. History has a hard time being made correctly. Time does not help. In a nation like the United States, we have millions of Monday morning quarterbacks, and for those who don't understand football, they are the spectators who on Monday tell the quarterback who played on Sunday how he should have played the game. And we've been told this morning how President Johnson should have played the game. I don't think that President Johnson at the time would have admired that. I think that he had a multitude of problems on his mind, and the fact that he didn't do this or didn't do that or the dog that didn't bark—I simply can't deal with those matters. But I think we have enough facts so that we have a pretty good idea what transpired.

The issue of collusion between Israeli intelligence and American intelligence takes me into the field of intelligence service relationships, but I'm not going to get into "Intelligence 101" here. That isn't what this conference is about. But I'd like to point out that intelligence services don't last long unless they serve their masters, and they do have masters. This whole "rogue elephant" concept that came up in 1975 is absolute bilge and garbage. Any plots, covert actions, and so forth have always been dutifully cleared by the CIA with its masters. That started on day 1, and anybody who wants to come along and tell me that it isn't true, that there was this exception and that exception. . . . I'm not all-wise; all I know is that I worked there for twenty-five years, and I can assure you that this is the case. It doesn't help to have fellows in another agency saying, well, you know, Jim Angleton had that close relationship with the Israelis and therefore, you know, he was giving them a lot of information which they shouldn't have had, etc., etc., etc. I want to tell you that the Israelis know what goes on in the U.S. government from top to bottom, and they didn't need Jim Angleton to tell them.

Meir Amit: Jim Angleton's main thrust was the Russians, not the Israelis. That's what I want you to remember.

Richard Helms: There is a relationship with the Israeli intelligence, but General Amit is correct. The interest was in the Russians who came to Israel, from whom we hoped to get some additional information about what was going on in the Soviet Union, a perfectly sensible arrangement. Angleton has been blamed for a lot of things recently. You know, it's inconvenient to die. I promise you, if you're interested in your own history, don't die.

There's a point here that I think gets overlooked and consequently focuses attention on Angleton. And I'll take responsibility for the decision that early in the years of the agency it was thought that it would be wise to have the Arab account—the Arab countries—handled in one part of the CIA and the Israeli account in another. That is why they were divided, and that is why Angleton is associated with the Israeli account, and it's been blown out of all proportion. He was simply dealing with [Israel] in the same way another part of the agency was dealing with Egypt, Jordan, the United Arab

Emirates, and so forth. So let's keep this whole thing in perspective and not demonize this man, who was representing this country and his agency as faithfully as he possibly could. To think that he conspired with Meir Amit to start the war is ridiculous. He had his orders. He knew he wasn't making policy. He wasn't going to tell the Israelis what the Americans could or couldn't do, and besides General Amit didn't need this kind of help. He had plenty of people around the United States who could have told him better than Angleton what was going on.

It also seems to be forgotten that President Johnson—a point I made yesterday—was a great fellow with the telephone. It was amazing how many people he talked to in the course of a day, and it was impossible to figure out who it was he had last talked to when he approached you on some problem. I don't want to go into the details of something that's irrelevant, but he once attacked me and told me he was going to close down an important operation. I have yet to figure out who it was he talked to last on that subject. But it was difficult to deal with sometimes, and in late May and early June, the air was blue with people with whom he was talking.

While I'm talking here about relationships between intelligence services, I'd like to point out that the CIA had a good relationship with Egyptian intelligence during the months leading up to the '67 war and in the period thereafter. You say, how do you know this? I simply know it. I'll give you some evidence. When the war was over and diplomatic relations between Egypt and the United States had been broken off, obviously the United States had an interest in having somebody to report from Cairo. The precise dealings on this, Ambassador Battle or Ambassador Parker can tell you in greater detail. What ended up was that the CIA man who had been declared to Egyptian intelligence when he went to Egypt was the only person that the Egyptian intelligence chief, Salah Nasr, would accept to remain and represent the U.S. government, as head of a U.S. Interests Section in the Spanish Embassy. So a fellow named William Bromell, because his name is well known, was a sort of acting ambassador in Cairo for some weeks until things could get straightened out with the Egyptians and the normal diplomatic relationship resumed. So there is no truth in the [allegation] that we were holding off the Egyptians and loving the Israelis. The agency was simply trying to carry out the wishes of its masters, which were to have good relationships with all these countries.

Before I conclude, I want to take up this business about the Stephen Green piece, which is in the reading material for this conference but which hasn't been discussed. I'm referring to his allegation that a U.S. Air Force reconnaissance unit based in Britain was taken to Spain, its uniforms changed to civilian clothes, flown on to Israel to work with the Israelis performing photo reconnaissance during the Six-Day War. It is is totally untrue. There isn't a shred of truth whatsoever in it. In the first place, let me point out that any secret in the U.S. government of that sensitivity could not have lasted twenty-five years. Secrets hardly last twenty-five hours in this country, in this town, if they're sensitive. Second, if one looks at what was allegedly involved—taking an officer of the U.S. military out of uniform, putting him into civilian clothes, and sending him into hostile territory—it simply means he becomes a spy and he and his family and friends lose all government appurtenances, salary, insurance, hospitalization, everything that he is signed up for. There are those who say that if the president ordered it, that would make it legal. That is nonsense. This is a country of laws, and you have to abide by the laws. Even the president has to abide by the laws.

I happen to be an expert in what is known as "sheep-dipping." That's changing a soldier from his military uniform to a civilian uniform. I've been involved in this over the years. It's a complicated legal procedure that takes a lot of paper and a lot of work with various elements of the U.S. government. It is not something you do with a snap of the fingers.

Examining the facts as outlined in Stephen Green's book, I can only say that it's an interesting story that's been made up out of whole cloth. I guess I forgot to say that since those fellows were photographing in an area where there was a war going on, they could easily have been taken prisoner by the Egyptians and shot on the spot as spies. Now what kind of a commander sends a bunch of fellows into a situation like that, totally unheralded and unsung and without the permission of anybody? McNamara never heard of this thing. I never heard of this thing. If between the two of us we didn't have enough connections in the U.S. military to have heard something like this, I just can't understand how anybody could believe it.

Last, let me speak a moment about conspiracies. I suppose that, like many words in the dictionary, conspiracy has various meanings, but to me a conspiracy involves several people who intend to commit a single, particular act. If you really want to enjoy a conspiracy theory, go and see this "JFK" movie, which I refuse to see because I won't put one single dollar in the hands of Mr. Oliver Stone. I think the movie is an outrage. The idea that the vice-president, the chief justice, the director of Central Intelligence, and other senior officials would conspire to hire Oswald, give him a rifle, put him in the textbook depository, and let him shoot at the president of the United States—that's just plain sick.

In the first place, all of these books that have been written always have some reason why the establishment in Washington wanted to get rid of President Kennedy. One was that he was backing off in Vietnam. Hell, I don't know anybody who knows that he was backing off on Vietnam. It's alleged one way or the other, but there isn't any substantiation for this. Another book says it was because the Cubans wanted to "get" him. I don't know why the Cubans wanted to get President Kennedy, as Castro himself pointed out not long ago. He said, "You know, that would have been a very silly thing for me to do, because the next thing you'd know, the whole American air force would be over Cuba and we would be obliterated." This is just utter nonsense. I do think that sensible Americans ought to try to deal with everybody under thirty who goes to that movie and believes it's true.

As for conspiracies with foreign intelligence services to do X, Y, and Z, there may be some joint operations, but I don't know about any conspiracies. You know, you have to be careful in this intelligence business. The guy who puts his hand in yours one day may be the guy that's got a knife in your back the next. This is not a game for children or for dreamers. And as General Amit pointed out yesterday, you have various ways of doing things and various relationships, but they're in various grades, depending on the country you're dealing with. And the allegation here is that we were in bed with the Israelis. Not true.

In response to Mr. Cockburn's remarks that the Foreign Broadcast Information reports of this period were thin on one particular area. ... I'd like to point out that the Foreign Broadcast Information Service is not a conspiratorial organization. It is simply an organization that listens to radio and television broadcasts and reads newspapers and magazines and translates them and reports on them. It has no capacity for conspiracy. If the reports are thin, it's because they had no way of making them otherwise. But they do monitor things that are going on, and they do do a pretty good job. U.S. intelligence learned that the Israeli air force had attacked the Egyptian air force on June 5 from the Foreign Broadcast Information Service. The news did not come from NSA; it did not come from secret agents; it did not come from anything except the public broadcasts.

This has been a most interesting and useful conference that Ambassador Parker has organized. I think there's been a lot of static in the air. There's been a lot of back and forth, but I wouldn't be surprised if, when the scholars got through, they couldn't clean this thing up pretty well. And I think that if they would just work a little bit on the facts and less on the conspiracies, we'd all be better off.

Discussion

Lucius Battle: I would like to make two comments. First thing, with respect to the period after the break in relations with Egypt: Our first plan was to leave Dick Parker there as head of the American Interests section in Cairo, but the Egyptians thought he was CIA and refused to let that go through, and we had to send our other expert, Don Bergus, out in lieu of Parker. Neither one, I quickly add, was CIA or had any connection with it. But the one known CIA man [William Bromell] was the one the Egyptians quite happily accepted.

Now, as the American who had more to do with Nasser than any of the others here, I feel I have to comment. The statements made today about the extent to which Americans hated Nasser and hated Arabs and hated Egypt are absolute nonsense. There was a strong division in the government and in the public with respect to Gamal Abd al-Nasser. I have licks on my back now from testifying on behalf of aid to Gamal Abd al-Nasser, and I wanted to continue the kind of relationship we'd had with him since the beginning. We were overall, from '62 on, quite a good friend to Nasser. We gave him a lot of help of all kinds—financial help, a lot of food aid, a lot of technical assistance, a lot of advice that he wanted. He was not an easy man for us to deal with. He never understood that we had to go to the Congress and get appropriations to cover all the aid that we were handing out to him and that there had to be a reasonable climate in relationships between the United States and Egypt in order for us to have any chance of getting it through. He simply could not understand the impact of his speeches on American public opinion, particularly on congressional opinion. I was a recipient of several of the attacks in his speeches; they were not pleasant listening, and I did not like having them come my way.

I talked with him at great length. You say we all hated him. I rather liked him. He drove me up the wall in some respects, but he was an intelligent man. He was not well educated in a Western context, and he never had a clear sense of where he wanted to take Egypt or himself. That was one of his big weaknesses. He never had a clear philosophy, either economic or political. Arab socialism was whatever he wanted to do that day. It didn't matter that it was different from yesterday and from tomorrow. There was a gap in that context.

I asked him, "Mr. President, why do you make those speeches?" I said, "I worked for six months trying to improve our relationship and you undo everything I've done with one speech." He said, "Mr. Ambassador, I'm only talking to my people." I said, "Mr. President, you can't speak only to your people. You're the president of a great nation. When you speak, the whole world listens and reads and tries to understand." And I said, "We don't understand those speeches."

Before the speech that finally led to the withdrawal of aid, he went nearly a year without making a speech, without making a single attack on the United States. That was something of a record. But there was a strong body of opinion in the U.S. government, and outside it, that saw many good qualities in Nasser and that wanted to maintain a reasonable relationship with him, and he made it as difficult as he could for us to maintain that.

Richard Parker: I'd like to make one clarification about the acceptance of Bill Bromell as indicating how fond the Egyptians were of the CIA. I don't question that fondness, but just for the record, Bromell was a courageous and competent officer, low key, unobtrusive, and I think the Egyptians just couldn't believe that he was really the chief of station. He was just too modest.

Several years ago I went back to Cairo, and at first the Egyptians were reluctant to tell me why I had been kicked out—by Nasser personally. It wasn't Salah Nasr, it was Gamal Abd al-Nasser who kicked me out. He insisted. They had detectives down at the train to make sure that I got on it with the other people in the middle of the night. And I said, why me? A close friend who was in the intelligence business there said, "Well, you didn't act like a diplomat. You were too active, and we just couldn't believe that this fellow [Bromell] was the American *dimagh al-mufakkir*, the thinking brain behind all the evil things that you [Americans] were doing. It couldn't have been Luke Battle and it couldn't have been Dave Nes, so it must have been you." It was not any Egyptian love affair with the CIA that allowed Bromell to stay.

Talcott Seelye: I was not involved directly in any of this operation because I was in Jidda at the time, and the only thing that happened to us at the embassy was that a bomb was planted in the corner of our compound. It did no damage to anybody and we survived very well. But I have a few points I want to make.

General Amit, I appreciate your cogent and concise presentation that conformed to the time constraints and could be heard by everybody. General Amit started out this conference by saying that it was his impression that the purpose of this conference was to vindicate Gamal Abd al-Nasser. I think now you'd be the first to agree, General Amit, that this has not been the purpose of the conference. If anything, the reverse has been true.

I sense that a number of people here have come to the conclusion that

Nasser was wholly responsible for this debacle, although Dick Parker has made a comment suggesting that the United States may have provoked him. I would submit that to blame one person wholly for this war is too simplistic. Maybe we need to understand better what I think some of our Egyptian colleagues were alluding to earlier, namely, the context of Gamal Abd al-Nasser, the phenomenon of Nasser, how he got to power, and why he followed certain policies.

For example, there were important changes in the Middle East as radical Arab nationalist regimes came to power in the 1950s. This [shift in power] resulted from the Arab defeat in 1948 and the creation of Israel, which discredited the previous Arab governments. Nasser came to power to a great extent as a result of that defeat and of the creation of Israel. Later, certain actions by Israel contributed to Nasser's turning away from the West and associating Egypt with the Soviet Union. I think we all know that in 1955 the major cross-border strike into Gaza, during which an Egyptian unit was decimated, contributed to Nasser's request for military aid [from the Soviet Union] to improve Egypt's defenses. Another reason that Nasser turned to the Soviets was that the United States had attached strings to its offer of military aid to Egypt. It was Nasser's close Soviet connection that led to his taking seriously the famous message passed to him by the Soviets in May 1967, which indicated incorrectly that the Israelis were mobilizing along the Syrian-Israeli border. This was a key factor in the buildup of tensions.

In other words, there were some explanations for Nasser's actions. Also, let us not forget that in the early 1950s, after Nasser came to power, we were working closely with him. During this period, Nasser extended peace overtures to Israel that were rebuffed. What might have happened if those overtures had been accepted? Maybe all the subsequent wars could have been avoided, with Nasser's moving in a constructive direction.

History, of course, cannot be repeated. I was surprised that Ambassador Tomeh yesterday did not refer to the proposal by the Syrian leader, Husni Zaim, in 1949, during the cease-fire armistice negotiations. He proposed that in place of a cease-fire agreement, a final peace agreement with Israel be signed. This initiative was rebuffed by the Israelis. These are aspects of the situation that should be kept in mind.

I have received the impression from the American and the Israeli interlocutors here that somehow the Israeli attack on Egypt was inevitable, was desirable, and was for the good of Israel. I would like the record of this conference to show that not all of us agree with this judgment. We cannot hypothesize now, obviously, about what the alternatives might have been. However, we have heard that such Israeli statesmen as Ben-Gurion had reservations concerning the planned attack. His views were dismissed by one of the Israeli representatives as being unimportant because he was not then in the government. But were the views of an elder statesman not important? It was mentioned that Ambassador Harman felt the same way. Is it not possible that if the Israelis had pursued the diplomatic course, if the United States had pushed harder for that course, that the long-run outcome would have been better and Israel might be better off today?

Israel has less security now than it had before the '67 war. It has more problems now than it had before the '67 war. The moderate Israeli regimes of the past have been replaced by an uncompromising regime, and instead of being the object of the affection of the American people, as so eloquently described by Mr. Bundy yesterday [in speaking of the 1967 period], Israel is now widely criticized in the United States. Because of the way the Israelis have acted in the last several years—beating up Lebanese and Palestinians, stealing American secrets, and thumbing their nose at the United States, Israel has become almost a pariah in certain circles. No longer is Israel admired as it was before the 1967 war. I'm suggesting that things might have been better.

My final point is a controversial one, but let's have a little controversy. Mr. Cockburn has referred in passing to the incident of the USS *Liberty* in 1967. I hope my Israeli colleagues will not sit here and claim that the Israelis did not know the identity of the ship. If they do, they will be laughed out of this room because we have incontrovertible evidence from intercepts between Israeli pilots that the Israelis knew that this was an American ship. We have the testimony of President Lyndon Johnson, of Dean Rusk, of Admiral Moorer, then the chairman of the chiefs of staff, that this was clearly an Israeli attack, a cold-blooded attack on American naval personnel, killing fifty or so and wounding one hundred fifty.

What I want to know is why our close ally and friend, Israel—and people here have been emphasizing our special relationship—would do such a thing to its closest ally. Certainly the families of those killed on the USS *Liberty* do not have deep affection for Israel. There was an explanation for this action given by Mr. Cockburn, namely, that the Israelis did not want us to know that they were about to break the cease-fire and attack the Golan. That may or may not be the correct explanation, but even if it is, it does not justify what happened.

Shimon Shamir: Having heard Ambassador Seelye, I would like to refer to one point in his statement: the allegation that opportunities for making peace between Nasser and Israel had been missed. The subject happens to be one on which I've done extensive research, and I think I can speak on it with some authority.

Let me say bluntly that opportunity for concluding formal peace between Nasser and Israel never existed. I made thorough investigations of this question. I went through all the available documents and testimonies on the secret contacts that took place, mostly between '54 and '56. I found that there were indeed several opportunities for concluding, secretly, agreements on various types of de facto arrangements. It is true that not all the signals and messages that were exchanged at the time were properly understood, that the Israelis made mistakes and the Egyptians made mistakes. But let me set the record straight: At no point in Nasser's career was there a real possibility of concluding a formal peace with Israel.

I would like to speak about conspiracy theories. Not so much about their substance, for most of these theories—and we heard here enough examples— are so outlandish that they shouldn't be dignified with a serious discussion. But the *phenomenon* of conspiracy theories is an interesting subject. Even when such theories are entirely imaginary, they do affect reality. It has already been noted that "things that are perceived as real—are real in their consequences." We come from a part of the world where conspiracy theories are common. They play an important role in public life and influence the way people see politics. Some say it is cultural. I am not sure. The wild conspiracy theories that spread about the Kennedy assassination have been mentioned here. I think it's a good example of the rule that, in extraordinary circumstances, people everywhere will be inclined to generate such theories and to believe them.

My opinion is that the diffusion of such theories depends very much on the type of political regime under which people live. When people do not trust their newspapers and disbelieve the official line, they tend to conjecture explanations of their own. Going by their own experience, they assume that the truth is always more complex and sinister than what they are told—so they invent and consume conspiracy theories. It is their way to defy the propaganda of the dignitaries in power. This may be the explanation of the proliferation of such theories in a number of authoritarian Arab states. But this may have been true also under the communist regimes. You may observe this disposition in Israel among Jews from the former Soviet Union. A year ago, when the abortive putsch was taking place in Moscow, and the media turned to Jews from Russia to get expert analysis, many of the interpretations they offered wildly missed the mark. They came up with conspiracy theories. Apparently, in totalitarian regimes people are brought up on the belief that there is always a fierce power struggle behind the scenes, that there is always a grand design, and they become accustomed to looking for it.

Conspiracy theories in the Middle East have certain characteristics that deserve attention. Let me point out three of them. First, like those that were mentioned here this morning, many conspiracy theories oversimplify the identity of the actors. They see them as monolithic, schematic protagonists who behave according to deeply ingrained stereotypes. Conspiracy theories, as we have heard, usually speak about actors like "Israel," "the United States," or "the Soviet Union." They claim that "*Israel* targeted Nasser," "*the United States* laid a trap for Saddam," "*the Soviet Union* wanted the Arabs to be defeated," and so on. In fact, as the deliberations in this forum have shown clearly, there is no "Israel," no "United States," and no "Soviet Union." In each of these entities decisions are made, and actions are taken, by a large number of persons who may have different, or even contradictory, orientations. In the case of Israel, for example, there was the prime minister, the general staff, influential ministers, the Mapai Party, intelligence, and several others. Conspiracy theories usually fail to pinpoint and identify the people who really made the decision and took the action.

Another characteristic of these theories is that they tend to reverse conventional wisdom. When the apparent facts create some uneasiness, or even embarrassment, a good conspiracy theory can straighten things out. Here again the May 1967 affair offers examples. Conventional wisdom would say that Nasser was trying to change the status quo—in Sinai, in the Gulf of Elath, and perhaps in the whole strategic arena—whereas Israel was trying to defend the existing situation. In the broader context, the Soviet Union was trying to undermine the pro-Western regimes in the region, whereas the United States was trying to protect the status quo. Against this background, the colossal failure of [the attempts in] both [contexts] makes them look foolish. Along comes the conspiracy theory to put things in order: If the whole conflict was the machination of a secretly contrived Israeli-American scheme, as the conspiracy theories purport, then the losers are no longer the victims of their own doing, of their own miscalculated initiatives, but just the innocent victims of a diabolical grand design.

Finally, one of the attractions of conspiracy theories is that they draw a picture in black and white. They may be telling a complicated story, but at the end it always transpires that the good guys were good and the bad guys were bad, and the whole picture becomes clear and satisfying. I'm not trying to say that only conspiratorial theories do this; on different levels of sophistication, even historical interpretations indulge in the same practice. It may be useful to remind ourselves of the wise words that were written in the introduction to the Harvard core curriculum: "There are very few heroes and very few villains and only forged history makes easy judgment possible."

Carl Brown: I completely agree with Shimon Shamir's appraisal, and I want to add a bit. As a historian, I have always admired the statement of Arthur Schlesinger, Jr., that the historian is going to get a lot farther down the pike with the confusion theory of history rather than the conspiracy theory. To answer why the United States was so passive, we need to look at the way bureaucracies react, to take the lesson that Graham Allison brought out in his classic study *Essence of Decision.* To discover how we develop in a crisis something that passes for a policy is to reconstruct carefully who the various parties involved were and what they were doing. The same holds for Israel, and theirs. Another good maxim for any historian is Occam's razor: things are not to be made more complicated than they have to be.

I get a little nervous about even the rubric of this panel because I think it can easily divert us. We are coming close to understanding, in a genuinely Machiavellian way—as Francis Bacon said, we are indebted to Machiavelli for telling us how people act instead of how they ought to act—how people acted. It seems to me it's diversionary to look for conspiracies.

I agree that when great numbers of people believe in conspiracies, that very belief can have a dramatic impact on developments. That gets us into public opinion.

Conspiracy theories are often allegations that so-and-so is manipulating so-and-so. I would suggest that, seemingly paradoxically, so-called regional clients have an ability to manipulate their so-called great-power patrons. I am reminded of the statement of a Soviet ambassador to Syria: "Syria takes everything from us except advice." Something along that line could be said about many of the so-called client states in the area in dealing with their outside great-power patrons.

Ephraim Evron: As I was listening to the presentations, I couldn't help recalling that fellow in Tel Aviv who went up to somebody at the café and said to him, "Look, your sister is a prostitute." The man said, "But I don't have any sisters!" And the first fellow said, "That doesn't matter, she's still a prostitute" [laughter].

I sympathize with Dick Helms and the others, and I suggest and hope that researchers and future historians will look at the facts as they are and see the documents and pass judgment then. I shall not go into great analysis of Ambassador Basheer's historical record. I just want to remind him that after the armistice agreement—and that's also for Ambassador Seelye—

Israel, as you all know, especially you, Luke, tried to get our Arab neighbors to come to peace terms with us on the basis of the armistice lines. It was rejected. On June 19, 1967, the Israeli government passed to the American government a proposal—and Mr. Begin agreed to it at that time, he was one of those that supported it—that, in exchange for peace, Israel will give up every inch of the Sinai and Golan Heights and be ready to begin negotiations about the West Bank. We got the Khartoum resolution [by the Arab leaders rejecting negotiations or reconciliation with Israel]. But that is history, and I don't want to pursue it any farther.

A word about the Rabin statement on the radio: It's a figment of the imagination. I repeat it as firmly as I can. I asked General Rabin about it. He never made that statement on the radio on May 11. Nothing can change this fact.

I didn't quite understand the connection between the young man at Oxford and the collusion theory, but maybe we can hear about that.

We were told that the Israelis had penetrated all levels of the American government. This is what embassies are for, to try to find out what goes on in [the host country's] government. And I want to take my hat off to Sam Lewis, who made us all look like bumbling amateurs. He knew much more about what was going on in Israel than Prime Minister Begin. And you should have seen the queues of all the Israeli officials and nonofficials waiting outside his office and his residence.

I'll take up the challenge of the *Liberty*, with your permission. Why would Israel do such a terrible thing? We may be crazy, but we are not fools. For Israel in the middle of a war, when the Soviet fleet is on the horizon, to come out and shoot up and try to sink and bomb and kill American sailors is worse than a crime, it's a damned folly. [As for] the reason being that we were going to attack the Golan Heights: that this was a reason good enough to provoke this kind of horrible thing, which would do incalculable damage to Israel, is unimaginable. The Americans had many ways of finding out what our plans were. They knew what was going on, and anybody who knows Israel knows that even a truck that goes up the single road to the Golan could be spotted. We don't have to sink an American ship for that. At the risk of being laughed out of this room, I have to repeat to you that it was a terrible tragic mistake.

William Quandt: I don't have too much to add to what Carl Brown and Shimon Shamir said about conspiracies. I think it's important to remember, though, that the willingness to believe conspiracies, particularly in the Arab world, has a lot to do with Suez. Because Suez did happen, one can't just say at the outset of any discussion that conspiracies should be laughed out of court. But what disturbed me a little bit about the tone of the panel was that the distinction between a genuine conspiracy, of which we have seen some examples in the Middle East, Suez being the most interesting, and various other forms of cooperation—attempts to manipulate, attempts to influence—is almost being swept away as irrelevant. I think it makes an analytical hodgepodge if you say there is no real difference between a conspiracy or collusion, as one category, and any kind of cooperation and manipulation and trying to influence as another.

It seems to me that various forms of cooperation, contacts, joint planning, manipulation, and feeding distorted information are what governments do to one another because they're trying to influence, trying to persuade [each other]. And sure, we sometimes exaggerate, and we sometimes selectively inform. If that's what a conspiracy consists of, then we've trivialized the entire concept. I think some of the discussion this morning erased the distinction between conspiracy—which fits the Suez case and fits it correctly—and what governments commonly do to one another in pursuit of their national interests.

I also think there's a difference in saying that in the end the United States assented to Israel's acting on its own against Egypt. That doesn't strike me as being alarming in its implications unless it implies that from the beginning, somewhere back in the fall of 1966, the United States and Israel were cooking up a joint strategy that would end with this kind of American blessing of Israel's going to war against Egypt. Assent occurred, I have no doubt of it. But it happened late in the day, late in the crisis. That's different from the similar-sounding argument that there was instigation, [meaning] that the United States set the whole thing up in collusion with the Israelis. Unless I am mistaken, Mr. Cockburn's book argues the collusion theory.

Andrew Cockburn: You are mistaken.

William Quandt: Well, then, I misread it. I will have to go back and read it more carefully. But there is a somewhat stronger statement in your book than simply that the United States assented to Israel's attacking Egypt late in the crisis because it had nothing else to suggest. If that's really all you're saying, that we assented to Israel's taking action because all else had failed, then there's really no difference between you and me. But as I read your account, it seemed a little more dramatic than that. It had Angleton playing a significant role in planting an idea—[rather than] Israel acting in its own interest—to go out and topple the Nasser regime. Maybe he said that. We have people here who have talked with him who say that he did not. That's an important distinction. Did we support Israel going to war to defend its perceived national interest vis-à-vis the Strait of Tiran and the Egyptian mobilization of forces, or did we want the Israelis to topple the regime of Gamal Abd al-Nasser? I don't know; I wasn't there, but I haven't heard from any of the Americans who were close to the decision making that we wanted the war and that the purpose of the whole yellow light, green light, whatever it was, was to bring about the downfall of Nasser's regime. And I do think you subscribe to that theory.

Ambassador Helms mentioned that we can't get a clear picture of what happened because LBJ was on the phone all the time, and that's true. There are logs of his phone calls, but not the content of them. What we do have, and what I have consulted and found extremely useful, is the log of whom he talked to. It doesn't tell you what he discussed, but at one point when I was deep in figuring out this crisis, I made a tally of whom LBJ talked to. I didn't bring it with me, but some of you in the room were on the other end of those phone calls. You might find it interesting: who his frequent contacts were during this period, especially calls that he initiated. First, Walt Rostow, as national security adviser, got far and away more calls than anybody else. I have no way of knowing if they were about Vietnam or about the Middle East or anything else. Dean Rusk was second, Robert McNamara was third, and Matilda Krim was probably fourth. She doesn't show up in the histories because we don't know what they talked about. But she spent a lot of time with LBJ, as did her husband, over a long weekend at the ranch. She was a committed pro-Israeli person. LBJ talked a great deal with her and she sent him memos on the Middle East during the crisis.

He also talked to Ambassador Helms a number of times, but not as often as to Mrs. Krim. He talked to Ambassador Goldberg quite a bit. He talked to Justice Fortas frequently. This is a man who reached out to a lot of people, but we simply don't have any way of knowing the content [of his telephone calls] unless there was a taping system that recorded it, but none of that has been released if it existed. We simply don't know what he talked about. But it is interesting that most of his contacts were with the official hierarchy.

Brian Urquhart: After all that's been said, I'm afraid what I'm going to say is rather simple-minded, but never mind. It seems to me there are two things about conspiracy theories. They do play a large part in events before they happen, by getting people off on the wrong track. I think that after disasters a lot of people find conspiracy theories comforting, and they proliferate. After Dag Hammerskjöld was killed . . . there is still a cottage industry in conspiracy theories about how he was killed. The fact that he was killed by pilot error is almost unquestioned, but it has nothing to do with the enthusiasm of the theorists. And the thing about conspiracy theories is that if you accept one, all the others are bogus. That seems to me to put a rather considerable practical limit on their value.

Like everybody in this room, I've lived through a fair share of disasters, and the thing that's always impressed me, particularly working in the UN, not to mention in World War II, was that in most disasters, almost no one after the first day has a clear policy about anything. They're simply living from day to day. That even applies to a great world power like the United States or the former Soviet Union. What we're really talking about here is a sort of [classification by] percentages of misleading things. I think about 70 percent of most disasters are miscalculations—preconceived ideas, ill-considered reactions, often personal ambitions of one kind or another, and downright stupidity. About 15 percent are misinformation and, sometimes, manipulation through misinformation. I would say that bad luck and unfortunate coincidence account for about 10 percent, and maybe somewhere, down at the bottom, about 5 percent could conceivably be some kind of conspiratorial idea, but very seldom.

I think it's all far less important than the basic dynamics of any great international disaster, which is what I hope we concentrate on here, particularly trying to distill, if possible, some lessons from the 1967 disaster. International politics and international relations are a whole rambling structure of deals and understandings and intrigues and fears and animosities and special relationships, and often governments are influenced by public perceptions of what is going on and by public preferences. Then, of course, there are other preoccupations, in this case the Vietnam War for the United States, that play an enormous role in the way the government feels, when it wakes up in the morning, about how it's going to deal with the next twenty-four hours.

Perhaps I might say one word here about the situation of people in the UN, international civil servants at the level of secretary-general, or someone like Ralph Bunche, or later on, myself, come to that. In this kind of situation in the UN, in the Secretariat, in the international civil service, we have a rather old-fashioned rule that we're not allowed to conspire with anyone, and we do, on the whole, try to respect agreements that we have been a party to in the past, which often leads us to be unpopular. Now the secretary-general is playing a major role in situations all over the world, and I think that the situation of being an international civil servant—of trying to act objectively and impartially in a situation where everybody else feels absolutely passionately one way or the other—is a very difficult situation to be in. It's usually unpopular, and it automatically deprives even the secretary general of a lot of those supports, in terms of information or things handed under the counter, and so on, that all governments have one way or another.

I hope that one thing that may come out in your conclusions is a look at the importance of international institutions, for example, UNEF in this case. The extreme lack of interest in UNEF before this disaster took place . . . I know because I used to be sent out every year to reduce UNEF because the British and the Americans who were paying for it thought it was too expensive at whatever it was—11 million a year or something. In fact, the British treasury the year before, when I had come back, had taken me to task for not having taken the Swedish company out of Sharm al-Shaykh. They said, "How can you possibly justify having these chaps in Sharm al-Shaykh? It's very expensive to feed them, because stuff has to be flown in; you had to build an airstrip. They have a primitive desalination plant because there's no water in Sharm al-Shaykh. It's an outrageous expense. What are they doing?" And I said, "Well, the whole point is, they're there. They're not doing anything; that's the whole point." And they said, "No, no, no, we've got to find a justification." So finally, the year before 1967, we gave UNEF a task, which was counting the ships going through the Strait of Tiran and writing down on a little pad, if they could see them, the flag and the name of the ship. Well, of course, you can get all that from Lloyd's, so it was completely pointless. Nonetheless that's what we were doing. This was the level of government understanding, I'm sorry to say, in my own country, as to what the hell we were doing in the Middle East.

The next year, people would happily have given $30 million to have had the Swedes back in Sharm al-Shaykh, but it really didn't impinge much on people's consciousness at the time. That is the kind of confusion and basic misunderstanding that I think tends to get overshadowed a bit by conspiracy theories of who did what to whom and whose fault it was. It really isn't much like that at the time when you're struggling. Even a powerful government is struggling to get some level of stability out of the situation, which has grown in all directions unexpectedly, which has caused all sorts of horrendous disasters to a whole lot of innocent people on the ground. I'm all for discussing conspiracies, and I suppose they do have a part, but I think the important thing is to try to get a handle on the web of complicated relationships and reactions that actually do fuel and run major disasters.

Alfred Atherton: I'm prompted by some of Tahsin Basheer's remarks to reflect again the view from the working level. Let me say I was glad to hear you [Tahsin Basheer], after you outlined all the conspiracy theories, make clear that you don't necessarily agree with them, because I don't either.

I did appreciate your attempt to describe the mindset of Americans—and I'm speaking of both government and people—toward the Arabs, particularly Nasser and Egypt, on the one hand, and toward Israel on the other. I'm sorry McGeorge Bundy isn't here today because I think his comments tended to reflect what I consider part of the problem in oversimplifying the view of Nasser as the evil spirit. I was glad to hear Luke's comments about this. I spent a great deal of my time in those days, when I was working-level, trying not to be an advocate for, or even to justify, necessarily, Arab positions and Egyptian positions and policies, but trying to explain them to people in the United States—trying to explain why there was a historical background for what we saw as hostile policy toward the United States. We were partly responsible for this, particularly, I think, in the Eisenhower-Dulles era. We helped create the situation that led to these attitudes and to these conflicts and grievances.

I spent a long time trying at least to explain that there was a historical background, there were two sides. I used to quote what I thought was a good piece in the introduction to one of Nadav Safran's books, where he said, "Because of my background people will question my qualification to speak objectively on this issue. Let me state my belief. I happen to believe that both the Arabs and Israelis have unassailable moral arguments, and anyone who does not understand how this is true cannot understand the true nature of tragedy." That used to get people's attention. One of the circuits I was on was known as the ZOA circuit, because the Zionist Organization of America used to have a series of meetings, usually on Sundays. The format was a speaker for ZOA, usually a man named Jacques Torcziner, who was a fiery orator, then someone from the Israeli Embassy or consulate, if there was one in the city. Then I was there. My role was theoretically to explain American policy, but it soon became apparent that I was viewed as the surrogate for the Arabs, that I became the target. What I was really trying to do was explain, not justify. And I think it important to make that distinction.

Having said all of that, and I do agree with a lot of what you [Tahsin Basheer] have said, I'd have to make one point that I don't think you did make, or if you did it was made sotto voce. One of the problems—and it was a problem for those of us trying to help people understand American policy at the time, or to understand where the Arabs were coming from—was precisely the fact that the Arab world had not at that point, from '64 to '67 and right afterward, made the decision to accept Israel. There are historical reasons for this, but the fact of the matter was that the Arab world had not made the decision, and the implication was that if the opportunity came, we would see Israel disappear. The hope was that somehow history would repeat itself. The two-hundred-year crusader kingdom [of Jerusalem] was often cited as an example of how it would come about.

Those of us who were trying to explain the Arab position found it difficult to deal with that issue [nonrecognition of Israel] because it was, of course, a major factor in our strong support for Israel. We saw Israel as something we could not separate ourselves from. We were committed to its survival, and if we could not keep Israel strong enough to survive on its own, if that day came when there would be a showdown, if Israel's existence would be threatened, we would then be drawn in, and obviously that was something to avoid. This was a major obstacle to Americans who were trying to help make American public opinion and policymakers in those days understand that there was an Arab side to the issue as well as a well-presented Israeli side.

Salah Bassiouny: During all the discussions this morning, we tended to forget an uncontested political-military fact. From the outset of the crisis, the U.S. position, which was communicated to Egypt on several occasions directly, and indirectly via the Soviet Union, was a warning to Egypt not to start any hostilities. At the same time, that was the position also of the Soviet Union, which consistently informed Egypt that enough is enough— Egypt should de-escalate and should find a way out from the closure of the Strait of Tiran. So from the United States and the Soviet Union, and even from the assessment of Nasser himself—as explained to Mr. Anderson in the last meeting between an American and Gamal Abd al-Nasser—he was clear that Egypt will not start the war.

The key element for the success of the Israeli attack on Egypt was to have the initiative, and that was something that was well known to the American administration, from the president to all the other departments dealing with this question. The United States was in the know regarding Israeli preparations. The United States, whether the CIA or the Pentagon, was evaluating and assessing every two or three days the capabilities of Israel to defeat the one front or the two fronts or the three fronts, within a week or within two weeks and so forth. The exchange of information between General Amit and Mr. Helms was also to confirm and reconfirm this situation. On June 1 it was final that Israel would start the war. Israel was unleashed, while Egypt was under much pressure from the United States and the Soviet Union not to start the war. My question is, how do you describe this situation? The United States did have diplomatic relations with Egypt, the United States did have interests in Egypt, but the United States failed to tell Egypt for five days before the war that there was a serious situation, or at least to give Egypt the type of warning warranted by such circumstances. How do we explain and how do we describe such a situation?

Janice Stein: My comment follows directly on Ambassador Bassiouny's and Bill Quandt's points. It addresses the issue of the dog that didn't bark, and dogs that don't bark are equivalent to collusive theories or conspiracy theories. Let's take one other historical example directly related to the Middle East, in which some of the participants are reversed. We now have good historical evidence that the Soviet Union tried hard to restrain Egypt and Syria through much of 1973. We also have good evidence that the Soviets were informed and their intelligence assessments were that war, an attack by Egypt and Syria on Israel, was coming, was likely. They got hard information of this attack on October 4, forty-eight to seventy-two hours before the war started. I think it would be inaccurate to charge that the Soviet Union conspired, or colluded, with Egypt and Syria under those circumstances. [The Soviets] also sold military equipment that Egypt and Syria repeatedly and insistently requested throughout this period.

Carl Brown has made clear that in the context of close relationships with allies, the superpowers were often more managed than they were managers. There was great frustration in Moscow about the inability to get Soviet advice heeded. Their advice was listened to but it wasn't heeded, and there was great frustration in Cairo over the Soviets' attempts, repeatedly, to make their voice heard and to deliver a message that was unwelcome in Cairo. It's a far more complex and nuanced set of relationships. If one looked simply at the outcome, and at the argument that Soviet government officials and the intelligence agency knew seventy-two hours before the fact that an Egyptian and Syrian attack was coming and did not tell other interested governments, one would have to draw a conclusion of conspiracy or collusion. In fact, that would be, I think, a historically inaccurate judgment, and that's why in this kind of discussion we need some criteria of evidence.

Dennis Kux: I want to follow up on the subject that we touched on before: the *Liberty*. I wonder whether Secretary Rostow, Mr. Helms, and General Amit want to comment on that, to fill in some of the picture for the record as to what happened and why.

Eugene Rostow: At the time [of the attack on the *Liberty*] I was chairman of the committee that I referred to yesterday, and on receiving the news I immediately pursued it with the Israelis and finally got the text of the court-martial proceedings, as well as numerous documents from the Israeli Embassy and from our own government. I did a fairly thorough job at that time, and I remained interested necessarily thereafter and read some of the books and articles about it. My recollection is clear about the court-martial proceedings. They were full and impressive and sober, and they portrayed the picture of accident. I was convinced, and I am convinced, that it was a pure accident.

The story went, as I recall, that there was a long table in the headquarters of the Israeli naval authorities or the combined authorities indicating the positions, troops, and ships in the area. They swept the board clear during the lunch break and reconstituted it from new information or information that was newly confirmed. In the morning the table showed an American ship, the *Liberty,* with an American flag, and when they came back after lunch the American ship wasn't there, so the operations orders were given on the basis of the second display table, not the first. When the Israeli torpedo boat approached the *Liberty,* which had been badly damaged by Israeli bombing, one of the sailors on the torpedo boat saw a circular lifesaver that said USS *Liberty* on it. The Israeli boat immediately stopped, and of course the situation had changed. They asked if they could help. Of course the people on the *Liberty* were mad as hell and said, "No, we don't need your help." But I never read anything in all the voluminous literature—I don't pretend to have read it all—that contradicts the testimony of those concerned in that court-martial proceedings.

There are strong emotions on the subject, as there always are when people are killed by friendly fire, as we can now see in Britain and in our own forces. But the great difficulty always was to find any conceivable reason. I could never imagine any Israeli, no matter what his politics were, deliberately firing on the American flag. And the theory that it was done to prevent the United States from knowing about the attack on Syria seems even less plausible than the totally fantastic theories that were advanced in some of the earlier books, particularly those by the former Illinois Congressman [Paul Findley in *They Dared to Speak Out* (Westport, Conn: Lawrence Hill & Co., 1985)].

Lucius Battle: I do not believe that it was an accident. I do not know what the exact motive was unless it was the Syrian matter.

Richard Helms: My distinct impression is this: The Israelis have their position, a lot of the Americans have their position. This has been discussed and rediscussed and rehashed and worked over, and it's a debate that gets nowhere. The Israelis are stuck with their position, we are stuck with our position. The external evidence was relatively clear. It was a bright sunny day. The American flag was flying, and this plane came in and attacked. Now, if it was an accident, or if it was a mistake, if it was a misidentification, or whatever the Israeli case may be, they've got that case. We've got our case. But you can discuss this until the moon comes down on the eastern front and we won't be any farther ahead than we are now.

Talcott Seelye: I think you are not being frank. The fact is that you have intercepts. The Israelis were actually aware that this was an American ship. The Israeli pilots knew that this was an American ship. We have the testimony of Lyndon Johnson, of Dean Rusk and . . .

Meir Amit: Do we have these documents?

Talcott Seelye: Yes, there are intercepts.

Gideon Rafael: The story has been spread. There is no intercept. If you introduce them, I would be glad.

Talcott Seelye: Okay. Talk to our ambassador in Beirut, Dwight Porter.

Dennis Kux: I was just wondering, Mr. Helms, what you thought personally about it? Just as Secretary Rostow gave his view, what was your personal view?

Richard Helms: I don't know what use my personal view has. I mean, I've just told you what I believe happened and I don't understand how it was that this was an accident. I'm just saying that by discussing it back and forth, back and forth, it was an accident, it wasn't an accident, you do, you don't, you do, you don't. . . .

Lucius Battle: This is an issue that has not gone away, but I think it's time to go away from it here. I don't see any point in pursuing it farther, and I think that the views have been stated by several of us. Mine are considered and are not going to change. I have several more names on the list. Dr. Dawn.

Ernest Dawn: Well, conspiracy theories have been around a long time. They are still publishing books on who actually killed Abraham Lincoln. They come out every year. I asked a question in an earlier session but, unfortunately, there wasn't time to answer. I asked General Amit or others, did the Israelis actually devote any contingency planning to what would happen in case they did preempt without the approval of, in fact against the wishes of, the United States? And what could the United States have done to them? I'd like to ask, did anyone in the American government devote any attention to finding what they could do in case they wanted to prevent or counter an Israeli preemption? I don't think they did, but it is still a vital question.

Mr. Cockburn and all of them here are taking the stand that the Israelis needed a green light or at least a yellow light; they had to have it. That is strongly suggested . . . by the argument. The reason I'm asking my question is, what really could the United States have done if we'd said don't do it?

What could we have done to Israel to keep it from carrying out the campaign it obviously was able to do? Mr. Cockburn points out, as others have, that the United States presumably did not approve of the attack on Syria, and yet we couldn't do a damn thing about it. Getting an infantry company into motion is one hell of a hard job, but it's not just bureaucratic bumbling; it's war. Even small wars are big things. It takes a lot of work to get them into being. And one thing I know about this whole question from the beginning: Zionists, Israelis, on the one hand, Arabs on the other, and their various friends, have always said that the British could have done this, the Americans could have done that, when the simple fact of the matter is that much of the time the great powers were not able to do a single thing that would have changed the situation at that time.

Victor Israelyan: I am perturbed listening to this discussion and sometimes surprised by the lack of ability or desire to understand the Soviet perception. Today, Ambassador Basheer, speaking of the conspiracy theories, said that one of these was the Soviet double standard toward Nasser. I do not agree with that completely, and I would like to try to strengthen your understanding of how the Soviets sometimes think. It seems to me that was the case in this particular event.

Fifty years ago—fifty-one, to be exact—the prime minister of Britain, Churchill, warned Stalin of a great concentration of German troops along the Soviet western border. And there were other indications to Stalin of the same thing. How did Stalin react? He didn't react. He didn't care and the result was the catastrophic defeat of the Soviet army in '41–'42.

Now, how have the Soviets seen the situation in the Middle East? Soviet representatives in Israel, Syria, and Egypt have either heard of or witnessed certain indications of Israel's growing militant activity, and nobody will challenge that. [The indications were] Rabin's declaration, some mobilizing measures in Israel, and so on. I'm not challenging Ambassador Kornienko's oath that he didn't see the instruction to Pojidaev, but let's accept that there was a warning. What's wrong with that? It was a warning to a friend that there are some measures, military measures, undertaken by Israel. Exaggerated? Yes, but do you think that all the information that Stalin got, or any leader gets, was accurate? Not necessarily. Certainly, if it was sixteen divisions, that's nonsense, but there was a warning to a friend.

How did Nasser react to that? He overreacted. And what was the attitude of the Soviets to that? They wanted to cool him down as a friend, and that was consistent with the friendly attitude of Moscow toward Nasser. I do not see here any double standard toward Nasser. In general, my feeling is that, in many statements, this perception, this vision of the world by the

Soviet leaders is ignored, disregarded. Unfortunately, many politicians and researchers measure the Soviet behavior from the Western point of view, and that is wrong.

This tragic historical experience of Russia, of the Soviet Union [in 1941], played a certain role when the Soviet leaders felt that since something was going wrong in Israel, the Arabs had to be prepared for the worst. The Soviet Union warned them, but their reaction was unexpected.

Gideon Rafael: Let me at the outset comment on this statement [by Talcott Seelye]: It is as inaccurate as it was offensive to Israel. Israel is not a pariah state. The policy of the Arab states before President Sadat made that great long jump over the barrier was the defamation of Israel, its isolation, and eventually its elimination. Israel, which has established in recent months relations with China, with India, which has relations with nearly all Asian and all European states, with nearly all the new republics of the former Soviet Union—is this a pariah state? And, I must say, it is not exactly expressing the spirit of this meeting to characterize Israel this way.

The second point, on a more scientific note, is this. We are discussing here conspiracies. Conspiracy means . . . that one pretends something but does something completely different. It is a theory to mislead your enemy or your friend. Permit me to quote the message that we gave to Secretary-General U Thant on May 22, 1967, the morning when he set out for Cairo. That message was formulated in a way that it should reach President Nasser. This is the text: "The freedom of passage of Israeli-bound ships in the Strait of Tiran is of supreme national interest and right, which it will assert and defend, whatever the sacrifice. Israel's refusal to return to a position of blockade is firm and unconditional. We urgently request the secretary-general to consider methods of ensuring the retention of a suitable United Nations presence at Sharm al-Shaykh." I must state, to my regret, after having seen the minutes of the meeting between the secretary-general and President Nasser, this message was never in this form brought to the attention of President Nasser when the president of Egypt met with the secretary-general in Cairo. The message did not leave any doubt about the position of Israel. [U Thant did inform Egyptian Foreign Minister Mahmoud Riad of Rafael's *démarche* when they met on May 24.—*Ed.*]

I want to say something about conspiracy. The breeding ground for conspiracy is suspicion, distrust. And I didn't find any better description of this situation than by a man who is now prominent in Russian affairs, the Russian foreign minister, Andrei Kozyrev. He wrote in 1988 in the Soviet journal *International Affairs,* when he was deputy chief of the International Organizations Administration in the Soviet Foreign Ministry, "It is difficult to trust a society gripped by total suspicion and it is as difficult to trust a regime which does not trust its people in any matter. The problem of confidence knows no state boundaries and admits no reference of sovereignty and non-interference in internal affairs." I think he put his finger exactly on the point. Conspiracy theories are emanating from countries that are gripped by suspicion, suspicion toward regimes, both international and domestic regimes.

Was it a conspiracy when Egypt, Syria, and the Gulf states entered into a coalition with the United States in order to defeat Saddam Hussein's aggression? It was a coalition of cooperation. And, in the same sense, I can speak about the coalition in 1956 between Israel, France, and England—not that I justify the action as it happened, but it was not a conspiracy. Was it a conspiracy when the United States cooperated with the Soviet Union after it was attacked by Hitler? It was an alliance; it was fighting together. So, I think we should be more careful about using the term "conspiracy."

On attacks from Syria: I think there is no controversy that there were attacks, terrorist attacks and so on, but to acquit the Syrian government of any responsibility is not correct. Attacks were carried out by organizations, not only Fatah, but Saiqa, an organization under the command of Syrian officers, equipped with Syrian arms, financed by Damascus. It participated in the harassment of Israel. The situation reached the point that, in April 1967, the secretary-general of the UN issued a very strong warning in regard to these terrorist incursions into Israel and, as a matter of fact, indicated that they could lead to grave complications.

Speaking about Syria, Husni Zaim was mentioned. Well, Husni Zaim really made an effort to find an overall solution, not exactly on the terms we would have liked, but he didn't survive his initiative more than two months. He was assassinated. Yet fortunately he still managed to conclude the armistice agreement with Israel in July 1949.

I will finish with one thing:

I had been in the 1950s in charge of contacts with President Nasser and Egypt on peace, and I can only fully confirm the conclusions of Professor Shamir, that there was no Egyptian opening we could see at the time—neither myself, directly involved, nor the intermediaries of the United States, Anderson, Jackson, and others.

Eugene Rostow: I've heard the discussion about conspiracy with great interest, and I sympathize strongly with and support Bill Quandt's comments. All I can contribute on the subject is the legal definition, which might have helped if it had come earlier. Conspiracy, our courts say, and the

British courts say the same thing, I think, is a contract to achieve illegal ends by legal means or legal ends by illegal means. And that's all. You have either an illegal end, or illegal means, or both.

Tahsin Basheer: I started by saying I don't believe in conspiratorial theory, but not because conspiracies don't happen. They happen, but they don't give enough explanation to the complicated and complex reality. In the Middle East, the relevance of conspiratorial theory, whether in the perception of the people or in the reality of history, is more abundant, and I start with Sykes-Picot—you know, the whole theory of how the British in secrecy negotiated two totally incompatible agreements. But it did not end there. I wish Mr. Helms were here.

The first time, what did Nasser know of America, an Egyptian colonel who had never met foreigners before, aside from Israelis in the '48 war? It was Kim Roosevelt, [William] Lakeland. What was the first gift of America to Nasser? Twenty million dollars cash in a bank by a CIA agent. They thought that he was another colonel who could be bribed. He counted every bloody dollar, and when ten dollars were missing, he asked [Hassan] Tuhaimi, where the hell are the ten dollars? He didn't know what to do with them. He built a tower for communications.

For a long time America was seen through the optic of CIA and intelligence, and Nasser was plagued by the Lavon affair. I agree with Eppy about his proposal and with Shamir, but the first experience of a young people trying to be independent was the Lavon affair. That cast Israel not as a nationality trying to find a home after thousands of years of homelessness, but as a people finding their home by doing the Arab in and now by doing Egypt in. The Lavon affair [an Israeli attempt to disrupt U.S.-Egyptian relations in 1954] tended to undercut a trend that existed, well documented, in the RCC, the Egyptian military command, to play down the Arab-Israeli conflict. We reduced our military budget for two years, and that's important.

I agree that in '49 we did not accept the armistice as a permanent settlement. In fact, we wanted a return, somewhere, to negotiate between the status quo of the armistice agreement and the partition plan. Nasser accepted that when [British Prime Minister] Eden proposed it in the Guildhall speech in 1955; Israel at the time, Ben-Gurion, would not cede an inch. But with Lavon . . . and then the Suez attack . . . Suez—unlike what Rafael is saying, that the Sevres agreement was another deal—was a secret agreement. There is a difference between countries, but what Bill Quandt was saying is that the difference between conspiracy and arrangements or cooperation is the degree of secrecy. Nasser never expected the British to double-cross him. He discounted this, and when he heard propellers of the British planes, he went up on the roof and said, "Uh, it happened." Then the idea of cross and double cross became a phantom that existed in the Middle East, and it continued. Saddam Hussein is a victim, a doer and a victim, of this.

But where do we have conspiracies in the Middle East? Kim Roosevelt has a whole story of how he toppled Mossadegh. That is not fiction. That happened. *Centerpiece* is a book that the CIA stopped, and there's a watered-down version of that book. Who is Husni Zaim? Syria under a parliamentary system would not have concluded an armistice agreement with Israel. Then there was a coup, and now we have an Israeli professor who has a well-documented book about how the CIA got rid of the parliamentary system and got Husni Zaim [instead]. That's why Husni Zaim rushed to find a final settlement, but the man didn't have enough time to do it. So, let's leave that. Now, in peace, we can cooperate better on this.

What irritates me, as a civilian, is that the first know-how of new regimes and new leadership about power in the West was through the technology of secrecy, the technology of control and propaganda. And every Arab government perfected, not the technology of knowledge, of research, but the technology of control. The Arabs have good [security], you know—the systems are almost foolproof, they all existed, they don't change. Where did they learn this? From America, later from Russia. Where did even Qadhafi get his intelligence service? From a former CIA man who turned. So, we would wish that any future cooperation would have the Americans sending us the CIA, because there is a role, a limited utility for intelligence, but we will need also some unlimited utility for democratic practices and legalism, which we never got. Not yesterday and not today. Not from the British, not from the Americans.

What exactly did Nasser do in '67? He never shot the first bullet. To him, he did not commit an aggression. America told him not to commit it. Russia told him not to commit it. He obliged, and then the story turned. The theory that preemption is permitted is something new in the world. It was new until '67; that's when it started. You attack somebody and then say, but he planned to attack me, and that's the difference between Johnson and de Gaulle.

Now, when I said the United States targeted Nasser, the United States until today never understood what the Arabs want. The Arabs are people. I'm not talking only about regimes and government. The Arabs need more integration of their economies and politics. These little states here and there, or statelets . . . I mean, the United States now is in a ridiculous agreement to defend certain shaykhs who own countries and who use the United States, as poor grocers say in some parts of Brooklyn, to buy protection from above. And they think that by paying American money, they can use you to do that. By doing that, you are intervening in the normal, internal domestic affair of a fragmented nation that wants to reintegrate. We have to find a way to do it, and that's why I want peace with Israel, exactly, to be able—the Israelis do their thing, we do our things, with rules of the game respected by both.

Now, the same mindset that did not understand the Arab nationalism of Nasser's days is not understanding the forces of Islam today. There are many Islams. It is complex, but many think that Islam is the new enemy, like Japan was the yellow enemy. These things are [a matter of] internal debate in the Muslim world—whether it needs reformation or counter-reformation. It's complex. It is [mistaken] for any superpower to think that it can manipulate whose shaykh is right and whose shaykh is wrong; it needs a lot of understanding.

Now, after June 9, Israel had a fantastic chance to offer the Arabs, and especially the Palestinians, any reasonable settlement. Yet Israel came with the idea to go with Egypt alone to reach a contracted peace. It was impossible for Egypt at the time to accept it. That would have been surrender. We never accept surrender. To make people accept compromises, they have to feel that they are strong, that they are successful. Sadat could not have made Camp David without having the perception of victory, or at least some degree of it. The Arabs cannot be cowed. If you give them a sense that, in a historical compromise with the Israelis, both will win, it can work. If you dictate it, it will never work.

In historical justice, Nasser never had a contingency plan of any kind to eliminate Israel. I asked Mahmoud Riad, what did you expect in June? What to do? He didn't know. They wanted to improve, to return to the status quo ante of 1956. And Israel, the mirror image, wanted to correct the mistakes that it made in 1956 by not getting American approval. I personally think Nasser miscalculated, but he did not necessarily act illegally. There is a difference between these, but what did Nasser want to do? I think the best interpretation of his escalation . . . is that he escalated, and he wanted to de-escalate, and while he was de-escalating Israel caught him, and America gave the yellow light or whatever light. What he wanted to do was written by Robert Stephens in a book [presumably *Nasser: A Political Biography*, by Robert H. Stephens (New York, 1972)—*Ed.*]. He [Nasser] said he had risked war above all because he believed that sooner or later the Arabs, particularly Egypt, must turn and face the power of Israel or live forever at the mercy of Israel's political will and her supposed international backers. He ran the risk and failed. That's why, to end conspiracies, you have to be active and sensitive about seeking the workings of peace, and when we do that, we will be talking about joint projects and not joint conspiracies.

Andrew Cockburn: I understand now that it is important to label an analysis of any series of events you don't like as a conspiracy theory and then take a hefty swig of political science and move on smartly to the cultural phenomenon thereof. What I was doing—and I didn't ask to be called a conspiracy theorist—was simply trying to point out certain facts, many of them more or less unanimously agreed on around this table, although people may label them in different ways. What I was trying to inject is the notion that perhaps, first of all, Israel had taken the initiative in a number of areas, particularly on the Syrian front. As Dr. Rafael, I think, said, we should not excuse Syrian behavior. I quite agree. Nor should we excuse or ignore Israeli behavior there.

Richard Helms, I think, is keener to find, to detect conspiracy theories than I am, since I certainly wasn't accusing FBIS of being part of a conspiracy to censure Yitzhak Rabin's speech, just that FBIS wasn't very good there.

On the *Liberty* issue: I am sure lots of people don't want to reopen that, but I think it's worth saying that I agree with Luke Battle and Mr. Seelye. The evidence is incontestable that it happened, that there was the American flag. It took six hours. There were, we have it on good authority, intercepts to suggest the Israelis knew exactly what they were attacking. I agree it's a mystery, why it happened. To take such a phenomenal risk seems to me extraordinary, but it's hard to argue. It's impossible, I believe, to argue, honestly anyway, that it could have been an accident.

I mentioned my friend at Oxford simply because I was reminded of him by hearing again in the last few days the notion that Israel's survival was at stake. We've had good testimony here that it certainly wasn't at stake. No intelligence estimate held that Israel could not defeat any combination of Arabs. The closing of the strait, even if that had endured, wouldn't have threatened the survival of Israel. Israel had functioned perfectly well prior to '56 without access through the strait. So, I was just interested to hear this [notion about Israel's survival] popping up again, which was of course the whole image the world carried away from the June '67 war. I don't agree with whoever said that Israel's reputation went down after the '67 war. It went up because of this extraordinary story, as everyone perceived it, of David defeating Goliath. As we now know, that was not really the case, but it's an important part of the mindset, the mythology of '67.

Ambassador Bassiouny, I think, has really put it better than I can. When you have a set of agreed-upon facts about General Amit's visit, the warnings to Egypt not to fire the first shot, the assent, the go-ahead to Israel to fire the first shot, what do we call that? I think we might possibly consider calling it a contract to secure legal ends by illegal means, or the other way around.

There was an interesting idea that, if you took a look at the parallel of 1973, one could, therefore, using the same criteria, accuse the Russians of conspiracy. I don't. I've seen no record—I could be wrong—of Sadat in Cairo in '73, or Assad in Damascus, sitting around and waiting for whomever they might have sent to Moscow to give the news, to come back to decide whether to go ahead. That was, we have on numerous Israeli accounts, what was happening in Jerusalem: When General Amit got back, they were all waiting for him at Eshkol's house to know if they could go ahead. That seems to me one important difference. I mean, the whole thing did depend on American assent. The Egyptian-Syrian attack in '73 did not, so I don't think it's a clear, a good, parallel.

Dr. Dawn raised the question of its not being complicity, because what would the Americans have done if the Israelis had ignored them? Well, the Israelis didn't ignore them and felt they couldn't ignore them. The dramatic accounts of what was going on in the Israeli inner cabinet, and the meetings with the Israeli generals in those last weeks before the war, were of Eshkol desperately holding on, of the generals saying, let's go, let's go, let's go, and Eshkol saying, no, we have to wait for LBJ. Some people may feel the Israelis could have gone ahead anyway. Prime Minister Eshkol, who was certainly no fool, didn't think so.

It's interesting, what Dr. Rafael had to say about the notion that Suez was not a conspiracy but a coalition. I think we're getting some interesting definitions here. Supposing I were the arch-conspiracy theorist, it would make my task in analyzing '67 easy if we simply said any coalition is a conspiracy. Maybe it is.

I knew I was going to attract brickbats for quoting anonymous intelligence sources to the effect that Jim Angleton had talked to the Israelis about what to do about Nasser. I find it bizarre, the proposition that he never did that in all these many conversations. He spent a lot of time in Israel and the Israelis came here. Dr. Amit was saying to me yesterday that he always made a point [of seeing] Angleton when he came here and he valued him as a friend and brilliant man. Are we to believe that they never discussed what Nasser might be up to? What could be done about the threat of Nasser? What could be done about the threat of Nasser and the Soviets? I think they almost certainly did. Otherwise, we are left with this bizarre notion which I find odd (and I did ask the question yesterday and I got an answer, but I still find it hard to understand, and I've never been in government or a national security person or even the lofty heights of a political science professor): that everyone, sort of, marched into this war, certainly on the American side and perhaps on the Israeli side too, with no idea of what was to happen except that Israel would win.

Was there no one—no one at the top, no one in this room—who had any idea, or even bothered to think, what might happen on day seven after the well-predicted Israeli victory? No one thought of what effect this will have on Nasser's position in Egypt? I wonder. No one thought if this will lead to a change of position of Jordan, and possibly the West Bank will get occupied? In those last days, when General Amit was here or even before, these questions really crossed no one's mind in Washington? No one sat down and thought about it? No one talked to the Israelis about it? No one asked the Israelis about it? We have high authority that that, indeed, was the case. I find it hard to believe, but then I'm that sort of pariah conspiracy theorist, I guess.

CHAPTER 7

🥄 Conclusions

Richard B. Parker

The conference has raised more questions than it has answered, and that is perhaps a measure of its success. As a number of participants pointed out, it has demonstrated the need for (1) more study of the underlying causes and the global and regional contexts in which the war occurred and (2) more information about decision making and motivation in all of the states involved, particularly in Syria, the former Soviet Union, and Egypt, in that order.

While we know a good deal more today than we did in 1967 about the inner workings of the Egyptian government at that time, there is still no satisfactory answer to the question, what made Gamal Abd al-Nasser act as he did? Specifically, how could he have thought, as seems to be the case, that his military forces were strong enough to confront Israel's with one hand tied behind them, so to speak, because of their involvement in the Yemen? To what extent did he actually control the decisions being made, and to what extent was Abd al-Hakim 'Amr running things? Was there a concerted Egyptian plan to react, or were Nasser and 'Amr merely stumbling into catastrophe? Was there something else that could have been done that would have pulled the parties back from war?

Tahsin Basheer argued in this panel and the previous one that Nasser was trying to de-escalate toward the end of May but ran out of time. If that was in fact the case, it was not apparent to diplomats in Cairo at the time. In retrospect, U Thant's visit of May 23–24 was probably Nasser's last chance to stop the rush to war. His failure to seize it and the escalation in Egyptian rhetoric in the following week raise serious questions as to how interested he was in taking steps to avoid a military confrontation. As William Zartman commented in this panel, it was as though someone who had rushed over the brink and was falling fast kept saying that he expected someone to stop him because he had had no intention of hitting the ground when he jumped.

We also know more about the Soviets than we did in 1967, but not much. Soviet intentions in particular remain obscure, but as we have seen there is not even agreement on what they actually did. There is much work to be done in the archives of the Central Committee, of the Foreign Ministry, and the military and intelligence establishments, as well as interviewing survivors, if we are ever to know with any certainty what the Soviets had in mind and why they passed the false warning of an Israeli troop buildup to the Egyptians on May 13. Perhaps they had nothing particular in mind and there is some banal operational or bureaucratic explanation for what happened. At this point we can only speculate, given the absence of documentation or the reliable testimony of knowledgeable survivors, who are scarcer with each passing year, and none of whom seems to have written memoirs on the subject.

Syria remains a black hole. We know almost nothing directly from Syrian official sources about the motives and actions of the Syrian leaders at the time, many of whom are either dead or in prison. The theory put forth by Patrick Seale in his book *Asad*—that the Syrians were victims of a U.S.-Israeli plot—is popular with some, but Ernest Dawn in his commentary in panel 3 discussed the internal situation in Syria that could have led Damascus to provoke the crisis. Neither thesis was discussed in the conference, and Ambassador Tomeh indicated that we would have to await his memoirs to know his views. [He has since died and we have no word of his memoirs.] That the radicals in Damascus were behind the report of Israeli troop concentrations is a plausible proposition, but we need a good deal more information before this or any other conclusion about Syrian behavior can be drawn. There is a major task of historiography to be performed here.

On the other hand, some answers did emerge from the discussion. There seemed to be general agreement that miscalculation was a major cause of the war. Shimon Shamir, for instance, saw miscalculation and misperception on the part of all parties as the reason that war broke out when it did. Nasser's misreading of Israeli capabilities and his own, and the Israelis' misreading of his probable reaction to what they were doing, led both to misjudge the results of their policy decisions. This was hardly a new phenomenon. As Raymond Garthoff pointed out, the same forces were at work in the Cuban missile crisis of 1962. He saw both crises as particularly clear examples of the miscalculation syndrome.

The misperceptions and miscalculations were in part an outgrowth of the continued hostility and noncommunication between Israel and its neighbors, as well as of time-honored stereotypes and conspiratorial analyses. They were also the result of unrealistic expectations and perceptions regarding the roles of the great powers, which were not borne out when the time came. In particular, Nasser's obsession with what he saw as the hostility of the United States, and Israeli disillusionment with American failure to force the blockade of the Strait of Tiran, were in different ways factors driving the parties to decisions that made war increasingly likely. In this regard, Carl Brown suggested that we needed to step back and look at the broader context, to see the perceptions and assumptions regarding the rules of the game, bearing in mind the inability of statesmen to control events and the dynamics of the patron-client relationship in which the former is manipulated by the latter.

Bernard Reich listed a variety of factors which he thought led to a war that all parties said they did not want. There were problems of perception and communication, both horizontal and vertical, the problem of messages that never got delivered, the asymmetry of access to American leadership on the parts of Israel and Egypt, U.S. failure, as seen by the Israelis, to honor the commitment regarding the Gulf of Aqaba, and the vagaries of the patron-client relationship.

Lucius Battle responded to Alexander Cockburn's expression of disbelief that the Americans had no clear idea what the aftermath of the war would be by saying that he could not recall any war in which the United States had a clear vision of that sort when the war began. We never knew what would happen when crises ended. In this case he felt there were no victors, but everyone lost. He said the crisis illustrated the need for better coordination internally and better communications externally.

William Zartman commented that Brian Urquhart had told us very eloquently why the UN could not have done more to prevent the war from happening but that we really needed to look at that question in more depth and detail. The fact that a given course of action may not seem bureaucratically possible or useful should not necessarily determine whether it should be followed.

The most interesting discussion in panel 7 centered on Alfred Atherton's question, raised here a second time, as to when and where U.S. policy changed, in the period June 5–19, from its eighteen-year reliance on the

1949 armistice regimes to one of acquiescence in Israeli retention of the territories seized until such time as the Arabs came forward with an offer of peace. William Quandt said he could not answer the question satisfactorily, but the idea that the United States should hold out for full peace rather than calling for a return to the armistice agreements, which had proven inadequate, was contained in a handwritten message to President Johnson, apparently from Abba Eban, on the second day of the war. Quandt had found no record of any discussion of this concept. Rather, it simply became the way Johnson and the people closest to him began to see things. (See the note on this subject on p. 318.)

Lucius Battle said he did not know where the idea had originated but recalled telling his staff, "We've got to take another look at this, because you're not going to get the Israelis to withdraw the way we did in 1956, on the basis of assurances that once again we'll come to their assistance. We've got to think of a more comprehensive solution to the whole problem before there's any chance of there being a withdrawal." He said he could not remember whether that was his own reaction or whether someone on high had said it to him.

Samuel Lewis commented that no political scientist or historian would dare write in his book that policy changes could be made in the fashion described by Messrs. Atherton, Quandt, and Battle.

Panel 7

Conclusions

Richard Parker: I'm going to start off with some observations, then throw it open to the other panel chairmen for comments, followed by a general discussion.

I think we all agree that we've had a fascinating set of exchanges here. Gideon Rafael pointed out, for instance, that this was the first time that Meir Amit has revealed outside Israel the details of his mission to Washington and what he was told and what he came back with.

Some things have been clarified. Others remain obscure. A number of people have asked why we are paying all this attention to these historical details, some of which seem fairly minor. The short answer is that these details were important. The first step in discovering what lessons there are to be learned from this crisis is to establish what actually happened. The macro aspects are, of course, of overriding importance in explaining why, for instance, war may have been inevitable. Given the nonresolution of the basic issues, it was clear to most of us on the ground at the time that sooner or later there was going to be another round. But we always thought in terms of *later*. It was always three years down the pike.

We haven't really discussed these basic issues because there hasn't been time, for one thing, but the micro details are important to understanding and evaluating some of the macro concepts. If we start, for example, from the macro view that there was a grand Soviet strategy to take over the Middle East—a plausible cold war scenario that was set forth by Gene Rostow in his article and by others in this conference—what are the details that prove it? We have a lot of speculation about what the Soviets were planning to do, but little or no hard data to support it. Shimon Shamir has given us an insight into the ability of the Israeli military to hear selectively and to decide that the Americans were going to tell them this or that by innuendo, and then to deduce what our intentions were, as we deduced from statements by Kremlin leaders what they were really going to do. There has been a great deal of similar deduction from innuendo in composing the bigger pictures of the Six-Day War.

One of the details adduced to support the Soviet grand design theory is that the Soviets planted an obviously false story on the Egyptians, and they must have done so deliberately. They did it three times in the same day. They gave it to the director of intelligence, Salah Nasr, they gave it to Ahmad Hassan al-Feki at the Foreign Ministry, and they gave it to Anwar Sadat in Moscow. It is not possible, the theory goes, that the Soviets did all of these things on the same day in this manner without thinking it through and without having approval at the highest level. Therefore, they must have decided deliberately to mislead the Egyptians.

I've always doubted this interpretation, because I didn't think the Soviets were quite that reckless. We had a long conversation about this with Georgiy Kornienko and Vitaly Naumkin and our Egyptian colleagues last night. When dinner was over, I was convinced that transmission of the report was done routinely and haphazardly and was not a deliberate step directed by the highest government levels of the USSR, but I can't prove it. [Four years later, I am persuaded that history will eventually prove me correct, Ernest Dawn's contrary essay for panel 4 notwithstanding.]

The second fact adduced for the theory of the grand strategy is the Gromyko visit to Cairo starting on March 29, which Gene Rostow thought was important. We don't really know what went on during that visit. Ambassador Bassiouny recalled that the discussions centered around the Israeli threat, although the timing seems a little early for that. We need more details, preferably from the memoranda of conversation, before we can assess the significance of that visit fully. In the absence of such details, I think we can say that the thesis that Gromyko was organizing a takeover of the Middle East is unproven. My own view that there was not a great Soviet plot has been strengthened by what I've heard here. Some of you may feel differently.

We still don't know, for another example, where the story of the twelve Israeli brigades originated. I don't think we'll ever be sure until we see the KGB report that was passed to the Egyptians, or until the man named Sergei, the KGB man in the Cairo embassy, comes forward and says where the report came from. Knowing the way our own Central Intelligence Agency works, I doubt that we will ever hear from the KGB, but it seems to me that this is something our Russian colleagues should be interested in tracing to its source for the sake of clarifying their own record. In the meantime, an effort should be made to find what is in the Egyptian Foreign Ministry archives on the subject.

There are various questions we haven't discussed or haven't discussed enough. Other questions remain unanswered. What did Nasser have in mind? Who was leading, Nasser or 'Amr? How could Nasser have thought his army was ready to take on Israel? That still boggles the mind.

Andrew Cockburn expressed his incredulity that the Americans did not take the time to think through the consequences of what was going to happen if there was a war and Israel won, or Israel lost, or whatever. Sam Lewis and I decided that the reason for Andrew's disbelief is that he hasn't had any real exposure to the American government. In the first place, when we're in a terrible crisis and everybody is dealing with the details minute by minute, nobody important has time to think about anything at all. You've got to make a decision in five minutes, a decision that is literally a matter of life and death for someone, and you haven't time to stop and think, where is this all leading us? You may think about this on your way to the bathroom, but by the end of the day you are so exhausted you haven't time or energy for serious thinking about it.

Andrew has made me think back on what was going on in my mind in Cairo at that time. I think we all believed there's going to be another war and God knows how it's going to turn out. We really expected that the Egyptians would put up a better fight than they did. So did a lot of other people. We thought that it was going to be a difficult war and that it would end, somewhere in the middle of Sinai, in a cease-fire, and people would withdraw. That's about as far as we got in our thinking. [Ruminating on this a year after the conference, I recall that I assumed the war would go on for some time, that the Egyptians would break relations with us, and that our embassy personnel would be interned. I packed a suitcase with spare clothes and left it in my office, just in case. It was provident of me, because I never got back to my residence from the time the war started until I was expelled.]

A related question is the one raised by Sam Lewis and Roy Atherton about the reason we Americans didn't decide early that we really couldn't stop the Israelis and there was no sense in trying, that we should stop trying to restrain them and let them go ahead. Personally I am appalled at this thought, which I think runs contrary to all our philosophy about conflict resolution—that you've got to keep people talking. Who was it who said, "Jaw, jaw, is better than war, war," Theodore Roosevelt? [In fact, Winston Churchill.] But in the backs of our minds—and this is a question Roy [Atherton] brought up that we ought to spend a little time discussing, and it's too bad Gene Rostow is not here—in Cairo certainly we took seriously the repeated reiterations of our intent to honor the obligations of the 1950 Tripartite Declaration [a U.S.-British-French declaration that the three governments would take action both within and outside the UN to prevent violation of frontiers or armistice lines in the region]. We even tried to revive it in 1967, but the French and British refused to do so [having renounced it in 1956 at the time of their participation in the Suez affair]. Our public and private statements at the time were full of Tripartite language. Gene Rostow, Arthur Goldberg, Secretary Rusk, and President Johnson himself all repeatedly said to the parties, this has been the policy of four administrations and we are going to oppose the use of force in the Middle East. But when the time came we did not do so. Why not? You'll have to ask LBJ.

Gene Rostow talked about a decision taken not to go back to a simple cease-fire but to insist on peace, on withdrawal in exchange for peace. This was not the policy, as far as I can tell, before June 5. It was the policy by June 19, by the time of LBJ's meeting with Kosygin at Glassboro, where Johnson kept insisting that withdrawal must be in the context of peace, and Kosygin kept insisting on withdrawal, period. When did the U.S. position change? The decision to change took place in the White House, not in the Department of State. That's a question we might discuss later.

Two years afterward, in the Rogers plan, we were still talking about withdrawal with "insubstantial" changes in the borders, and the idea that twenty-five years later Israel would still be in occupation of the West Bank is something I do not think occurred to any of us in 1967.

Another question that has not come up and that seems to me germane to the U.S. position is the point raised by Leonard Meeker, then the State Department legal adviser, in a memorandum in May 1967, that the Egyptian occupation of Sharm al-Shaykh did not, in itself, constitute justification for

President Lyndon Johnson and Soviet Premier Aleksei Kosygin, Glassboro, New Jersey, June 19, 1967, meeting to discuss resolution of issues created by the Six-Day War. The Soviet foreign minister, Andrei Gromyko, and Ambassador Anatoly Dobrynin stand behind Johnson. Llewellyn Thompson, U.S. ambassador to the USSR, is in the rear. *U.S. News and World Report* photo, Library of Congress collection.

a general war. If I understand his position, as amplified by his remarks yesterday, if an Israeli ship had tried to go through the strait, as General Amit proposed, and had been fired on, the Israelis would have been justified in attacking the garrison at Sharm al-Shaykh and occupying Sharm al-Shaykh in order to guarantee passage. That, I think, is the most that the Egyptians expected. There is a quantum difference between that and the sort of offensive that the Israelis launched. I don't know what happened to Mr. Meeker's memorandum, but it seems to me a valid legal argument that we've let pass. What would have happened if the Israelis had just occupied Sharm al-Shaykh ? If the issue was freedom of passage through the strait, why didn't they just do that?

Commentary

Ernest Dawn: I think it might be worthwhile to say a bit about the 1967 war as a case of inter-Arab politics and Arab nationalism. Whatever else that crisis was, I think almost everyone will admit that there was an inter-Arab dimension to it. Nowadays it has become rather common to say that Arab nationalism and Pan-Arabism are dead and have no influence. Yet I think that nationalism, Arab nationalism and Pan-Arabism, are as alive today as they were in 1967, when they played an important part in leading to this war—I think the major part. It created the crisis. Without that inter-Arab crisis, there would not have been a war. There would have been, at least, no opportunity for a war.

We have a notion of nationalism as a unifying force that brings people together, makes them strong, vigorous, progressive. This is a part of the Euromythic version of history. It's a myth. A nation is a political construction, and all nations are divided against each other. Most of them, probably all of them, have been unified by military force, held together by military force. Unification hasn't been possible in the Arab world, although there have been many contenders for it, and this [idea] is going to go on.

It is true that Arab nationalism has never unified the Arabs for a war, but if you think the American soldiers were all unified in favor of the war in 1941, you weren't in the army. There were a lot of people, some of them in high places, who thought that that was the wrong war all the way through.

Arab nationalism has led governments to do things that they think are against their own interests. This was true in 1948. It was true in 1967. It is very much a part of the situation today. Arab nations may not be able to unite and go to war, but they can break off diplomatic relations. They can create disturbances. They can make things difficult for people on the outside who want to be in there doing something, and that will happen unless. . . .

Sam Lewis put forward the hypothesis that if Israel had gone ahead and attacked earlier, if it had not occupied the West Bank, the world would be better off. That is a correct hypothesis, although it is counterfactual. But I think it's a mistake to think that all the bad parts of the situation today came from the Six-Day War. I think, perhaps, it may be better to say that the war created the situation, a chance to improve the situation, but that chance has been lost through subsequent actions by governments.

The basic problem is that the Israeli government and the Arab governments have had irreconcilable aims from the beginning and essentially still do. Each of them has limited capabilities to achieve its full aims. Neither really can. The Arabs cannot destroy Israel, which—there is no point in hedging about it—most of them would like to do, and nobody before Sadat in 1973 would ever say otherwise. The Israelis have limited capability to impose a peace. In fact, they have no capability to impose a peace on the entire Arab world.

The more important thing I tried to bring out is that the great powers have limited capabilities of influencing these people directly. You'd have to mobilize an enormous military force, incur enormous obligations, to exert your will directly in that way. We can do some things but, the way most governments are situated, there isn't really a lot that can be done in a crisis that comes up suddenly like this one. The Israelis were supposed to be so fearful that they had to have American permission to go ahead and attack, yet at the same time they go ahead and attack Syria when they know damn well that they don't have American approval, so much so that they are prepared to attack the *Liberty* in order to keep us from knowing what they are going to do. These are what I think may be the two most significant elements to think about in the future.

Lucius Battle: I was a bit troubled by the criticism, made by my colleague this morning, that we had not planned for the aftermath of the war. First of all, there has been no war that we've entered where we knew what was going to happen thereafter. The things that we thought might happen, that were going to be so good, did not happen. Look at Panama, where we thought the problem of drugs would be resolved. It wasn't resolved at all. We thought that we would free up the economy, that it would be improved by virtue of the change in administrations. It wasn't true at all. You might argue, I suppose, that we did what we said we were going to do in Grenada. I think even that campaign was sort of Gilbert and Sullivan, undertaken mainly for domestic [U.S.] political reasons more than anything else. Certainly in the Gulf war, it seems to me, we had not thought through what we were trying to do, and what we thought was going to happen in a simple way didn't happen at all. You've still got two nations destroyed and Saddam Hussein's still in power.

I think we obviously should have planned, but I don't think we planned for any war. In World War II we certainly didn't know what was going to happen. The Four Freedoms and the unconditional surrender and such ideas were rather sweeping, but not really very precise . . . and if anything the unconditional surrender may have been a mistake.

As I think about this, I'm rather surprised to find that I have not believed for a long time that the 1967 war really produced any victors. I'm not sure that any of these wars that we are talking about have produced victors. They have really worsened the situation; while I agree with my colleague here that everything in the Middle East can't be blamed on the Six-Day War, I think a good deal of it can be. I don't think it has enhanced Israel's position in the world or America's position in the world or the Arab position in the world. And I think it's caused a lot of suffering and a lot of hardship, and development in directions we did not contemplate and did not want.

Two rather trivial points nevertheless seem to be rather fundamental. One, it is clear there needs to be better coordination within governments, and somewhere there ought to be somebody who has "policy spokesman" stuck on his head, so you'll know who's supposed to be able to tell what policies are. The numbers of times we had confusion about what policy was and about who told what to whom is really astonishing. Better coordination and a firmer hand within the governments are needed. The broader question is better external communications. A lot of what went wrong in this case simply had to do with governments not understanding what other governments were thinking.

Carl Brown: I don't want to argue against micro analysis, but I do want to suggest that the one dimension that was less well covered than it needs to be—especially in this kind of meeting, where so many participants could recall what they remembered and how they saw things—is the wider context. We need to integrate better the crucial eyewitness accounts with efforts at general interpretation, which is never easy. Alexis de Tocqueville once noted: "I have come across men of letters who have written history without taking a part in public affairs, and politicians who have concerned themselves with producing events without thinking about them. I have observed that the first are always inclined to find general causes, whereas the second, living in the midst of disconnected daily facts, are prone to imagine that everything is attributable to particular incidents, and that the wires they pull are the same as those that move the world. It is to be presumed that both are equally deceived."

We have emphasized here almost exclusively the effort to find out exactly who did what, when, to whom, and why. Just as historians say intellectual history, properly understood, is not just the history of intellectuals, so diplomatic history is not just the history of diplomats. We have to get into the systemic aspects. What are the perceptions, often unconsciously held, of oneself, or of a group self, and the outer world? What are the assumptions, often unconsciously held, about the rules of the game? An equally important issue, never quite brought into focus (some of the comments, if I understood them correctly, of my colleagues from Egypt, were touching on this), is that we are not paying enough attention to the psychological dimension, to the group mindsets. To some extent this touches on the topic that Andrew Cockburn was afflicted with, and I use that word advisedly.

I have in mind the speech that Eshkol made late in the 1967 crisis. I remember several analysts pointing out that he made it at a time when he was very tired. He'd been in meeting after meeting. He looked like a defeated man, and apparently the speech was a disaster in terms of Israeli public opinion. So I see nothing wrong with two quite different viewpoints—that the military were confident, for good reason, hawkish, ready to go, but that the Israeli body politic was dealing with a badly shaken up, even traumatized, society. Equally, I think we have to pay more attention than we have, as Ernest Dawn mentioned, to what would go and what wouldn't go within the Arab body politic—the Egyptian, the Jordanian, and various others. This can be done without getting into apologetics or stereotyping. It's not as easy to pin down as this or that document, but I think we badly need that kind of dimension if we are going to move from the micro analysis that we've done so effectively here to the necessary big picture.

I have long been persuaded that the Middle East, and especially the Arab-Israeli portion of the Middle East, is properly to be characterized as a distinctive international relations subsystem that shows certain approaches to conflicts and negotiations, and to the daily diplomacy and crises as well, approaches that are not lacking in other parts of the world but that are present in a more pronounced way in the Middle East. I've already said that Middle Eastern so-called clients are in a good position to manipulate their outside great-power patrons more than, or at least as much as, the other way around. One can go even further and say that small groups—numerically, politically, militarily weak groups—can often exploit situations in ways that cause stronger groups to take actions that they would not otherwise have chosen. We need to factor that point into our understanding of this issue.

The pattern of what I call fait accompli politics is strongly marked in the Middle East. I'm not being whimsical or paradoxical in saying that anybody who wants to understand modern Middle Eastern politics should study the origins of the Crimean War, starting with monks fighting in the Church of the Nativity in Bethlehem over who gets which altar, and so on. That kind of fait accompli politics was very much involved here. As one of us pointed out, if we look at it in a cold-blooded way, there was an effort on the part of one party to change the status quo and then to say, "Let's negotiate on the basis of the new situation." The interesting point, which I still cannot completely understand, is that Nasser didn't seem to be interested in stopping and then trying to de-escalate the crisis on the basis of the fait accompli.

The patron-client relationship, the penetration of the great powers into the Middle East, which is older than America's move into world diplomacy in a big way after World War II—we simply picked up and built on all the mistakes of the British—is a better way of trying to appreciate in a larger dimension what's going on in this one fascinating, important, and certainly tragic case study.

I feel that any conference can be only a partial success. If it's a total success, we didn't plan ambitiously enough, but it was certainly not for lack of effort. I think we have covered one aspect thoroughly, and certainly I have learned things, in greater detail than I ever knew before, about the American and Israeli dimensions of the Six-Day War. I think we are woefully weak, not for lack of trying, in our understanding of the Syrian dimension. We need to know more about the inner workings of the Egyptian bureaucratic system, including such factors as the Nasser-'Amr relationship.

Richard Parker: And we don't know enough about the Soviets.

Carl Brown: And we don't know enough, surely, about the Soviets.

Bernard Reich: We have achieved something unique. This is probably the first Arab-Israeli conference that I've attended where there has been more light than heat. Despite that there are some things left to look at.

We should come back to this matter of perception for a moment. Some years ago a noted political psychologist wrote a book about the Vietnam War entitled *Nobody Wanted War* [Ralph K. White (Garden City, N.Y.: Doubleday, 1968)]. It struck me, as we were talking over the last few days that nobody wanted this war either, but as in the case of Vietnam, the perceptions of the various parties and the failures of communication between and among them were such that war resulted nevertheless. Why did we end up with a result that nobody really wanted in the first place, if we take at face value all of the assertions that nobody did want it? (These assertions are one of the points that I think also need more investigation.)

Clearly, the perceptions of the parties within the U.S. government, as we heard yesterday, were not as clear and precise as they may be today, twenty-five years later, although even today we're not clear on exactly what all the perceptions were. Part of this, I think, is due to a failure of communication, both horizontal and vertical failure. Roy Atherton kept saying yesterday that he was at the working level, not knowing exactly what was going on with LBJ, and Bill Quandt was telling us that LBJ probably didn't care what Roy Atherton was worrying about.

In any event, I think what we have is a problem of communication within these systems, which may be part of the reason we don't know exactly what took place. I think there are exceptions to that, though. My impression, in listening to the various parts of the Israeli presentation, was that because it was a relatively small group of individuals involved in the decision-making process, with reasonably good communications between and among them, a good deal more was known within that system about who was doing what, when it was being done, who was communicating with whom, what was said. Even if some of the interpretations were not always identical, they were similar to each other. This I find unique, because every time you have two Israeli officials, you have three points of view, at least.

So, we have this problem of communication and then, of course, this problem of the missing messages. Several times in the last few days people have talked about communications that didn't quite get to where they should have gone in time to prevent something from happening. It would be interesting to know, for example, why U Thant did not deliver a message as asked, when he was supposed to [as noted earlier, U Thant did in fact deliver the message, but to Mahmoud Riad instead of Nasser—*Ed.*], or exactly how many messages were delivered to Egypt and how many different mechanisms, and who that famous missing Soviet interlocutor was. The same thing on the U.S. side: who was doing what and when? The problem here, I think, is partly a disconnect between the so-called high policy elite and the working levels. Ambassador Helms made clear a number of times that there were communications at one level that simply did not show up again at another. And that comes to the point of outside influences.

Bill Quandt told us this morning of the relative weight of communications in terms of number of contacts. This is an old political science technique of measuring the number of interactions and trying to deduce [on the theory] that there must be quality along with the quantity. I'd still like to know about that fourth person [Matilda Krim], on the [LBJ telephone] list, much more than about the first three.

One of the interesting things is that, as Ambassador Helms seemed to suggest, the vice-president [Hubert Humphrey] played a more significant role than Bill Quandt seemed to suggest by virtue of the number of contacts. We've barely mentioned him, and it would be interesting to see if he was more of a factor than we know about. Who was, in fact, the dominant influence on the president of the United States? Was it the intelligence information coming in, the specialists of the Department of State, the outside political influences, the neighboring ranch owner, or the vice-president?

The decision-making context of U.S. policy is most intriguing, especially if we try to compare it with that of the other countries. Were we writing a different book, I think it would be fascinating to look at the decision-making processes in each of the capitals. We heard a good deal about Jordan, for example, which would be wonderful to compare with the facts in Egypt and in Syria in terms of three systems where, in effect, a single individual was making the judgments. Yet in the United States, where we are supposed to have multiple involvements—we kept mentioning yesterday the president's concern that we go back to the Congress—we've talked not at all about Congress except inadvertently and by footnote, with some comments by Luke Battle on congressional discussions and presentations. Where was that factored? How did these two different decision-making processes work?

And, while we have talked a good deal about Israel, we haven't really said much about the Eshkol-Dayan interaction, for example, beyond the fact that, of course, the prime minister was forced to accept a defense minister who didn't exactly comport with his views. We've had little discussion about Mr. Eban and about what may have taken place in other capitals that may have affected Israeli decisions. We basically left out France. We've left out a number of other factors as well that may have influenced that context of decisions.

Another element to be considered is the U.S.-Israel relationship. Tahsin Basheer kept talking about the uniqueness and the special nature of the relationship. All relationships are by definition unique. The question is, what makes the Israel relationship special? The specialness was well defined yesterday by, I think, Bill Quandt. It's the amount of access you've got at a particular point of crisis to the people who make the real decisions. And here, I think, Tahsin Basheer's comment about Egypt is most crucial: "There was a dramatic asymmetry." Israel had access to the most senior levels of the U.S. government, where the decisions were really being made—even to the point, as Ambassador Evron suggested, that Israel didn't need a justice of the Supreme Court to intercede, or the vice-president, or anyone else, because there were enough points of contact. Egypt, by contrast, had virtually none. Ambassador Battle described his inability even to see the president of Egypt over a multimonth period, never mind the lack of ambassadorial presence in Cairo during those last weeks—where, by the way, there were other high-quality people left in the embassy. The fact of the matter is that we had little symmetry of discussion, and that does nothing to prevent a crisis from erupting into conflict.

There's one more point of importance: reliability, which was mentioned a number of times yesterday. Most important, despite Bill Quandt's attempt to remind us that we did meet the obligations of the letter of 1957, I see our Israeli interlocutors reminding us that, in Israel's view, that was not the case, and that's the crucial difference. Whatever we may think we were doing correctly from the U.S. perspective, from the Israeli perspective we did not meet the obligations that we had undertaken. As Sam Lewis pointed out, this was a constant subject of discussion during his long and distinguished tenure in Israel. What we have, if you will, is again a question of perception and the relationship between a large state and a small one.

Carl Brown mentioned the patron-client relationship. This whole subject area of political science is well understudied. In this crisis, we have three sets of patron-client relationships that would be wonderful to examine—Israel-U.S., Egypt-Soviet Union, and the one we haven't talked about at all,

Soviet-Syria. We have kept mentioning how important Syria was to the Soviet Union, yet we have not examined that statement, that dimension, that decision making, that relationship in any respect at all. Did it have an influence? Clearly it didn't prevent Israel from dealing with Syria in the 1967 war, despite other factors that were there.

One last set of observations, on disproving conspiracies. I don't like the term *conspiracy*. I've never particularly liked the term, partly because everyone is eventually accused of being part of one, but how do you prove that something didn't happen? And I've never quite understood how, logically, that can be made to take place. We mentioned FBIS this morning. Here is the FBIS summary for a few days ago. I looked through it for a particular statement that I know was made, but it's not there. In 1967, as I recall, the far more useful summary of radio broadcasts for the Middle East was not that of the FBIS but of the BBC, which had a longer and, I think, more distinguished history of tracking the region. [In terms of reliability,] these two have now, I think, reversed their positions. The fact that a report wasn't listed doesn't mean that it wasn't broadcast, and the assumption that [the absence of a listing means] that for some reason a judgment was made [against listing what was, in fact, broadcast] . . . both pose problems in trying to determine what took place. I don't know what the convincing explanations of certain events are. The *Liberty* is, perhaps, a good example. The facts are well known. The interpretations [cause us to] wind up in totally different places. But maybe it comes back to the ultimate point that there are facts and then there are true facts, and perhaps it's those true facts that have eluded us.

After reading Bill [Quandt's] paper and most of the other works and after listening to General Amit, it seems to me that the light [the supposed U.S.-to-Israel signal] was either nonexistent, green, red, amber, or acquiescent—which must be a new color—or some of the above, all mixed. What I suspect is that it's a matter of perception, as Bill suggested in his presentation. In any event, whether it is one or the other, I leave the conference far more enlightened than when I got here.

William Zartman: I think you should all be grateful to Mr. Cockburn for reminding you that you are being observed, and sense is being made, by lofty political scientists.

We're grateful to all the people who came here and brought their memories, checked their notes, and illuminated things, throwing an awful lot of light—not green, red, or yellow but just plain incandescent—on the events. We have opened up some questions that go beyond the simple details of who said what to whom and what happened. If we hadn't opened up new questions but had simply closed the box, the conference wouldn't have been a success. Pushing on to new kinds of things, I think, is the greatest mark of success.

I start out with the question of what the Egyptian intent was. And, then, could Nasser have accepted a face-saver? I've heard Mr. Bassiouny's assertion that Egypt would not start the war. There seems to have been, however, a kind of rush toward the edge of the brink and falling off in the hope that somebody might catch the falling body, but proclaiming all the way down that one had never intended to land on the ground below. Yes, perhaps Nasser would have taken a face-saver; that's an impression one gets from the proceedings, but it opens up a larger question, which takes a different kind of conference. What kind of face-saver would have been possible? What kind of reaction from the UN or through the UN would have been able to deal with the request to take out UNEF as the first step? What we need is not a conference to establish what happened but rather a different kind of brainstorming process, to look again, as people were trying to do under the pressure of the crisis, at what kind of alternatives would have been possible.

Brian Urquhart did a wonderful job of showing us that history was absolutely authoritative. Nothing else could have been done except what was done, and all alternatives that were conceivable were blocked by some impossibility or incapability. If we are going to learn from this kind of crisis, I don't think we want to stop at that point; I think we want to go into a different type of reflection.

In regard to the second step, the declaration of the blockade, the idea of living up to obligations was raised. I think it's not a question of legality, whether one thing was done or not done, but a question of creativity that we want to address. Ambassador Parker has correctly stated that our policy is looking for ways to avoid crisis rather than saying, wouldn't it be best just to let it run? If we want to learn something from the Six-Day War, it is how to be creative, how to find the nonobvious alternative that would have been a face-saver.

Similarly, in that period after the Strait of Tiran was declared closed, what could the United States have done? We have plenty of descriptions or discussions about whether the United States could have stopped Israel, what kind of lights we gave, and so on, but we paid less attention to the single [problem-solving] idea that was identified: the multilateral fleet, which was sinking before our eyes. Again, creativity [was lacking]. What other things could have been done to fill up the two-week period that we thought we had [after closure of the strait]? What could have been done to extend the period or to make it, in fact, two weeks rather than something shorter?

Dick Parker yesterday came out with a cri de coeur that the field did not feel supported by Washington, but we didn't push that one farther. Supported in what? What were specific measures that could have been taken, and what kind of support was the field looking for?

Similarly, we were reminded of how Vietnam was preoccupying us and, indeed, dramatically reminded at one point that Vietnam was taking all our time. Other than accepting that on faith—and it certainly wasn't something we could go into in this conference—we never got into a detailed examination of the ways in which time and effort were taken up by Vietnam during this period. [Such an examination would have given us] a more precise notion of how little time was left [for concerns other than Vietnam].

We didn't look at the aftermath except to say that we hadn't looked at the aftermath. Dick Parker raised the question about U.S. plans for or attitudes toward the postwar Arab-Israel situation and about Johnson's goal of a complete peace rather than simply a temporary arrangement. As I understand it, that was a presidential decision that happened sometime during the war and was probably very different, indeed, from what was communicated to the working level: an acknowledgment that he couldn't stop the war, along with the resolve to contribute to a more lasting peace rather than going back to the situation as it was after '48 or '56.

A greater examination is needed of the question of how much one looks in the nontime that's left at the aftermath, the consequence of immediate decisions. Is there a way of cranking in that necessary but never practiced aspect of war planning?

The thing that shakes me up the most has to do with the general [popular knowledge and understanding] of what we're talking about. I went home last night and talked to people completely unassociated with anything like this conference—upper-middle-class businesspeople, who told me I was completely wasting my time in these three days, that the subject interested only people who were defending their actions, that there was no sense in going over this business, and that we were all essentially hoodwinking each other. [At this conference, however,] we hear the conspiracy theories of the Middle East, which say that if a lot of people out there believe it, there's prima facie evidence that it must be true. We don't even have a smoking gun; we have only smoke, or maybe a smell of smoke, and if so, there must be a gun, and there must be a body.

As practitioners and analysts of events like this crisis, we are doing a catastrophically bad job of informing the people in the democracies that we live in—who, after all, we believe as an article of faith, determine, and should determine, the course of our national action—about what government and diplomacy are about. There is a woeful lack of understanding of what cannot be done by weak superpowers, such as the United States, weak, devious little powers, such as Israel, and weak big countries in a powerful, oil-filled world, such as Egypt. It is only because people don't understand the limits of the capabilities of states that we have people sopping up conspiracy theories and continuing to do so, not only in the Middle East but also in the United States. That's a big challenge for us to overcome.

Discussion

Ephraim Evron: First, Ambassador Parker, a few answers to some of the points that you raised.

The Tripartite Declaration was one of the casualties of the '56 war. For better or for worse, that was the end of the joint U.S., French, and British policy and, indeed, both the British and the French said so in '67.

About the American policy of opposing the use of force: Gene Rostow referred yesterday to the message that President Johnson received from President Eisenhower that had an impact on Johnson's decisions in the last week before the war started. I asked him [Rostow] what was in that message from President Eisenhower, and he said . . . Eisenhower told Johnson that the 1957 arrangements between the United States and Israel were a debt of honor that he felt that the United States was obliged to implement. That debt of honor, those arrangements, also included the American recognition that in case of the closure of the Strait of Tiran, Israel would be right to treat it as an act of aggression and to act in accordance with article 51, self-defense. I can't speak for either President Eisenhower or President Johnson, but I assume that that [view] played a role in the American behavior.

As for the idea that the Israelis overreacted, I don't know of any way, once a war begins—and the war began, I believe, on May 23 or 22—of measuring the hostility. [How could anyone have] expected that we would just drop on Sharm al-Shaykh, take over the Egyptian garrison, and stay there with the whole Egyptian army behind us? To get to Sharm al-Shaykh you have to go through the Sinai, and in the Sinai there were seven Egyptian divisions.

I was a little surprised to hear Dick Helms refer to Vice-President Humphrey's intervention. To the best of my recollection, he didn't play any role at all during the 1967 crisis. I know that we in the embassy met with him only once, on May 23, to urge him to get the president to issue the statement he had promised us that he would issue after the closure of the strait. Humphrey then said to us that he just couldn't believe that a president who was going to war in Vietnam in order to assert the American commitment would desert Israel. As far as I know, that's the whole of his intervention.

I'll make two or three short remarks about lessons that Israel might have learned from this war. One is that international assurances, including clear commitments by the U.S. government—certainly also by France, Britain, and Canada—evaporated in the face of new realities and changing national interest.

Second, Israel's military forces did not pass the test of Arab recognition of their deterrent power before the Arabs chose the option of war. What we believed would deter them from going into war failed that test, and that means that in the absence of real peace and normal relations with all our neighbors, Israel is bound to be on constant alert. I also think that the Arab illusion of Israel's nonfuture was punctured somehow during this war and that the war provided Israel with means to bring about a change in some basic Arab assumptions. It started us on the road that led to [the 1991 negotiations in] Madrid. It took a long time but we got there.

Leonard Meeker: Dick, you spoke just a bit ago about a memorandum of May 1967 saying, first, that closing the strait would be a violation of international law, and, second, that while Israel would not be justified by that violation in launching a full-scale war against Egypt, measures locally to deal with interference of shipping would nevertheless be justified. General Amit yesterday said that when he went back to Jerusalem, he recommended the first step should be sending an Israeli ship through the strait to see what would happen. I asked him today, if that had been done, you would have to expect that Egypt would interfere by military means with the ship; then what? His answer was quite clear: In that event a full-scale attack would take place, as General Dayan had made clear to him. General Dayan said in answer to General Amit's proposal that it was foolish to wait any more— we are mobilized, we can't stand still, we have to go ahead.

I suppose this raises a further question about U.S. policy. Suppose during that period before June 5 the United States had said to Israel, we understand your taking measures locally to ensure free passage, but we really have to say, strongly, no to a full-scale attack. Would that have made a difference? Perhaps with the appointment of General Dayan to be defense minister, the answer would have to be no.

Richard Parker: Yes.

Sam Lewis: I think you have to understand the topography of the military situation to answer that question. I don't think General Dayan, or Eshkol himself, or any defense minister would risk putting a couple of hundred soldiers at Sharm al-Shaykh, in an isolated position, and leaving the Egyptian army 300 kilometers behind them. No American general would do it, either. It's a militarily unacceptable proposition for any defense minister to approve, so I think the question is purely hypothetical.

Richard Parker: But you could have had a retaliatory raid—simply gone ahead and wiped out the garrison and then withdrawn. There was a lightly armed Egyptian garrison, and it would not have been difficult to overcome. I think that's what the Egyptians expected them [the Israelis] to try.

Ernest Dawn: In the midst of the war an Israeli mechanized force got bogged down in the desert just outside Sharm al-Shaykh, and you can still see some of the remains there. No, militarily totally impossible.

Samir Mutawi: In talking yesterday, at length, about who started what and when, our discussion seemed to concentrate on a belated point in the series of developments that led eventually to the 1967 war. As far as Israel is concerned, the starting point was Rabin's statement, or the denial that the statement took place, [accompanied by the denial] that there was any intention on the part of the Israeli leaders to launch a full-scale war at that stage. This might be the starting point from a theoretical point of view, but the whole Middle East theater was beginning to develop progressively into a situation that was bound to lead to war—since 1964, since the first Arab summit meeting. We haven't really dealt with that.

In other words, we haven't given sufficient attention to the background that most of us here had been watching or observing in that area at that time. The seeds of the 1967 war were sown in the first Arab summit meeting, by way of inter-Arab differences.

I think perceptions were extremely important at that particular time, not only to Jordanian decision makers but also to Syrians and Egyptians. Unfortunately, I haven't heard much about perceptions from the other two sides except what Mr. Basheer told us yesterday—but not enough.

[As for reticence on] the Egyptian side, I don't know whether it is deliberate or [whether it reflects a] lack of information or a lack of will on the part of certain people to reveal information. Not much has been done to explore what led the Egyptian leadership to make an all-of-a-sudden change. Nasser, only one year earlier, was saying, I'll never go to war unless I'm ready for it, and the Arabs are not ready for it. The report submitted to Nasser and his Arab colleagues by the Unified Arab Command in 1965 stated clearly that the Arabs would not be on a par situation with Israel before 1970—

that is, that neither strategically, militarily, nor operationally could they launch war against Israel and hope to achieve even a stalemate, let alone victory. Nasser as well as the other leaders knew all these facts.

Perhaps the Syrians, in their conception of a people's war of liberation, didn't want to hear or chose to ignore the realities that Arab professional officers were able to conceive and present to Arab leaders. Nevertheless, the Arabs in general, and I'm talking here particularly about Nasser and the Jordanian leadership, knew full well that they could not confront the State of Israel in any state of war and hope to win. That was clear, and Nasser said it on more than one occasion.

Then all of a sudden there was a chain of developments in a short period of time: first, the expulsion of UNEF, second, the closure of the Strait of Aqaba, and third, a flurry of activity that led eventually into the war. That sudden change has not been fully developed during our conference, and I think it deserves special attention because it's not only misreadings or misperceptions or misinformation or disinformation, as Mr. Rafael called it yesterday, that caused this change.

We also haven't talked about [the perceptions in] Israel itself. How did the Israelis perceive what the Arabs had been doing since the summit of 1964? How did they interpret each movement? Ambassador Shamir, for example, had explained to me about Samu', which I seem to have dwelt on in some detail. But I went into such detail because I felt Samu' was extremely important in Jordanian thinking, in making the Jordanians shift from the position of desperately trying to preserve the status quo to a position of allying themselves with Nasser. But how did the Israelis interpret, or how did they think the Arabs would interpret, every move that they made?

There has been a lot of talk in Jordan about a conspiracy theory—of the Americans being behind the Jordanian rapprochement with Egypt. Three respected Jordanian politicians confirmed that Richard Murphy talked to them personally, trying to convince them to advise King Hussein to patch things up with Nasser. This they said took place during April 1967.

Richard Parker: Murphy was political officer in Amman.

Samir Mutawi: I did mention the matter in passing in my book, but I didn't develop the theory because, like many of you, I don't believe in the conspiracy theory—or, at least, I believe that the Arabs have for a long time been convincing themselves that it's part and parcel of their political structure.

Richard Parker: All the points you've raised are valid. It's just a question of time available. All these things should be discussed. Shimon Shamir gave some time to the doctrine of retaliation and described it as a dead-end street.

Certainly there are divisions of opinion in Israel on that, but I agree it is something that should be looked at.

Lucius Battle: First, I was the one who said that under certain circumstances I thought Nasser could have accepted a face-saver, but it couldn't originate with him; it had to be imposed on him. What I had in mind was something that would have been all things to all people, such as a mandate from on high—that is, the United States, the UK, and France or the UN—that there be UNEF forces stationed on Israel's side as well as on Egypt's, which would have been a big face-saver for him, and that there be enforcement of [navigation] rights in the Strait of Tiran . . . a combination of things, plus throwing in that we would force the Strait of Tiran, and in exchange for that Nasser could get UNEF stationed on [Israel's] side, which would have helped him with the rest of the Arab world. If there was something like that that could be imposed from the outside, giving you [Nasser] a face-saver with the Arab world, made you [Israel] unhappy but still wasn't really crucial. . . .

Second, the question of Hubert Humphrey: I talked with him several times during this whole period, and he was sympathetic to Israel, without any question. I did not know him to take any particular part in anything. He came to one meeting I attended in the White House with the president, and he said at that time exactly what Dick Helms told us. He did say one other thing: "The domestic political consequences of this are horrendous, and we've got to get it behind us." But I'm not aware of any active participation at any point other than that.

Shimon Shamir: I have a feeling that in time many details of the 1967 affair—questions like exactly what happened in Sharm al-Shaykh or in the demilitarized zones—will become less and less interesting, while the issue that will always remain relevant and meaningful is why this war, which nobody wanted, broke out. I think that in the longer perspective this will become the crucial question. As I see it today, the answer should be sought in the direction pointed out by Samir Mutawi: the misperceptions and miscalculations that took place in this affair. I do not necessarily mean miscommunications. The term *miscommunication* seems to imply that a good understanding of the situation exists but somehow is not communicated well. This may be so in many cases, but it was not the root of the problem in our case. Here the problem was clearly a large accumulation of misperceptions and miscalculations. The two are, of course, connected, but there is a difference between them. As we all know, misperception refers to the way one sees the other or one's self; miscalculation happens when a decision is made or an action is taken without having sufficiently or correctly considered the consequences. We have many examples in history of disastrous results issuing from both. What is typical of the 1967 affair is the striking proliferation of both misperceptions and miscalculations.

The misperceptions: We don't have to go into great detail—the story is well known. The Soviets had a distorted image of Israeli capabilities and intentions. Israel and the United States did not perceive the desperate mood of Nasser. The Arabs, both Egyptians and Syrians, did not grasp the Israeli concept of security. The Israelis could not comprehend the Soviets.

The miscalculations: When the Syrians started their Popular (or People's) War of Liberation, they should have understood that this type of guerrilla warfare could not go on without eventually leading to full-scale war and that they were not ready for an all-out confrontation with Israel. The Soviets, Victor Israelyan told us, only wanted to warn their friends, but it didn't occur to them that the warning might generate a chain of events that would get out of control. The Egyptians made the most famous of all the miscalculations—we don't even have to mention them. The Israelis conducted a dual policy of employing secret diplomacy, on the one hand, and issuing militant warnings, on the other—both designed to restrain the Syrians. They did not consider the possibility that this [their dual policy] might bring about exactly the opposite result: instead of pacifying their borders, it would bring about escalation and the activation of an Arab war coalition against Israel.

Some of the decisions made by actors in this affair seem logical only on the assumption that a certain scenario would take place, but they completely lacked a convincing answer to the question of what happens if another scenario materializes. Let me give you an example. Nasser sent his army to Sinai to deter Israel and prevent an operation against Syria. Fine, I accept this. If subsequently Israel had refrained from any military action, Nasser's move would have been considered a great success. But suppose the Israelis did take an action against Syria, what could Nasser have done? Suppose that the big operation, which everybody believed the Israelis were preparing, was executed while Nasser had his army in Sinai, how would he react? Remain inactive and look foolish? Launch an all-out attack on Israel? There is evidence that Nasser believed his army was capable of absorbing an Israeli first strike, but it's quite obvious that Nasser could not imagine that his insufficient forces had the capability of launching an offensive against Israel.

Richard Parker: Have you read Rikhye's account of the conversation between Nasser and U Thant? It was Nasser who said, "My generals all say they are ready to go to war now."

Shimon Shamir: The expression "ready to go to war," I believe, is generally interpreted as readiness to absorb the first strike and stop an Israeli offensive.

But to go on the offensive, to attack Israel, required forces that the Egyptian army, largely deployed in the Yemen, did not have. They certainly did not have an offensive capability.

Richard Parker: As Samir Mutawi brought up, and it's a great mystery, how could Nasser have believed that he was ready to confront Israel?

Shimon Shamir: This is my question.

Richard Parker: You find differences of view among the Egyptians on this score. We'll come back to that in a minute. To me that's one of the great mysteries.

Shimon Shamir: Well, I wouldn't call the behavior of the actors in this affair a mystery. They were responsible for downright miscalculations, pure and simple. Why should we dignify this with the word *mystery*? But let me use this opportunity to correct an impression that my words may project. I am not trying to pass judgment on the behavior of the decision makers in this affair, to condemn their morality or wisdom. They were human beings making human mistakes, miscalculating their moves, as many before them had done. There was nothing exceptional about it. This is the way the world is run. It is easy to say retrospectively that this decision or that action could have been avoided, but such mistakes are the material that history is made of. It was Adenauer who said that "history is the sum total of all the things that could have been avoided."

What *is* important is to draw lessons from this war, to study its misperceptions and miscalculations, because they may be instructive. That decision makers are human beings and make mistakes is a trivial observation. Much more interesting is to find out in which circumstances such mistakes are made and what their manifestations are on the ground. If this conference can come up with some new insight on these questions, I think it will make a great contribution.

Ernest Dawn: I want to make it clear that I do not approve of the post-1967 situation, and certainly not the current one, with regard to Israel and the Arab states. I said I agreed with Ambassador Lewis's hypothesis that it would be better if Israel had not occupied the West Bank, but they did occupy the West Bank. I think that Ambassador Evron also said something that is close to what I was trying to indicate. As a result of that war, there was a situation where there could have been some movement. There was some movement. There were many opportunities later. The fault is not the '67 war. The fault is . . . there were opportunities between September 1970 and October 1973 that were missed and, to be blunt, the '80s are just filled with horrors that, with a different administration in the United States, we could have avoided. Put blame on Israel and the Arabs, but in this case we do have some capabilities that in other cases we didn't have. This is a situation where the United States does have some leverage, much more so than it has had in the past, but it has not been used; that's looking into the future. I think we would have been better off without the '67 war, but it did create a new situation that could have been utilized and has been, tragically, allowed to go to waste.

Janice Stein: I want to come back to the question that Samir and Shimon raised: Why did the leaders miscalculate? There is an interesting pattern here that we haven't talked about. We have confident militaries in all the major countries except for Jordan. We have a confident military in Israel. We clearly have a confident military in the United States. We have a confident military under 'Amr in Egypt, certainly in the month of May, and we have a confident military in the Soviet Union, although we know least about that, if you take Grechko as a representative of that particular group. On the other hand, you have cautious civilians. You have Eshkol, clearly more cautious than the military, troubled, worried about American reaction right through. You have Johnson, as Bill Quandt so forcefully demonstrated, skeptical of military estimates. You have Soviet civilians not at all confident, pulling back, trying to pull Egypt back as you move into this last period. Therefore, there was in place at least a pattern that might have permitted the avoidance of miscalculation.

The one exception is Nasser, and in him there is a dramatic change. I remember reading an interview that you did, Luke, with Nasser when he talked about Egypt's inability to enter into military confrontation. That was early March 1967, and when you read carefully what he is saying at the end of May, it seems inconceivable that he could change so much. There is an explanation, I think, for why he changed his estimate, and that was the crucial change. If Nasser's estimate of Egypt's military capability had not changed, you could not have had a war. That is the rock bottom question when we look at this whole series of interrelated calculations, and, I think, the answer is that he was in an impossibly tough situation. He had no good diplomatic option, not dissimilar to Johnson at the end, and Bill's choice of words is careful: Johnson resigned himself. When top leaderships find themselves in a situation, pressed, conflicted, and they simply cannot identify a good option, they begin to change their estimates in ways that solve their political problems for them. If you read Nasser's interviews and his statements, what we hear from him is "My generals tell me that we are ready to go to war." There is a tinge of reservation, but essentially he buys the military estimate as the month of May continues, and I think he buys it because there is simply no face-saver, no good diplomatic option.

It might be worthwhile paying attention to the asymmetries between the military estimates and the civilian estimates and to trace that as carefully as you can. And then to look carefully at what happens to Nasser within that ten-day period. I think there is an answer there.

Raymond Garthoff: Four brief comments. (1) I want to concur strongly and underline what Shimon Shamir just said about the force of misconception and miscalculations. While this is undoubtedly true to a greater or lesser extent in all historical events, it's more true in some than in others, and this is one case in which it was especially true. We also found it to have been the case, strongly, in another historical episode that I have been working on lately, the Cuban missile crisis.

(2) It has been suggested that Sharm al-Shaykh could have been attacked or taken as a reprisal step, perhaps coupled with a warning that if that threat were restored and interference made at a later time, a strong reprisal would be made. In fact, Sharm al-Shaykh was taken from the sea, I think on the second day of the war, by landing from Israeli patrol boats, not overland.

Ephraim Evron: After the Egyptian army was destroyed.

————: The air force was destroyed also.

Raymond Garthoff: Well, it is true that it would have been a different situation without the destruction of the Egyptian air force, in particular. Nonetheless, it wouldn't have been necessary, for that matter, to occupy it. It could have been destroyed in a bombing raid.

(3) For the record, concerning assessments afterward about miscalculations: The deputy Soviet representative to the UN, Ambassador Platon Morozov, on or about June 9, commented to a Yugoslav colleague that every Soviet military attaché in the Near East ought to be shot for their misleading reporting on Arab military capabilities. That was his reaction to a misevaluation.

(4) On May 24, Ambassador Nikolai Federenko, the Soviet UN representative in New York, made a statement in which he called for the withdrawal of the American Sixth Fleet from the Mediterranean. Ambassador Rafael tells me that in conversations Federenko explicitly tied this . . . saying if the American Sixth Fleet were withdrawn, that might create conditions under which something could be done about calling off the blockade of Aqaba.

Now, I don't know, but I'm very much of the opinion that Federenko's speech was made on his own initiative. He was following through on a call for the withdrawal of the Sixth Fleet from the Mediterranean that had been made by Leonid Brezhnev in a speech in Czechoslovakia on April 24. I'm sure Brezhnev's comment had not been related to events that were happening, or would be happening, in the Middle East, but was part of a broader political offensive at the time. But whether by coincidence or on his own initiative, that element was brought back into the picture on May 24 by Ambassador Federenko.

Tahsin Basheer: I go to the question, what would happen if Nasser didn't do anything? Did not cause the battle, did not react to Hussein, did not react to Syria? He was in a difficult position. His view of the Americans was that they were intent on cutting him down to size. His view of the Soviets was that they were friendly but not reliable. His view of the group in Syria was that they were playing havoc. But he was in a psychological seizure himself, I think. He was feeling that the revolution was declining, and every time he found threats around him, he reacted by overescalating. He did what he did in 1960, in the [Khirbet] Tawafiq thing; he moved that army to Sinai, Israel backed down, and nothing happened.

Ephraim Evron: But not without contact.

Tahsin Basheer: Yes, but the situation was different. He moved his forces into Sinai. All along, in the discussions with the army, unlike those who were saying that war will ensue and that war is inevitable if you do that, Nasser was always discounting them, saying after the strait was closed that the likelihood of war was only 60 percent. 'Amr, for example, said that means war, even when he just sent the forces into Sinai. What is interesting is that nowhere in the discussions that I could find is [there any indication] whether any of the civilians, Mahmoud Riad or Mahmoud Fawzi, referred to this communiqué [of February 7, 1957, regarding navigation in the Gulf of Aqaba] between the Americans and the Israelis. Nowhere is anyone raising it.

Nasser felt all the forces on him and decided to escalate. That was a game he initiated: I will send the forces; I will threaten Israel because the only way America moves is if Israel is in trouble. That's his perception. He acted upon the model of '56. Okay, [he thinks] at the worst there will be a little war, but my army will be able to take it. Even if we lose half of Sinai, we will still retain the passes. Some Egyptians accuse him of trying to cut the army down to size, [of thinking] it doesn't matter if they get a blow or two. He had no idea at all that the army would collapse, and when it collapsed, he said, "My army had a stroke, a heart attack." He was calculating a risk, and he was always trying to put the blame [elsewhere], as you indicated rightly. "My generals say, ask 'Amr." Well, since when does he ask 'Amr? And during the war he didn't go to the command center. He avoided it. But he estimated that America would intervene, and his fight was really to bring America to a reconciliation with him. I think that is the key.

Now, Eppie Evron, I take issue with you on Sadat. It is not this policy that led to Sadat's going to Jerusalem. If we had remained defeated like the rest of the Arabs, neither Sadat nor anybody else would have gone to Jerusalem. Once we had the '73 war, we were able to convince ourselves more than everybody else did that Israel is defeatable: Israel after two days of war sent an SOS to Nixon: come and help us, we need this and this and this. Sadat was able to go because he had a total picture; he was able to say, Israel is not a great threat.

Ephraim Evron: Didn't it help him [Sadat] when we suggested that he can exchange the rest of the Sinai for peace? The fact that we had real estate and gave it back to him, don't you think that this was also a factor in the equation?

Tahsin Basheer: I'll come to that. He [Sadat] had the courage to go to his people and to his men and say that the Egyptians never thought that you [Israelis] will keep the real estate of Sinai forever. I mean, you [Israelis] can dream of it, but we would have fought for it for many years to come. You know, peasants don't leave the land.

Once I tried, in the third day of the [1973] war, to stop the war. He [Sadat] was mad, and I don't know why, because, in any [way of] thinking, the third day of the war finished it in '73. Once we ended the war and Kissinger came, we thought, look, we reach now a delineation. We cannot defeat Israel; Israel cannot defeat us. Let us not waste effort. Let's make up with America and settle the problem, and that's why he accepted it.

And when the Americans could not deliver a peace, Sadat started going to Jerusalem. He did it out of confidence, not out of a sense of defeat.

Nasser was trying to de-escalate when the war came, but he was never willing to have peace with Israel. The Arab public does not forget its hurts. The background to this crisis is important, and we cannot understand what happened without discussing it.

Salah Bassiouny: We have been discussing the lessons of the past, the questions of miscalculation and misperception, the lessons of the June War. Now we are in 1992. Are we approaching a similar situation now?

Alfred Atherton: I want to be sure that my question is not ignored. For eighteen years the United States had the policy of maintaining a structure embedded in the armistice agreements that had at least maintained a status quo and a reasonable amount of stability. Sometime between June 5 and 19, when Johnson made his speech, there was a major change in U.S. national policy, and I think it would be useful to know how this change happened. It was perhaps logical, when you look back, that we were not going to restore the status quo ante, but that was not necessarily the assumption. Those of us at the working level operated on the assumption, how do we get this back to the situation when the war started? And suddenly we learn that at some other level a decision has been made that we wouldn't go back to the structure but would establish the principle that the new status quo of Israeli occupation would be accepted until the Arabs were ready to change their policy and make peace, to recognize Israel's legitimacy, and then there would be a famous land-for-peace exchange.

I think it would be useful to know how that change started. Where did it start? In whose mind did it first germinate? It had to start with somebody. I think it would be enlightening to know.

Richard Parker: Can you answer that, Bill [Quandt]?

William Quandt: I can't answer it satisfactorily, but I can give you a hint of when it first showed up. On the second day of the war, there was a hand-written note passed to Johnson, a message, I think, from Eban, saying, Eban hopes the president understands that the United States would serve the cause of peace well by not calling for any withdrawal of Israeli forces in the aftermath of the conflict. [The note said that] this time there should be no return to the armistice agreements, which were not adequate; this time the effort should be to get full peace.

This [note] is the first time I saw this formulation. The amazing thing is, I don't think it was thereafter discussed, but it was assumed that this was the policy. It was simply the way Johnson and his associates saw the new situation. Whatever had prevailed before June 5 was not satisfactory. There was no reason to go back to it. There is no record of it [the policy] being discussed. Hal Saunders in his postmortem says that the most interesting thing was the questions that were never raised. Never discussed early on was, why not just let the Israelis do it? It's their problem. They can take care of it. Let them do it on their own. Nor was this issue [of withdrawal to the armistice lines] discussed. It was just assumed. Perhaps the most important thing to know is, when top policymakers don't think they need to discuss something, it is just understood. But then it doesn't leave any traces.[1]

1. On reading Quandt's explanation, Harold Saunders comments that in the numerous conversations among Ephraim Evron, Walt Rostow, President Johnson, and himself in the days before the war, Evron repeatedly took the position that the situation should be used to end the Arab-Israeli crisis once and for all. "As I pointed out in my introduction to the collection of White House documents now in the Johnson library, the first official statement of this point as a U.S. position can be found in the first public statement made by the White House after the outbreak of the war. The fact that this public statement incorporated that language without policy debate suggests that—even by the morning of June 5—this perspective had become embedded in the thinking of top U.S. policymakers. It was only after the war, in one of the meetings of the NSC Executive Committee, that another top U.S. policymaker caused those around the table to reflect seriously on the consequences of that policy, which was already deeply embedded in the public record" (Saunders, note to Walda Metcalf, UPF, August 24, 1994).

Richard Parker: How was this communicated? Did you learn it by osmosis, Luke?

Lucius Battle: One thing you have to recognize—there's a bit of realism in the fact. I said to my staff meeting, "We've got to take another look at this because you're not going to get the Israelis to withdraw the way we did in 1956, on the basis of assurances that once again we'll come to their assistance. We've got to think of more comprehensive solutions to the whole problem before there's any chance of there being a withdrawal." I don't know whether I made that up myself or whether someone on high told me, but it seemed clear to me that there was no point in our going on with "you have to get out of there quickly" unless we had something more than that to offer. I can remember saying at a staff meeting, "Isn't it time we go for a full peace?"

Every Arab ambassador came to see me every hour on the hour to ask, "When are you going to make the Israelis withdraw?" I kept saying, "It's impossible. We can't tell the Israelis to withdraw. They're not going to do it [just] because we say so." We obviously didn't like the occupation situation we were facing, but I don't remember any great big discussion that we're going to change policy. I think it was more an outgrowth of realism and natural development than it was a conscious decision.

Summaries

Gideon Rafael: Unilateral withdrawal was excluded from the beginning. The fruits of war were UN resolutions 242 and 338. There was miscommunication as well as miscalculation in this crisis. Messages were not delivered or understood properly.

Philip Mattar: There is need for more attention to underlying causes. The ultimate causes are as important as the immediate.

Don Peretz: The war changed not only the whole basis of political discussion but also the negotiating positions of all the parties. The old status quo disappeared.

Samir Mutawi: Ambassador Rafael said Israel had offered to return Sinai and the Golan, but not the West Bank. This serves to confirm Jordanian suspicions regarding Israeli intentions.

Ambassador Goldberg told King Hussein, "If you accept resolution 242, you'll get the West Bank back in six months." The king received the same assurances from President Johnson.

Samuel Lewis: I have a nonsubstantive, procedural comment. One of the things this conference has reinforced for me is the utility of getting together policy practitioners and scholars in this sort of fairly relaxed, searching examination of a set of events. It should be absolutely crystal-clear to every-one how different we are in the way we approach issues. . . . There was never any more dramatic demonstration of how scholars don't usually under-stand how American policy is actually made than what went on here just a few minutes ago. I dare say that no historian or political scientist would ever have dared put into his book how U.S. policy changed in the way it was described here by Luke Battle, Roy Atherton, and Bill Quandt. It just kind of happened . . . "people assumed, things changed, there were no option papers." No one would believe that. I think this is one of the values of this kind of exchange.

Appendix

The Panelists: Where They Were in June 1967

General Meir Amit was chief of Mossad, the Israeli intelligence agency. Today he is a businessman in Tel Aviv.

Ambassador Tahsin Basheer was a member of the United Arab Republic (Egyptian) mission to the UN. Today he is a writer and lecturer in Cairo.

Ambassador Salah Bassiouny was a special assistant in the office of the Undersecretary of Foreign Affairs in Cairo. Today he is practicing law in Cairo.

Ambassador Lucius Battle was the assistant secretary for Near East and South Asian Affairs at the Department of State. Today he is chairman of ANERA (American Near East Refugee Aid).

Ambassador Donald Bergus was the country director for UAR Affairs in the Department of State. Today he is retired and lives in Strathmere, New Jersey.

Dr. Carl Brown was finishing his first year as a faculty member at Princeton University. He is still at Princeton, where he has been director of the Near East Program.

McGeorge Bundy was recalled to the staff of the National Security Council. Today he is with the Carnegie Corporation in New York City.

Andrew Cockburn was a student at Oxford University. Today he is a writer and journalist in Washington, D.C.

Dr. Karen Dawisha was a high school graduate. Today she is a professor in the Department of Government and Politics at the University of Maryland.

Dr. C. Ernest Dawn was a research fellow in Beirut, studying Syrian politics. Today he is an emeritus professor of history at the University of Illinois.

Ambassador Ephraim Evron was minister counselor of the Israeli Embassy in Washington, D.C. Today he is retired and living in Jerusalem.

Ambassador Richard Helms was director of Central Intelligence. Today he is a consultant in Washington, D.C.

F.T. Liu was the UN political officer in Jerusalem. Today he is with the International Peace Academy in New York City.

Dr. Samir Mutawi was working for the BBC Arabic Service in London. Today he is a writer and lecturer in Amman and London.

Dr. Vitaly Naumkin was a student in Cairo. Today he is director of the Russian Center for Strategic Research and International Relations.

Ambassador Richard B. Parker was political counselor in the American Embassy in Cairo. Today he is a writer and lecturer living in Washington, D.C.

Dr. William Quandt was doing research for his Ph.D. thesis in Algiers. Today he is a fellow at the Brookings Institution in Washington, D.C.

Dr. Bernard Reich was a consultant to the Army Chief of Staff's task force on the Middle East. Today he is a professor of political science at George Washington University.

Eugene Rostow was undersecretary of state for political affairs. Today he is a fellow at the U.S. Institute of Peace in Washington, D.C.

Ambassador Shimon Shamir was an officer in Israeli military intelligence. At the time of the conference he was a fellow at the U.S. Institute of Peace. Today (1996) he is the Israeli ambassador in Amman.

Dr. Janice Stein was a visiting scholar at the Center for International Studies at Princeton. Today she is a professor at the University of Toronto.

Dr. George Tomeh (deceased in 1994) was the Syrian delegate to the United Nations. After he retired, he lived in Washington, D.C.

Sir Brian Urquhart was in the office of the undersecretary general for special political affairs at the UN. Today he is with the Ford Foundation in New York City.

Dr. I. William Zartman was a professor at New York University. Today he is teaching at SAIS Johns Hopkins in Washington, D.C.

Note: "Today" as used above refers to June 1992, except as noted.

Observers (invited)

Current or former State Department (with 1967 position when pertinent)

Norman Anderson
Granville Austin (INR)
Alfred L. Atherton (director Israel/Arab-Israel Affairs)
Perry Baltimore
Eugene Bovis (UAR Desk, NEA)
Timothy W. Childs (donor)
William Crawford (Rabat)
Raymond Garthoff (G/PM)
Brandon Grove, Jr.
Paul Hare
George Harris (CIA)
Fred Hill
Thomas Hughes (INR)
Andrew Killgore (Baghdad)
Lucien Kinsolving (State Task Force)
Robert V. Keeley (Athens)

David A. Korn (NEA)
Daniel E. Kurtzer
Dennis Kux
Glenn W. Lafantasie (Historian's Office)
James Leonard
Samuel Lewis
Mark Lissfelt (Embassy, Tel Aviv)
Leonard Meeker (Legal Adviser)
Joseph Montville
Kendall Myers
Robert B. Oakley
Talcott W. Seelye (Jidda)
George Sherman
Roscoe S. Suddarth (Taiz)
Richard N. Viets (Tunis)

Other Governmental

Ambassador Georgiy Kornienko (American Affairs, Soviet Foreign Ministry)
Captain L.P. Blasch (assistant naval attaché, Haifa)
Ambassador Victor Israelyan (Soviet Diplomatic Academy)
Robert Komer (National Security Council)
Ambassador Gideon Rafael (Israeli delegate to UN)

Academics and Others

Joan Bingham, International Human Rights Law Group
Robert Freedman, Baltimore Hebrew University
Philip Geyelin, journalist
Martin Indyk, Washington Institute
Elie Kedourie, Wilson Center
Robert Litwak, Wilson Center
Phillip Mattar, Institute of Palestine Studies
Donald Neff, author, *Warriors for Jerusalem*
Don Peretz, U.S. Institute of Peace
Deborah Rivel, Brookings Institution
Stephen Rosenfeld, *Washington Post*
Merle Thorpe, Foundation for Middle East Peace
Milton Viorst, journalist
Samuel Wells, Woodrow Wilson Center
Irena Zviagelskaya, Oriental Institute, Moscow

Selected Bibliography

Bar Zohar, Michael. *Embassies in Crisis: Diplomats and Demagogues Behind the Six Day War,* Englewood Cliffs, N.J.: Prentice Hall, 1968. Written shortly after the June War and based in part on interviews with participants. Bar Zohar, now a member of the Knesset, was a journalist at the time.

Brecher, Michael, and Benjamin Geist. *Decisions in Israel's Foreign Policy.* London: Oxford University Press, 1974. A well-documented and carefully researched study of a series of crises, including the June War. Perhaps the most serious single published account of the process leading up to the Israeli decision to strike.

Bull, General Odd. *War and Peace in the Middle East: The Experience and Views of a UN Observer,* London: Leo Cooper, 1976. General Bull was the commanding officer of UNTSO, the UN Truce Supervision Organization, at the time of the June War.

Burdett, Winston. *Encounter with the Middle East: An Intimate Report of What Lies Behind the Arab-Israeli Conflict.* New York: Athenaeum, 1969. A serious piece of journalistic research that includes a long section on the June War. Burdett was extensively briefed by officers of the Department of State on their view of what happened.

Burns, William J. *Economic Aid and American Policy Toward Egypt, 1955–1981.* Albany: SUNY Press, 1985. A carefully researched and documented study of the ups and downs of U.S.-Egyptian relations and the role of economic aid therein.

Brown, Leon Carl. "Nasser and the June 1967 War: Plan or Improvisation?" In *Quest for Understanding: Arabic and Islamic Studies in Memory of Malcolm H. Kerr,* edited by Seikaly, Baalbaki, and Dodd. Beirut: American University of Beirut, 1991. A carefully reasoned article which argues that Nasser stumbled into the war.

Cockburn, Andrew, and Leslie Cockburn. *Dangerous Liaison: The Inside Story of the U.S.-Israeli Covert Relationship.* New York: HarperCollins, 1991. Chapter 6 deals with allegations of U.S.-Israeli collusion in the attack on Egypt.

Dagan, Avigdor. *Moscow and Jerusalem.* London: Abelard-Schuman, 1970. An account of Soviet-Israeli relations and exchanges prior to the June War.

Dawn, C. Ernest. "The Egyptian Remilitarization of Sinai, May 1967." *Journal of Contemporary History* 3 (July 1968): 201–44.

Draper, Theodore. *Israel and World Politics: Roots of the Third Arab-Israeli War.* New York: Viking, 1968.

Dupuy, Trevor. *Elusive Victory, The Arab-Israeli Wars, 1947–1974.* New York: Harper and Row, 1978. Perhaps the best-known of the American military commentators who writes on the Israeli military machine, Dupuy has been given unusual access to Israeli military information. He is less informative about the Arab military.

Eban, Abba. *An Autobiography.* Jerusalem: Steimatsky's, 1977. Eban was the Israeli foreign minister in 1967. His memoirs have a useful account of the events leading up to the war and of Israel's exchanges with the Americans.

Ennes, James M., Jr. *Assault on the Liberty.* New York: Random House, 1979. Ennis was the executive officer of the *Liberty* and this detailed account of what occurred makes chilling reading. This book has played an important role in keeping alive the controversy about whether the Israelis knowingly attacked an American ship.

Fawzi, General Muhammad. *Harb al-Thalath Sanawat* (The three years war) from the June War to the cease-fire in 1970. Vol. 1 of Fawzi's memoirs. Heliopolis: Dar al-Mustaqbil al-Arabi, 1980. Fawzi was the Chief of Staff in 1967 and replaced Marshal 'Amr as Deputy Commander in Chief when the war ended. Important military details by a professional.

Geist, Benjamin. "The Six Day War." Ph.D. thesis, Hebrew University, 1974. The most comprehensive study in English of the Israeli sources. Geist contributed importantly to the Brecher book listed here.

Green, Stephen. *Taking Sides.* New York: William Morrow & Co., 1984. A readable account of the special relationship of the United States with Israel. Provides alleged details of intelligence cooperation on the eve of and during the June war, but the details have yet to be corroborated.

Hamrush, Ahmad, *Kharif 'Abd al-Nasir* (The autumn of Abd al-Nasser). Cairo: Maktabat Madbuli, 1984. One of a number of books dealing with the decline of Abd al-Nasser following the June War.

Heikal, Mohamed Hassanein. *Nasser: The Cairo Documents.* London: The New English Library, 1972. Heikal is always readable, in either Arabic or English. On pages 205–24 he describes the relationship between Nasser and Johnson and the deterioration of U.S.-Egyptian relations under the latter.

————. *The Sphinx and the Commissar: The Rise and Fall of Soviet Influence in the Middle East.* New York: Harper and Row, 1978. An informative account of the Egyptian-Soviet relationship, with anecdotes about Khrushchev and others. Contains the first published account by an insider of the details of Soviet-Egyptian contacts on the eve of the June War.

————. *1967-Al-Infijar* (1967-The explosion). Cairo: al-Ahram, 1990. A massive (1,089 pages) and often fascinating insider's account, supported by 149 pages of documents, of the events leading up to the June War. Heikal's selective use of sources to support his contention that Egypt was the victim of a U.S.-Israeli conspiracy throws doubt on other aspects of his narrative, but it is the most authentic-looking account we have from Egyptian sources to date.

Howard, Michael, and Robert Hunter. "Israel and the Arab World: The Crisis of 1967." Adelphi Papers Number 41. London: The Institute for Strategic Studies, 1967. A first-crack-out-of-the-box study of the events leading up to and the consequences of the June War. Worth reading as reminder of how much detail we have forgotten.

Hussein, Ibn Talal. *My War with Israel*. London: Peter Owen, 1969. King Hussein of Jordan's account of his side of the June War.

Imam, Abdallah. *Nasir wa 'Amr* (Nasser and 'Amr). Cairo: Ruz al-Yusuf, 1985. An account of the Nasser-'Amr relationship, with many details, some not original.

Kimche, David, and D. Bawly. *The Sandstorm: The Arab-Israeli War of 1967, Prelude and Aftermath*. London: Secker and Warburg, 1968. Another early work in popular style that has been given more weight than it should because of Kimche's intelligence background. Not very serious.

Laqueur, Walter. *The Road to War, 1967*. London: Weidenfeld and Nicolson, 1968. A serious study by a well-known student of the area.

McLeish, Roderick. *The Sun Stood Still*. New York: Athenaeum, 1967. McLeish, a well-known commentator on National Public Radio, was one of the few early writers on the June War who actually talked to a Soviet official about the Soviet role.

Murtagi, General Abdul Muhsin Kamil. *Al-Fariq Murtagi Yarwa al-Haqa'iq* (General Murtagi narrates the facts). Cairo: Dar al Watn al Arabi, 1976. The commander of the Sinai front gives his version of events. A useful account of the problems of command and decision under Marshal 'Amr.

Mutawi, Samir A. *Jordan in the 1967 War*. Cambridge: Press Syndicate, 1987. Mutawi was given access to the documents in the Jordanian military archives relating to the war. A carefully researched and responsible book that gives Jordan's side of the question.

Nassif, Ramses. *U Thant in New York*. London: C. Hurst & Co., 1986. Nassif accompanied U Thant on his trip to Cairo in May 1967 and describes their discussions there. Includes the memorandum of U Thant's conversation with Nasser.

Neff, Donald. *Warriors for Jerusalem: The Six Days that Changed the Middle East*. New York: Simon and Schuster, 1984. Probably the best single account of the June War published to date. Based on extensive interviews and declassified documents as well as the public record.

Nutting, Anthony. *Nasser*. New York: E. P. Dutton, 1972. A sympathetic account of Nasser's role in Middle East politics from the 1952 revolution to his death.

Parker, Richard B. *The Politics of Miscalculation in the Middle East*. Bloomington: Indiana University Press, 1993. The first half of the book deals with the 1967 crisis.

———. "The June 1967 War: Some Mysteries Explored." *Middle East Journal* (Spring 1992). An examination of some of the questions discussed in the conference.

————. "The June War: Whose Conspiracy?" *Journal of Palestine Studies* (Summer 1992), a discussion of various conspiracy theories.

Quandt, William B. *Decade of Decisions: American Policy Toward the Arab-Israeli Conflict, 1967–1976.* Berkeley: University of California Press, 1977. A former NSC staffer's well-researched and authoritative study of American policy based on declassified documents, interviews, and personal knowledge.

————. *Peace Process: American Diplomacy in the Arab-Israeli Conflict Since 1967.* Berkeley: University of California Press, 1993. An updated and broader treatment of the subjects dealt with in *Decade of Decisions.*

————. "Lyndon Johnson and the June 1967 War: What Color Was the Light?" *Middle East Journal* (Spring 1992): 198–228. A close look at LBJ's decision to acquiesce in the Israeli attack on Egypt.

Rafael, Gideon. *Destination Peace.* New York: Stein & Day, 1981. Israel's former UN delegate's recollections of a long and distinguished diplomatic career.

Riad, Mahmoud. *Amrika wa al-Arab* (America and the Arabs). Cairo: Dar Mustaqbil al-Arabi, 1986. The third volume of Riad's memoirs. In the first 43 pages he interprets events leading up to the June War and American responsibility for it.

————. *The Struggle for Peace in the Middle East.* New York: Quartet Books, 1981. The first volume of memoirs of the former Egyptian Minister of Foreign Affairs.

Rikhye, General Indar Jit. *The Sinai Blunder.* New Delhi: Oxford & IBH Publishing Co., 1978. The commander of the UN Emergency Force describes the critical events of May and June 1967 from his perspective.

Rostow, Eugene. *Peace in the Balance: The Future of American Foreign Policy.* New York: Simon and Schuster, 1972. Rostow was Undersecretary of State for Political Affairs in 1967. In pages 250–82 he deals with the 1967 crisis.

Rouleau, Eric, with Jean-Francis Held and Jean and Simonne Lacouture. *Israel et les arabes: le 3ᵉ combat.* Paris: Editions du Seuil, 1967. Knowledgeable French journalists give their version of events.

Rusk, Dean. *As I Saw It.* New York: W.W. Norton, 1990. The memoirs of the Secretary of State at the time of the 1967 crisis.

Sadat, Anwar. *In Search of Identity: An Autobiography.* New York: Harper and Row, 1977. Not as many details about the Soviet warning delivered to him in Moscow as one would like.

Safran, Nadav. *From War to War: The Arab-Israeli Confrontation.* New York: Pegasus, 1969. A well-known student of the area writes on Israel's wars up to 1969.

St. John, Robert. *Eban,* New York: Doubleday, 1972. A sympathetic biography of Abba Eban.

Sam'o, Elias, ed. *The June 1967 Arab-Israeli War.* Wilmette, Ill.: Medina University Press International, 1971. A collection of articles on the June War.

Schleifer, Abdullah. *The Fall of Jerusalem.* New York: Monthly Review Press, 1972. An eyewitness account by a journalist.

Seale, Patrick. *Asad of Syria: The Struggle for the Middle East.* Berkeley and Los Angeles: University of California Press, 1988. The most authoritative biography of Syria's ruler, by a well-known British writer on the Middle East. Gives the Syrian view of the 1967 crisis.

Springborg, Robert. *Family, Power and Politics in Egypt*. Philadelphia: University of Pennsylvania Press, 1982. A study of Sayyed Marei and his family.

Stein, Janice, and Raymond Tanter. *Rational Decision Making—Israel's Security Choices, 1967*. Columbus: Ohio State University Press, 1980. An in-depth study of the factors affecting Israel's decisions in the 1967 crisis.

Urquhart, Sir Brian. *A Life in Peace and War*. New York: Harper and Row, 1987. Urquhart was Ralph Bunche's principal deputy in 1967. These memoirs have a brief account of the June War crisis as seen from New York.

Walter, Dennis. *Not Always with the Pack*. London: Constable, 1989. A British member of parliament, Walter met with Nasser well after the June War and has an interesting account of Nasser's explanation for his miscalculation.

Yost, Charles W. "The Arab-Israeli War: How It Began." *Foreign Affairs* 46 (January 1968): 304–20. Perhaps the most insightful single article explaining the circumstances that led to the June War, by a senior retired diplomat who was sent to Cairo as a special envoy during the crisis.

Zayyat, Muhammad Abd al-Salam. *Al-Sadat, al-Qina' wa al-Haqiqa* (Sadat, the mask and the truth). Cairo: Kitab al-Ahali, 1989. An attack on Sadat by a former deputy to Sayyed Marei in the Egyptian National Assembly. Gives a few personal details of Sadat's reaction to the 1967 crisis.

Index

Note: Italicized page numbers refer to photographs or maps.

Akopov, Pavel, 38–39
Allison, Graham, 269
Allon, Yigal, 221
Amit, Gen. Meir, *136;* and Angleton, 259–60, 287; CIA visit by, 124, 138–40, 193–94; on conspiracy theories, 238, 262; on context, 165, 176–77; on differences of opinion, 150–52; Helms's contacts with, 50, 136, 193–94, 276; on Hussein's role, 177, 180; on intelligence, 137–39, 142, 145; on Israeli intentions, 10, 145, 180, 221; on Israeli perceptions, 136–41, 144–45, 177; McNamara's meeting with, 140, 148; on Nasser's resignation, 20; recommendations of, 149, 296, 308; role of, 146, 210; and Samu' raid, 62, 102–3; on Soviet intentions, 216–17; on Soviet policy, 19, 49–51; on UN response, 103, 115; on U.S.-Israeli relations, 124–26; on U.S. response, 144, 239; on Ustinov's role, 64; Washington visit by, 144, 210, 256, 286–88, 292
'Amr, Field Marshal Abd al-Hakim, *43;* alternatives for, 7; Battle's meeting with, 218–19; on closure of strait, 316; death of, 55; and Jordanian communication, 158–59, 175, 181; motives of, 46; on Nasser's responsibility, 45; orders from, 67, 142, 171–72; Pakistan visit by, 56; rivalries of, 19–20, 44–45, 49, 55–56, 76, 301; role of, 289, 294; and Soviet warning, 18–19, 53; and UNEF withdrawal, 42–43, 45–46
'Amr, Ali, 181, 183
Anderson, Robert B.: Nasser's relations with, 112–13, 129, 211–12, 214, 276; role of, 191, 252
Andropov, Yuri, 47–48, 50, 68
Angleton, James, 136, 225, 239, 246, 256, 259–60, 271, 287

Arafat, Yasir, 162
Argov, Shlomo, 147
armistice agreements: attitudes toward, 283; collapse of, 104–5, 117; and demilitarized zones, 248; effectiveness of, 97, 164, 318; and Israel, 97, 99, 104–5, 108; legacy of, 195; meetings of, 83, 96, 163; memorandum on, 201–2; negotiations in, 1, 195; participants in, 282; versus peace, 228, 292, 295; revival of, 99; termination of, 97; terms of, 197, 233. *See also* demilitarized zones (DZs); peace
Asad, Hafez al, 127
Associated Press, 68–69
Atassi, Nuredin, *10,* 127, 247
Atherton, Alfred L.: on conspiracy theories, 274–75; on point of no return, 60; role of, 275–76, 301; on U.S. policy, 291–92, 317–18; on U.S. response, 222–23, 295
Austin, Granville, 60
Australia, and multinational fleet, 218

Ba'ath Party: and Egypt, 66; in Iraq, 161; and Nasser's South Arabian efforts, 162; propaganda of, 161–62; in Syria, 25, 54, 64, 97, 137, 155, 157, 161, 250
Badran, Shams: on Egyptian military strength, 66; evaluation requested by, 72; Moscow visit by, 16, 18–19, 38–39, 40, 44, 46, 73; motives of, 46; Pojidaev's meeting with, 37–38, 51–52; rivalries of, 56; and Soviet warning, 18–19
Balfour Declaration, 110, 112–13, 185, 244
Ball, George, 207
Barkovsky, Ambassador Anatoly, 36, 61
Basheer, Tahsin, *182;* on conspiracy theories, 238–39, 244–52, 283–86; on deescalation, 113–14; on Gulf navigation, 113, 242; on Hammarskjöld memo, 93; on Hussein, 160; on Israeli intentions,

Basheer, Tahsin (*continued*)
64; on Jordanian actions, 153; on Nasser, 55–56, 289–90, 316; on 1957 agreement, 226–27; on Sadat, 316–17; on
UNEF withdrawal, 20; on UN response,
92, 108–9; on U.S.-Israeli relations, 244–
45, 249, 251, 303
Bassiouny, Salah, *23;* on conspiracy theories, 239; on Egyptian response, 17–19,
41–46; on Gromyko's Cairo visit, 293;
on Jordanian actions, 153; on microhistory focus, 21; on Pojidaev, 53–54; role
of, 142; on sequence of events, 65; on Soviet cautions, 38; on UN response,
103–4; on U.S.-Israeli relations, 231–32;
on U.S. response, 276–77
Battle, Lucius, *248;* on aftermath, 291,
298–99; 'Amr's meeting with, 218–19;
on congressional approval, 219–20; on
conspiracy theories, 244; departure from
Cairo of, 229; on Israeli intentions, 292;
Johnson's meeting with, 207; on multinational fleet, 218; on Nasser, 218–19,
263–64, 311; on possibility of peace,
128–29; Riad's meeting with, 72, 218–
19; role of, 264, 303; Sadat's meeting
with, 218–19; staff of, 222; on UNEF
withdrawal, 114; on UN response, 111–
12; and U.S. policy, 200–202, 217–19,
319; on USS *Liberty,* 278–79
Battov, General, 50
BBC (British Broadcasting Corporation),
304
Begin, Menachem, 165–66, 225, 270
Ben-Gurion, David: and armistice agreement, 195; concerns of, 265–66; and diplomacy efforts, 1, 128, 250, 283; letters
to, 132; strategy of, 221
Bergus, Donald C., *193;* on congressional attitudes, 219; and 1957 agreement, 109,
113, 201; role of, 186, 231, 263; on U.S.
context, 189, 196–97; on U.S.-Egyptian
relations, 242; on U.S. response, 224–25
Bet Katzir (Israel), 25
Bhutto, Zulfikar Ali, 245
Black, Eugene, 245
Boulding, Kenneth, 25
Bourguiba, Habib, 1
Boutros-Ghali, Boutros, 75
Brecher, Michael, 29
Brezhnev, Leonid Ilyich: and Afghanistan,
37; alliances of, 19, 50; encouragement

from, 39; rise to power of, 4; role of, 47–
48, 50; and Soviet Middle East policy,
20, 61, 315–16
British Mandate for Palestine, 120
Bromell, William, 260, 263–64
Brown, George, 200
Brown, L. Carl, *23;* on bureaucratic politics, 49, 277, 291, 303; on conference
purpose, 23; on conspiracy theories, 269;
on context, 299–301; origins of war summarized by, 13–19; on point of no return, 60; on UN response, 107
Buffum, William, *105*
Bull, Gen. Odd, 100, 164, 184
Bunche, Ralph: on armistice agreements,
117; attitudes toward, 86; goal of, 90;
and Hammarskjöld memo, 91–92; role
of, 96, 99, 107, 163; on UNEF forces,
83, 85, 87–89; and UN response, 93–95
Bundy, McGeorge: role of, 152, 200; on
U.S.-Israeli relations, 239, 244; on U.S. response, 213–16; and Vietnam, 247; on
war origins, 222
Burns, Gen. E. L. M., 87, 164
Burns, Findley, 177, 186
Bush, George, 187, 209

Camp David accords, 231, 251, 285
Canada: Johnson's visit to, 133; and UNEF
forces, 87, 91–92, 104, 111
Canadian House of Commons, 92
Caradon, Lord, 104, 116
Carter, Jimmy, 145–46, 227
Castro, Fidel, 262
cease-fire: acceptance of, 8, 45; call for,
194; Johnson's support for, 222; negotiations on, 184; versus peace, 228, 265,
295; timing of, 230–31; UN resolutions
on, 166–67, 184–85
Chernyakov, 54
Churchill, Randolph, 254
Churchill, Winston, 150, 280, 295
Chuvakin, Ambassador Dimitri: inspection
visit refused by, 28, 59; Israeli meeting
with, 19; prediction by, 50–51
CIA: accusations against, 239, 259, 261;
Amit's visit to, 124, 138–40, 193–94; departments in, 259–60; Egyptian attitude
toward, 264; estimates by, 255; and Middle East tensions, 253; misinformation
for, 256; and Mossad report, 216; and
Nasser-'Amr rivalry, 49; personnel in,

263; and Soviet warning, 58; writing about, 257–58

Clifford, Clark, 207

Cockburn, Andrew: on aftermath, 287–88, 291, 294; on conspiracy theories, 239, 252–57, 286–88; on U.S. estimates, 227–28; on U.S.-Israeli relations, 279–80; writing by, 144, 205, 271

Cockburn, Leslie, 239

Cohen, Eli, 246

cold war: and call for cease-fire, 194; as context of war, 35–36, 47–48, 118, 200–201, 252–53; description of, 127; interests in, 2–3; and Israeli attack on Syria, 230–31; Soviet-U.S. relations in, 146–48; and UN response, 75, 81, 88, 91, 111–12, 115, 118, 126, 150, 201, 203, 233

communications: between ambassadors and governments, 59, 61; between Egypt and UN, 88–89; Egypt's use of, 179; failure in, 112, 290–91, 301–3, 311, 319; importance of, 299; Jordanian difficulty with, 179–80; with public, 307; between United States and Arab world, 242, 246

conspiracy theories: accusations of, 124, 158, 160, 181, 204–6, 241; characteristics of, 267–69; versus collusion, 286–88; components in, 240, 244–45; context for, 252–57; definition of, 240, 261, 281–84; denial of, 239–40, 256, 304; documentation on, 238; effects of, 272–73, 286; examples of, 260–62, 267–69, 272, 277, 279, 310; participants in, 153; and public opinion, 267–68, 270–71, 282; summary of, 237–43, 246–47

Copeland, Miles, 257

Cuba, and conspiracy theories, 262

Cuban missile crisis, 23, 46, 49–50, 290–91, 315

Czechoslovakia: Soviet invasion of, 46–47; Soviet pressure on, 67

Damascus (Syria), air battle over, 6, 83, 97, 103, 155, 164, 253

Davies, Rodger, 132

Dawisha, Karen: on Andropov, 50, 68; on Israeli troops, 186–87; on Soviet-Egyptian relations, 67–68; on Soviet leadership divisions, 46–49; on Soviet role, 19, 293

Dawn, C. Ernest: on aftermath, 313–14; on Arab politics, 296–98; Arab responses

summarized by, 153–61; on causes, 56–57; on conspiracy theories, 279–80; on Pan-Arab nationalist dimension, 161–63; on press reports, 20; on Syrian situation, 290

Day, Arthur (Pete), 112

Dayan, Gen. Moshe: accusations by, 247; appointment of, 55, 165; influences on, 221; motives of, 64; role of, 121, 123, 128, 140–41; staff of, 152; strategy of, 149, 220–21, 308–9; on war origins, 222

de Gaulle, Charles, 5, 45, 122

demilitarized zones (DZs): escalation in, 163, 186; Israeli expansion into, 248–49, 253–54; land disputes in, 97; status of, 164

deterrence warnings, 34

Dimona (Israel), nuclear facility at, 251

diplomacy: components in, 49; versus defense, 27–28, 33–34; versus military action, 212–13; peace as goal of, 201; and public opinion, 191

Dobrynin, Anatoli, 54, 201, 296

Dulles, John Foster, 2, 130–31, 192, 201, 242

Eban, Abba, 134; and cause of war, 60; diplomacy advocated by, 34; diplomatic trip by, 94; Dulles's meeting with, 131; and Israeli intentions, 243; on Israel's survival, 135; Johnson's meetings with, 122, 126, 133, 192–93, 205, 207–9, 214; message to Johnson from, 292, 318; and predicted Egyptian attack, 142; role of, 303; and Security Council meeting, 100; on "spirit of Tashkent," 27; and U.S. aide mémoire of 1957, 130–31, 242; on U.S. policy, 318; Washington trip by, 124, 133–35, 143, 147, 149–50

Eden, Anthony, 250, 283

Egypt: American Embassy in, 45, 190–91, 229, 242; Anglo-French attack on, 2; attack on Israelis in Sinai by, 277; characterization of, 17; documentation in, 37; economic development in, 189–90; foreign relations of, 41; influences on, 156–57, 277; Israeli attack on, 265, 276; Jordanian relations with, 156–57; leadership divisions in, 17–19, 21, 44–46, 55–56, 67, 76; military strength of, 16, 38–39, 48, 51, 57, 66–67, 216, 228, 309–10, 312–14; misinformation from, 172–74,

Egypt (*continued*)
176–78; motives of, 9, 142, 286, 305;
public opinion in, 86, 241–42; response
of, 17–19, 41–46; and right to demand
UNEF withdrawal, 82–83, 85–87, 90–
92, 116; Syrian relations with, 27, 62–
64, 103, 156; U.S. assistance for, 190,
196, 227, 229, 283; warnings to, 192,
239, 241–42, 276–77. *See also* Egyptian-
Syrian treaty; Gaza Strip; Sinai Peninsula;
U.S.-Egyptian relations
Egyptian air force, destruction of, 174, 315
Egyptian army: destruction of, 315; Jordanian troops commanded by, 100, 106,
160–61, 170–74; Soviet pressure on, 67,
72. *See also* Sinai Peninsula
Egyptian Foreign Ministry: decision-making
process in, 43–45; on Israeli military
strength, 42; and Soviet relations, 67–68;
and Soviet warning, 16–18, 20, 43–44,
71–72; and Syrian-Israeli tensions, 67
Egyptian-Israeli Mixed Armistice Commission, 96–97, 195
Egyptian-Israeli relations: changes in, 127;
and Nasser's response to Samu', 101; and
peace attempts, 265, 267, 270
Egyptian-Jordanian agreement: implications
of, 106, 143, 152, 191, 193, 202, 247;
motives for, 159, 169, 182–83; signing
of, 106–7, *171;* terms of, 172, 174; and
timing of Israeli attack, 159–60, 225
Egyptian-Syrian treaty of 1956: Egypt's failure to honor, 6; impact of, 175–76, 182;
Israeli response to, 103; as threat, 27
Eilat (Israeli port), 93, 95n, 120, 122, 243
Eisenhower, Dwight D.: and aide mémoire
of 1957, 202, 242, 307; Johnson supported by, 152; and Jordan River, 185;
and 1956 Israeli attack, 11; and Suez legacy, 214; and U.S.-Egyptian relations,
189
Eisenhower doctrine: confrontation over,
41; and congressional role, 203
embargo, by United States, 152
Eshkol, Levi, *98;* cautions to, 149–50; diplomacy advocated by, 34, 59, 132, 287,
314; on Israeli intentions, 243; Johnson's
June 2 letter to, 210; as moderate, 15,
27, 121; and moratorium, 95, 115–16;
papers of, 129; policies of, 126–27; pressures on, 124, 225; promises of, 203;

speeches of, 30, 299; style of, 128; and
UN response, 94; warning by, 164–65
Eveland, Wilbur Crane, 182, 246, 256, 257
Evron, Ephraim, *128;* on aftermath, 308,
316–17, 318n; and alliances, 145–46; on
conspiracy theories, 269–70; and Fortas,
212; on Israeli response, 123, 126–36,
167, 252; on Israeli-U.S. relations, 129–
32; on Israeli warning to Jordan, 157,
180–81; Johnson's meetings with, 126,
207, 214; on Jordanian response, 178;
meeting with E. Rostow, 132; meeting
with W. Rostow, 210; and 1957 agreement, 201; on point of no return, 152,
307; and predicted Egyptian attack, 142;
role of, 140, 146; on Sadat, 316–17; on
UNEF withdrawal, 114; on U.S. response, 223, 225, 307; on war with
Syria, 225–26

face-saving: devices for, 117–18; issues in,
76, 114–15, 305, 311
Fakhr, Col. Ahmad, 44
Faisal (king of Saudi Arabia), 162, 225,
227, 229
Fatah: leadership of, 162; operations of, 25,
27, 56, 75, 100, 253, 282
Fawzi, Mahmoud, 88, 113, 242, 316
Fawzi, Gen. Muhammad: and Marshal
'Amr, 45; on military situation, 67; and
report on Israel-Syria border, 18, 28, 42–
43; Syria visit by, 176; UNEF withdrawal
request by, 75, 83, 99
FBIS (Foreign Broadcast Information Ser-
vice), 254, 262, 286, 304
Federenko, Nikolai, 61, 315–16
al-Feki, Ahmad Hassan: and Grechko's en-
couragement to Badran, 44; Pojidaev's
meeting with, 42; Semenov's meeting
with, 18, 44; and Soviet warning, 17–19,
37–38, 293
Feron, James, 32–33, 69
Findley, Paul, 278
Folger, Kay, 219
Foreign Broadcast Information Service
(FBIS), 254, 262, 286, 304
Fortas, Justice Abe: influence by, 212; Johnson's calls to, 272; meetings of, 207; role
of, 70, 135–36, 208, 225–26
France: Arab relations with, 5; Egypt attacked by, 2; intelligence service of, 139;

and Israeli response, 122; Middle East policy of, 200, 244
Freedman, Robert, 54
friendly fire. *See* USS *Liberty*

Gamasy, Gen., 50
Garthoff, Raymond: on context, 315–16; on Cuban missile crisis, 290–91; on Israeli response, 148–49, 158, 176; on U.S.-Soviet relations, 230–31
Gaza Strip: casualties in, 82; Israeli occupation of, 243; military observers in, 99; 1955 attack on, 265; situation in, 87, 89, 115; UNEF forces in, 83; UNTSO in, 96–97
George, Alexander, 34
Ghalib, Murad, 73
Golan Heights: control of, 97, 221; Israeli occupation of, 194, 230, 243, 254, 319; offensive against, 33, 97; and peace negotiations, 270
Goldberg, Arthur, *105;* Johnson's calls to, 272; and military assistance, 234; role of, 104, 116, 150, 200, 203, 216, 245; on use of force, 295
Gomulka, Wladyslaw, 50
Gonen (kibbutz), 25
Goodpaster, Col. Andrew, 202
Gorchkov, 47, 49
Great Britain: and Anglo-French attack on Egypt, 5; Israeli relations with, 2, 127; and Israeli response, 122–23; Middle East policy of, 57, 120, 244, 252–53; and multinational fleet, 8, 193, 202, 207, 218; and UNEF in Egypt, 243, 274; U.S. relations with, 200, 213, 244
Grechko, Marshal Andrei: alliances of, 19, 50; encouragement from, 16, 18, 39, 44, 73; rise to power of, 19, 67; role of, 47, 67–68; on Soviet military, 314
Green, Stephen, 205, 239, 260–61
Gromyko, Andrei, 296: Cairo visit by, 21, 58, 67, 293–94; caution urged by, 187; role of, 48
Gulf of Tonkin resolution, 134, 204

Hammarskjöld, Dag: death of, 272; memorandum by, 90–94; on peacekeeping forces, 79; role of, 75; and UNEF deployment, 82, 86–87
Ha'on (kibbutz), 25

Harman, Avraham: contacts of, 140; on Eban's Washington trip, 133, 148; Eisenhower visit by, 152; and Fortas, Abe, 212, 226; reservations of, 266; Rusk's meeting with, 211
Harriman, Averell, 200
Hashemite regime, 102, 177, 253
Heikal, Mohamed: on conspiracy theories, 246; contacts of, 218; on Hussein, 11, 175, 181–82; on moratorium, 241; and U.S. commitment on Gulf of Aqaba, 242; on withdrawal versus redeployment, 89
Helms, Richard, *258;* Amit's contact with, 50, 136, 193–94, 276; on communications, 302; on conspiracy theories, 238–39, 257–62; Johnson's calls to, 272; on military assistance, 233–34; role of, 207, 257; on U.S. intelligence estimates, 216–17; on U.S.-Israeli relations, 248; on USS *Liberty,* 278–79
Hickenlooper, Sen. Bourke, 227
Hitti, Philip, 60
Hod, Gen. Mordechai, 165
Holmes, Julius, 200
Humphrey, Hubert, 113, 233–34, 302, 307–8, 311
Hussein, Saddam, 32, 250, 282, 284, 298
Hussein, Sharif (of Mecca), 249
Hussein ibn Talal (king of Jordan), *171;* alternatives for, 159, 168–69; conspiracy accusations against, 246–47; and inter-Arab politics, 159, 169–70, 310; and Israeli intentions, 100, 102–3, 156, 169–71, 183–84; Israeli messages to, 11, 157, 180–81, 183–84, 186; misinformation sent to, 157–58, 172–74, 175–77; motives of, 11, 169–70, 181–82; Nasser's meeting with, 106–7, 174; and Palestinian problem, 168–70, 177; propaganda against, 102–3; and Samu' raid, 60, 180; on Syrian trap, 175; warning from, 159, 175–76, 181–82, 246. *See also* Egyptian-Jordanian agreement
Hutchinson, Elmo H., 164
Huwaydi, Amin, 55

Idris (king of Libya), 219
India: caution urged by, 66; UAR supported by, 76, 85–86; UNEF casualties from, 82; and UNEF withdrawal, 86, 90, 96, 111, 115

intaharuh, 55

intelligence services: attitudes toward, 197,
264; cooperation among, 138–39, 216,
239; information sources for, 262; relationships among, 259–60, 262, 271; role
of, 284; workings of, 138–39, 145. *See
also* CIA; Mossad; KGB; Soviet warning

International Court of Justice, 77, 108, 191,
226–27

international politics: brinkmanship in, 16,
19, 49–50, 109, 178–79; bureaucratic
politics in, 49–51, 277, 291, 300, 303–4;
and communications, 242, 299; crisis
management in, 273–74, 277; decision
making in, 302–3; nature of, 239–40,
269, 307–8; psychological dimension in,
299–300; role of, 297–98; and technology of control, 284; war's impact on,
319. *See also* communications; diplomacy

Intrepid, 218

Iran, Soviet relations with, 47

Iraq: Ba'athists in, 161; 1958 revolution in,
41, 161, 189

Irgun Zvi Leumi, 166

Islamic Pact, 162

Israel: borders of, 26, 112–13, 166, 169,
243; and diplomacy, 93–95; internal politics in, 4, 33, 159–61, 240; Jordanian relations with, 157, 178; leadership differences in, 21, 27–28, 33–34, 46, 62, 128,
138, 141–42, 147, 150–51, 303; motives
of, 10, 28–29, 60–64, 101–2, 154, 156–
57, 183–84, 186, 254, 285, 319; perceptions of, 136–41, 144–45, 154, 177; policies of, 60, 64, 120–21, 177, 281;
provocation by, 253; public opinion in,
61–62, 121, 123–24, 137–38, 310; response of, 120–36, 141–44, 148–49,
158, 167, 176, 210–11, 233, 252; responsibility of, 251; and Soviet warning, 39;
and strike decision, 147; survival of, 1–2,
24, 36, 106, 119, 135, 138, 146, 255,
275–76, 286, 297; Syrian relations with,
6, 25, 27, 67, 163–64; terrorism by, 153;
terrorist attacks on, 27–28, 201, 253,
282; threats against, 162–63; and UNEF
deployment, 86, 105–6, 116–17; U.S. recommendations to, 122–25, 128–30, 132–
35, 138, 147–49; and U.S. response,
119–21, 125–26, 144; U.S. support for,
70, 139–41, 146–47, 279–80, 287; warnings by, 25, 33–34, 177, 180–81, 187–

88; and water rights, 25, 106–7, 113,
185–86, 248. *See also* armistice agreements; Israeli Defense Forces; Israeli
"threat"; retaliation strategy, Israel's;
U.S.-Israeli relations

Israeli air force: over Damascus, 6, 83, 97,
103, 155, 164, 253; Jordanian troops
bombarded by, 173, 180

Israeli Communist Party, 19

Israeli Defense Forces (IDF): alleged troop
movements of, 28–30, 32, 37–38, 42–43,
52, 58–59, 99, 154–57, 241, 254; mobilization of, 165, 225; preemptive strike by,
152, 203, 210–11, 276; strategy of, 14,
29, 60, 220–21, 296, 308–9; strength of,
36, 41–42, 49, 154, 161, 192, 217, 251,
255, 276, 317; and U.S. military assistance, 192, 233–34. *See also* Syria: Israeli
attack on; USS *Liberty*

Israeli military intelligence: assessments by,
121, 128, 142–43; and U.S. green light,
146–47

Israel-Jordan Mixed Armistice Commission,
97

Israeli National Water Carrier scheme, 25,
106–7, 248

Israeli Radio, 30

Israel-Soviet relations, 27–28, 33, 35–36

Israel-Syria Mixed Armistice Commission
(ISMAC), 83, 97, 163–64

Israeli "threat": alleged origins of, 30–32;
context of, 24–25; and diplomacy, 27–
28; impact of, 32–34, 60, 75, 154; media
reports on, 20, 68–69; summary of, 14–
15, 34–35, 71

Israelyan, Victor: on conspiracy theories,
280–81; on Soviet policy, 20; on Soviet
warning, 61, 312

Izvestia, Egyptian action encouraged in,
63–64

Jarring, Gunnar, 88

Jerusalem: and Jordanian operations, 172–
73; UN enclave seized in, 8

Johns Hopkins School of Advanced International Studies, 11

Johnson, Lyndon B., *134, 198, 296;* administration of, 191, 199–200, 301; on Arab
military strength, 192; and Arab relations, 3, 111; Canada visit by, 133; CIA's
reports to, 216–17; and communication
with Egypt, 229, 242, 246; constraints

on, 133–34, 139; Eban's contacts with, 122, 126, 133, 192–93, 205, 207–9, 214, 292, 318; Evron's meetings with, 126, 207, 214; influences on, 202, 207–9, 211–12, 216, 247, 255, 272, 302, 307; and Israeli attack on Syria, 221–22; on Israeli borders, 166; and Israeli relations, 5, 11, 37, 70, 123, 125, 130–31, 204–12; Israelis' meetings with, 124, 134–35, 143, 149; motives of, 250–51, 254–55, 306; policy of, 201, 213–14, 314, 317–20; role of, 120–21, 195–96, 203–11; signals from, 210–12, 256, 271–72; Soviets' meetings with, 187, 295; stereotype of, 206; style of, 208–13, 260, 272; and Suez crisis, 110; on use of force, 295; and USS *Liberty*, 266

Johnston, Eric, 185–86, 248

Jordan: Arab forces in, 172, 174, 183; Egypt criticized by, 56, 159, 162, 188; Egyptian relations with, 156–57; and guerrilla movements, 27–28; internal politics in, 41, 159–60, 168–69, 177; Israeli attack on, 6, 8, 257; and Israeli intentions, 319; Israeli negotiations with, 1; Israeli relations with, 157, 178; and Israeli retaliation, 56, 62–63, 160–61; Israeli warnings to, 157, 177, 180–81, 187–88; misinformation sent to, 172–74, 176–78; motives of, 11; and Palestinian cause, 159; and propaganda, 158–59, 177–81; response of, 153, 157–60, 168–78, 199; threats against, 6–7, 29. *See also* Egyptian-Jordanian agreement; Hussein ibn Talal; Samu' (Jordan) raid; West Bank

Jordanian Army: air bombardment of, 173, 180; air cover for, 170–71; Egyptian command of, 100, 106, 160–61, 170–74; Fortieth Armored Brigade, 172, 173; Sixtieth Armored Brigade, 172, 173, 180

Jordan River: diversion of, 106, 177, 185–86, 248, 250; rights to, 113, 153

June War. *See* Six-Day War

Kennedy, John F.: assassination of, 261–62, 267; and U.S.-Egyptian relations, 3, 189–90, 196, 250

Kerr, Malcolm, 3, 49

Kfar Szold (kibbutz), 25

KGB (Soviet intelligence): influence by, 59; leadership of, 47–48, 50; misinformation

by, 68; and Soviet warning, 16–18, 37, 42, 52–53, 64–65, 71, 294

Khammash, Gen. Amor, 176

Khartoum resolution, 270

Khirbet Tawafiq incident, 316

Khomeini, Ruhollah, 250

Khrushchev, Nikita: criticism of, 148; Nasser's relations with, 66, 129, 148; ousting of, 4; rise to power of, 2

Kissinger, Henry, 199, 317

Komer, Robert, 158, 229–30, 251

al-Kony, Muhammad Awad: and cease-fire, 45; and moratorium, 95; role of, 245; and UNEF withdrawal request, 83, 85–86, 88, 107

Korean War, influence of, 203

Korn, David, 60

Kornienko, Georgiy, 52; on ambassador's orders, 59, 280; on Soviet role, 70–73, 155; on Soviet warning, 20, 51–52, 293; on UNEF withdrawal, 114

Kosygin, Aleksei, 296; alliances of, 50; Badran's meeting with, 38; and blockade of strait, 40; caution urged by, 73, 187; Egyptians supported by, 38–39; on Egyptian-Syrian relations, 156; and Israeli response, 135; Johnson's meeting with, 295; on Middle East policy, 47–48; rise to power of, 4; role of, 47–48, 55; warning by, 16, 73

Kozyrev, Andrei, 281–82

Krim, Arthur, 255, 272

Krim, Matilda, 255, 272, 302

Kuwait: Iraq's challenge to, 189; Nasser's role in, 250

Kux, Dennis, 277, 279

Lakeland, William, 283

Lavon affair, 283

Law of the Sea, UN conference on, 77

LBJ. *See* Johnson, Lyndon B.

League of Nations, 185

Lebanon: and guerrilla movements, 27–28; uprising in, 41

Lehi, 166

Lewis, Samuel: on aftermath, 294; on communications, 59; on Israeli actions, 220, 297; on military situation, 308–9; on 1957 agreement, 231; on policy changes, 292; role of, 270; summary by, 319–20; on UN response, 104; on U.S. response, 295, 303

Libya, politics in, 219
Lior, Gen. Israel, 144
Liu, F. T., 96; on UNEF withdrawal, 114–15; on UN response, 95–97, 99–100
Lodge, Henry Cabot, 130, 242
Lorch, Netanel, 166
Lourie, Aryeh, 100

Ma'ariv, reports in, 29
Madrid, 1991 negotiations in, 308
Majali, Brig. Atif, 172
Malik (Soviet ambassador), 61
Malinovsky, Marshal, 19, 50
Mapai Party, 30, 165
Mapam Party, 141
Mardor, Meir, 185
Mattar, Philip, summary by, 319
McClure, Associated Press, 32, 68–69
McNamara, Robert: on alternatives, 210; Amit's meeting with, 140, 148; on congressional resolution, 203; and Israeli attack on Syria, 222; Johnson's calls to, 272; operational plan by, 209; role of, 200; on secret missions, 239, 261
media: alleged statements reported by, 7, 14, 30–33, 59, 71, 154; characterizations by, 20; Egyptian action encouraged in, 63–64; on Egyptian military forces, 101; Egyptian use of, 179; and intra-Arab criticism of Egypt, 56; on Israeli threat, 68–69; reliability of, 163, 304; as source for intelligence reports, 262; and Soviet warning, 56–57. See also radio transmissions
Meeker, Leonard: on Amit, 149; on Israeli force, 202; on UNEF, 92; on U.S. position, 295–96, 308
Meir, Golda, 8, 130–32, 203
Middle East Institute, 11
military equipment: Soviet-Egyptian agreements on, 2, 38, 65–67; from Soviet Union, 38, 66–67, 147, 277; from United States, 192, 233–34, 250
miscalculation syndrome, 290–91, 311–15
Moorer, Adm. Thomas, 266
moratorium: and Egyptians, 95, 114, 242–43; support for, 92–93; terms of, 243; Thant's request for, 94–95, 115–16, 243
Morozov, Platon, 315
Moscow Radio, Israeli troop movements reported on, 63–64
Mossad (Central Institute for Intelligence and Special Missions): accusations

against, 259; defense of, 137; and Soviet brinkmanship, 19; workings of, 138–39, 145
Mossadegh, Mohammad, 283
Mt. Scopus, and Jordanian operations, 172
Muhieddin, Zakariya, 109, 113–14, 191, 195, 212
al-Mukabbir Hill, and Jordanian operations, 172–74
Mukhitdinov (Soviet ambassador), 61
Murphy, Richard, 310
Murtagi, Gen. Abdul Muhsin, 156–57
Mutawi, Samir: on causes, 309–10; on conspiracy theories, 310; on Hussein, 159–60, 181; on Jordanian response, 153, 157, 168–76; on propaganda, 178–80, 182; on Samu' raid, 100–102; summary by, 319

Narkiss, Gen. Uzi, 180
Nasr, Salah: reports to, 65; Soviet warning delivered to, 42, 54, 293; and U.S. contacts, 260, 264
al-Nasser, Gamal Abd, 43, 173; actions of, 5–6, 128–29, 137, 151, 198, 207, 227, 289–90, 312–13, 316; alliances of, 106–7, 143, 169, 174, 265; alternatives of, 219; anticommunist policy of, 66; on Arab war readiness, 3, 9, 309–10, 312–14; and communication channels, 112, 117, 157–59; description of, 211–12; and Hammarskjöld memo, 91–93; Hussein's meeting with, 106–7, 174; influences on, 97, 99, 158–59; on Israeli threat, 29–30, 32–33, 71; motives of, 62, 127, 137, 162, 165, 219, 285–86, 294, 305; overcommitment by, 76–77, 79; and Pan-Arab nationalism, 161–62; and peace attempts, 265, 267; plot against, 175–76, 181–82, 237–39, 241, 245–47; Pojidaev's meeting with, 38, 52; preemptive plans by, 38–39; propaganda against, 158–62, 170, 177–81; resignation of, 20, 51; responsibility of, 45, 51, 65–67, 214–15, 219, 265; rivalries of, 19, 20, 44–46, 49, 55–56, 76, 301; role of, 41, 161, 246–47; speeches by, 229, 263–64; Thant's contacts with, 117, 281, 289, 312; and UNEF withdrawal, 21, 42–43, 181; UN relations with, 78, 82, 85–86, 89–97, 99, 113–14, 117; U.S. attitudes toward, 125, 256, 263–64, 275; U.S. rela-

tions with, 189–90, 196–97, 206–7, 229, 291, 316; warnings to, 50, 55, 159, 181, 241, 245–46, 258. *See also* Egyptian-Jordanian agreement; Egyptian-Syrian treaty

Nassif, Ramsis, 95n

National Security Council (U.S.), 199, 205, 207

NATO (North Atlantic Treaty Organization), 200

Naumkin, Vitaly: on Soviets in Syria, 156; on Soviet situation, 64–65; on Soviet warning, 15–18, 35–41, 293

Nes, David, 241, 264

Netherlands, and multinational fleet, 193, 218

New York Times, reports in, 69, 93

Nixon, Richard M., 317

Nolte, Richard, 45, 93, 112, 229

Norway, and UNEF withdrawal, 111, 115

Nuclear Non-Proliferation Treaty (NPT), 47, 251

nuclear weapons, and Israel, 158, 250–51

Oakley, Robert, 59

O'Ballance, Edgar, 179

occupation, Israeli, 185, 228, 318

October War. *See* Yom Kippur War

oil: and moratorium terms, 243; as strategic cargo, 8; U.S. access to, 2–3; and U.S.-Egyptian relations, 190; and U.S.-Israeli relations, 224; and U.S. opinion of Nasser, 196

Operation Nachson, 166

Operation Tariq, 172–74

Pakistan, 'Amr's visit to, 56

Palestine: borders of, 166, 169; Jordanian commitment to, 170; Nasser's support for, 175–76; not a hot issue, 222–23; and Pan-Arabism, 159, 162; partitioning of, 1, 244–45, 249; refugee problem, 177, 248–49; voice of, 249, 251. *See also* Israel: borders of

Palestine Conciliation Commission, 117, 249

Palestine Liberation Organization (PLO), 162, 231

Palestinian guerrilla movements: effects of, 312; increased incursions into Israel by, 6, 27, 41, 83, 253; retaliation against, 68–69, 99–100; Soviet encouragement of, 41; Syrian support for, 6, 27, 57, 83,

100, 127, 137, 156, 162, 177, 197, 201, 253, 282, 312; and UN response, 75

Panama, U.S. intervention in, 298

Pan-Arabism: concerns of, 159; description of, 161–63; influence by, 153, 296–97

Parker, Richard B.: on conference purpose, 22–23, 51; conspiracy theories summarized by, 237–43; on context, 228–29; on Egypt and CIA, 264; on point of no return, 60; role of, 263; on Syrian-Soviet relations, 54

parochialism, 229–30

peace: versus armistice, 228, 292, 295; components of, 235, 245, 317; as goal, 201, 306, 318–19; and land-for-peace exchange, 318; Middle East process of, 194–96, 199; and occupation issue, 185, 228, 270, 318; opportunities for, 266–68; planning for, 228; as political condition, 197; resistance to, 1

Pearson, Anthony, 158

Pearson, Lester, 91–92, 104, 133

Pentagon, and multinational fleet plan, 209

Peres, Shimon, 128

Peretz, Don, summary by, 319

Persian Gulf, British in, 57, 252–53

Persian Gulf War (1991), 137, 298

PLO. *See* Palestine Liberation Organization

Podgorny, Nikolay Viktorovich, 48

Pojidaev, Ambassador Dimitri: 'Amr's meeting with, 53; Feki's meeting with, 42; instructions to, 20, 51, 59, 72, 280; Nasser's meeting with, 38, 52; replacement of, 20, 61; Riad's meeting with, 37–38, 51–52; role of, 40; and Soviet warning, 16–18, 37–38, 53–54, 65, 72

Ponomarev, Boris, 47, 247

popular liberation war doctrine, 25, 156, 312

Porter, Dwight, 279

Pravda, Egyptian action encouraged in, 63–64

pro-Israeli demonstrators, 215

propaganda: in Arab world, 158–62, 170, 177–82; of Ba'ath Party, 161–62; and conspiracy theories, 267–68; against Hussein, 102–3; against Nasser, 158–62, 170, 177–81

public opinion: after Six-Day War, 214, 306–7; and casualties, 142; and conspiracy theories, 267–68, 282; and diplomacy, 191; in Egypt on United States, 86,

public opinion (*continued*)
241–42; and Eshkol's speech, 299–300;
influence by, 22; in Israel, 61–62, 121,
123–24, 137–38, 310; on Israeli intentions, 101, 266; and Jordanian response,
168–70; and June 5 attack, 165; versus
military estimates, 255; and retaliation,
25, 103; and Samu' raid, 62–63, 102;
and UNEF in Egypt, 90; in United States,
192, 196, 204, 214, 256, 263–64, 275

Qadhafi, Muammar, 284
Qalqilya raid, 25
Qasim, Abd Karim, 250
Quandt, William: on communications, 302;
on conspiracy theories, 239–40, 270–72;
on Israeli response, 144; on Jordanian response, 177–78; on peace negotiations,
292; on Rusk's position, 224; on U.S.-Is-
raeli relations, 303; on U.S. policy, 318;
on U.S. response, 223, 235–36; on White
House context, 204–13, 302

Rabin, Gen. Yitzhak: accusations against,
247; alleged statements by, 6–7, 30–31,
254, 270, 280, 286, 309; Dayan's meeting with, 55; memoirs of, 152; motives
of, 64; and retaliation plans, 29
Radio Cairo, 179
Radio Damascus, 32
radio transmissions: Egypt's use of, 179;
Eshkol's statement in, 30; fabrication of,
157–58; Israeli troop movements reported on, 63–64; UPI dispatch reported
in, 32
Rafael, Gideon, *106;* on conspiracy theories, 281–82; on context, 57; on Israeli-
Jordanian relations, 157; and Israeli message to Hussein, 157, 183–84; on Israeli
response, 233; Moscow trip by, 21; role
of, 140, 167; on Soviet warning, 58–59;
summary by, 319; on UNEF forces, 116–
17; on UN response, 93–95, 104–7; on
U.S. policy, 149–50
refugees, 177, 248–49
Reich, Bernard: on causes, 291; on communications, 301; Israeli response summarized by, 119–26
retaliation strategy, Israel's: components of,
14–15, 33; context for, 29, 71; effectiveness of, 20, 56, 62–63, 310–11; impact

of, 1–2; and public opinion, 25, 103; ra-
tionale for, 24–25, 119, 123
Revisionist Zionism, 159–60
Riad, Gen. Abd al-Mun'im: alliances of,
182–83; appointment of, 11, 106; messages to, 157, 175, 176; role of, 170–71;
strategy of, 172–73
Riad, Mahmoud, *248;* Battle's meeting
with, 72, 218–19; evaluation requested
by, 72; messages to, 241; plans of, 285;
Pojidaev's meeting with, 37–38, 51–52;
role of, 316; and UNEF withdrawal, 43,
89, 94; on war origins, 222; Yost's meetings with, 191, 211, 229
Rikhye, Gen. Indar Jit: messages to, 99,
241; orders requested by, 75; role of, 96,
104; on UNEF withdrawal, 95; and withdrawal request, 7, 78, 83, 85, 89, 99
Rogers plan, 295
rogue elephant concept, 259
Roosevelt, Kim, 283–84
Rostow, Eugene, *198;* on attack on Syria,
221–22; on conference purpose, 235; conspiracy defined by, 240, 282–83; on context, 197–204; Evron's meeting with,
132; and food supply program, 227–28;
Johnson's meeting with, 209; on multinational fleet, 219; on negotiations, 295;
role of, 130; on Soviet report, 54, 186;
on UN response, 109–11; on use of
force, 295; on U.S. response, 224–25; on
USS *Liberty,* 277–78
Rostow, Walt W.: Evron's meeting with,
210; on influences on Johnson, 202; Johnson's calls to, 272; on relations with Nasser, 158; role of, 133, 152; on U.S. response, 205
Rouleau, Eric, 31
Rusk, Dean: on alternatives, 207; on Israeli
borders, 243; on Israel response, 210–11,
224; Johnson's contacts with, 216–17,
272; memorandum by, 134; and multinational naval force, 209; and resolution
242, 110; role of, 45; on UNEF withdrawal, 82, 89; on use of force, 295; and
U.S. policy, 200, 202; on U.S. response,
205, 208; and USS *Liberty,* 266; writing
by, 70, 73
Ryevsky (Soviet military intelligence), 65

al-Sabah, UNEF withdrawal from, 85
Sabri, Ali, 247

sacrifice trap, 25
Sadat, Anwar: actions of, 316–17; Battle's
   meeting with, 218–19; delegation led by,
   58, 72; Nasser compared to, 215; peace
   agreement by, 251, 281, 285; and Soviet
   warning, 18, 55, 155, 293; and support
   for Syrians, 156
Safran, Nadav, 275
Saiqa (organization), 282
Sakharovsky (KGB), 71
Salim, Gen. Mohammed Ahmed, 179–80
Samu' (Jordan) raid: context of, 28; Egypt's
   response to, 6; impact of, 21, 75, 101–2,
   180, 222; interpretations of, 101–3, 176,
   310; Israeli initiation of, 60; Jordanian re-
   sponse to, 101–2, 170; motive for, 62–
   63, 100
Sasson, Moshe, 99–100
Saudi Arabia: versus Egypt, 3; Egypt criti-
   cized by, 56, 159, 162; Egyptian troops
   on border of, 252; U.S. relations with,
   224–25
Saunders, Harold, 210, 224, 318
Sawt al-Arab (radio), 179
Schiborin, Alexei, 39
Schlesinger, Arthur, Jr., 269
Seale, Patrick, 217, 290
Seelye, Talcott, 264–66, 279
Semenov, Vladimir: caution advised by,
   187; on Egytian-Syrian relations, 156;
   Feki's meeting with, 18, 44; Rafael's
   meeting with, 58; report delivered by, 72;
   role of, 39
Sevres agreement, 283
Seydoux, Roger, 104
al-Shadhli, Saad, 137
Shamir, Shimon, 23; on causes, 290, 311–
   13; on conspiracy theories, 268–69; on
   Hussein, 107; on intelligence, 146–48; on
   Israeli intentions, 60–64; on Israeli
   threat, 14–15, 20, 24–25, 27–28, 60; on
   microhistory focus, 21; on peace possibilities, 266–68; on retaliation, 310–11; on
   Soviet role, 63–64; on U.S.-Israeli relations, 123, 126, 293; on U.S. response,
   240; on war readiness, 312–13
Sharm al-Shaykh (Egypt): control of, 93,
   202; Egyptian occupation of, 7–8, 11,
   73, 76, 88–89, 295–96; and Egyptian-
   UNEF near clashes, 114; Israeli attack
   on, 307–9, 315; UNEF presence in, 83,
   110–11, 122, 274; UNEF withdrawal

from, 7, 11, 18, 42–43, 45–46, 53, 66,
   72, 85, 87, 93–96, 114–15, 183, 191,
   198
Shoukri, Muhammad, 42
Shuqayry, Ahmad, 162
signals exercise, 29
Simon, Eliav (UPI), 69
Sinai Peninsula: buffer zone in, 87; Egyptian
   troops deployed in, 39, 62, 67, 72, 83,
   137, 139, 144–45, 151, 191, 198, 201–
   2, 316; Israeli occupation of, 194, 243,
   319; Israeli withdrawal from, 6, 8, 122,
   131–32, 317, 318–19; and peace negotiations, 270; UNEF troops in, 84. See also
   Sharm al-Shaykh
Sisco, Joseph, 112, 200
Six-Day War: alternatives to, 305–6, 311;
   casualties predicted in, 124, 138, 140,
   142, 147, 151; compared to Suez War,
   151–52, 204; and crisis mismanagement,
   46; diplomacy prior to, 93–95; escalation
   prior to, 25, 27, 109–10, 125, 199, 265,
   312, 316; events of, xvii–xix, 6–8, 100,
   153, 194, 220, 310; as inadvertent, 34–
   35; as inevitable, 142–43; lack of predic-
   tions of, 3–5, 228–29; legacy of, 168,
   194, 199, 220, 224, 231, 288, 313;
   length estimates for, 217, 228, 276, 294;
   misperceptions/miscalculations leading to,
   51, 290–91, 311–15; planning for aftermath of, 285–86, 291–92, 294, 297–98,
   306, 308, 318; point of no return in, 6,
   59–60, 75, 100, 125, 150–52, 307, 316;
   as premeditated, 61–62; timing of, 203,
   206; and UN resolutions, 166–67. See
   also cease-fire; Egypt: response of; Israeli
   "threat"; Soviet warning
Smitchasni (head of KGB), 50
Sneh, Moshe, 19, 50–51
South Arabia and Nasser, 161–62
Soviet-Egyptian relations: and arms agreements, 2, 38, 65–67; communication in,
   277; definition of, 145; Nasser's role in,
   129, 148, 252–53, 265, 280–81; nature
   of, 17, 64–66, 121; and possible Egyptian attack, 38–39; questions about,
   66–68
Soviet Foreign Ministry, and ambassadors'
   orders, 61
Soviet Politburo, 37–38
Soviet-Syrian relations: importance of, 54,
   304; and Israeli policies, 14–15; role of,

Soviet-Syrian relations (*continued*)
304; and Syrian politics, 155–56; and
UN ambassadors, 186–87; and U.S. role
in war, 230–31, 233; and warnings to
Syria, 32
Soviet Union: administration of, 16–17, 37–
38, 59, 61; alleged conspiracy by, 247;
caution urged by, 32, 38–39, 44, 47, 52,
65–66, 129, 187, 276; Communist Party
in, 37, 40, 64; and crisis management,
273; and Egypt's 1973 attack on Israelis
in Sinai, 277; Egypt supported by, 148;
encouragement from, 16, 18, 39, 44, 66–
67, 73; influence by, 55, 121, 277; and Israeli attack on Syria, 230–31, 233; and Israeli threat, 32; leadership differences in,
19, 21, 39, 46–50, 64; Middle East policy of, 2–4, 20, 39–41, 47–51, 61–64,
200–201, 252–53, 280–81; motives of, 9,
15–16, 19, 35–36, 53, 155, 216–17, 247,
290, 293–94; response of, 47, 49–50; responsibilities of, 34–35, 315; role of, 19,
63–64, 70–73, 155, 293; Syria supported
by, 27, 194, 230–31, 233; and UNEF
withdrawal, 108–9, 111–12, 114; and
UN response, 76. *See also* Soviet warning
Soviet-U.S. relations: and cease-fire, 194;
and Israeli attack, 70, 230–31, 233; and
Middle East policies, 15–16, 19, 53, 195;
nature of, 146–48. *See also* cold war
Soviet warning: confirmation of, 42–44,
71–72; and escalation, 56–59; inaccuracy
of, 93, 124, 154–55, 198, 280, 312; influence by, 65, 72, 137; motives for, 9,
15–18, 39–40, 238, 290; real meaning
of, 148, 155–57, 247; role of, 6–7, 40,
73; and Soviet Middle East policy, 40–
41; Syrian role in, 154–56; transmittal
of, 16–19, 20, 37–42, 51–55, 61, 64–65,
72–73, 155, 293; versions of, 35–38, 48,
51–52
stalling: context for, 108–9; possibilities of,
89–90, 92, 103–4, 113–15
Stavropoulos, Constantine, 85, 92
Stein, Janice: on conspiracy theories, 239,
277; on Israeli policies, 60; on Israeli response, 141–43; on miscalculations, 314–
15; on stalling, 108; on use of force, 231
Stephens, Robert H., 285
Sterner, Michael, 202
Stern gang, 166
Strait of Tiran: and blockade as casus belli,

79, 93–95, 99–100, 124, 131, 144; control of, 7–8, 113; freedom of navigation
in, 8, 122–23, 181, 232, 235–36; importance of, 18, 44, 53, 189, 191, 198, 223,
316; Israeli response to closure of, 122–
25; Israeli use of, 195; Johnson's statement on, 133; and legal considerations,
232; multinational fleet for, 8, 142–43,
192–93, 195, 202–3, 207–10, 214, 218–
19, 305; Nasser's closure of, 7–8, 60,
72–73, 76, 79, 88, 94, 100, 109–10; negotiations over, 109–10, 113, 116; and
point of no return, 59–60, 202; possibility of sending Israeli ship through, 149;
recommended UNEF deployment to, 131;
and Soviet influence, 55; and UN response, 76, 108; U.S.-Israeli agreement
on, 120, 122–26, 130–31, 192, 206. *See
also* Eisenhower doctrine
Suez Canal, 189, 226, 233
Suez Canal Convention, 232
Suez War (1956): causes of, 1, 270–71; legacy of, 41–42, 96, 109–10, 189, 204,
270–71; and negotiations, 104; participants in, 2, 32, 110; Six-Day War compared to, 151–52, 204; and UNEF deployment, 91
Suslov, Mikhail, 16, 40, 47
Sweden, and UNEF withdrawal, 111, 115,
274
Sykes-Picot agreement, 244, 283
Syria: attack on Israelis by, 277; Ba'athist regime in, 25, 54, 64, 97, 137, 155, 157,
161, 250; borders of, 26, 106–7, 163–
64; complaints against, 163–64; and departure from UAR, 189; Egypt's relations
with, 27, 62–64, 103, 156; guerrilla
movements supported by, 6, 27, 57, 83,
100, 127, 137, 156, 162, 177, 197, 201,
253, 282, 312; hostility toward Israel of,
127; internal politics in, 97, 155–57,
162, 253, 290; Israeli attack on, 83, 97,
103, 153, 155, 166–67, 220–22, 225,
230–33, 253–54, 257, 280, 298; Israeli
influence in, 56–57; Israeli relations with,
6, 25, 27, 67, 163–64; and Israeli threat,
29–33, 36, 68–69, 154, 254; leadership
of, 247; military strength of, 57, 156,
162; motives of, 9, 247, 290–91; and negotiations, 97, 99, 184; and Palestinian
cause, 159, 310; press in, 20; propaganda
in, 162; response of, 156, 163–68; role

of, 153, 215; secession of, 250; Soviets
in, 156; Soviet support for, 27, 194,
230-31, 233; trap laid by, 175-76, 181-
82; warning from, 154; water diverted
by, 106-7. *See also* Damascus; Egyptian-
Syrian treaty; Golan Heights; Israeli
"threat"; Soviet-Syrian relations

Talas, Gen. Ahmad, 162
Tass, and Syrian situation, 56
Tel, Wasfi, 102, 178-79
terrorism: origins of, 166, 177; retaliation
against, 69; by states, 185; UN condem-
nation of, 282
Thant, U: alternatives for, 75-80, 99, 103-
4, 107-9, 111, 113, 115-18; and armistice agreements, 83; Cairo visit by, 76,
86, 88, 94, 100, 129, 302; criticism
against, 99; and Hammarskjöld memo,
91-94; on Israeli-Syrian situation, 97,
164; on Israeli threats, 165, 245; and Israeli troop concentration, 28, 99; moratorium requested by, 94-95, 114-16, 243;
Nasser's contacts with, 117, 281, 289,
312; proposals by, 105-6; recommendations to, 104, 111, 219, 281; responsibilities of, 80-82; role of, 85, 87, 99, 104,
107-12, 273-74; six-point response by,
78; and Soviet veto, 150; stalling by, 89-
90, 92, 103; and Syrian response, 163-
64; on terrorist attacks, 282; and UNEF
withdrawal, 7, 11, 43-44, 65-66, 73, 75,
78-80, 86, 93-94, 99
Thompson, George, 200
Tomeh, George: on Balfour Declaration,
112-13; and cease-fire, 184; on conference purpose, 234-35; on Israeli troops,
186-87; on Syrian situation, 153-54,
163-68, 290; on UNEF withdrawal,
114
Tonkin resolution, 134, 204
Torcziner, Jacques, 275
Tripartite Declaration (1950), 11, 243, 295,
307
Tsur, Abraham Ben, 50
Tuhaimi, Hassan, 283
Tunisia, Nasser taunted by, 159, 162

Ulbricht, Walter, 50
UNEF. *See* UN Emergency Force (UNEF)
Unified Arab Command (UAC), 101, 106,
160, 181-82, 309

United Arab Republic (UAR): military
strength of, 75, 162; support for, 75-76,
85-86; Syrian departure from, 189; trap
for, 175; U.S. relations with, 196
United Nations: cease-fire resolutions by,
166-67, 184-85; and closure of strait,
76, 108; and crisis management, 273-74,
291, 305-6; failure of, 74, 80, 120; and
Israeli threat, 32; Law of the Sea conference by, 77, 227, 232; limitations of, 80,
83, 243; military observers for, 88, 99;
motives of, 11; Nasser's relations with,
78, 82, 85-86, 89-97, 99, 113-14, 117;
purpose of, 78-79; reports to, 253; response of, 81-82, 93-100, 103-11, 134-
35, 291; responsibilities of, 74-75, 79-
81, 251; Soviet role in, 61, 72, 201; and
Syrian response, 163-64; U.S. role in,
200-201. *See also* cold war: and UN response; UN Emergency Force (UNEF);
UN Security Council; Thant, U
UN Charter: Article 24, 197; Article 51,
131-33, 167-68; Article 99, 99, 103;
and occupation, 185
UN Emergency Force (UNEF): Advisory
Committee for, 77-78, 85-87, 90-92;
and Arab propaganda, 159; deployment
of, 6, 41, 82, 84, 85-93, 105-6, 116-17,
131, 189; establishment of, 81; failure of,
120; illusions about, 82, 92; importance
of, 274; legal status of, 82-83, 85-87,
90-92, 116; partial versus total withdrawal of, 75, 78, 82, 93, 107-9, 117;
and point of no return, 60; purpose of,
78-79, 85, 105, 122, 181; regulations
on, 82-83, 85, 90-92, 96-97, 195; success of, 189; withdrawal of, 7, 11, 18,
21, 42-46, 48, 53, 66, 72, 93-96, 111-
15, 181, 183, 191, 198. *See also*
Thant, U
UN General Assembly: Palestine partitioned
by, 1, 244-45; recommendations to, 131;
responsibilities of, 74-75
UN Security Council: and cold war context,
75, 81, 88, 91, 111-12, 115, 118, 126,
150, 201, 203, 233; complaints against
Syria in, 163-64; and Egyptian-Israeli
talks, 58; recommendations to, 150; resolutions of, 108, 110, 166-67, 184-85,
197, 199-201, 319; responsibilities of,
74-75; and state of belligerence, 104;
and Suez Canal, 233; and Syrian situa-

UN Security Council (*continued*)
tion, 57–58, 155; Thant's report to, 116;
and UNEF withdrawal, 76–77, 82, 87,
92, 99, 103, 108; U.S. role in, 103, 109
UN Truce Supervision Organization. *See*
UNTSO
United Press International (UPI), on Israeli
warning, 7, 14, 32–33, 59, 71, 154
United States: alliances of, 41; assessment
by, 45; British relations with, 200, 213,
244; commitments of, 8, 231, 235–36,
241–43, 295, 303, 307–8; and crisis management, 220, 223–25, 249, 273; demonstrators in, 215; documentation in, 38,
205, 238; embargo imposed by, 152; foreign policy of, 66, 120–21, 149–50, 158,
213; Israeli relations with, 5, 70–71, 93,
116, 136–37; and Israeli response, 122–
25, 143, 149–50; Israel supported by, 36,
119–20, 123–26, 129–32, 139–47, 144,
146, 192–94, 233, 240, 271, 279–80,
287; leadership differences in, 46; Middle
East policy of, 2, 196, 200–208, 226–27,
246–50, 253, 276, 284–85; motives of,
10–11, 142–43, 205–6; Nasser's relations
with, 189–90, 196–97, 206–7, 229, 291,
316; planning by, 218, 222–23, 228,
288, 294, 298; policy changes by, 194–
95, 291–92, 295, 317–20; public opinion
in, 192, 196, 204, 214, 256, 263–64,
275; response of, 121–24, 144, 205–8,
213–36, 239–41, 252–55, 269, 276,
295–96, 303, 315; responsibility of, 229–
30, 239; Saudi Arabia relations with,
224–25; signals from, 136–41, 146–48,
210–12, 256, 271, 279–80, 304; and Soviet warning, 54; and UN response, 76,
79, 103–4, 109–11; and use of force,
295, 307–8. *See also* Eisenhower doctrine; Johnson, Lyndon B.; Soviet-U.S. relations
U.S. Air Force, reconnaisance by, 260–61
U.S. Congress: attitudes in, 219–20, 250,
263; House Foreign Affairs Committee,
219–20; Johnson's relations with, 206;
and military support for Israel, 192; and
opening the strait, 203, 219; role of, 302;
and support for Israel, 133–34
U.S. Department of Defense (DOD), and
multinational fleet, 202, 214, 219
U.S.-Egyptian relations: after Six-Day War,
260, 263–64; communication in, 241–42;

deterioration in, 42, 190–91, 196, 229;
and diplomacy, 190–91; improvement in,
189, 265; Israeli attempt to disrupt, 283;
and Israeli preemptive strike, 276–77; limitations of, 303
U.S.-Israeli relations: ambiguity in, 122–33,
279–80; and closure of strait, 120, 122–
26, 130–31, 192, 206; and coming confrontation, 65; commitments in, 231–32;
as conspiracy, 245–46; consultations in,
191–92, 239, 271; definition of, 145–46;
deterioration in, 266; Johnson's influence
on, 133–35; knowledge of, 181; motives
in, 224–25, 251; nature of, 17, 240, 248,
255–56, 259; and 1957 agreements, 197,
201–3, 206, 210, 231; perceptions of,
153; Shamir on, 123, 126, 293; and special nature of, 212–14, 239, 303; stability of, 41; uniqueness of, 244–45
USS *Liberty*: and court-martial proceedings,
277–78; facts on, 304; intercepts regarding, 279; Israeli attack on, 158, 257,
266, 270, 286, 298; symbolism of, 248
U.S. Public Law 480, 190, 196, 227, 229
U.S. State Department: and ambassadors to
Egypt, 229; and communication with
Egypt, 242; Foreign Service Institute at,
11; meetings at, 132; and "missing" file,
201–2, 226, 232–33; perspective of, 197–
204, 226; recommendations from, 207
U.S.-Syrian relations, at UN, 187
Uniting for Peace procedure, 76
UNTSO (UN Truce Supervision Organization): and cease-fire line, 184; contingency plans by, 99; leadership of, 95,
100; perspective from, 253; report on border by, 28, 77, 99; role of, 96–97, 107;
and UNEF withdrawal, 95–96
UPI (United Press International), on Israeli
warning, 7, 14, 32–33, 59, 71, 154
Urquhart, Brian, *81*; on armistice agreements, 195; on British response, 243,
274; on conspiracy theories, 272–74; on
face-saving, 117–18; on Hammarskjöld
memorandum, 91–92; on moratorium,
115–17, 243; on redeployment versus
withdrawal, 89–90; role of, 99, 305; on
UNEF withdrawal, 117; on UN response,
80–83, 85–92, 291; on U.S.-Soviet consultations, 118
USSR. *See* Soviet Union
Ustinov, Dmitry Fedorovich, 50, 64

Versailles Treaty (1919), and proposal for Jewish state, 112–13
Vietnam War: as context for Six-Day War, 204, 229–30, 306; effects of, 273; and Johnson's position, 130; Soviet opposition to America in, 67; strategy in, 247–48; U.S. troops in, 3–4, 48, 53, 123, 190, 229; writing on, 301
Vinogradov (ambassador), 61
Von Horn, Gen. Carl, 164, 253

wars: Arab-Israeli (1948–49), 1, 161, 265; Crimean, 300; Korean, 203; Persian Gulf (1991), 137, 298; World War II, 297–98; October or Yom Kippur (1973), 184. See also cold war; Six-Day War; Suez War (1956); Vietnam War; Yemen civil war
water: confrontations over, 25, 106–7; Israeli scheme for, 25, 106–7, 248; rights to, 113, 185–86
Weizmann, Chaim, 244, 249, 254
West Bank: and Israeli intentions, 101, 153, 157, 159, 181, 186; Israeli occupation of, 8, 194, 243, 295, 313, 319; Jordanian control of, 159–60; Jordanian operations in, 171–74, 183; and Jordanian politics, 168–69; and peace negotiations, 270; and Samu' raid, 101–2
Wheeler, Gen. Earle, 208–9, 217, 218
White, Ralph K., 301
Wilson, Harold, 122
withdrawal versus redeployment, 83, 89–90. See also UN Emergency Force (UNEF)
World Bank, 245
World Zionist Organization, 112–13, 166, 185–86

Yariv, Gen. Aharon: briefing by, 7, 10, 31–32, 59; recommendations by, 138; on retaliation plans, 29
Yemen civil war: context of, 41; Egyptian military in, 3, 161, 190; Egyptian-Saudi Arabian conflict in, 189, 229; and Nasser's options, 196, 219
Yom Kippur War (1973), 184, 317
Yost, Charles: Nasser's relations with, 129, 229; report from, 209–10; Riad's meeting with, 191, 211, 229; role of, 112, 252
Yugoslavia: caution urged by, 66; UAR supported by, 76, 85, 86; and UNEF withdrawal, 15, 86, 90, 96, 111

Zaim, Husni, 265, 282, 284
Zartman, I. William, 23; on alleged number of brigades, 60; on conference results, 304–5; on Nasser's actions, 290; on UN response, 74–80, 107–8, 291
Zeroni, Benjamin, 166
Zionism, as origin of terrorism, 166
Zionist Organization of America (ZOA), 275
Zu'ayyin, Dr, Yusuf, 247

Schmitt (replacement)